PLAYBOOK

Maxine Klein   **Lydia Sargent**

Howard Zinn

SOUTH END PRESS

First edition
Production by South End Press, USA
Manufactured in the USA
Cover art by Pat Andreotti
Cover design by Lydia Sargent

The graphics used on the title pages are taken from the play's promotional poster.

Set drawings for "Emma," "The Furies of Mother Jones," "Split-Shift," "New Rise of the Master Race," and "Windfall" are by Michael Anania.

Library of Congress Cataloguing in Publication Data

Klein, Maxine.
    Playbook.

        Bibligraphy: p.
        1. American drama—20th century. 2. Political Plays, American. 3. Women—drama. I. Sargent, Lydia. II. Zinn, Howard. III Title.
    PZ627.P65k55   1986   812'.54'080358   86-6754
    ISBN 0-89608-309-8
    ISBN 0-89608-308-x (pbk.)

South End Press   116 St. Botolph St   Boston MA 02115

*Dedicated to the tradition of political theater
which has spoken throughout history with
courage and passion to all humanity.*

Table of Contents

Preface

George Santayana has said that the purpose of art is to consecrate what heretofore was unconsecrated. There are thousands of plays in the Western World that consecrate—give honor to kings and queens; to the rich and powerful, young and "beautiful"; to the gentry who have time and money to explore the dark recesses of their private neuroses; to those who believe that history is made by the innately superior few who fight against the "stupidity" of a chaotic rabble; to the male protagonist who struggles alone against his own "fatal flaw" to become the accepted ideal hero.

There are very few plays in this country that consecrate miners, factory workers, waitresses; the powerless, the poor, and the "plain"; those men and women who fight for their rights; those who believe that history is also made by the collective efforts of the disenfranchised. In a word, there are very few plays which consecrate the lives of people like Mother Mary Harris Jones, Emma Goldman, Agnes Smedley, Billie Murphy, Mae Black, Marie Rogers, and Biddie Gazinski.

While reliable authority preaches that theater ought to hold up a mirror to its age, too many contemporary American playwrights turn a deaf ear to our national and global crises; to the economy; to the quality of life, of work, of the environment, and of the national psyche. Today's theatrical mirror is rendered opaque. And today's *critical* playwrights are too often silenced or permitted to be heard only when they present a mirrored image in soft-pink lights that pleases critics and theater elites while it etherizes a theater-going public. Today's critical playwright is too often pressured, coerced, influenced, and seduced into supporting the status quo in form and content. The artist is shackled, the audience robbed, the theater empoverished.

The plays in this volume are part of a "political theater" that really does mirror the problems and potentials of our age. They consciously reflect the oppressive and liberatory sides of life and so consciously consecrate the heretofore unconsecrated. While respecting aesthetic norms, they challenge stifling theatrical conceits. Their publication is intended to contribute to a tradition of political theater and to a new cultural community of people who want mirrors that don't lie. We hope the seven plays in this volume will be performed as widely as possible with passion, humor, and courage.

Maxine Klein
Lydia Sargent
Howard Zinn

ACKNOWLEDGEMENTS

With gratitude and admiration I would like to thank every actor who has performed in my plays. But most particularly I wish to thank James Oestereich, Ellen Field, and David Carl Olson for their extraordinary commitment to and performance in realizing both these plays and the larger vision of which they are a part. They are, in every sense, the heart of the matter. I would also like to commend the commitment and editing skills of Renee Herberle.

Maxine Klein
Boston, 1986

Thanks to South End Press and to Jade Barker and Mike Prokosch for their production of this book. And grateful acknowledgement to the women and men whose practice of the craft of acting continually enriches the final production and content of each play. Who must use their bodies, voices, emotions, hearts, and minds to portray characters, plots, events, themes, and ideas with pace, timing, rhythm, and energy in costume and makeup moving in a space filled with props and furniture to be used in character in the company of and with sensitivity to other actors who are all using their bodies, voices, emotions, hearts, and minds in the presence of anywhere from one to five hundred people who have come to the theater to be moved emotionally and mentally beyond themselves.

Lydia Sargent
Boston, 1986

DAUGHTER OF EARTH

Adapted by Lydia Sargent
from Agnes Smedley's novel

To Agnes Smedley

Daughter of Earth is adapted from Agnes Smedley's autobiographical novel. Until its republication by Feminist Press, most of us had never heard of Agnes Smedley or been able to find her books. According to Paul Lautner's afterword to the reprinted novel, hers were among the first works to be hunted down by the bookburners of the early 1950s. Her books disappeared from library shelves. Publishers allowed her books to go out of print. She was called a "Red sympathizer" for her writings and her participation in the Chinese Revolution. She was a feminist who described marriage as a "relic of human slavery" in a time when women were being forced back into the home, and when abortion was only whispered about. Although her books had been praised in the past—called fiercely honest, urgent, and savage in tone—under the avalanche of McCarthyism, her life and books were buried. This play is dedicated to this remarkable woman: a frontier child, tobacco stripper, waitress, teacher, student, activist, and revolutionary.

"Daughter of Earth" was first produced in Boston by The Newbury Street Theater in May 1978. Second and third productions were performed in April 1980, and March 1984. All three productions were directed by Lydia Sargent. The cast for the 1984 production was as follows:

Marie Rogers .... *Lydia Sargent*
Elly Rogers
Fran
Rich Woman
Clothilde .... *Elissa Forsythe*
Student 1
Landlady
Irish Prostitute
Florence

John Rogers
Antoine .... *Justin Kaan*
Juan Diaz
Detective

Annie Rogers
Sally
Nurse
Couple next door .... *Tamara Harper*
Leila
Student Adams
Alcie
Margaret

Beatrice Rogers
Aunt Helen
Rich Woman .... *Jan Connery*
Karin
Student 2
Old Forger

George Rogers
Robert Hampton
Raphael .... *Derek Stearns*
Assistant
Student 3
Dan Rogers

Lou
Mr. Turner
Frank
Clerk
Justice of the Peace .... *William Harris*
Couple next door
Luther
Sardar Ranjit Singh
Interrogator

Sam
Big Buck
Jim Watson
Knut .... *Jim Mullen*
Jackson
Detective
University Professor
Anand
Student 4

Lighting by Cassandra Dixon. Sets by William Harris, Jim Mullen, and Lydia Sargent.

PART I

The Rogers family home inside and out. Early 1900s. In Missouri, then in Colorado.

PART II

Marie's environment. First at teacher's school in Phoenix, then in California, then a park in St. Louis, then apartments in New York City, a classroom at the University, and the Tombs prison. Just before and after World War I.

STORY OF THE PLAY

"Daughter of Earth" is a drama set in the early 1900s in the West, then in New York City. It tells the story of Marie Rogers and her recurrent struggles to transform herself. As the play begins, Marie is stands looking out over a Danish sea contemplating thirty years of pain and unhappiness. As she considers ending her life, she relives it. "I write," she says, "of the joys and sorrows of the lowly. Of loneliness, of pain, and of love." She tells her story beginning with her family and their struggle to survive, as they move from mining town to mining town in search of work and the realization of her father's dream of "becoming a doctor so they'll be rich." But poverty and hard work and grasping employers take their toll. Marie's father becomes a drunk who threatens his family with physical violence; her mother dies of overwork and malnutrition; one of her sisters dies in childbirth; her aunt becomes a prostitute to "pay for the things she wants" and to help support the Roger's family. Marie, unable to "accept her lot as ordained by God and marry a working man and bear him five children to wander the face of the earth," deserts her family to realize her own dream of becoming a great writer some day.

Marie studies to be a teacher in Phoenix and is befriended by Karin and Knut Larson. Impressed by their beauty and intelligence, influenced by their Socialist politics, Marie becomes involved in social movements of the day. She is also admitted to the University of California. She marries Knut with the agreement that they will both work and study. But the fear of having children breaks their marriage apart and Marie goes alone to New York where she continues to study. Patronized by rich radicals in Greenwich Village, she finds a place for herself among the men from India who are fighting to free their country from the British. During World War I, she is imprisoned, suspected of being a spy. On her release, she becomes the only woman writer for *The Call*, a Socialist newspaper. She meets and marries an revolutionary from India, a man whose "revolution extends to women." Yet, his jealousy and traditional attitudes about women, in the end, destroy not only their love but Marie's ability to do political work in the United States. She flees to Denmark and, as in the beginning of the play, stands looking out at the sea, contemplating suicide. But she decides otherwise for she belongs to "those who do not die for the sake of beauty. She belongs to those who dies from other causes— exhausted by poverty, victims of power and wealth, fighters in a great cause." And so, haunted continually by the spectres of her mother and aunt—the grim alternatives for most women of her class—Marie does not submit to needless oppression and brutality and struggles to survive through her writing and her involvement in movements for social change.

DESCRIPTION OF CHARACTERS

MARIE ROGERS: a thirty-year old journalist, Socialist, feminist, and revolutionary who tells of the earth on which "we all happen to be living." When she narrates she is the writer, spinning out her story. When she acts out her childhood, she is clearly a strong, independent, imaginative young girl who fights injustice and who will not succumb to the "traditional" role women are supposed to play.

JOHN ROGERS: Marie's father. At first, he is a farmer, then he excavates for mine owners while he dreams of becoming a wealthy doctor. He is a colorful man who knows all the songs, who tells stories, and who is considered dangerous with women. Later, poverty turns him into a drunk who carries a doubled up rope which he uses to threaten his wife and his children into obedience.

ELLY ROGERS: Marie's mother. A slender woman who raises her children and who contributes to the family income by taking in washing. Her hands are black and worn. Her tired face is lit by beautiful eyes. She is thirty but looks fifty. Her one dream is to see that Marie gets an education and she stands up to her husband in order to realize this. She has a profound hatred for the rich, and a profound love for her sister, Helen.

ANNIE ROGERS: Marie's older sister. A physical young girl who cares little for school. As she grows into a young woman, she becomes independent, defying her father. She does not have Marie's dislike of men, sex and women's role in life (much to Marie's disgust).

BEATRICE ROGERS: Marie's younger sister. She is only six in the play—long-legged and thin with rough hands and a rough way of talking.

GEORGE ROGERS: Marie's younger brother. He is favored by his father, as a son. And he has an unwavering faith, trust, and confidence in Marie. He is rough and uneducated.

AUNT HELEN: Marie's aunt, Elly's sister. She is a proud, independent woman, afraid of no one. She loves and teases the kids, the way an aunt should. She adores her sister above all others. She is a prostitute, giving much of her money to Elly to help buy nice things for the kids.

DAN ROGERS: Marie's youngest brother. He, like George, trusts and believes in Marie. He appears only briefly in Part II.

LOU and SALLY: A farming couple who attend the Harvest Dance. Lou is a flirt, Sally likes to gossip. Both do so with affection.

SAM: A farmer who courts Aunt Helen at the Harvest Dance.

MR. TURNER: A mine owner who employs John to haul coal and who cheats him, taking advantage of the fact that John can't read the contract he signed. He is a small man with a quiet voice and a prim manner who remains unaffected by the angry men and weeping women he has to "deal" with.

BIG BUCK: A cowboy turned mechanic who teaches Marie how to shoot and ride. A big man who cuts a romantic figure and who is like an uncle to Marie, helping her to go to teacher's school.

8

JIM WATSON: A lean, lanky cowboy in his late twenties who has left his ranch to see the world and who works for Marie's father for a time. He takes a romantic interest in Marie, asks her to marry him, and is ultimately rejected.

KARIN LARSON: A teacher and a Socialist. She is tall, dignified, and beautiful. She influences Marie, exposing her to new ideas

KNUT LARSON: Marie's first husband. A Socialist. Beautiful and educated, kind and gentle.

JUSTICE OF THE PEACE: A round, perspiring man who rushes through the marriage ceremony so he can get back to his dinner. He has seen many young couples, a process that has wearied him.

FRAN: His wife, a loud, cheerful woman. While she has witnessed many, many marriages, she still delights in each new romantic young couple.

ANTOINE: A marxist intellectual from the upper classes who tries to teach Marie political theory.

LUTHER: An upper class anarchist who tries to introduce Marie to anarchism.

JACKSON: An upper class Bohemian who enjoys culture and who has become fascinated with Freud and psychology and longs to analyze Marie.

LEILA: An upper class Bohemian, involved in theater and literature, who is also attempting to write "working class" plays and to bring culture to Marie.

CLOTHILDE: An upper class "free spirit" who is currently inspired by Isadora Duncan.

RAPHAEL: A painter and an eccentric anti-social man.

ROBERT HAMPTON: A clerk in an office, and childhood "pen pal" to Marie. When they finally meet later in life, he is not the romantic educated man she thought he was, but a small man in a shabby coat who chatters enthusiastically in a thin, eager voice. His politics are traditional and he is shocked by Marie's radicalism.

UNIVERSITY PROFESSOR: A middle-aged man, who enjoys the classroom debate but who's politics are racist and imperialist in a time in history when students and faculty are deep in heated debates on social issues.

STUDENT ADAMS: A student who argues for the inferiority of the Negro.

SARDAR RANJIT SINGH: A teacher and a leader in the movement to free India from the British living in exile. His origins are upper class but he identifies with the common people of India. He is passionate in his dedication and convincing in his arguments for his beliefs.

JUAN DIAZ: A Eurasian and a participant in the movement to free India from the British. He is cynical and contemptuous of women. Later he turns out to be a spy.

INTERROGATOR: A government man, contemptuous of Asian people and women. He has a hard face and thin lips.

DETECTIVE: A short, thick-set man. Brutal expression and hard eyes that watch every movement.

IRISH PROSTITUTE: A resident of Tombs prison in New York City. She is worn out, pocked-marked with a voice like a fog horn.

OLD FORGER: A resident of Tombs prison. She is a large woman who weeps bitterly.

ALCIE: A resident of Tombs prison. A young woman with delicate features.

FLORENCE: A poet who shares an apartment with Marie. She is a lover of music and literature who also loves Marie. She is upper class.

MARGARET: A manicurist who rents a room in Florence and Marie's apartment. She is blunt, direct and practical.

ANAND MANEVEKAR: Marie's second husband. A revolutionary whose revolution extends to women. His speech and movements are quick and gentle. His jealousy and traditional values about women gradually dominate his interactions with Marie.

NURSE: A severe woman who works for an illegal abortionist who makes fortunes off rich women.

WOMEN IN DOCTOR'S OFFICE: Rich women who have come for illegal abortions.

STUDENTS 1-4: Attend the University and have various reactions and responses to the political debate that ensues, first between Marie and the University Professor; then to the dialogue between Marie and Sardar Ranjit Singh.

10

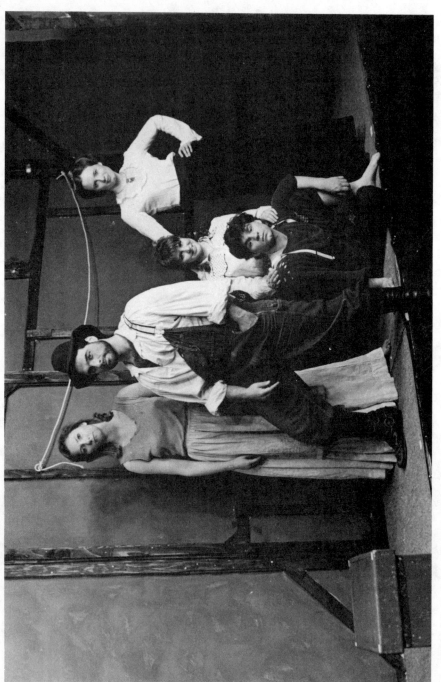

From left to right: Elissa Forsythe, Justin Kaan, Derek Stearns, Tamara Harper, Jan Connery in "Daughter of Earth."
Photo: Lydia Sargent.

Part I

Fragment 1: "I Write Of The Earth"

MARIE. (*standing center on the platform*) Before me stretches a Danish sea. Cold, gray, limitless. The sea and the gray sky blend and become one. A bird with outstretched wings takes its way over the depths. For months I have been here watching the sea...and writing the story of a human life. It is the story of a life written in desperation and in unhappiness. I write of the earth on which we all by some strange circumstance happen to be living. I write of the joys and sorrows of the lowly, of loneliness, of pain, and of love. (*ELLY enters upstage left and hangs a quilt on the clothesline, then exits*) I recall a crazy quilt my mother once had. She made it from the remnants of gay and beautiful cotton materials. She also made a quilt of solid blue. I would stand gazing at the blue quilt for a little time, but the crazy quilt held me for hours. It was an adventure. I shall gather up these fragments of my life and make a crazy quilt of them. This, too, will be an adventure.

(*ELLY and ANNIE enter upstage. ANNIE watches as ELLY takes the quilt from the clothesline. ELLY takes ANNIE'S hand and they cross to the bed.*)

MARIE. (*continuing to talk while ANNIE and ELLY work*) We were very poor. But that I did not know. For all the world seemed just like our home. At least that world of ours that stretched for some two hundred miles across northern Missouri. The rolling stony earth that yielded so reluctantly seemed to stretch far (*ELLY unfurls quilt*) beyond the horizon and touch the sky where the sun set. The northern frontier was a town of a few hundred people. The south ended...well, my father's imagination reached to a mysterious city called St. Joseph on the Missouri River. (*ELLY and ANNIE exit*) But then he was a man with the soul and imagination of a vagabond. People listened to his stories but they didn't always believe them.

13

(ELLY re-enters with more laundry and crosses to the clothlesline)

MARIE. Because he wasn't one of them. He was almost a foreigner in fact. His family wasn't farmers. Some said they were a shiftless crew...that was the Indian blood in their veins. Oh, you could never trust a foreigner or an Indian.

(ELLY crosses to kitchen shelf. ANNIE and BEATRICE enter chasing each other in a game of Cowboys and Indians. ANNIE grabs the quilt from the bed and begins teasing MARIE with it. MARIE chases after ANNIE trying to get the quilt away from her. THEY are wrestling with it at the clothesline when JOHN enters platform right.)

Fragment 2: "I'm a Rogers"

JOHN. *(smiles around at his family, then talks to MARIE, clearly his favorite)* Marie, come on over here.

MARIE. *(yanking the quilt away from ANNIE and moving toward JOHN trailing the quilt along after her)* Coming, Pa. *(she is no longer the narrator but has become a child again)*

(ANNIE and BEATRICE sit under the clothesline, hiding in the shirts)

JOHN. You see that pile of stones away off there? *(pointing way off)*

MARIE. *(excited about the story they both know is coming)* Yes, Pa. I see it. *(looks at him, then off at imaginary pile of stones)*

JOHN. Do you know what that mound of stones is?

MARIE. *(shaking her head)* No, Pa.

JOHN. That's a burial mound of the Indians. They fought a great battle over there. They come from far away...the Rockies, I think. Some of 'em came naked, some in blankets *(dramatizing the story)* and skins, an' some layin' down on their horses, hanging from the mane with one hand and a foot. *(demonstrating)*

(MARIE, ANNIE, and BEATRICE smile at each other. ELLY, in the kitchen, is disapproving but affectionate.)

JOHN. And they fought and they fought and they fought until not one of them was left to tell the tale. *(looking around for approval from the kids)*

ELLY. *(crossing to the washtub bench)* What're ya tellin' her that for? That mound of stones ain't no burial ground. It's a den for rattlesnakes.

JOHN. *(putting one foot up)* Sure it is. I ought to know, my ancestors being Indians.

(MARIE imitates him)

JOHN. One day, Marie. I'm gonna take you out to the Rockies. They got this huge peak there, Fisher's Peak. It's a half a mile high. We'll go campin' and huntin' and shootin' deer. *(putting his arm around her as they both stare off in the direction of Fisher's Peak)* Would you like that, Marie?

MARIE. *(nods)* Yes, Pa.

ELLY. *(beginning to set the table for supper)* Can't see why you want to go way out there. Can't farm the land. And I always thought farming was a good way to make a living.

JOHN. *(crossing down the stairs to the table and trying to involve ELLY in his dream)* That's 'cause you're a Garfield, Elly. Just tied to one place. Not me. I'm a Rogers and I'm gonna make the most of it. One day I'll get down to St. Joe. They got fancy doctors there and I hear you can train with 'em. *(grabbing his hat from hook in kitchen and using a dishcloth for a tie)* One of these days I'm gonna hitch up the horses and offer my services as a driver for one of those fancy eye specialists. I'll drive for him, and he'll teach me to be an eye specialist, and I'll come back rich. Wearin' store bought clothes, and one of those store bought hats. *(strutting around)* Wear it down over my left eye. And a black tie that flies in the wind. And a fancy belt buckle like those cowboys wear. And Elly, *(coming toward ELLY and putting his arms around her from behind)* I'll get you some black silk and you can make yourself the prettiest dress, prettier than anyone around here. Then won't we be the ones.

ELLY. *(briefly caught up in the idea, then reality hits)* I don't want to live in some far off place like St. Joe. *(pulling away and crossing to the washtub bench, then heads to the clothesline)* Farming here is all right with me.

JOHN. *(looking after her, then crossing to the kitchen to rehang his hat on the hook and untie the dishcloth "tie" and put it back)* Well, you might as well get used to it. 'Cause it'll happen some day. I ain't workin' like a dog all my life.

(ELLY and JOHN stare at each other from opposite ends of the stage. ANNIE, MARIE, and BEATRICE look from one to the other as the lights fade. In the dark, JOHN exits up right, ANNIE and BEATRICE cross to the bed and lie down, ELLY crosses to kitchen.)

Fragment 3: "She Said That I Lied"

MARIE. (*kneeling on platform center using her quilt as a fire*) I remember vaguely of love, of the color red. I was building a fire—a lovely fire made of stones and it burnt brilliantly between two tall cedar trees until my mother found me and tapped me on the head with her steel thimble. She said that I lied and as the years of her marriage increased and more children came she began to hit me more and more.

(*ELLY crosses to clothes line with a shirt*)

And I learned to tell her only the things I knew she wanted to hear. She began to threaten me with my father. But she failed. For he had never struck me and I knew he never would. (*whispers her father's story about the the mound of stones to the wind*)

ELLY. Marie. (*getting no response*) Marie. What are you doing?

MARIE. (*exaggerated innocence*) Nothing, Mama.

ELLY. Marie, you were talkin' to somebody. Who were you talkin' to?

MARIE. To the fire, Mama. (*trying to continue her game*)

ELLY. You can't talk to fire, Marie. You're lyin' to me. (*coming closer to MARIE*) Who were you talkin' to?

MARIE. (*beginning to be frightened but sticking to her story*) I was just talking to the trees, Ma. And the wind. (*smiling, remembering her father*)

ELLY. (*crossing to grab MARIE'S arm and yank her down the stairs to the bench below the platform*) You can't talk to the wind, Marie. Admit that you lied, Marie. (*hitting MARIE on the back*) I want you to stop lyin' and tellin' those stories. I'm gonna tell your pa. (*hitting her again*)

MARIE. (*crying out*) Stop hittin' me, Mama. Please, stop hittin' me. All right. I lied, Mama. (*pulling away from her and trying to run away*) I lied. Now stop hittin' me.

ELLY. (*going after MARIE and grabbing her arm to hit her one last time*) Next time, Marie, you admit it right away (*exits down right*)

(*MARIE climbs on the washtub bench and begins defiantly talking to the wind, clutching her quilt, still crying from the beating. The lights begin to change to suggest a coming cyclone.*)

Fragment 4: "But We Were Spared"

(*ANNIE and BEATRICE get up from the bed and run around MARIE grabbing her quilt. THEY chase around the stage, the quilt flying out after them, when ANNIE senses the cyclone.*)

ANNIE. Marie, it's a cyclone comin'.

JOHN. (*entering the platform on the run*) Cyclone, Elly.

(*ELLY enters downstage and crosses to the kitchen*) ›

JOHN. Grab some things, Elly. I'll get the kids.

(*JOHN grabs ANNIE and BEATRICE but they pull away and rush to get their treasures. MARIE runs for her quilt. JOHN grabs them and shoves them under the platform.*)

ANNIE. (*hushed tone*) It's cold in here.

MARIE. Are we gonna die, Pa?

JOHN. Quiet. If we're buried, I got the axe.

ELLY. What if something falls on the air hole?

JOHN. I'll cut us out, I'm tellin' you. There ain't no need losin' your head until something happens.

BEATRICE. Pa, I saw a mouse, Pa.

MARIE. Don't be frightened, Beatrice.

ANNIE. I'm hungry, Mama.

ELLY. It'll be over soon, Annie.

JOHN. Sounds quiet out there. Let me take a look.

ELLY. Be careful, John.

JOHN. (*poking his head out*) Aw, it ain't no cyclone. The house is still standin'. Cedars must have broke the wind. There ain't no danger. I told you not to worry. Come on out.

ELLY. Wait a bit, John. You can never tell.

JOHN. (*starting to pull ELLY and the KIDS from under the platform*) I can tell. I seen lots of cyclones.

(*MARIE, ANNIE, and BEATRICE wander around the stage looking to see what's still standing. ELLY goes to the kitchen. MARIE soon listens with admiration to her father's story.*)

JOHN. This wasn't anything like the cyclone that struck St. Joe. That was a cyclone! It sucked up cattle and horses and men and houses and fences and set 'em down miles away. (*climbing the stairs to the platform*) It cut right across the country for sixty miles and they tried to dynamite it to break it up. You could see it comin' for miles. A long black funnel. It sucked up a smokehouse in one place and left the house standing ten feet away...clean as a whistle. I think there must have been well nigh a hundred people lost in that there cyclone.

(*JOHN smiles at MARIE, his only audience, then exits to go back to work. ELLY exits. ANNIE and BEATRICE wander to the bed and lie down.*)

MARIE. (*crossing to where JOHN told his story*) One time we were in cyclone. It swept our house fifty feet away and left it standing as clean as a whistle. (*embellishing the story for an imaginary audience*) We saw houses and fences and cattle and people fly by. You should have seen it. Horses and Indians and sheep just tumbled out the air. Well nigh a million people were killed in that cyclone, but we were spared. (*bows her head thankfully as the lights fade*)

Fragment 5: "Secrecy and Shame"

MARIE. (*sitting on platform*) Slowly I was learning the secrecy and shame of sex. When my little brother George was born, we were hurried off to the next farmhouse and secrecy and shame settled like a clammy rag over everything.

(*ANNIE drags BEATRICE to the clothesline*)

ANNIE. (*whispering mysteriously*) Come on, Beatrice. Mama's havin' a baby and we can't see.

BEATRICE. Why?

ANNIE. Don't know why. Marie, come over here.

(*MARIE joins them and THEY hide in the shirts hanging on the clothesline*)

BEATRICE. But I wanna see the stork.

ANNIE. (*laughing*) The stork?

BEATRICE. I thought the stork brought babies?

MARIE. Yea.

ANNIE. Uh, uh. That's not how babies get born.

BEATRICE. It's not?

ANNIE. Nope.

BEATRICE. How then?

MARIE. Are you sure, Annie?

ANNIE. Sure I'm sure. I'll tell you how babies get born. First, Ma and Pa have to have sex.

MARIE. What's that?

ANNIE. Well, first Ma lies down on the bed and then Pa goes and gets something pointy.

BEATRICE. What?

ANNIE. A stick or something. Then he comes over to the bed where mama is layin' down and he starts breathin' hard like this. (*demonstrates*)

BEATRICE. (*enjoying it*) Then what?

MARIE. Pa doesn't breathe like that.

ANNIE. Yep. I heard them one night. Then he takes the stick and puts it in her. (*demonstrating*)

MARIE. (*disgusted*) Uuh.

BEATRICE. Where's he put the stick? In her mouth?

ANNIE. No, somewhere around her belly button and it makes her blow up like a balloon.

BEATRICE. And then? When does the stork come?

ANNIE. In a year maybe.

MARIE. A year?

ANNIE. The stork comes flyin' through the air and into the house and settles on the edge of ma's bed. And she starts screamin' (*throwing her body around to scare BEATRICE and MARIE*) and yellin' and twistin' around and all the women come from miles around and hold her arms and shove a rag in her mouth. And then the stork takes his long beak and pops open ma's stomach and pulls the baby out. And blood and goo and other stuff comes with it. And the baby hollers.

(*BEATRICE and MARIE are listening raptly: BEATRICE is delighted, MARIE is horrified.*)

ANNIE. If the baby is a boy, the men light up cigars and drink whiskey and if it's a girl they just go back to work. (*smiling at MARIE proudly*)

MARIE. (*throwing the quilt aside and jumping up*) No. I don't believe you. That's awful and horrible and disgusting.

Fragment 6:"Git An Education"

MARIE. (*walks along the edge of the stage as if balancing on railroad ties*) In winter we went to school and each day I took my little brother, George, by the hand...

(*GEORGE enters, takes MARIE'S hand, and the CHILDREN form a line as they balance along the edge of the platform*)

And guided him there and we knew that we were treading holy ground for my mother constantly spoke of it as such.

(*eventually GEORGE falls and MARIE tries to cheer him up*)

MARIE. Don't feel bad, Georgie. Come on, we'll play a game. What shall we play?

BEATRICE. Indians.

ANNIE. Dress up.

GEORGE. Cowboys.

MARIE. No, I know. Let's play school. And I'm gonna be the teacher. Teacher said if I worked hard I would be the best in the class so I'm the teacher.

ANNIE. I'm the oldest so I should be the teacher.

MARIE. You know you don't give a damn about school, Annie. I'm gonna git an education and be a famous writer some day. So I'm the teacher. (*very firmly*)

GEORGE. Let Marie be the teacher, Annie.

ANNIE. All right. You can be the teacher.

BEATRICE. I wanna play Indians.

MARIE. You can be Jane Lockwood, Beatrice.

BEATRICE. Who's that?

ANNIE. You know. She's the stuck up girl with the doctor father.

BEATRICE. (*making a snooty face*) Oh.

GEORGE. Let me be Clarence, Marie. (*imitating CLARENCE who is clearly a snob*)

MARIE. You be Clarence, Georgie and...

ANNIE. And I'll be you, Marie (*pleased with herself for besting MARIE*)

MARIE. (*squaring off*) You can't be me. I'll be me.

ANNIE. You can't. You're being the teacher.

MARIE. (*making a quick decision*) All right. You be me. Now children (*tapping the table in her best teacher imitation*) let's have quiet, please. Let's say our names and tell what our fathers do. Jane, would you go first?

BEATRICE. *(playing JANE)* My name is Jane Lockwood. And my father's a...*(looking around for help)*

GEORGE. *(whispering)* Doctor.

BEATRICE. My father is a doctor. *(sneering at ANNIE playing MARIE)*

MARIE. Thank you, Jane. Clarence, would you tell us what your father does?

GEORGE. *(playing Clarence)* My name is Clarence Livingston the third and my father is a...lawyer *(rushing to say this before ANNIE can remind him)*

MARIE. Thank you, Clarence. You show such promise. Now, Marie, would you tell what your father does?

(CLARENCE and JANE snicker)

ANNIE. *(playing MARIE as a tough girl)* My name is Marie Rogers and my father farms, hauls bricks, excavates...

GEORGE. *(taunting her, as CLARENCE)* Your father hauls bricks. Your father hauls bricks. Marie's father hauls bricks.

BEATRICE. *(looking down her nose as JANE)* How disgusting.

ANNIE. *(as MARIE)* What the hell is wrong with that? *(coming over to GEORGE and shoving him on the floor and then sitting on top of him while she pummels him)*

GEORGE. *(laughing and yelling)* I bet you live over by the train tracks in one of those beat up shacks. Ha, ha. Your father hauls bricks.

ANNIE. *(getting into it as MARIE)* You shut up, you shut up.

MARIE. Children, stop that. Marie, get off of him. What do you mean by using that disgusting language? *(pulls ANNIE off GEORGE and they all begin to laugh)*

ANNIE. Anyway, he's gonna study to be a doctor soon. An eye specialist. Over in St. Joe.

(the CHILDREN laugh over what is clearly a recent incident)

MARIE. *(getting them back to the game)* Settle down, children. *(addressing ANNIE)* Marie, you are a smart child. You're in the third reader. If you worked hard, you could be the best in the class and sit right here in the front seat.

(ANNIE sticks out tongue at GEORGE and they disintegrate into a free-for-all because that's what they like to do best. BEATRICE is feeling left out.)

BEATRICE. Do the part where teacher shows us directions.

MARIE. What's that, Beatrice?

BEATRICE. You know, north is facing...

MARIE. Oh yes, that's a good one.

(*ANNIE and GEORGE remember it too and they all settle down for the next part of the game*)

MARIE. Now children, we're going to learn directions. Everyone face the blackboard and repeat after me. Ready?

ALL. Ready.

MARIE. Facing the blackboard is North.

ALL. Facing the blackboard is North.

MARIE. South is back over your shoulder.

All. South is back over your shoulder.

MARIE. East is to the right and West is to the left.

ALL. East is to the right and West is to the left.

(*THEY imitate MARIE'S gestures during this and end up in a heap on the floor*)

GEORGE. (*from the middle of the heap*) You sure do make a good teacher, Marie.

MARIE. I know. What I want to know is what happens when you're walking around and get lost and there's no blackboard? How do you know which way is North?

ANNIE. You pretend you're in the classroom, silly. (*begins again*) Facin' the blackboard is North...

BEATRICE. (*interrupting*) Marie, let's play the part where the teacher reads from the book of manners...

GEORGE. Do that part, Marie.

(*THEY all gather around the table for what is clearly the favorite. MARIE spreads quilt like a tablecloth.*)

MARIE. All right, that's a good part. First, we must all learn to eat with a fork. This is the proper way for ladies and gentlemen to eat.

(*THEY all try to eat like ladies and gentlemen*)

MARIE. You must keep your mouth closed when you chew. After meals you must wash your teeth.

ANNIE. (*breaking out of the game for a minute*) What's that, Marie?

MARIE. I don't know. I seen mama do it once in a while. I think you rub some yellow soap on your teeth with your finger.

(*THEY all make faces*)

MARIE. Finally we must learn to take daily baths so we are fresh and clean for school each day.

ANNIE. (*as MARIE again*) Excuse me, Teacher, but how am I gonna do that. Mama only does the wash once a week. That's the only time we get to wash. In the dirty clothes water.

(*CLARENCE and JANE are disgusted at this concept*)

BEATRICE. I take a bath every evening.

GEORGE. So do I.

ANNIE. I can tell. Yer skin's about to fall off. Look at it.

(*ANNIE and GEORGE start to disintegrate into a brawl again*)

BEATRICE. Wait, stop it, Georgie. Marie, tell the part about sleepless nights.

GEORGE. Yes, tell that one.

ANNIE. Yea, sleepless nights.

MARIE. Oh yes. Sleepless nights. Let's see. For those who are sleepless at night they should get up and take a walk (*getting up*). If you have two beds in the room, change to the other bed. Fresh sheets produce sleep.

(*THEY lie on the table and the benches, have trouble sleeping, then move to another spot, ending on the bed in a free-for-all*)

MARIE. (*popping out from under the quilt and sitting up*) Hey, we can't play this game. We don't have any sheets.

(*more tossling and laughing*)

ELLY. (*entering*) Children, fix up that bed. (*CHILDREN hasten to neaten up and look innocent*) Tommorrow's the Harvest Dance and we're havin' it here. You know that, Marie. Marie! Have you been tellin' those stories again?

MARIE. No, Mama. Just talkin' about school.

ELLY. (*very serious*) Marie, you git yourself an education. You promise me now. You got to git an education. (*pauses and waits for an answer*) You promise me.

MARIE. I promise, Mama.

(*The lights begin to dim. GEORGE and BEATRICE fall asleep. ELLY pauses to watch as MARIE gets a book from under the bed, then crosses to get the wash on the line, then exits down right. MARIE begins to read out loud as the lights fade.*)

Fragment 7: "The Harvest Dance"

(*ANNIE exits in the dark and becomes SALLY in the Harvest Dance. The lights come up on MARIE reading while GEORGE sleeps next to her. AUNT HELEN appears on the platform dressed for the dance, carrying a beautiful shawl over her arm.*)

HELEN. Marie. You awake?

MARIE. (*excited*) Aunt Helen.

HELEN. Ssh. Don't wake George. Is Elly around?

MARIE. She's in her room gettin' ready for the Harvest Dance.

HELEN. Is she alone? I mean, where's John?

MARIE. She's alone.

HELEN. I brought her a present. (*holds up the shawl*) Go get her will you, Marie?

(*MARIE admires the shawl then starts off to get ELLY*)

HELEN. And Marie, don't tell her about the shawl. I want to surprise her.

MARIE. I won't. (*stops, then continues off*) Mama, Mama. Aunt Helen's here.

ELLY. (*entering with a tablecloth*) Helen, you're early. It's good to see you. You look lovely. (*gives HELEN a hug*)

HELEN. I brought you a surprise, Elly. Turn around and close your eyes.

(*ELLY looks at MARIE with delight. MARIE wakes up GEORGE so he can watch the surprise. HELEN, with MARIE'S help, puts the shawl around ELLY'S shoulders*)

HELEN. All right, Elly. You can open your eyes now.

ELLY. (*opening her eyes and seeing the shawl*) Oh, Helen, it's beautiful. But it cost a lot of money. You shouldn't be spendin' yer hard earned money on me.

HELEN. I'll spend my money on whatever I want, Elly. Now you need nice things.

JOHN. (*calling from offstage*) Elly, they're comin'. (*entering from the fields*) Where's my whiskey? They'll be thirsty after their long ride. (*sees HELEN*)

JOHN. Helen. Nice to see you.

HELEN. How are you, John?

GEORGE. Pa, look at the present Aunt Helen brought for ma.

ELLY. Ain't it beautiful, John?

JOHN. It's nice all right. (*goes to kitchen to find his flask*) Don't see how you can be buyin' such fancy presents with the wages you make as a hired girl.

HELEN. How I spend my money is my business, John Rogers.

JOHN. I don't need you to be buyin' pretty things for my wife.

ELLY. Now, John, she just wanted to get me something for the dance.

HELEN. I suppose you're gonna buy her nice things, John Rogers.

JOHN. That's none of your business, Helen.

(*JOHN and HELEN argue across ELLY*)

MARIE. Pa's gonna be an doctor some day, Helen, gonna be an eye specialist down in St. Joe...

GEORGE. Yea, and we'll be rich and wear store-bought clothes.

MARIE. Pa's gonna have a hat and a tie that flies in the wind...

(*VOICES come from offstage as the neighbors arrive for the dance. LOU and SALLY enter with bowls of apples, JOE enters and joins up with HELEN. SAM and BETTY bring a guitar and fiddle. They greet JOHN and ELLY, then MARIE and GEORGE. The WOMEN gravitate to the table and the MEN start to tell stories on the platform.*)

SALLY. Help me with these apples, ladies, while I tell you the latest news. I know you didn't hear about Gladys and I'm gonna split if I don't tell someone about it. You know Gladys, Elly, don't you?

ELLY. Why yes. Marie works over her house now and then.

MARIE. I haven't been there in a long time, Mama.

(*MARIE and GEORGE are on the platform trying to listen both to the men and the women depending on which gets more interesting: the gossip or the stories. The WOMEN are at the table peeling apples.*)

ELLY. I heard she wasn't lookin' too well lately.

HELEN. Didn't she quit workin' right after she got married?

SALLY. You bet she quit workin'. Her husband said, "No wife of mine is gonna work."

ELLY. Fine thing. Bein' married and relaxin' all day like that.

SALLY. You're right there. She doesn't do a thing now. Just lays in her bed all day. Sometimes she doesn't get dressed 'til afternoon. Catch me layin' around like that. (*getting another bowl of apples from the kitchen*)

ELLY. What's her husband say?

HELEN. I can imagine.

ELLY. Helen, we know your views about marriage.

SALLY. Listen to this. A few weeks after they were married, they started to fight. All the time, according to the neighbors. Fight after fight. He says, "What're you fussing about, fer Christ sakes?" She says, "I want to go back to work. Yer gone all day and I just sit here at home..."

ELLY. What's the matter with her?

HELEN. She came to her senses, if you ask me...

SALLY. Well, nobody did, Helen. So he says, "What? Go to work and have people saying I can't support my wife? I don't know what you want. You've got duds enough and you hardly have to put yer hands in water."

ELLY. She shouldn't just lay around like that...

HELEN. Well, it's her husband's fault asking her to stay home like that.

(*LOU has come over to snatch some apples and to hear what they're talking about*)

JOHN. What are you women talkin' about? I hope you aren't tellin' tales on people. Georgie, come on over here.

(*GEORGE is delighted to join the men*)

LOU. That's my wife, John. She picked up some tired old story and she's wakin' it up over here. (*trying to snatch some apples from the bowl*)

SALLY. (*hitting his hand playfully with her apple peeler*) I am not, Lou. You mind yer own business over there. We're just exchangin' recipes.

(*the WOMEN smile over SALLY'S lie*)

ELLY. Yes, John, Sally here is just giving me a new recipe for apple pie.

HELEN. Why don't you tell the men one of those stories yer always tellin' about how you're gonna be an eye doctor...

LOU. (*returning to the men upstage*) Not that one.

GEORGE. Tell about the time you were in the flood, Pa, and you saw a stick poking out of the water and you went over to get it and it turned out to be a man's arm. (*acting out his words*) Tell that one, Pa.

JOE. I think you jist told that one for him, Son. Looks like he's gonna take after you, John.

(*the MEN laugh and the WOMEN get back to their gossip and apple peeling*)

SALLY. So she says back...wait, where was I?

MARIE. You were tellin' how he said, "You hardly have to put your hands in water."

SALLY. Oh, yes. So she says, "I want to work." He says back, "An' gad about the streets and stick yer money under my nose? You give me back the clothes I bought." She says, "Damn it, you know I love you. I just want something to do."

ELLY. She should mind her husband although I don't see why she can't find things to do around the house. There's plenty of work.

MARIE. She could take in washin' like we do, Ma.

HELEN. (*sarcastic*) That's a real good livin' now isn't it, Elly?

ELLY. Well...

SALLY. She ought to start havin' babies, if you ask me. That'd keep her busy.

HELEN. That'll put her in her grave...

ELLY. Now, Helen...

SALLY. (*confidentially*) 'Course I heard that now she's expectin' so she couldn't go back to work even if she wanted to.

LOU. (*coming over to flirt with the WOMEN as he's heard John's stories before*) Come on, John, let's see what these pretty women are up to.

SALLY. Get away from here, Lou. We're not done yet.

JOHN. Come on, we want to dance. My feet just won't keep still.

LOU. Mine neither. (*doing a little jig step*) I'm gonna dance the first dance tonight, John, and I swear you're wife is lookin' so fine I just might elope with her. (*sneaking off with ELLY*) Come on, Elly. Get rid of that husband of yours and come dance with me.

(*MUSICIANS begin to improvise as LOU and ELLY twirl*)

JOHN. (*crossing over to retrieve ELLY*) Sorry, Lou, this here is my house, my harvest dance, and my wife. She's dancing the first one with me.

(*JOHN grabs ELLY and they dance a polka center stage. EVERYONE grabs hands and circles around them. The last DANCER grabs JOHN'S hand and they form a circle. MARIE and GEORGE watch from upstage, sneaking apples. JOHN calls the dance.* After the dance and one final swing, the COUPLES go to various corners to talk.*)

LOU. (*after a pause*) Seems like a long time since the last Harvest Dance, doesn't it, John?

JOHN. Sure does.

JOE. Be a long time until the next one, too.

SALLY. Remember now, next year's gonna be at our place.

JOHN. Don't know if we'll be there but we'll sure try.

ELLY. We'll be there, Sally.

SALLY. What's that pretty song you used to sing, John?

LOU. "Sweet Marie."

*See p. 104.

SALLY. Sing that for us, John.

JOHN. That's a pretty song. You'll help me out won't you?

LOU. (*affectionately*) Sally wouldn't miss a chance to use her voice, would you honey?

SALLY. (*softly*) Oh, Lou.

(*Musicians begin to play "Sweet Marie" music.* JOHN sings the first time through then EVERYONE joins him. During the song, MARIE walks along the platform behind her father, watching him proudly, convinced that he is singing to her.*)

> Come to me, Sweet Marie
> Sweet Marie, come to me.
> Not because thy face is fair
> Love to see.
> But because thou art so sweet
> Makes my happiness complete
> Makes me falter at thy feet
> Sweet Marie.

SALLY. (*after a pause*) Come on, Lou. Time to be going.

(*EVERYONE moves to leave, saying goodbye to JOHN and ELLY, then to MARIE and GEORGE, then exits. ELLY begins to clean up the table. MARIE and GEORGE cross to platform right and she puts her arm around him. JOHN stands center watching ELLY work.*)

Fragment 8: "Wandering"

ELLY. (*clearing the bowls of apples*) That was a nice dance, wasn't it, John?

JOHN. It was a nice dance, all right.

(*ELLY senses something is wrong and stops working*)

JOHN. Elly, I got to git away from this farm. It's just endless pettiness.

ELLY. (*busying herself with the wash which she puts back on the wash bench*) It's a steady livin', John.

JOHN. Damn it. There's only three or four dances a year. The rest of the time I have to plow the soil in my bare feet. Stumblin' over the damn stones. I want shoes, Elly. I want to wear shoes year 'round.

*See p. 104.

ELLY. (*crossing to the clothesline*) If we work hard, save a little...

JOHN. (*crossing to ELLY at the clothesline*) Save what? A few pennies a year? I want to make money, Elly. Lots of it. An existence like this is death. (*again, with more feeling*) An existence like this is death. This ain't no kind of life for a man.

ELLY. (*crossing to kitchen*) You're always complainin'. It don't matter to you what we do, you're always complainin'. I carry two buckets of water at a time from the well. That's a mile walk, in my bare feet. I can do that work because it has to be done. Why can't you?

(*They face each other across the stage: JOHN on the platform, ELLY in the kitchen. MARIE and GEORGE are in the middle, watching them.*)

JOHN. All right. If that's what you think of me, I might as well go down to St. Joe and study with that doctor fella. George, Marie, how'd you like to come down to St. Joe and live with yer dad while he studies to be a doctor? I'll make lots of money, we'll be rich. Come on with me. Georgie?

GEORGE. (*looks at MARIE who shakes her head and grabs hold of his hand, but he pulls away and goes over to JOHN*) I'd like that, Pa.

ELLY. You oughta be ashamed of yourself, tellin' such things to the children. If you want to run away and leave us, just go. Don't come tellin' stories for an excuse.

JOHN. Marie? Come on with yer pa. We can see Fisher's Peak after I git to be a doctor. Daughter? Yer ma treats ya like dogs anyway.

(*ELLY crosses wearily to the washtub bench and sits. She is crying softly. MARIE watches her.*)

JOHN. (*softly*) Marie? I thought you always dreamed of going to St. Joe with me.

(*MARIE looks one last time at JOHN then crosses to stand behind ELLY who turns and sees her. The lights change as MARIE narrates.*)

MARIE. My father didn't go away then, and I thought it was because I would not go with him. But he won at last for we all went away and from that moment our roots were torn from the soil and we began a life of wandering, searching for success and happiness and riches that always lay just beyond where we were not. Finally one winter he did go away. The shining railway tracks stretched to the horizon, melted together and plunged over the edge of the world. Over there where my father had gone; into the distance where happiness was. Only since then have I heard the old saying, "where I am not, there is happiness."

(*ANNIE and BEATRICE enter up left and stand by the clothesline. ELLY turns toward JOHN. MARIE turns after ELLY. GEORGE stands up. JOHN exits as the lights fade on the tableau.*)

Fragment 9: "You're a God Damn Thief"

(*MARIE is upstage right reading to GEORGE. ANNIE is doing the washing. ELLY hangs the wash. BEATRICE plays with her doll near the clothesline.*)

MARIE. My father returned and we settled on the outskirts of Trinidad, Colorado. He spoke no more of his dreams of becoming a doctor, of dressing my mother in silk. He had his own team and wagon now and he signed a contract to haul coal for a mine owner.

ELLY. Git that wash done, Annie. Mr. Turner be here soon to pay yer pa for haulin' coal.

(*GEORGE sneaks over to dip his fingers in the pot of stew*)

ELLY. Git outta that pot of stew, George. That's for Mr. Turner.

GEORGE. What're we havin' fer dinner, Ma?

ELLY. Git away from that food, George.

MARIE. Come on, Georgie. I'll read you about a handsome cowboy with a shiny silver belt buckle and a six gun slung at his hip.

GEORGE. (*walking over to the clothesline and running his hands along the rope*) What's a mine owner look like?

MARIE. (*engrossed in her books*) Mean and ugly.

ANNIE. (*crossing platform bench where she keeps her mirror*) And fat.

GEORGE. From eatin' too much. Rich people eat all the time, don't they, Ma?

ELLY. (*bitterly*) They ain't starvin'.

BEATRICE. They eat whole pigs, and turtles, and sometimes, I heard, they eat little boys. Juicy little boys.

ELLY. Annie and Marie, come help me with this pot. (*to kitchen*) George, why don't you see if yer pa's comin' with Mr. Turner.

GEORGE. Sure, Ma.

(*MARIE and ANNIE hurry to set the table. GEORGE starts off at a run and runs right into MR. TURNER whose hat falls sideways.*)

JOHN. Look where yer goin', Georgie.

GEORGE. (*backing toward MARIE and whispering loudly*) Look, Marie, it's the mine owner and he's got a gold watch and chain.

ELLY. Hush, Georgie.

JOHN. Mr. Turner, I'd like you to meet my wife, Elly.

(*ELLY curtseys from the kitchen. MR. TURNER nods.*)

JOHN. And here's my daughters, Annie, Marie, and Beatrice. And my son, George. And my baby, Dan, is off sleepin'.

(the CHILDREN nod and/or curtsey to MR. TURNER who looks at them with patronizing disgust)

MR. TURNER. Quite a family you've got there, John.

JOHN. Come on over to the table, Mr. Turner. Elly's fixed up a nice meal fer you.

(JOHN and TURNER cross to the table. MARIE hurries GEORGE over to the platform bench and they are joined by BEATRICE. ANNIE brings plates of beans and bread and sits. ELLY serves TURNER.)

GEORGE. *(taking the plate handed to him)* Beans and bacon again.

ANNIE. Hush, George.

(TURNER takes out a handkerchief and surreptitiously cleans the bench and the silverware before eating)

JOHN. *(making polite conversation)* It's been a pretty good year, Mr. Turner. Good group of men workin' with me.

TURNER. Haulin' coal takes a good group of men, John.

JOHN. Haven't had any trouble. Had to shoot a rattler, now and then.

TURNER. Rattlers can cause some trouble, Rogers.

ELLY. Would you like more stew, Mr. Turner?

TURNER. Yes. Mighty good food, Mrs. Rogers.

(KIDS eye the food as TURNER eats stew while they eat beans and bacon)

JOHN. *(excited about the money he thinks he's getting)* I got me a good team of horses.

TURNER. Haulin' coal takes a good team of horses. *(wipes his mouth carefully and takes out a wallet filled with money)* You're a good worker, John. No doubt about it. You've earned your pay, that's for sure. *(takes out money, counts it softly to himself, then puts it in front of JOHN)*

(KIDS and ELLY stare at the money which seems like a lot to them. JOHN counts.)

JOHN. Is this all yer givin' me? Me and my wife have been workin' like dogs.

TURNER. *(taking the money out of JOHN'S hands)* Isn't it all there. *(counts it)* Yep, it's all there. Look at the contract, John. I believe that's what we agreed on.

JOHN. This isn't enough to buy my wife a shirt.

TURNER. Look at the contract. Look at the contract. *(starts to get up)*

JOHN. *(rising)* God man, I worked from daylight 'til dark since May with my own team and wagon, fer you.

TURNER. (*getting his hat which ELLY has hung on the hook in the kitchen*) You seem to be able to afford good food here. You're not starving.

ELLY. We never have such things. I made them special fer you.

GEORGE. We always have beans and bacon.

TURNER. I'm holding you to your contract, John. Here's your signature (*takes contract from breast pocket and puts in front of JOHN*)

JOHN. Damn you, you know I can't read that thing. I trusted you. I come from a place where a man's word is his honor. He don't need no piece of paper. (*shoves contract aside*)

TURNER. (*picks up contract then looks at his gold watch*) Let's keep our temper, now. I have expenses too.

JOHN. So we're to work to buy silk dresses for yer wife and kids. Look at my wife. (*goes to kitchen and pushes ELLY forward*) She's thirty and she looks fifty. Think of it, man. And you come here and show me a piece of paper. You're a god damn thief, stealin' bread out of the mouths of children. (*crosses to KIDS on the bench and grabs a plate of food*) Look at this. That's what they been eatin' every night. Beans and bacon. (*shoves plate under TURNER'S nose, then slams it on the table*) God damn you, Turner. You god damn lyin' dirty thief.

(*Grabs TURNER by the throat and throws him against the wall. ELLY rushes to interfere. The KIDS silently cheer JOHN on.*)

ELLY. John, don't. They'll put you in prison.

TURNER. I'll have you arrested for this, John Rogers. Let go of me.

JOHN. I don't care. You're a god damn thief. There's not enough money there to feed a dog.

ELLY. John, please.

TURNER. Let go of me.

(*JOHN struggles and then realizes he's lost and releases TURNER who straightens his clothes, hunts for his hat*)

TURNER. You've got your money, Rogers. (*nods to ELLY*) Ma'am. (*looks at his watch, at the KIDS with disgust, then exits*)

ELLY. (*as she cleans up*) We can't live on that money, John. That ain't enough fer food fer the kids, let alone shoes and clothes.

JOHN. I heard of a job over in Tercio. Excavatin'.

ELLY. (*stops working*) Yer leavin' again.

JOHN. (*getting his hat and a doubled up rope from the kitchen*) I got to git out of here, Elly. I got to git some money. Don't look at me like that.

ELLY. You got some woman over there. That's why yer leavin'.

JOHN. I'll send fer you, when I git settled.

ELLY. You'll send fer me? I'm supposed to pack up and move the kids? What about their education?

JOHN. (*looking guiltily at the kids*) I told you I'll send fer you. It's none of yer business what I do. (*exits*)

ELLY. (*crying*) Please don't go...

(*JOHN looks at her, turns away and exits. ELLY crosses to the washtub bench. ANNIE and MARIE start to clean the table then stop as ELLY crosses slowly to the bed and lies down as the lights spotlight MARIE. The OTHERS freeze in tableau as MARIE crosses to stairs*)

Fragment 10: "I'll Be Paying My Own Way"

MARIE. We moved to Tercio, a Colorado Coal and Mine Company camp. My father would contract for work excavating for mine owners. He was making money now. I would stand at the edge of an excavation and watch him through the cloud of dust below. He was deaf to all things but his work. Had I gone close to him, he would not have seen me. His mind was working in great circles and I knew that back deep it was sweeping over the horizon of his life, far beyond. He was digging not just a hole in the ground but uncovering marvelous things, all that lies in the earth. And that I knew for I knew him. Because I was my father's daughter. After a time, lured by enthusiastic letters from my mother, Aunt Helen came to join us.

(*MARIE grabs GEORGE crosses the platform to find her book. ANNIE sits at the table. BIG BUCK enters and bumps into MARIE.*)

BUCK. Marie, I been lookin' for you.

MARIE. Buck. I thought you were out workin' with pa.

BUCK. I'm goin' soon. I know you wanted to go out shootin' squirrels so I brought you a present.

MARIE. What is it? Let me see it? George, Buck's got a present for me.

GEORGE. (*tries to look behind BUCK'S back*) Let me see, Buck.

BUCK. Calm down, Georgie. Here it is, Marie. A gun fer your very own. To replace that plaything you been carrying around.

MARIE. A real gun of my own. Thanks, Buck.

BUCK. Don't mention it.

GEORGE. Aunt Helen's comin' to stay, Buck. I bet she brings *me* a present.

BUCK. Sure she will. And when yer old enough, George, I'll bring you a gun and teach you to shoot, like Marie.

MARIE. Wanna go huntin' with me, Buck?

BUCK. Can't. Got to work. Yer pa's got us excavatin' over on the edge of town. (*exits*)

GEORGE. When's Aunt Helen comin', Ma? Bet she's got a present for me.

ELLY. (*getting her sewing from under the bed*) I don't know what's keepin' her, Georgie. But don't you be askin' for any gifts.

HELEN. (*entering on the platform*) Gifts? Did I hear something about gifts? Who's getting gifts. I hope there's one for me.

(*EVERYONE gathers around as HELEN goes to hug ELLY. The KIDS are happy to see HELEN but disappointed that there are no gifts.*)

HELEN. My, it's good to be here. Where's my room so I can unpack. Oh, well, I'm not shy. I'll just unpack right here. (*puts her suitcase down on the table and starts to rummage around in it*) Now what have I got in here? (*pulls out some lotion*) My, I didn't mean to bring this. This is cream for a young girl trying to beautify herself. I sure don't need that. (*tosses the lotion in ANNIE'S direction who catches it*) Now what's this? I sure don't need this. I got plenty of dresses and this isn't my size anyway. Now how'd that get in here? (*throws the dress in MARIE'S direction who catches it*) And look, what am I doing with a pair of young men's shoes? How embarrassing. Don't need these at all. (*tosses them in GEORGE'S direction who catches them*) My goodness, I didn't do a very good job of packing because I seem to have put this calico in here and everybody knows I don't wear calico. (*places the calico in ELLY'S hands, then closes the suitcase*) Well, I'm glad I got rid of that stuff. Where's my room, Elly? Time's a wasting. Gotta get me a job.

(*EVERYONE is so excited about their new presents that they don't notice JOHN entering platform right*)

JOHN. What's going on here?

HELEN. Hello, John.

JOHN. (*nodding*) Helen.

ANNIE. (*interrupting*) Pa, Aunt Helen's come to stay for a while and she brought us presents. Look.

(*ANNIE holds up lotion, MARIE her dress, and GEORGE his shoes*)

JOHN. That's nice of you, Helen.

HELEN. Thank you, John.

ELLY. She brought me some calico to make some new dresses.

JOHN. Wonder where you got the money fer all this stuff, Helen.

HELEN. That's my business, isn't it, John?

JOHN. Not if yer stayin' in my house, it ain't...

ELLY. Now, John...

MARIE. (*interrupting quickly and crossing to the washtub bench with GEORGE*) Where are ya gonna get a job, Helen?

ANNIE. (*joining MARIE and GEORGE on the washtub bench*) Yes. Why don't you work in the laundry, Aunt Helen?

HELEN. The laundry. (*crosses behind the washtub bench and rests hands on ANNIE'S shoulders*) What do they pay? Remember, I've been gettin' six dollars a month as a hired girl. And the oldest son even wanted to marry me.

ELLY. (*sitting on the bed and busying herself with sewing*) The laundry ain't a respectable place for a woman to work, Helen.

JOHN. (*puts his foot on the platform bench and plays with his doubled up rope*) Besides, it's real hard work. Why don't ya git a job as a hired girl agin. Plenty of nice families around here.

HELEN. I am not afraid of hard work, John Rogers. And I can take care of myself anywhere. What do they pay at the laundry, Annie?

ANNIE. Seven dollars a week on the mangle.

HELEN. And the stiff shirt machine?

ANNIE. Eleven.

HELEN. Eleven dollars a week! That settles it. I'm going to work in the laundry. It's better hours and better pay. Workin' as a hired girl, I gotta work from sunrise to sunset and sometimes to midnight. At least at the laundry it's only ten hours a day.

ANNIE. Let me go with you down to the laundry, Helen.

HELEN. All right, Annie. (*takes ANNIE'S hand and they start up the stairs*) You know what we're going to do with my first paycheck? (*turns back*) We're going to buy you a new dress, Marie, and one for Annie too, and then the rest of my paycheck I'm giving to you, Elly.

ELLY. Helen, I can't let you do that. It's yer money. You keep it. I won't be takin' money from you.

HELEN. All right, Elly. I'll take the first ten dollars for myself but the rest is for you and the kids. I've got nice things and the kids don't. You can't be living like tramps all your life. (*starting off again*)

JOHN. You watch yer tongue, Helen. We're doing all right. We don't need yer money.

ELLY. She's just tryin' to help.

JOHN. Well she ain't helpin'. I know where she gits her money...

ELLY. John...

HELEN. Don't you tell me what to do, John Rogers. And who are you to tell me where I can and can't get my money? You keep going off and leaving Elly. You may be able to boss your wife but you won't boss me. Because I'll be paying my way here. Get that straight. No man ever bossed me around and no man ever will, as long as I pay my keep. (*turning and flipping her skirts at him*) You hear me? (*exits then pokes her head back in*) Come on, Annie. Let's get me a job. (*flips her skirts again and exits*)

ANNIE. Comin', Aunt Helen.

(*ANNIE runs after HELEN. GEORGE and MARIE exchange looks of admiration for HELEN. JOHN shakes his head at ELLY who starts back to work as the lights fade.*)

Fragment 11: "He Was a Lean Lanky Cowboy"

(*ELLY, JOHN, and GEORGE exit in the dark. MARIE crosses to the platform and as the lights come up, JIM WATSON enters on the platform, leans against the wall, and smokes a cigarette.*)

MARIE. He was a lean lanky cowboy of twenty-eight and he worked for my father. He had left his cattle ranch in New Mexico for a time to go out and see the world. He, like many of the men who worked for my father, tired of one place or one kind of work and moved on to the next. The cowboys were men who, as a rule, carried all their possessions with them. I was a friend of all these men. I admired and envied them. When they received their wages, they spent them in one night on the hill where women sell themselves to men's desires. When they married, which was rare, they married only virgins. Women had nothing but virginity to trade for a bed and food for the rest of their lives and fathers protected their daughters as men guard their bank accounts, with a gun slung at the hips and a gleam of warning in the eye.

(*MARIE checks her gun then starts off left. JIM calls to her.*)

JIM. Marie, where you going in such a hurry?

MARIE. Goin' up the canyon to look fer squirrels. Big Buck give me a gun and he's letting me borrow his pony.

JIM. Buck give you that gun?

MARIE. Yep.

JIM. Let me see it.

MARIE. Jim Watson, I'm in a hurry...

JIM. Well, then, mind if I come along?

MARIE. I guess I don't mind.

JIM. (pleased with himself) Good.

MARIE. Come on then, I'm in a hurry.

JIM. We'll go in a minute. Let's just sit a minute while I roll me a cigarette.

MARIE. Jim Watson, I told you I'm gonna hunt squirrels.

JIM. I got something for you.

MARIE. What?

JIM. Come on over here, I'll show you.

MARIE. (interested) Is it another gun? Buck already gave me a gun.

JIM. It's not a gun.

MARIE. Well, what then?

JIM. I brought you a gold chain for around your neck.

MARIE. (with a poor attempt at enthusiasm) A gold chain? Thanks, Jim. (MARIE hangs chain around her neck and THEY both stare off at the scenery, embarrassed)

JIM. (squatting down and rolling a cigarette) I sure wish you could see my cattle ranch down in New Mexico, Marie. It's mighty pretty. Got a hundred acres of land. Horses, cattle, plenty of squirrels for shooting.

MARIE. (kneels and examines her gun) Sounds great.

JIM. Ever seen a cattle ranch, Marie?

MARIE. Not lately. Can't say as I ever have. I read about 'em in books, though.

JIM. Think you'd like to come down and see my cattle ranch some day?

MARIE. Maybe.

JIM. Maybe? Is that a yes or a no?

MARIE. Just maybe.

JIM. Well, what would you think about getting married to me? (checks for a reaction, then hurries on) Then my ranch would be half yours. (sees her unenthusiastic expression and starts piling it on) And you could have a pony of your own...

MARIE. (getting interested) A pony of my own?

JIM. And I'll get you a regular .45 instead of that thing Buck gave you.

MARIE. A .45? (*puts gun in her belt*)

JIM. Well, what do you say to getting married?

MARIE. Maybe.

JIM. Maybe? Well, how about I get you some nice gloves and a new hat. What do ya say?

MARIE. A ranch, a pony of my own, a gun, some gloves and a new hat?

JIM. And a regular .45.

MARIE. Well...sure.

JIM. Honest?

MARIE. Sure.

JIM. (*rising and taking off his hat*) Yahoo! My pony is yours now and as soon as I get into town I'll get you a .45 and gloves. Then you can give Buck back that gun he give you.

MARIE. (*touches her gun protectively*) What did you say?

JIM. I said you could give Buck back that gun he give you.

MARIE. (*rising*) Not by a long shot I don't. What's wrong with this here gun?

JIM. Well, it's give to you by another man and when you're going to marry me...

MARIE. (*squares off*) Well, you can just take a running jump at yourself, Jim Watson. There ain't nothin' wrong with this here gun. (*looking ready to draw on him*)

JIM. (*laughs to cover up*) Oh, Marie, I was just joshing. Just to see what you'd do. When I give you a gun, you'll have two guns. It ain't every girl that's got two guns.

MARIE. Well, all right. (*very politely*) Thank you.

(*THEY gaze ahead*)

JIM. (*trying to assert his sexual power over her*) Ain't you gonna...ain't you gonna kiss me? (*approaches her*)

MARIE. (*disgusted, moving away*) Am I supposed to?

JIM. You're supposed to.

(*JIM gets ready to kiss her. MARIE looks disgusted but braces herself by closing her eyes, making fists, and tilting her head up. JIM kisses her on the lips then releases her with great satisfaction. MARIE turns away from him, wipes her mouth, spits, then narrates.*)

MARIE. It never occurred to me that marriage for myself meant what it did for other people. Ordinary marriage was something too awful even to think about. But it wouldn't be half bad to have someone love me. The idea caught in my blood as a hook catches on a snag in a stream.

Fragment 12: "Dooties?"

(*Lights up full as ELLY enters and crosses to kitchen area. JOHN enters and heads for the table. FRANK and GEORGE enter and stand along the platform watching JIM and MARIE with romantic interest. ANNIE enters and goes to help ELLY put the food on the table.*)

ELLY. Marie, help me git the supper on the table. And bring in the wash.

(*MARIE starts for the clothesline, sees JIM as he starts for the table, and grabs his arm*)

MARIE. Where you goin', Jim Watson.

JIM. Going to talk to your pa.

MARIE. (*talking softly so JOHN and ELLY can't hear*) Yer not gonna blab about our gittin' married are ya?

JIM. Well, sure. I got to ask your pa. That's the proper way to do it.

JOHN. (*looking up from his meal*) Ask me what?

JIM. (*crossing to JOHN*) I asked Marie to marry me and she said she would so now I'm asking your permission.

(*JOHN looks at ELLY who shakes her head. GEORGE and ANNIE are smiling. MARIE is angry. JIM is pleased*)

JOHN. What do you mean you asked Marie to marry you? Marie!

MARIE. Yes, Pa?

JOHN. Marie!

MARIE. (*suddenly very busy with the wash*) I'm busy, Pa. Gotta take down the wash.

ELLY. Marie, your father's talkin' to you.

MARIE. Oh. Well, then I gotta clean up. (*very busy cleaning dishes from the table*)

ELLY. Marie, we haven't had our supper yet.

JOHN. (*very firmly*) Marie!!

MARIE. Yes, Pa. (*jumps, drops dishes but stays near ELLY*)

JOHN. Marie, Jim here has told me that you and he is goin' to git married. (*rises and brings JIM forward*)

MARIE. Yes, Pa. (*shyly taking JIM'S arm*) And we're gonna live on his cattle ranch and it'll be half mine.

GEORGE. (*worried*) Is Marie gonna leave us, Pa?

ELLY. Hush, Son.

JOHN. Marie?

MARIE. I'll have a gun, two guns, and a pony of my own...

JOHN. You're too young to get married.

MARIE. I'm near fifteen.

GEORGE. Are you leavin', Marie?

ELLY. George...

JOHN. Nobody's leavin', George. Marie, that's too young. You're not of age 'til yer eighteen.

ELLY. That's right, Marie.

MARIE. Lot's of girls get married before eighteen. Annie's practically engaged.

ANNIE. I am not.

JOHN. Annie's more grown up than you. Besides, there's things in marriage you don't know nothing about.

GEORGE. Marie knows about everything, Pa.

MARIE. Things? What things? Ma, what things?

ELLY. Listen to your father, Marie.

(*ANNIE and FRANK snicker. GEORGE is worried. JIM is embarrassed.*)

JOHN. There's...well, there's...uh...dooties.

(*ANNIE and FRANK can hardly contain themselves. ELLY tries to hush ANNIE.*)

MARIE. (*looking around in horror and disgust at EVERYONE*) Dooties?

ANNIE. Yep. Dooties.

GEORGE. What's dooties, Pa?

ELLY. George...

MARIE. Dooties, Pa?

JOHN. Now, Marie...

MARIE. (*to ELLY*) Ma?

ELLY. Yes, Marie.

MARIE. (*sees JIM smiling and realizes finally what dooties really are*) Dooties. I won't have nothin' to do with dooties. Dooties be damned. Some things make me sick (*runs past Jim to the platform, then stops*) Annie. Annie. Come here. Give Jim back his gold chain and tell him I don't want no ranch, no pony, no gun, no gloves from him.

ANNIE. (*gets chain from MARIE, then crosses back to JIM who is looking baffled*) Jim, Marie says to give you yer gold chain back. She says she don't want it, and she don't want no ranch, no pony, no gun, and no gloves from you.

MARIE. And no hat, neither.

ANNIE. No hat, neither.

GEORGE. And no dooties, right, Marie?

(*FRANK begins to hum "Red River Valley" as JIM looks at JOHN, then at MARIE, and slowly climbs stairs to the platform. He exits after one last look at MARIE.*)

Fragment 13: "I'll Maul Hell Out of You"

(*The lights change as MARIE crosses to the platform, gets her book, and sits on the bench to read. ANNIE and JOHN and FRANK exit. ELLY goes to the bed to begin sewing.*)

MARIE. Come on, George. Sit here and read to me. I'm gonna teach you and git you an education.

GEORGE. (*crossing left and sitting*) I can't read, Marie. You know I'm not as smart as you.

MARIE. You got to git an education, George, so you can go be a doctor like pa. Try to read, and I'll help you.

(*GEORGE starts to read aloud. HELEN enters carrying a new dress for MARIE.*)

HELEN. Marie, you're an insurrection. You're always reading. Put that book down and let me see how this dress looks on you.

MARIE. (*stands up and HELEN holds dress against her*) It's pretty, Aunt Helen. Do you like it, Ma?

ELLY. It's nice, Marie. You shouldn't be spendin' your money on us, Helen.

HELEN. She's got to start looking nice, Elly. She's growing up. She'll be looking for a husband one of these days. Say, Marie, how would you like to shampoo your hair with eggs, the way I do. (*playing with MARIE'S hair as MARIE knees down*)

GEORGE. (*making a face*) With eggs?

HELEN. Don't worry, George, I got something different in mind for you. It's time you started looking like a man...

MARIE. You think my hair will ever look nice and soft like yours, Aunt Helen?

HELEN. Sure it will.

GEORGE. Aunt Helen?

HELEN. What is it, Georgie?

GEORGE. (*putting the book away and getting up*) How come you never married?

ELLY. George, that's none of your business.

HELEN. Why would I want to marry, George?

(*JOHN enters on the platform pushing ANNIE ahead of him into the room. ELLY puts her sewing down and gets up.*)

JOHN. You git in here.

ANNIE. Stop it, Pa.

JOHN. I'll maul hell out of you. I wouldn't care if you were twenty-five years old and as big as the side of a house, I'd still maul hell out of you.

ANNIE. I told you a thousand times I went to the dance and stayed all night with Millie. Go ask her ma if you don't believe me.

JOHN. You're lying. (*takes a swig from flask he keeps in his back pocket*)

ANNIE. (*coming back toward JOHN*) I'm lyin', am I? Then what you ask me for?

JOHN. (*putting flask back in his pocket*) I'll let you go this time, but next time if I hear of you goin' to that dance and dancin' with pimps and stayin' out all night, I'll maul hell out of you.

ANNIE. You look out for yourself, Pa, and I'll take care of myself. You're always in the saloon. You ain't got nothin' to say to me, Pa. I'm makin' my own money now.

JOHN. Yea, you earn your own money all right, and a lot of good it does us. Helen gives her money to yer ma but you spend yours on duds for paradin' about the streets.

ANNIE. Why don't you give yer money to Ma, I'd like to know, instead of spendin' it in the saloon?

JOHN. (*grabbing her arm with one hand and getting his rope from his back pocket with the other*) No back talk from you, Miss. You do as I say or I'll maul hell out of you.

ANNIE. (*trying to free herself*) You leave go of me. I told you I'm payin' my own way now and you can't say nothin' to me. You're not goin' to boss me anymore. (*frees herself and runs off*)

(JOHN looks at ELLY who is staring at him from near the bed. HELEN looks away. MARIE and GEORGE are scared.)

JOHN. Don't be so self-righteous, Elly. God damn you. Why're you starin' at me. I swear, Elly, you're accusin' eyes are gonna drive me into the mines. *(slams his rope on the table and exits)*

ELLY. *(after a pause)* I'm just gonna sit a minute. The pains in my shoulders is pretty bad. *(sits on bed)*

HELEN. *(crosses to ELLY and gives her some money)* Elly, this is for you.

ELLY. No, Helen.

HELEN. Take it, Elly. I got nice things and you ain't. I know John's not bringing his money home. *(crosses to platform again, looks at ELLY, then at MARIE and GEORGE, then exits.)*

MARIE. *(goes slowly to the washtub)* Mama, let me take some of Helen's money and buy you a new dress. And some shoes.

ELLY. *(rising and crossing to the washtub)* No. That money's fer you kids. You'll need shoes fer school.

MARIE. Please, Mama. You don't have any nice things.

ELLY. I don't need nice things. I don't need nothin'. I don't go nowhere and I don't see nobody.

(MARIE watches ELLY as GEORGE comes forward and stands with MARIE in tableau as the lights change)

Fragment 14: "There Was a Mine Explosion"

(In dim light JOHN, FRANK, BUCK, and ANNIE enter. The MEN sit at the table, ANNIE sits with ELLY on the bed. GEORGE sits on the platform. THEY are in a tableau when MARIE starts her narration.)

MARIE. *(beginning a long circle around the back of the platform)* My life in those years that followed was gray and colorless. *(running fingers along the clothesline)* Never had I known such a lonely place. Up the canyon to the west lay gaping, gas-reeking mines abandoned after explosions that killed nearly a hundred men and burned the mines out. In the village, the saloon, the sign that Rockefeller civilization lay near. Beyond the saloon, the schoolhouse stood on the borders of Tercio, a Colorado Coal and Mining Company camp. To the miners, as to us, existence meant working, sleeping, eating what and when you could, and breeding. For amusement, there was the saloon for the men, and for the women, nothing.

(ELLY begins sewing. ANNIE is combing her hair. The MEN begin a game of poker after inviting GEORGE to play. BUCK deals first. MARIE sits and reads near the platform bench.)

FRANK. Damn strike. *(looking at his cards and getting two from the dealer)* Can't walk into town without passing those troops standin' around starin'.

BUCK. *(dealing three cards to JOHN)* Only food we can get is at the company store. And they're not giving any credit.

FRANK. Damn company owns the store, the saloon, the bank. Look at this here. *(pulls out "money")* They only pay in scrip, and you can't get full value for that. Even at the company store.

BUCK. That's the only place you *can* use the damn money—at the company store. *(gets two cards)*

GEORGE. Two, Buck. *(gets two cards)* Come on, Frank, ain't ya gonna bet something?

(the MEN laugh)

FRANK. Sure, Georgie, I'm bettin' two match sticks on this hand I got here.

JOHN. I'm out.

GEORGE. See ya two, and raise ya....*(thinking it over while the MEN exchange patient smiles)* two.

BUCK. *(whistles)* I don't know, George. *(checks his hand)* I'll stay with it. *(puts in match sticks)*

FRANK. Let's see what we got.

BUCK. Two pair. Jacks and fives.

FRANK. Beats me...*(throws his cards down)*

GEORGE. Pa, does this beat two pair?

BUCK. What's he got there?

JOHN. Full house.

(GEORGE smiles over at MARIE. ELLY and ANNIE look up from their work. JOHN deals the next hand.)

BUCK. I hear they closed the school on account of the strike.

JOHN. Only good thing they done. Always thought that school was no damn good.

FRANK. Only rich girls who are sickly and do nothin' go to school.

JOHN. Dudes and women. That's what school is for. *(looks over at*

ELLY)

BUCK. I don't know, John. Getting an education might be a good thing. Marie's getting an education and she's a real smart girl.

FRANK. What's she gonna do with that education anyhow?

ELLY. She's gonna be a great writer some day. And she's gonna vote in an election, 'cause women got the vote now. She'll be smart enough to vote for the right people.

FRANK. You plannin' to vote, Mrs. Rogers?

ELLY. One of these days, I just might.

FRANK. And who might you be votin' fer?

ELLY. Ain't gonna tell.

BUCK. Who's she voting for, John?

JOHN. She's not gonna be votin' at all, if I have anything to say about it. Now are we playing poker or not?

GEORGE. I'm bettin' two.

JOHN. I'm out.

BUCK. The kid's at it again, John. I'll see your two and raise you three.

FRANK. You don't scare me. I'll see your two and call your three.

BUCK. Full house.

FRANK. Damn. That beats me again.

GEORGE. I got four of these kings here.

(*The MEN all marvel at his hand. FRANK goes and gets a drink from kitchen shelf and brings the flask back to the table.*)

FRANK. I sure wish they'd get this strike over with. State militia's making me fearful about my daughter.

BUCK. Wouldn't let your daughter walk home from work alone, if I was you, Frank.

JOHN. I been thinking about this strike. Strikin' ain't no good seems to me. (*starts to deal*) Company just brings in strike breakers. They can outsmart ya every time.

FRANK. That's right. Ain't no point to this strike. Just git themselves starved.

BUCK. Or shot.

ELLY. It's the mine owners, they're all rich people.

FRANK. What workin' man can sit home for long and watch his wife and family starve to death? They'll all go back to work soon.

JOHN. It just ain't right to strike. A man's paid to do his job and he oughtta do it. You men are workin' for me and I expect you to do your work, ain't that right? You work hard enough and someday you git rich.

BUCK. You worked hard all your life, John, and you ain't rich. Mine owner's rich enough. Can't see where he's worked hard all his life.

JOHN. Some people don't think I've worked hard enough. (*looks over at ELLY*)

ELLY. It's the fault of the rich.

JOHN. I sure can't figure out how.

BUCK. They stole it. That's how. Just like this son of yours is getting rich robbing us blind at the poker table here.

FRANK. Come on, George, I call you...let's see those cards.

BUCK. (*looking at GEORGE'S cards*) I'm gonna take up drinkin' for the rest of the evening. He's got a straight.

FRANK. (*throws cards down*) I can't keep my mind on the game anyhow. Damn it, John, those miners ought to get a better deal. Every day when they go to the weigh boss, he weighs 'em low. The miners know they're being cheated. Hell, we all know they're being cheated but every day they come up to the weigh boss and he weighs 'em low.

BUCK. If I was them I guess I'd be on strike too.

FRANK. I'm surprised one of them bosses ain't been shot yet.

BUCK. (*squatting on the bench behind the table*) Not with the sheriff we got. You seen the gun he's carrying? It's the biggest gun I ever saw. He struts around town with that thing..."I'm letting you miners know that I am paid for doing my do-o-o-o-tie and I'm going to do it."

FRANK. (*imitating the miners*) "Yes sir, Mr. Sherriff, sir."

(*THEY laugh bitterly*)

ELLY. People get what they deserve. You work for the company, you get what you deserve. (*crosses to MARIE and holds up the dress to see if it fits*)

FRANK. Man's got to do what's necessary, Ma'am.

BUCK. State militia's outside your door, you do what's necessary.

JOHN. Something's gonna happen though. There's only so much a man can take.

BUCK. The other day this fella that works over in the mines forgot to meet his daughter after work at the laundry. She didn't come home. He waited awhile. Then he went to look for her. He found her in the possession of two soldiers away down between some piles of lumber in the lumber yard.

FRANK. I bet if there'd been a soldier murdered and they'd chosen a jury from our side of the tracks, no father would have been convicted.

BUCK. No man would have stood as a witness against him.

(*The MEN are drinking now. GEORGE plays with the cards. MARIE has forgotten about her book. ANNIE has stopped combing her hair.*)

JOHN. This ain't no kind of life for a man. I was gonna be a doctor once, Had a chance to train with one of them eye specialists over in St. Joe. I coulda been rich. With fancy clothes, a tie that flies in the wind and a silver belt buckle that shines in the sun.

(*ELLY crosses slowly back to the bed and sits*)

BUCK. (*sits on the edge of the platform*) I wish I was back on my ranch in Texas. When the weather was good, we used to sit outside my kitchen door, talking and singing. (*gradually he is lit by a blue spotlight*) The moon'd be coming up. Every now and then you'd hear some kind of animal off in the distance, making a soft sound 'cause it was so far away. One of the men would take out a French harp. Another would tell stories. I remember one man, he'd always get up and dance. He was the most beautiful dancer I ever saw. He'd bend over and dance and sway until the heels of his boots sounded like pistol shots on the ground. His face would be turned up to the moon. The moonlight would run up and down the leg of his black boots. That must have been fifteen...no, more like twenty years ago, come to think of it.

(*Lights begin to fade on this tableau. When the lights are almost out, there's the sound of an explosion in the distance and a bright light flashes. THEY stand and freeze in tableau as MARIE narrates.*)

MARIE. There was a mine explosion over in Primero. The road was black with coal dust. People were running through the streets. The windows of the company store where shattered into bits. The mine was belching black smoke. Men were drawing ropes around the base of the slag dump and trying to beat back the struggling women. The air shafts had been closed to save the coal but the fumes would smother the men trapped in the shafts to death. I heard the scream of a woman.

(*Offstage a WOMAN screams. Blackout. JOHN, FRANK, and BUCK exit.*)

Fragment 15: "You're a Whore"

(*ELLY takes wash from the clothesline and crosses to the washtub. GEORGE and MARIE cross to the platform. ANNIE crosses to kitchen shelf. THEY hear JOHN offstage and look at each other in fear.*)

JOHN. *(from offstage)* What the hell is going on here?

ELLY. Where's Helen?

ANNIE. She's out on the porch with that fella she's been seein'.

JOHN. *(from offstage)* Git inside you...

(JOHN drags HELEN in by the hair. HELEN pulls herself free and faces him on the platform.)

JOHN. *(taking a rope from his back pocket)* Look, Marie. Look at your Aunt Helen. I caught her lyin' out on the porch with that dago beau of hers. Payin' for her clothes. That's what she's been doing.

ELLY. What in god's name do you mean talkin' to a child like that?

JOHN. She's got to learn what kind of a sister her mother's got.

HELEN. You've got nothing to say to me when you spend all your money in the saloon.

JOHN. God, you're a whore.

(HELEN screams and attacks JOHN. ELLY tries to pull her back.)

ELLY. Let her go, John. Helen, come over here to me.

JOHN. Taking the part of a whore against yer own husband. *(goes to kitchen shelf to replenish his flask)*

HELEN. *(lunging for JOHN again but held back by ELLY)* Elly, let me go. If you call me that again, you low down dog, I'll choke you to death with my bare hands and Elly can't stop me. *(frees herself, getting control)* And if I was a whore, John Rogers, I want to know who made me one. You, John Rogers, you. Elly ain't had enough money to buy food and clothes for herself and the kids. I've given her my wages each payday. Yes, and you know it. If it wasn't for my money, she'd have starved to death while you were off dreaming of becoming a doctor. *(starts down the stairs)* Or off drinking in that saloon or coming home drunk with every cent gone. Then lying and threatening her if she complained. *(starts for the washtub)* How'd you think she was to live? Washing? *(hurls clothes in a rage)* Damn you. You're a lowdown dog. And you call me names. You...Where'd you think I got the money for clothes? On what they pay me at the laundry? I won't go in rags. I won't marry some man and depend on his money so he can boss me around and whip me and starve me to death. I've got a right to things. If I'm a whore, then you made me one.

JOHN. You pack your things and git out. Go to your dago pimp. Yer not fit for a dog.

HELEN. And I suppose you are? You call this a home, do you? You call this your home? You don't even pay the rent. You don't bring home nothing.

JOHN. You get out of this house or I'll throw you out.

ELLY. (*coming near HELEN*) If she goes out of this house, John, then I go with her.

JOHN. You're a nice wife to talk of goin' into the streets with a woman like that. Let go of her and come here. Come here or I'll get the axe and break every piece of furniture in this house. (*exits to get the axe*)

HELEN. (*hurrying to pick up the clothes she had thrown*) I'll go alone, Elly. John'll break up everything you've got. And he might kill you. (*starts off to the bedroom*)

ELLY. (*grabbing HELEN'S arm*) He can go, not you.

HELEN. He won't go. He'll kill us first.

ELLY. Then let him. I'd rather be dead than alive anyway.

HELEN. Don't, Elly. I'll go. I'll send money for you and the kids. Stay here. Think of the kids, Elly. What'll they do without you. Wait until I make money enough for all of us. I'll send for you. Annie, come on. Help me pack. Annie, come on. You want this place broken up and your mother with it? (*exits down right*)

ANNIE. (*runs off after HELEN and they talk in hurried whispers offstage*) I don't want you to go, Aunt Helen.

HELEN. Hush. Help me with this. Hurry, get those things from the drawers.

ANNIE. What'll we do without you. What'll mama do, Aunt Helen. You can't go.

HELEN. (*hurrying onstage*) Bring my suitcase, Annie.

ANNIE. (*entering with suitcase*) What'll you do, Aunt Helen?

HELEN. (*stroking ELLY'S hair as she sits on the bed*) Don't worry about me. I can take care of myself.

ANNIE. You could get married.

HELEN. A woman gets married, a man starts reminding her of her past.

MARIE. You could work in a laundry. Seven dollars a week.

HELEN. Seven dollars a week isn't enough for the things I want. And it ain't enough for you and your ma, Marie. (*goes to MARIE and GEORGE*)

ELLY. But Helen, you can't go on this way forever.

HELEN. (*crosses to ELLY*) Hush, Elly.

ELLY. I don't see how you can stand it.

HELEN. I make my living the same way married women make theirs, except I make a better living and I got more rights over my body and soul.

There's no man that dares mistreat me. You tell me what else I can do. Beggars can't be choosers. (*crossing to GEORGE and MARIE who are standing on the platform*) Besides, you kids are grown up now. Why, Marie and Annie are working and making money. And soon Annie'll be married to that nice boy, Sam. I'll send you money. I'm learning to roll dice so when I get too old, I can still make a good living.

(*JOHN enters with the axe. HELEN kisses ELLY goodbye, then says goodbye to the kids and with a last look exits as THEY watch in silence. JOHN sees HELEN leave, looks quickly at ELLY, takes out his flask and exits. ELLY lies down on the bed.*)

MARIE. (*crossing to the bed*) Ain't you gettin' up, Ma? We got lots of washin' to do. And the men'll be here soon for their supper.

ELLY. No, they won't. I can tell. Yer father's gonna leave again. I just want to lay in bed a little longer, Marie. Just a little longer. My back feels like it can't hold out.

(*MARIE begins washing at the washtub bench*)

ELLY. One of these days, Marie, I'm gonna git you a piano. And you can finish yer education.

(*MARIE takes a sheet and starts for the clothesline. ANNIE crosses the stage slowly as MARIE narrates. GEORGE enters and walks slowly across platform running his hand along the clothesline.*)

MARIE. Our house was a mass of steaming shirts and sheets. And we never ceased dreaming of a washing machine to save my mother's back from so much pain. But there were always shoes to buy and schoolbooks. (*crossing to the clothesline*) We decided that Annie would work in the laundry, and I would go to work in a cigar factory and my mother would work alone. (*ANNIE and GEORGE exit*) At the cigar factory one of the men was young and handsome. Perhaps, I dreamed, he would see me standing there and like a prince in a fairy tale ask me to marry him. I pictured myself sitting by his side rolling cigars. (*leans against the wall*) In school I was miserable and the worst in my class. On the playground I was herded with the tough girls from beyond the tracks. I fought with the boys and girls in the alley and I let nothing hurt me. (*crosses toward clothesline*) When my mother sent me to the store, I made good use of my time. I came to regard everything from the viewpoint of its stealing possibilities. (*exits*)

Fragment 16: "Stealing Possibilities"

(*Lights change and we hear store CLERK whistling "Red River Valley" offstage. He enters with a stool, some fabric, and some spools of thread which he puts down and examines. MARIE enters.*)

CLERK. Hello, Marie. How are you today?

MARIE. Fine. And yourself?

CLERK. Oh, just fine. Pretty dress you have on, Marie.

MARIE. Thank you. My Aunt Helen made it. Do you know my Aunt Helen?

CLERK. Why, yes, I do. What do you hear from her?

MARIE. She's living in Denver.

CLERK. That's nice. Well, what can I do fer you today, Marie?

MARIE. Let's see. Ma wants a spool of thread, a sack of salt, and some soap.

CLERK. (*starts off right, then comes back as he has a short memory*) Spool of thread? Oh, what color?

MARIE. Mmm. Purple.

CLERK. Purple. Pretty color. Don't have much call for it, though. Mayn't be able to find any. Take me a minute. (*exits humming*)

MARIE. That's all right. Take your time. (*begins pocketing items from the stool*)

CLERK. (*from off*) Sack of salt. Got that. Some soap. Got that. And purple thread. Let's see. I got blue. I got red. I got yellow. But I don't see any purple. Maybe in this box.

(*CLERK pokes his head out and MARIE looks innocent*)

CLERK. Can't find purple, will blue do?

MARIE. Blue's fine. Rather have purple but don't trouble yourself.

CLERK. I'll look again but I don't think we got it. (*disappears humming*)

(*MARIE collects more items*)

CLERK. (*re-entering*) Here you are, Marie. Sack of salt, some soap, and a spool of blue thread. That'll be ten cents.

MARIE. Here you are. (*hands CLERK the money and smiles sweetly*) See you in a few days. (*starts off*) Oh, and thanks for your trouble.

CLERK. My pleasure, Marie. No trouble at all. Such a nice child.

(*MARIE exits. CLERK picks up the stool with a depleted amount of items*

*on it; checks to see if it's all there; looks confused, then shrugs and exits
humming as lights change.)*

Fragment 17: "If You Dare"

*(ELLY enters and starts washing. JOHN enters drunk, a rope in his back
pocket, crosses to the kitchen and rummages around for a flask. HE finds
it and comes up behind ELLY who cringes. ELLY takes sheet and crosses
to clothesline, avoiding JOHN.)*

JOHN. Well, I've come back. What d'ya say to that? *(staggers after ELLY
and grabs her arms)*

(ELLY shakes loose and returns to washtub)

JOHN. I'm gonna move over to Primero. They need excavatin' done
there. *(starts down the stairs)*

(ELLY crosses to kitchen to start supper)

JOHN. *(following her)* Did ya' hear me? I'm movin'. *(watches her then
searches under the bed for a suitcase which he pulls out)* You're comin'
with me.

(ELLY sets table for dinner as JOHN exits to bedroom with suitcase)

Did ya hear me? *(from offstage)* I said yer comin' with me. I need ya to cook
for my men. *(enters with suitcase)*

ELLY. I heard you.

JOHN. Well?

ELLY. Git that woman you been living with to cook fer you.

JOHN. You'll need to start packin' today. Git the kids. *(grabs her arm
again)*

ELLY. *(pulls away and crosses to clothesline)* I ain't goin'.

JOHN. I said I need you to work for my men. Yer goin'.

ELLY. And take the children away from a decent school agin?

JOHN. Ain't no work here. *(takes rope out of pocket and starts rewinding
it)*

ELLY. *(folding sheets slowly)* They already missed a year of school. A
whole year wasted.

JOHN. Ain't no point to that damn school. Now git yer things.

*(JOHN smacks rope against the table, then moves toward ELLY as she
moves away)*

You're comin' with me.

ELLY. No.

JOHN. Yer my wife, Elly. You gotta do what I say. If'n you don't, then I got the right to make you. You disobey me, Elly, I got the right to beat you until you do what I say. (*tries to work himself up to it*)

ELLY. I ain't going with you.

(*JOHN starts up the steps toward her. MARIE enters on the platform. JOHN hesitates. ELLY moves right toward MARIE her eyes fixed on the rope.*)

ELLY. Marie.

MARIE. Yes, Mama?

ELLY. Marie, he's gonna hit me with that thing. Marie, if he hits me I'm gonna drop dead.

MARIE. (*crosses in front of ELLY, standing between ELLY and JOHN*) God, I hate you, Pa. You're a coward, Pa. You think you can beat a woman who's half yer size because the law gives you the right? I swear I'm gonna get my gun and kill you. (*starts down*)

JOHN. Git out of my way daughter. (*pushes MARIE, heads for ELLY*)

MARIE. (*shoving him aside*) You hit her, Pa, if you dare. If you dare.

JOHN. She's comin' with me.

(*JOHN starts for ELLY again. MARIE flinches but holds her ground.*)

MARIE. You gonna hit me, too, Pa? 'Cause if you do, I swear I'll git at your throat with my teeth. God damn you, Pa. If you hit me, I'll kill you.

(*JOHN looks at her and slowly lets the rope fall from his hand, stumbles to the kitchen to get his suitcase, exits. ELLY crosses slowly to bed and lies down. MARIE goes over to her, then to the washtub. After a few moments, ELLY comes to help.*)

MARIE. (*stops ELLY with her voice*) No, Ma. I just as leave finish it. There ain't much more.

(*ELLY starts back to bed, then turns and MARIE and ELLY look at each other as the lights change*)

Fragment 18: "I Got Malnourishment"

(*GEORGE enters and sits on platform bench. ELLY lies down. ANNIE enters and crosses slowly to the platform, stopping at the bed to look at ELLY.*)

MARIE. (*crossing to platform*) Silence began to settle more and more about my mother. Her existence was almost completely isolated now. My sister, Annie, married that year and went to live in western Oklahoma. She endured the life for two years and then went into the silence where all pioneer women have gone before her. She died a year later giving birth to her first child. And so my sister went into the darkness and I remained behind in what is called the light.

Had I not inherited my father's refusal to accept my lot as ordained by God, I might have remained in the mining towns all my life, married some working man, born him a dozen children to wander the face of the earth, and died in my early thirties. But settled things were enemies to me now and soon lost their newness and color. The unknown called. Within a year I found myself a school teacher. I, who had never finished grammar school. I was teaching children out in New Mexico on top of one of those purple-red-green mesas when a message came that my mother was very sick and I must return home. (*crosses to ELLY*) Mama, what's wrong. (*sits on the edge of the bed*)

ELLY. Doctor says I got malnourishment.

MARIE. You should take care of yourself, Mama.

ELLY. Don't matter about me, Marie. I'm so proud of you. Tell me about yer teachin'.

MARIE. Don't you think you should rest, Mama?

ELLY. I'm restin' but I want to hear about yer teachin'.

MARIE. Well all right, but I think you should rest, Mama.

ELLY. I will, honey. Now tell me.

MARIE. Well, I took the examination for teachin' and, Mama, I was real scared because all the other women were older and better educated than I was.

ELLY. You ain't never been scared, Marie.

MARIE. Well, I was then. Two days later, the county superintendent of schools sent for me. He was very kind, Mama. He told me, "You have low grades in arithmetic, grammar, and school law, but you can speak a little Mexican, so here's a school. It's lonely, and far from town, and it's cold—so cold that school is only held durin' the summer. You'll cook your own food and wash your own clothes. The life is rough—cattlemen you know." Well, Mama, I didn't understand what he was talking about but I listened and tried to look real smart.

ELLY. You are real smart, Marie. Teachers always said you were real smart.

MARIE. Maybe so, Mama, but I didn't understand what this superintendent of schools was talkin' about 'cause it was news to me that there were people who didn't cook their own food and wash their own clothes. And those rough people he was talking about, Mama? Well, when I got there, everybody acted just like I do. I guess rough people is the same as us.

ELLY. Well, I just know you're a good teacher, Marie.

MARIE. And, Mama, I found this picture postcard exchange in one of those ladies magazines. I picked out the most beautiful name, Robert Hampton. He lives somewhere in the East, Mama. And he's finished high school. He sent me his picture and he's so handsome and learned like men in books. Did you get those books I sent you, Mama? The ones on history and botany? It's good for you to know these things too.

ELLY. I got 'em, honey. I been readin' the one about history. But it takes such a long time. (*tries to sit up*) Marie, I don't know how I could have lived until now if it hadn't been for you, Daughter. (*moans with pain in her stomach and lies down*) Please, Marie, give me some of that bicarbonate.

MARIE. (*rising*) I'll get it, Mama.

GEORGE. (*rising*) No, Marie. The doctor said it was bad for her to take bicarbonate.

MARIE. Mama, doctor says you can't have the bicarbonate.

ELLY. The pains are real bad, honey. Marie?

MARIE. Yes, Mama? (*sits*)

ELLY. Promise me you'll go on and git a better education. You promise me.

MARIE. I promise, Mama.

(*JOHN enters by the bed with his flask and staggers to the table where he sits. ELLY sees him and cries out.*)

ELLY. Marie, git me the bicarbonate. I got pains in my stomach. It's on the kitchen shelf.

GEORGE. No, Marie. Doctor says no.

(*ELLY moans in pain. MARIE hesitates, then grabs the bicarbonate and gives ELLY a spoonful. GEORGE takes a few steps toward them but MARIE shakes him off.*)

MARIE. Here, Mama. I got the bicarbonate.

ELLY. Oh, Marie. (*sits up, then grabs her stomach in pain*) Daughter.

(*MARIE puts her arms around her mother*) Mama. No, Mama.

(*ELLY dies. MARIE buries her head. GEORGE sits. JOHN stands up. AUNT HELEN enters as the lights fade on this tableau.*)

Fragment 19: "A Black Curtain Descended Softly"

(*MARIE and HELEN set the table. GEORGE tries to read sitting at the platform bench. JOHN and ELLY have exited in the dark.*)

MARIE. What'll I do without ma, Aunt Helen?

HELEN. You could go back to Mexico and keep up your teachin'.

MARIE. Who'll take care of George, and Beatrice, and Dan? They got no one to take care of them now. Pa's off drunk half the time.

HELEN. You could find a rich man and git married.

MARIE. You never married, Helen, and you're doin' all right.

HELEN. I was engaged once.

MARIE. Why didn't you marry him?

HELEN. Why should I marry him, in God's name? I couldn't marry him. A woman gets married and can't make her own living.

MARIE. It's because of the other men, isn't it?

HELEN. Of course it is. And then I can't have a baby.

MARIE. Why?

HELEN. You are nosy, Marie. I've had two operations and I have to go down to the springs every year for treatment. There. Are you satisfied? It's not good for you to know these things. A young tree can't grow straight and beautiful if its roots are watered with acid.

MARIE. (*goes to washtub*) I don't want to have anything to do with men. Whether they're rich or poor, it doesn't matter to me. I want to go to college and study history and literature and economics.

HELEN. I thought you finished your education and knew those things.

MARIE. There's always more to learn.

HELEN. Will you make a lot of money, when you get educated?

MARIE. I don't know. Not much I guess.

HELEN. Then what's the use of getting more educated?

MARIE. (*goes to hang clothes on the clothesline*) Because I like to learn things. If I'm rich, it'll be from money I made myself. But it doesn't matter anyway. I'll have to take care of my brothers and sister. Instead of gittin' an education, I'll be here cookin' and washin' and sewin' and ironin' for years and years like mama did.

HELEN. (*gets her shawl and prepares to leave*) You know you're welcome to stay with me in Denver any time. Maybe I can help you get a job. I'll send you money, Marie. Like I did yer ma. (*exchanges one last look with MARIE, then exits*)

GEORGE. I can't do this arithmetic, Marie.

MARIE. Sure you can, George. I'll fix yer supper and you keep tryin'.

GEORGE. *(goes to sit at the table)* I'm not smart like you, Marie. Anyway, pa says he's gonna send us off to some farmer in Oklahoma. I heard him talkin' about it. I heard he beats the boys that work for him, Marie.

MARIE. Pa's not sending you to Oklahoma, Georgie. I'm stayin' here. I'm takin' ma's place now and nobody's gonna send you off to Oklahoma while I'm here.

JOHN. *(from offstage)* George, damn you. Where are you?

GEORGE. It's pa.

JOHN. *(enters with a doubled-up rope in his hand)* George, damn you, I asked you to harness my team and you ain't done it yet. *(swings rope and misses GEORGE by inches)* Git back here. *(picks up books)* So you're readin' instead of hitchin' my team.

(JOHN takes a swing at GEORGE who dodges the rope. JOHN chases him to the clothesline, swinging wildly, narrowly missing GEORGE.)

MARIE. *(runs in between THEM)* Stop hittin' him, pa.

(JOHN tries to get past MARIE. She keeps hitting him and hitting him.)

MARIE. God damn you.

(JOHN lets the rope fall)

MARIE. *(backing away from him)* Why did you ever bring me into the world. *(looks at GEORGE, then runs to the bedroom)*

GEORGE. Marie, you're not gonna leave. Pa, Marie's gonna leave.

(JOHN sits at the end of the table. MARIE enters with suitcase and heads for the platform.)

GEORGE. *(grabbing MARIE'S arm as she passes)* Marie, you're not leavin' are you? Marie, don't leave. Pa's gonna send us to that farmer in Oklahoma. You said you'd stay, Marie. You said you'd take ma's place. Marie.

MARIE. I gotta go, Georgie. *(frees herself with one fierce pull and climbs the stairs to the platform)* When I make enough money, George, I'll send for you and the kids. When I make enough money, I'll send for you.

(MARIE climbs stairs as GEORGE and JOHN freeze in tableau: GEORGE by the platform bench, JOHN sitting at the table)

And so I deserted them and strangled the emotion that tried to convince me that I should not. A black curtain descended softly and erased from my memory the faces of those I loved. I now began a process of reasoning that I kept up for years. I began to forget that I had a family at all. And I resented everything. I hated my father and mother for bringing me into a world when I didn't ask to come. I hated my brothers and sister for loading me with a responsibility that I refused to carry. And I hated myself most of all for having been born a woman.

(*lights out*)

END OF PART I

Part II

Fragment 20: "They Teach People Lies"

(low lights on MARIE straddling small bench on the platform)

MARIE. I went to Denver to stay with Aunt Helen and I studied stenography for a while. But the things I yearned for always lay just beyond somewhere. Finally Big Buck gave me the money to go to teacher's school down in Phoenix. One afternoon just as the sun was beginning to set I stood before the row of red brick buildings of the teacher's school. It and the little town to one side, clinging to the banks of the river sprang out of the desert like a mirage. The desert was indeed a gray and sinister place, but it lay there calling you to come on and on. Just beyond was something still more beautiful in the moonlight. And if you kept going, sometimes you could hear through the crystal clear air, the sad monotonous singing from the camp of Indians who had wandered over from New Mexico. The Arizona desert came closer to my spirit than any place I have ever known. *(swings her back foot over the bench)* I learned many things in that school. I took jobs in the daytime and I studied at night. Under the sympathetic interest of teachers, my mind began to work vigorously. And I was elected to the school newspaper. *(rises and crosses left of platform)* I learned other things too. I began to see that a girl could command respect by intellectual ability, a show of power, but that these were dry and tasteless things. I yearned for beauty, grace, and love.

(KARIN enters platform right, the epitome of beauty and grace. She surveys the room, her eyes finally resting on MARIE.)

KARIN. Sooo...

MARIE. *(trying to look like a tough cowgirl)* Sooo?

KARIN. *(coming forward to shake hands)* I'm Karin Larson.

MARIE. *(shaking KARIN'S hand)* I'm Marie Rogers.

KARIN. I'm from the East. Where are you from?

MARIE. Just about anywhere I guess.

(KARIN begins wandering around the room, looking at the books to see

what MARIE is reading and studying in teacher's school)

MARIE. Why have you come to Phoenix? Are you planning to study to be a teacher?

KARIN. *(laughing)* I am a teacher. I've spent most of my life in educational insitutions. No, I have come to Phoenix to see a little of life.

MARIE. *(following KARIN)* Phoenix is a funny place to come if you want to see the world.

KARIN. Well, I really came for the state debating contest on women's suffrage here in Phoenix. I thought perhaps your school newspaper would print a story about it. *(handing papers from her briefcase to MARIE)* And of course my brother lives out here. So I thought I'd come.

MARIE. *(taking papers from KARIN and looking them over)* Your brother lives here?

KARIN. *(strolling to table)* Yes, my brother, Knut. He works in the desert. Are you studying to be a teacher?

MARIE. Yes. *(moving to bench right)*

KARIN. And what do you think of school? *(leaning against table)*

MARIE. *(putting right foot up on bench)* School always seemed to me to be a way out of poverty.

KARIN. Yes. Perhaps. But I've begun to feel that teaching is static and uncreative. Even reactionary. What do schools teach, really? Do they teach us to think? To understand the world?

MARIE. I've learned many remarkable things in school.

KARIN. *(moving toward MARIE)* What things have you learned? Have you learned who Emma Goldman is? Have you learned what the free speech movements are about? Do you know what's going on in Russia? Do you know who the Wobblies are?

MARIE. Well, no. *(sits)* But people should know how to read and write and speak.

KARIN. For what? So they can spend their lives working in the mines or the factories? Or in some office somewhere? Typing? Doing what someone else tells them to do? Barely making enough to stay alive? No, I'm not sure that schools benefit society.

MARIE. *(coming toward KARIN)* Society?

KARIN. People. Society. The working class.

MARIE. *(impressed)* Oh. Well, why don't you think that schools...

(KNUT enters on platform, the male equivalent of KARIN. MARIE is impressed and a little shy.)

KNUT. Karin, there you are. I've been looking all over for you.

KARIN. (*crossing toward KNUT*) Ah, Knut. Come and meet Marie Rogers. Marie, this is my brother, Knut.

KNUT. (*crossing center to shake hands with MARIE*) Hello, Marie.

MARIE. (*shaking KNUT'S hand*) How d'ye do.

KNUT. Well, what were you discussing so fervently when I came in? Has Karin been lecturing you, Marie?

MARIE. We were talking...

KARIN. (*interrupting*) We were talking about schools. And whether they teach anything.

MARIE. And I said that I thought....

KNUT. And what did you decide?

MARIE. (*crossing to center bench and straddling it*) We didn't decide anything...

(*during the rest of the scene, KNUT plays right of MARIE, KARIN plays left, and they talk over her*)

KNUT. Well in my view they certainly teach something. The question is what do they teach and to what purpose? (*looking at the books on bench right*)

MARIE. Well, they teach about...

KARIN. I was telling Marie that I thought schools were static, uncreative, and reactionary.

MARIE. And I said...

KNUT. Agreed. They teach people to follow instructions, feel stupid, and they teach people lies.

MARIE. Lies?

KNUT. For instance, Emma Goldman. What do schools teach about Emma Goldman?

MARIE. I don't even know who she is. Well, I've heard her name but...

KNUT. You see?

KARIN. They teach that she is a terrible sort of person. A "free for all" character with a dangerous tongue.

MARIE. Well, is she?

KARIN. Of course not. She's a noted woman speaker, a writer, a fighter for social justice and for freedom.

MARIE. Oh.

KNUT. Take another example. (*coming close to MARIE with a book*) Take the Native American Indian. What do schools teach about them?

MARIE. Well, I...

KARIN. That they are stupid savages who massacred innocent white people.

KNUT. You see? Lies.

MARIE. But how else can one learn about the world? About culture and history?

KARIN. From life. From what's going on around us. From observing people working. From seeing culture that's about real people.

MARIE. Real people?

KNUT. For instance, we saw a play in San Francisco called the *Twelve Pound Look*.

KARIN. It's a wonderful play, Marie. You really should try to see it. The acting is so natural. And it's about working people. Like you.

MARIE. Doesn't sound very interesting to me. Who wants to watch people acting naturally? I seen enough of that.

KNUT. (*smiling at KARIN*) It depicts real life situations. It's about a woman who saves enough money to buy herself a typewriter so she can make a living.

MARIE. (*rising*) Why would anyone want to see a play about a woman who makes a living typing? What a silly thing to write a play about.

(*MARIE backs into KNUT who steadies her until she pulls away embarrassed*)

KNUT. (*laughing with KARIN*) Here's another example. Have you been to those amusement centers they have outside the big cities? There's one near San Francisco.

MARIE. You mean those places with merry-go-rounds and shooting galleries?

KNUT. And crowds of people, working people. Have you ever stopped to observe those people? Have you ever wondered why they go to such places?

MARIE. Yes, but I don't see that I can learn anything from that.

KNUT. Why do people go to those places, spend their hard-earned money, drink?

MARIE. Because they're cheap and ugly.

KNUT. Yes, some people are cheap and ugly. But what made them that way? Stop and think, Marie. What made them that way?

MARIE. Well, what did?

KNUT. The system.

MARIE. The system?

KNUT. (*taking her hands*) Yes, the system.

MARIE. Oh.

(*KNUT and KARIN smile at MARIE who looks at them in awe, then at KNUT'S hands holding hers as the lights fade*)

Fragment 21: "Aire You Willin'?"

(*MARIE frees her hands and comes forward to narrate. KARIN exits right. KNUT sits on the edge of the couchbed with a book.*)

MARIE. Knut and Karin left for San Francisco. I felt very humble before Knut and Karin. They were so beautiful and educated and intelligent. They incorporated the only independent thought I had ever known. It seemed to me that they just manufactured their thoughts as they went along and that was indeed a remarkable thing. They had no anxiety about making a living and hunger would have been an adventure for them. Knut wrote to me from San Francisco and he asked me to join them. He wrote of love and marriage but what he wrote sounded different from all the terrible things that I thought marriage was. All that I had longed for seemed combined in him. The fear of sex and children still barred the way but I really thought that a marriage without sex was possible. (*goes to opposite end of the couchbed*) A sort of romantic friendship. Two people working together and remaining friends.

(*KNUT rises*)

MARIE. And I want to make my own living.

KNUT. Of course, we will both work and study.

MARIE. And I don't want any children.

KNUT. Nor I, not for a long time anyway.

MARIE. I don't want any at all. There are enough children in the world.

KNUT. Fine. We're agreed on that, then.

MARIE. And I will have to earn my own money for my brothers and my sister, Beatrice. They will need money, too.

KNUT. Fine. We agree on that point also.

MARIE. I don't want a home, either. No cooking, washing, or scrubbing.

KNUT. We agree on that point, too. Anything else?

MARIE. (*thinking*) No.

KNUT. Then it's settled. Let's go and get the marriage license and get married before I leave for my new job.

MARIE. All right. But I insist on paying for half. I won't let you pay for our marriage as if I belonged to you.

KNUT. *(laughing)* Agreed. I'll save $2.50.

(JUSTICE of the Peace enters carrying a Bible and removes a napkin from under his chin. He hurries the ceremony, to get back to his dinner.)

JUSTICE. Well, now. Are we all set? My, aren't we a nice young couple. Have we got everything? That's a pretty dress.

MARIE. Marie...Marie Rogers.

JUSTICE. That's a nice name. And you?

KNUT. Knut Larson.

JUSTICE. Larson. All right. *(comes down the stairs)* Knut, you stand here. And Marie, you stand right over here. Now, that's nice. We'll need a witness. *(yelling)* Fran? We're about ready, Fran.

FRAN. *(from offstage)* Just a minute. I'm washin' up. Just hold your horses, now. *(enters)* There. *(drying hands on apron)* Oh, my what a nice young couple.

JUSTICE. Yes, they are. Knut, just move over a little bit closer to Marie.

FRAN. What a shy young couple.

JUSTICE. *(climbs the stairs and stands with FRAN on the platform above the couchbed)* Now we're ready. Knut Larson...

FRAN. Wait, dear. Can't be a witness without my hat. *(puts her hat on)* on hat)

JUSTICE. Ready now, Fran?

FRAN. Ready.

JUSTICE. *(briskly so he can get back to his dinner)* Knut Larson, aire you willin' to take this here woman fer your lawful wedded wife?

(KNUT and MARIE look at each other uncomfortably)

JUSTICE. What's wrong? *(exchanging looks with FRAN)*

KNUT. It's rather sudden.

JUSTICE. Sudden. *(another knowing look at FRAN)* Well, don't you know whether you want to get married or not?

(FRAN is amused)

KNUT. Yes, but you go about it too suddenly.

JUSTICE. Lord, man what do you want me to do? The hula hula?

(FRAN laughs)

KNUT. *(aside to MARIE)* Not a half bad idea.

JUSTICE. May we begin again?

MARIE. Yes.

JUSTICE. Knut Larson, aire you willin' to take this here woman as yer lawful wedded wife? (*waits patiently*)

KNUT. Yes.

JUSTICE. Good. That wasn't difficult, was it? Marie Rogers, aire you willin' to take this here man fer yer wedded husband?

(*MARIE hesitates*)

KNUT. (*aside*) Say yes. All you have to do is say yes, and we'll get out of this place.

JUSTICE. Ain't no use gettin' scared. People go through this every day, all day long. (*long suffering look at FRAN*) Now child, aire you willin' to take this here man fer yer lawful wedded husband?

MARIE. I guess so.

JUSTICE. (*to FRAN*) She guesses so.

FRAN. It's close enough.

JUSTICE. You got a point there. We'll leave it at that. Now, aire you, Knut Larson, willin' to support this here woman through all the vicissitoodes of life, through sunshine and rain, through storm and stress?

KNUT. (*trying to control a smile*) Uh, yes. (*to MARIE*) Vicissitoodes?

(*FRAN does not approve as MARIE and KNUT are clearly close to cracking up*)

JUSTICE. Marie Rogers, aire you willin' to obey this man through all the vicissitoodes of life, through sunshine and rain, through storm and stress?

MARIE. (*hating this whole thing*) Knut, he said obey?

KNUT. Never mind. It's just in the service that way. Say yes, so we can get out of here.

JUSTICE. Well, Marie. We haven't got all day.

FRAN. Yes, dear.

MARIE. All right.

FRAN. Well, don't force yourself, dear.

JUSTICE. (*to FRAN*) Ssh. Don't get her started up again. Now, that wasn't so hard was it? Have you got the ring?

KNUT. Ring. We haven't got a ring.

JUSTICE. Haven't got a ring.

FRAN. How do you expect to git married without a ring?

MARIE. We don't believe in rings.

JUSTICE. Oh, my. They don't believe in rings. Now I've seen everything. Well, fine. That's the ceremony. You're man and wife. You may kiss the bride. Or don't you believe in kissin'?

(*FRAN is laughing*)

KNUT. We can do without it.

MARIE. No kissing.

JUSTICE. No kissing? No kissing?

FRAN. Such a pretty young couple too. Well, that's five dollars.

KNUT. (*gives her his share*) Here.

FRAN. That's only $2.50.

MARIE. I'm paying the other half. (*gives FRAN the money*)

JUSTICE. Oh, my god. She's payin' the other half.

(*MARIE AND KNUT cross right*)

MARIE. He looks like a toad.

JUSTICE. Come on, Fran. I never seen a couple like that one.

KNUT. Easy way he has of making money. That only took two minutes.

FRAN. I give that marriage one year.

MARIE. I feel like going back and making him cancel our names and give us our money back.

JUSTICE. Six months if you ask me.

KNUT. We can't do that. It's legal now.

JUSTICE. And next time you come here, Knut and Marie Larson, come prepared. Marriage is a serious business.

(*lights out*)

Fragment 22: "People Call Me Mrs. Larson"

(*Lights come up on KARIN helping MARIE over to the table*)

KARIN. Marie, you must be more careful. You can't fight in the free speech movement if you are killed in the process.

(*MARIE sits. KARIN get bandages from the shelf.*)

MARIE. But how can I stand by when my friends are being beaten and imprisoned. I've always been the kind of person who acts first and thinks afterword.

KARIN. (*beginning to bandage MARIE'S left arm*) Yes. To physically attack the police was a stupid thing to do.

MARIE. I thought you admired people who acted naturally. Besides, how could I just stand there while the police beat this man. He was only demanding the right of free speech. I saw them throw him to the ground and hit him again and again. His face was turned upward and blood poured from his eyes. Then they dragged him to prison and accused him of attacking the police. (*crossing to bed*)

KARIN. Marie, I don't understand what you are doing. You remain in San Francisco while Knut is off in the desert building a canal. You are not only an idiot but you are doing my brother an injury by being married to him and not living with him as his wife.

MARIE. That kind of marriage means violence, children, nagging women, and complaining men. Our marriage is different from that. We agreed. If Knut doesn't like it, he can get a divorce.

KARIN. That's not what love is. Love means being with a man. Even when he goes to work in the desert.

MARIE. Love which means that is the enemy of women. My goal in life is to work and study, not to follow some man around.

KARIN. Oh, Marie. You know nothing of love.

MARIE. Thank God, I don't.

KARIN. (*Sighing, giving up for the moment. She climbs the stairs, then turns.*) You have my address in New York, if you need me. (*exits*)

(*MARIE lies on the bed and begins to read. The COUPLE next door begin arguing. MARIE sits up, waiting for it to stop. She lies down again. The arguing begins again, then stops. Soon the book falls to the floor and she dozes. KNUT enters with suitcase which he sets down. He crosses to the bed and touches MARIE'S hand.*)

MARIE. (*waking*) Knut. Did you just get here?

KNUT. Ssh. Go back to sleep. We can talk in the morning.

MARIE. How long are you staying?

KNUT. A few months at least. (*crosses to shelf, gets some tea*)

MARIE. (*sits up and watches him*) Knut.

KNUT. (*turns*) Yes, Marie?

MARIE. Karin says I should go with you to the desert and live with you as man and wife.

KNUT. And what did you tell her?

MARIE. I said I had no desire to be married if that's what love meant.

KNUT. You are right. Our life is our life and we have a right to live it as we wish.

MARIE. Perhaps...(*stands next to KNUT who sits at the table*) Is there a chance of making money down in the desert? Perhaps I could go with you and make enough money to return to school.

KNUT. (*takes MARIE'S hand*) There is a town near by where you could make more than you could here in San Francisco.

MARIE. Then perhaps I will go with you. Then in a year I can go to the University of California. I will be as educated as you. My mind will become crystal clear as though borne forward on the wings of light. (*frees her hand and sits on her knees on the couchbed*) And perhaps, one day, I'll be a great writer like I've always dreamed.

KNUT. (*standing by the bed*) Yes. I think, one day, you will.

(*As the lights fade, MARIE and KNUT look at each other. Tentatively he kisses her. MARIE tries to participate but she is scared. THEY kiss again. Then MARIE turns away from him and lies down on the bed. He lies on top of her and they kiss as the lights fade. When the lights come up, MARIE is sitting up with her back to KNUT who is still asleep. The couple next door begin shouting at each other. MARIE crosses to the shelf as KNUT wakes.*)

KNUT. What is that?

MARIE. It's the couple next door.

KNUT. Does that go on often?

MARIE. Every day. She stopped working when she married. She sits at home all day waiting for her husband to come home. They live a purely sexual existence. She is his wife, after all. (*bitterly*)

KNUT. Marie...

MARIE. Now, she's pregnant. There are sores on her mouth and on her face. We all know what disease she has. But syphilis in marriage is respectable.

(*the COUPLE begins shouting again*)

MARIE. Listen. Soon he will beat her. She is his wife and he will beat her. Yesterday she ran out into the hall screaming and no one came to help her.

(*screaming offstage, a thud*)

KNUT. Why doesn't someone help her? (*rising from the bed*)

MARIE. It wouldn't do any good. He'd only beat her more. She is his wife. No one dares interfere.

KNUT. Well, I'm going to do something.

MARIE. (*intercepting him in front of the bed*) I told you. She is his wife. That's what marriage is.

KNUT. Marie, you know our marriage isn't like that.

MARIE. People call me Mrs. Larson, as if Marie Rogers had just sunk into the earth. Karin accuses me of ruining your life, of doing you an injustice. God, Knut. There are times when I hate you.

KNUT. Marie, how can you say things like that to me. One day I'll kill myself if you say those things to me.

MARIE. Why don't you divorce me then. I won't object.

KNUT. Because I love you.

MARIE. Love. That's no excuse. That's a weakness.

KNUT. Why are you so cruel to me, Marie.

MARIE. Because I am afraid that I will be plunged back into the hell I came from. The hell of nagging, weeping women, depending on you for food and clothing. Losing all hope or desire to study.

KNUT. That won't happen. How could that happen to us. We won't let it.

MARIE. The fear of having children has always hovered like a bird of prey over my head...

KNUT. (staring) Marie. You're going to have a baby?

MARIE. I been trying to get rid of it. I stopped eating. I went to see a doctor. He said he couldn't help me, it was illegal. He gave me a prescription for something to take but I didn't know how to use it. He said if I tried to use it and something went wrong, then he could operate and finish it, for a hundred dollars. That's all the money I've saved.

KNUT. I know of a doctor. We can go there.

MARIE. I can't pay for that.

KNUT. Then I will pay.

MARIE. No. Oh, God, Knut. I won't have this baby. I'll kill myself first. This is your fault. Get me out of this. (falls into KNUT'S arms as the lights change)

Fragment 23: "Marriage is Too Terrible"

(Two RICH WOMEN enter on the platform and stand and wait. MARIE and KNUT join them. A NURSE enters right.)

NURSE. (softly) Next.

(One of the RICH WOMEN goes off left with the NURSE. MARIE and *the second RICH WOMAN wait, trying not to look at each other. The stage is dimly lit. The NURSE appears again with the first RICH WOMAN who crosses platform and exits right.)*

NURSE. *(softly)* Next.

(MARIE looks at the RICH WOMAN and then bravely follows the NURSE off. The second RICH WOMAN waits her turn. MARIE returns with the NURSE holding her arm. MARIE pulls her arm away.)

MARIE. I can walk.

(MARIE reaches the stairs, screams in pain and starts to fall. KNUT catches her with the help of the NURSE.)

NURSE. *(hisses)* Stand up, Mrs. Larson. People are looking. Please stand up. People will suspect this house. Walk. Walk.

KNUT. *(with unexpected vehemence)* Stand up, Marie. Do you want to make a scene in public. Stand up.

(MARIE looks at him, sees the look in his face as he orders her to stand. She walks angrily down the stairs. KNUT helps her to the bed.)

NURSE. Next.

(the second RICH WOMAN goes off left with the NURSE)

MARIE. *(staring straight ahead, not wanting to look at KNUT, who sits on the bed)* It was wrong of me to marry, Knut. I don't want to be married. Marriage is too terrible.

KNUT. I don't understand why our marriage has been a failure. I have always loved you, Marie.

MARIE. And I don't know what love is. *(pauses)* I want my name back.

KNUT. No, Marie. Please let's go on as we have been...

MARIE. You can charge me with desertion. It will be better that way in case you want to marry again.

KNUT. I can't. You have been my first love and I think you will be my last.

MARIE. I will never marry again. I want to be a free woman. My name is Marie Rogers. The world is my home. And the wind my companion.

(MARIE smiles sadly as she and KNUT stare off at the horizon. The lights fade out.)

Fragment 23: "I Thought You'd Be Different"

(*KNUT exits in the dark. MARIE climbs stairs to the platform with suitcase.*)

MARIE. I decided to go to New York to study at the University and to stay with Karin. On the way, I took a southern route to see Robert Hampton, a man I had never seen. It was this man who for years had sent me his old high school books and made it possible for me to pass my examinations. In my mind, he was still the distant hero. A man who, when he saw me, would gaze down from his noble heights and without speaking, wait for me to speak.

(*MARIE walks along the platform as if waiting for someone to meet her at the train. A small MAN in a bowler hat enters down right. MARIE ignores his stares.*)

HAMPTON. Uh, Marie? Marie Rogers?

(*MARIE avoiding this suspicious character*)

HAMPTON. Why, Marie, don't you know me? I would know you anywhere. You look just like your picture. Taller but that don't matter to me. Didn't you know me?

MARIE. Robert Hampton? Why, yes. I thought I knew you. (*amazed at how little he resembles his photograph*)

HAMPTON. Come and I'll take you to the hotel. How long are you going to stay?

MARIE. Oh, I can't stay. I have to be in New York as soon as possible. I'm taking the next train, in fact. (*an instant decision*)

HAMPTON. (*very disappointed*) So soon, Marie? I thought you were going to stay awhile. Well, let's sit in the park. You can stay for a little while can't you? We can talk.

(*HAMPTON tries to take MARIE'S suitcase but she holds onto it. Then he ushers her to the center bench which he cleans off for her with his handkerchief. She waits for him to sit. He waits for her to sit. Finally they sit at the same time. There is an awkward pause then THEY both start talking at once.*)

HAMPTON. Well, Marie. There's so much to tell you since your last letter so long ago. I live in the YMCA, Marie. High on the top floor. At the back. It's nice and cheap and the fellows treat you right.

(*HAMPTON looks at her eagerly. MARIE tries to look interested and encouraging.*)

MARIE. That's nice.

HAMPTON. When my father died, I left high school and came here. So I've been in this town since my father died.

MARIE. Oh, well, that's nice.

HAMPTON. I keep books in a big grocery firm. The owner says he doesn't know what he would do without me. When the other clerks fail to do the thing right, he calls me to do it. Just like that. (*snaps his fingers*) What's the matter, Marie. You're not interested?

MARIE. Oh, yes, I'm interested. I'm just tired. So, what do you do for amusement? Are there any movie theaters?

HAMPTON. No, there aren't any theaters here. But I don't know if I approve of theaters anyway. There are church socials in the basement of the Presbyterian Church twice a month. The women are nice and the older ones like me. I guess they know the right sort when they meet him.

MARIE. Do you read a lot? You used to send me such nice books.

HAMPTON. Oh, yes, I read a lot. The *Saturday Evening Post*. That's a nice clean magazine with no nonsense in it and good live stories. Have you ever read any of the stories in the *Saturday Evening Post*, Marie?

MARIE. No, I haven't.

HAMPTON. Do you know how much one advertisement in the *Post* costs?

MARIE. No, I don't.

HAMPTON. Do you know how many million circulation it has?

MARIE. No, I don't.

HAMPTON. No? Oh, well. (*trying another tack*) Tell me about you, Marie? What church do you go to?

MARIE. Oh, I don't go to any church. I went for three weeks when I was a child. I never understood the idea of God they taught in Church. God gives to those who have and takes from those who have not. No, I don't go to Church. Why should I go to Church?

HAMPTON. (*a little shocked*) I've never heard such a question. Then you don't pray?

MARIE. Pray? Why should I pray? To get rest for myself? Why should I rest? Why should the world rest? I'm not interested in rest today. Not until things are different. (*heated*)

HAMPTON. Prayer and belief in God would make them different.

MARIE. People have always prayed and believed in God. And look where they are.

HAMPTON. I hope you don't believe in socialism, Marie. You talk so hard.

MARIE. I am a Socialist. Or was. Now I'm thinking of joining the IWW. Their beliefs are close to mine.

HAMPTON. (*very angry but trying to remain polite*) Did they tell you all their beliefs, Marie? They're bums. They are. IWW means "I Won't Work." I'll bet they didn't tell you that.

MARIE. Well, if it means that, then why don't the rich belong to it? They don't work.

HAMPTON. (*rising in shock from the bench*) Marie, socialism and the IWW would destroy the home and the purity of women.

MARIE. (*rising and circling behind the bench*) Well, it didn't destroy my home, nor the purity of my aunt. Yet they were destroyed. You tell me who did that. What is purity anyway? I'd like to know. It means you don't live with a man. Then are all married women impure? I'm not going to let any man judge whether I'm pure or not. What right have you to judge me by my body? Your kind of purity means nothing.

HAMPTON. (*very upset*) Do you mean you wish you were not pure?

MARIE. (*equally upset*) I mean I won't let any man judge me by my body.

HAMPTON. (*pausing to collect himself*) I thought you'd be different, Marie. I thought you'd be someone I could talk to. If you stayed a day or two, I could explain. (*moves down right*) I could really explain my ideas. We could walk down by the river and talk. We could walk under the trees arm in arm and talk. I think a lot, Marie, but I've got no one to talk to. I thought you'd be different. You understand, I'm not saying anything against you.

MARIE. (*picking up her bag*) I'm sorry. You perhaps like to pray, I do not. (*crossing to stairs*) It wouldn't help me in any way. (*climbs to platform*)

HAMPTON. Marie, you'll be studying at the University. Would you remember to send me your old books when you finish with them? I could read and keep up with things. A fellow gets stuck in the mud. It wouldn't cost much if you'd send them. After you don't want them anymore.

MARIE. Yes. I'll send them.

(*HAMPTON turns and walks slowly off down right. MARIE watches him as the lights fade.*)

Fragment 24: "She Is a Worker"

(*KARIN enters on platform carrying a tray of sherry glasses and crosses to
table. LEILA and JACKSON enter and sprawl on the bed where he listens
to her read from her latest play. ANTOINE and LUTHER stroll on,
deeply involved in one of their political debates.*)

ANTOINE. The trouble with you Anarchists, Luther, is that you may
have a great deal to say about the state, but you don't have a fully
developed class analysis. Oh, thank you, Karin. (*takes sherry from tray
offered by KARIN*)

LUTHER. But Antoine, (*takes glass from tray*) I don't deny that every
society has a class structure in which some are the oppressors and some are
oppressed. But your analysis leads you to think that we merely have to
change which class controls state power.

(*ANTOINE tries to interrupt but LUTHER presses his point*)

And to quote freely from Kropotkin, (*looks to make sure EVERYONE is
listening*) "You cannot use state power to liberate labor any more than
you can use the Church."

ANTOINE. I am not denying that the state has as its highest purpose the
protection of private property.

(*LUTHER tries to interrupt but ANTOINE presses on*)

But it is merely an instrument for that purpose and not the creator of it.

LUTHER. You are wrong. They are intertwined. The state in itself is
oppressive.

ANTOINE. Only partially. You are so fixated on the state, Luther, that
you never think about who is going to run your society. Eh? You are
proposing chaos.

LUTHER. Not chaos, Antoine, but a glorious new form of political
organization that is decentralized, popular, and nearer, as Kropotkin
says, to the "folkmote" self-government than your Party-controlled
government can ever be.

KARIN. (*joins the debate*) Well, you can say all you want to about the
state but until you both realize the importance of institutions that exist to
oppress women, you are talking about the liberation of men only.

LUTHER. Ah, yes. Marriage must be done away with. That's obvious.

KARIN. As Emma Goldman says so eloquently, "Marriage is primarily
an economic arrangement. An insurance pact. If every woman's premium
is her husband, she pays for that premium with her name, her privacy, her
self-respect, her very life. Until death do us part."

MARIE. (*passionately, one foot on the platform bench*) Yes, Karin. Marriage makes women parasites, dependent on men.

(*EVERYONE looks at MARIE and smiles with delight*)

LUTHER. She is such a refreshing person, don't you agree, Antoine?

LEILA. She is so new. Marie dear, come over here and let me read to you from Gorky's new play, *The Mother.*

JACKSON. Oh, Leila. Spare her. Spare me. I've spent the entire day reading Freud. Not another word about mothers and fathers and oedipuses and the rest of it. Come here, Marie. Sit by me and let me tell you about your complexes.

(*CLOTHILDE shrieks a greeting from offstage, then enters on the platform in a whirl of scarves*)

CLOTHILDE. Karin love, I'm back. It was heaven. It was glorious. It was religious. (*dances each feeling*)

KARIN. (*brings sherry to CLOTHILDE*) You saw her, I take it?

CLOTHILDE. (*takes sherry and dances to each of THEM, hugging and kissing*) I saw her, I saw her. My whole life has changed. Why are you wearing so many clothes? Take off these clothes, these garments.

MARIE. Who did she see in Paris, Karin?

CLOTHILDE. (*spotting MARIE*) And who is this charming nymph?

KARIN. This is Marie Rogers.

CLOTHILDE. Marie. Marie. Marie. (*rushes up the stairs and takes MARIE'S hands and sways*) I have seen Isadora Duncan, you dear child. (*tries to dance with MARIE*) Come, let me gather the little girls around me and show them how to liberate their bodies and their minds.

LEILA. How marvelous.

JACKSON. What fun. Dance for us, Clothilde.

CLOTHILDE. (*forgetting MARIE*) Yes. I will perform dances of the peasants, (*dances*) the miners, (*dances*) the cowboys, (*dances*) the farmers, (*dances*), and workers of America. (*a final move to great applause*)

(*LEILA and JACKSON crowd around her. ANTOINE, LUTHER, and KARIN cross to table. MARIE eyes the group. RAPHAEL enters and jumps nervously when KARIN speaks to him.*)

KARIN. (*takes sherry to RAPHAEL*) Raphael.

(*Murmurs as EVERYONE stares at RAPHAEL. "Surprised he came," "I hope he doesn't smash the furniture this time," etc.*)

KARIN. How's your painting coming along?

RAPHAEL. Terrible. I hate it.

ANTOINE. Oh, Raphael. You hate all your paintings. That's a mark of genius. Come, (*takes RAPHAEL'S arm*) what you need is something to drink and some good conversation. Come and join the *Party*. (*laughs with LUTHER*)

LUTHER. (*takes ANTOINE'S arm and moves him to the bench right*) Antoine, you don't really believe in the vanguard party, do you? You're just replacing the ruling class with a class of technocrats, a new party bourgeoisie.

LEILA. Oh, you two are tiresome and dull. Marie, come, come, come. Sit with me and I'll read you my new play. Did you read that play I gave you last week?

(*RAPHAEL makes his way upstage left. THEY all stare at MARIE, smiling at this child of the West.*)

MARIE. Yes. I like Gawky very much. He seems to long for freedom.

ANTOINE. (*amused at her mispronunciation*) It's Gorky, Marie. Gorky. By the way, Marie, did you read that pamphlet I gave you on surplus value?

MARIE. Not yet. I don't have much time to study theory, the way you do. In the mornings I take dictation, in the afternoons I type, and in the evening I go to class at the University.

JACKSON. Marie, Marie. Don't bother with that stuffy old University. And those dreary little Marxist tracts. Read Freud. Understand the subconscious mind.

LUTHER. Would you ruin her? Marie, did you like that fellow, Joe, from the IWW? You know, the sailing man I introduced you to at the rally yesterday.

MARIE. Oh yes, I liked him. He's a worker, like me.

JACKSON. You know, (*studies MARIE*) there is something about Marie that suggests a classic Freudian obsession with her father.

ANTOINE. No. I think she needs to study more theory. Her actions are uninformed, lacking theoretical underpinnings. Marie, if you will visit me tomorrow, I have some books I'd like you to read.

CLOTHILDE. Would you destroy the child for life? Look at her. She's a free spirit. She's from the West. So at ease with her body.

LUTHER. "Classic working class," eh, Antoine?

KARIN. Marie is going to speak at the rally tonight.

MARIE. No, I don't think I can. Perhaps one day I will be able to write my ideas and feelings but I don't think I could talk before so many people.

LUTHER. But you must. You could move people.

MARIE. I don't think I know enough. I've heard you all speak about poverty and the suppression of the masses. I could never do that. You talk about the great of Europe as if they were your personal friends. And of the Russian Revolution as if it were your private property. No, I shall never be able to speak with such authority about the difference between left wings and right wings. I was talking to a man the other day and he said he was a statiktician.

(*THEY laugh at her mispronunciation*)

ANTOINE. Marie, it's statistician. Statistician.

CLOTHILDE. No, don't laugh. Words are so unimportant. She is so refreshing. And there are so few delightful things left in life.

LUTHER. Yes, we must stop trying to change her.

ANTOINE. She is a worker. She is our hope for the future. We all know that within the working class lies buried some magic force which will at the critical moment manifest itself in the form of a social revolution and transform the face of the world.

LEILA. (*raising her sherry glass*) To the working class.

(*THEY all toast the working class. It is a religious moment.*)

ALL. To the working class.

MARIE. Are we going to the rally now. Isn't it time? (*embarrassed by the attention and feeling very uncomfortable with these people*)

JACKSON. Marie, you are obsessed with the desire to be in perpetual motion. Come and sit. Sit, sit, sit. Let me analyze you. I really feel that there is something deeply subconscious. Something to do with your father. Come, Raphael, join us.

RAPHAEL. I don't talk, Jackson. I paint.

KARIN. I do think it's time to go.

CLOTHILDE. Wait a bit. It's early. The later we get there the fewer speeches we'll have to listen to. Words, words. What are they? Marie, remember that. Let life be your teacher, Marie. Let life be your teacher.

LEILA. Come. I will read from my new play.

JACKSON. Yes, let's hear your new play, Leila.

RAPHAEL. I'm leaving.

LEILA. No, no, Raphael. (*rises and brings him against his will to the couch*) Now, Act One, Scene One.

(*ANTOINE and LUTHER sit on bench right. JACKSON reclines on the center bench. RAPHAEL is imprisoned on the couch with LEILA. MARIE is on the platform. KARIN is at the table. CLOTHILDE is at the stairs ready to dance.*)

LEILA. We are in a factory. (*CLOTHILDE climbs the stairs*) Dim lights. Terrible conditions. Noise. Lots of noise. (*CLOTHILDE dances noises*) Then quiet. (*CLOTHILDE dances quiet*) A worker stands in a ray of sunlight from the one window. He begins to speak...''It's true that we are the wretched of the earth.'' (*CLOTHILDE dances*) His eyes wander around the factory, resting on the other workers, the machinery. ''We are the starving masses. We are the scum of the earth.'' (*CLOTHILDE dances*) He looks proudly up at the glass enclosed office where the owner sits watching his workers. ''But the scum always rises to the top.''

(*CLOTHILDE in final dance pose as THEY freeze in ecstasy. MARIE looks at them in disbelief as the lights fade.*)

Fragment 25: "One Has Only To Look At Them"

(*In the dark, ANTOINE and LUTHER exit right. The OTHERS shove capes and jackets under the bed and grab books. As the lights come up, STUDENTS are talking in twos waiting for the professor to arrive. The PROFESSOR arrives hurriedly and crosses to the table.*)

PROFESSOR. Take your seats please.

(*MISS ADAMS sits on center bench facing upstage. Another STUDENT sits with her. Two more STUDENTS sit at bench right. MARIE sits on platform bench.*)

PROFESSOR. Can we begin? Where is Miss Adams? Ah, there you are. Miss Adams, you were discussing your paper yesterday. Let's continue. Miss Adams?

ADAMS. Yes. I had reached the part in my paper where I talk about the Negro and whether there is any scientific proof of the inferiority of the Negro. And someone in the class, I believe it was Miss Rogers, questioned my presentation by saying that there is absolutely no proof of the inferiority of the Negro.

PROFESSOR. Yes. Now let's continue from there. Present your argument, Miss Adams.

ADAMS. I maintain that men of color are by nature inferior.

PROFESSOR. And your proof. What proof have you?

ADAMS. Observation. All you have to do is look at them to know it. (*responses from the other STUDENTS*)

PROFESSOR. Let's keep emotions out of this discussion. Now, Miss Adams, that is not the most scientific approach to the question.

(*MARIE raises her hand*)

PROFESSOR. Yes, Miss Rogers.

MARIE. I suggest that Miss Adams look at them a little harder. There are people from India on this very campus. There is an American Indian in my history class, a Negro in my math class, a Chinese in...

ADAMS. Would you marry a Negro?

MARIE. What has that got to do with anything?

ADAMS. If you wouldn't marry a Negro then you obviously think them inferior.

MARIE. If I were to marry at all, I'd rather marry a Negro than most white men I know.

(*response from Marie's SUPPORTERS in the class*)

PROFESSOR. (*enjoys the heated debate*) Please, let's discuss this more calmly and academically. Let me see if I can help answer this question of the inferiority of the Negro with a small example. I recently served as an advisor to a large international rubber concern (*begins to stroll informally among the STUDENTS who listen attentively except for the one next to ADAMS who keeps falling asleep and is nudged by her and by the PROFESSOR*) I won't mention the name but they have heavy rubber interests in South America. Now, the gathering of rubber is a very difficult operation. So difficult, in fact, that it could not possibly be done within the American eight hour day or the price of rubber would increase so much in our country that few could afford even to buy a raincoat. But in the Amazon, the Negroes are able to work in the terrible heat from dawn to darkness without objection.

MARIE. Your observations are as unscientific as Miss Adams'. What does that prove?

PROFESSOR. Why, simply that the Negro has a brain or an intelligence, if you will, that is much closer to animals. They can work in terrible conditions, not even notice it or complain or try to improve their lot. Why I have seen them take a licking and then trot off, perfectly satisfied.

MARIE. I don't believe it. But even if it were true, we should be ashamed.

PROFESSOR. I tell you, I have seen it.

ADAMS. So have I.

MARIE. Do you think that Negroes are less sensitive than we are because they are black?

PROFESSOR. I am suggesting that the evidence is strong that they are less intelligent.

MARIE. How can you see people toiling in the deadening heat for unearthly hours, for just enough to keep life in their bodies, and demand less for them than you demand for yourselves? Anyone of us could have been born slave not free. Black or white. How can you see these people and say that they enjoy their lives? If you can think that, then you are to be feared for you will never be convinced that the enslaved should be free. Your books and scientific observations have made you cynical to subjection of any kind.

(*responses from other STUDENTS*)

PROFESSOR. Your arguments are very emotional, Miss Rogers. You may win some people to your side with them but you forget one thing: you cannot judge them as if they were like you or me.

ADAMS. I believe I was trying to say that earlier. One has only to look at them.

PROFESSOR. Yes, Miss Adams, your paper has some good arguments but you must support them with further evidence. Now, whose essay is next? (*consults notebook*) Ah, Marie Rogers. I believe you are next. Perhaps you'll have a chance to give your views in more scientific detail. What is your essay, please?

MARIE. (*hunts for her essay*) Ah, here it is. I thought I had forgotten to bring it. You see, I toil in the deadening atmosphere of an office from dawn to dusk.

ADAMS. (*murmuring*) Oh, spare us.

PROFESSOR. Perhaps if you're not ready we could hear from someone else today?

MARIE. Oh, I'm quite ready. My essay is titled, "The Contributions the Chinese Have Made to Civilization When the White Race Was Savage."

(*responses from STUDENTS and PROFESSOR as lights go out*)

Fragment 26: "My Name Is Sardar Ranjit Singh"

(*STUDENTS are standing without books waiting for a speaker to arrive at an informal gathering. SARDAR enters down right and walks among the STUDENTS who nod to him as he bows to them. SARDAR climbs the steps to the platform and sits on the bench. STUDENTS take more informal positions around the room, some of them sitting on the floor with pillows from the couch. MARIE is at the table with the professor who has taken off his jacket and is now a STUDENT.*)

SARDAR. I have been invited to speak to you about my country. I am from the North of India. My name is Sardar Ranjit Singh. I and many others have spent our lives in the struggle to free our land from the British. Now you Americans are about to fight a war for democracy, or so you say. But this war will not help the people of India because the British are fighting the Germans for control of commerce to India. How will that free India? Do you Americans believe in freedom for yourselves only? You say your war is for democracy? I doubt it. Your principles do not extend to Asia, although Asia is three-fourths the human race.

STUDENT 1. But we are not responsible.

SARDAR. Can you Americans really be at peace in your minds when your system, your leisure rests on the enslaved bodies of others? If so, you are machines without a soul, without a purpose.

STUDENT 2. But what can we do? We are only students at a University very far from India.

SARDAR. India needs teachers very badly. Come to India and help us teach our people. I must warn you that the work is very hard.

STUDENT 3. We are not afraid of hard work.

SARDAR. And without reward.

MARIE. How can you work without reward?

SARDAR. Because I know it is right. Isn't that the only reason for work of any kind? It is the only basis for life. We all work for a lifetime and in the end we get nothing for it except death. So one must choose to work for what is fundamental and true.

MARIE. It's true that I would like to help for I hate poverty, ignorance and superstition but to work without reward, it seems too difficult.

SARDAR. Then stay in America and work only for money.

STUDENT 4. Would you have us work hopelessly?

SARDAR. If the thing you work for is great enough, and true enough, to work for its achievement is reward enough.

MARIE. It sounds to me as if you do not expect to see your country free. Isn't that a philosophy of despair?

SARDAR. Had I worshipped success I would have despaired long ago.

MARIE. Perhaps you have had enough to eat all your life and that is why you can speak of spiritual things.

SARDAR. It's true that I come from a wealthy family but I have not always had enough to eat.

MARIE. That's not the same thing.

SARDAR. Do you know what it is to love the very soil of your country?

MARIE. Well, I love the mountains of the West and the deserts. But most people mean the government when they talk about patriotism. I do not love the government. But the earth, yes. I love the earth.

SARDAR. If you were in exile and all this country were ruled by a foreign power, would you work for its freedom?

STUDENT 3. Of course. Yes, we would all work for freedom.

MARIE. But I wouldn't work to put it in the hands of a few rich men who would make the rest of us work for them and live in poverty and then tell us that this land was our country.

SARDAR. Living in exile, I cannot forget that India is a land of suffering people.

MARIE. If you were a peasant you would also remember the landlord and if you were a worker you would also think of the boss.

SARDAR. Yes, perhaps you are right. If any of you choose to enter our movement, I must warn you that you cannot play with it in the spirit of adventure for a few months. It is a life's work and it is dangerous. It requires knowledge and the ability to suffer for a principle. In this movement, one is hunted like an animal, and you never feel safe.

MARIE. (comes closer to SARDAR) I have known little else but suffering in my life. Perhaps I will always be too ignorant to fully understand all that you might teach me or that I might teach others. But I think that through you I might touch for the first time in my life a movement of unwavering principle and beauty—the struggle of a continent to be free. One day I would like to be able to convince the people of my country, with their worship of external things, that differences of race, color, and creed are like shadows on the face of a stream, each lending a beauty of its own.

SARDAR. I often hope that women also will work for freedom of all people. They should know, like the working class, and like all of Asia, what subjection means.

(lights fade slowly on SARDAR looking down at MARIE who sits on the couch in front of him)

Fragment 27: "I Am Looking For Talvar Singh"

(Lights come up on empty stage. Voices of the LANDLADY and JUAN DIAZ come from offstage right. Shortly after, THEY appear on the platform.)

LANDLADY. I'll let you take a look, sir, but I'm telling you Marie Rogers is not home just now. I saw her leave with one of her Indian friends.

DIAZ. Was he wearing a turban, this friend of hers?

LANDLADY. How should I know? I don't pay attention to what goes on here. I just know that there are many Indians who come to her apartment at all hours.

DIAZ. Please, try to remember. It is very important. I am leaving the country tonight and I must speak with him before I go. I have been trying to reach him for weeks.

LANDLADY. I think he wore a cap.

DIAZ. A cap? Do you think I could wait here for Marie? I am a friend of hers from the university. You must have seen me before. I wouldn't ask you but it is very urgent.

LANDLADY. I don't like to...

DIAZ. She won't mind.

LANDLADY. I'm sure of that. She doesn't seem to mind who walks in and out of her apartment. All right. But I'm just downstairs.

DIAZ. If I were a thief, I wouldn't come to Marie's apartment.

LANDLADY. (*laughing in spite of herself*) Well, you're right about that.

(*LANDLADY exits. DIAZ walks down the stairs and begins hunting for a notebook in the shelf. Then he crosses to the couch. MARIE enters during the search and crosses to the table, puts her books down, and begins to fix tea. DIAZ drops a book and MARIE reacts by dropping the tea kettle.*)

MARIE. Juan Diaz. How did you get in here?

DIAZ. Your landlady let me in. I have been waiting for you.

MARIE. (*too tired to argue*) For me? That's difficult to believe. What do you want?

DIAZ. I'm looking for Talvar Singh. It is very important that I reach him. I thought he might have been here.

MARIE. (*on her guard for SINGH is a revolutionary*) Talvar Singh? I heard he was arrested two days ago. (*gets book from table and crosses to couch*)

DIAZ. Your landlady said that a man had been here this evening and that she thought it was Talvar.

MARIE. She doesn't know who my friends are. She is mistaken. A friend called.

DIAZ. Why all this secrecy, Marie?

MARIE. What secrecy? It's you who come to my room late at night and look through my things.

DIAZ. You must know that I am also a revolutionary. I work with Talvar. He has a notebook with contacts that he was going to give me. Your landlady told me that the friend you left with tonight was an Indian and he wore a cap instead of a turban. Talvar Singh wears a cap.

MARIE. A friend called and we went to the university. Now, if you don't mind I am very tired. I haven't eaten all day.

DIAZ. I'm sorry, Marie. Here, sit down (*helps her sit, his hands lingering on her arm longer than necessary*) Let me make you some tea. (*smiles, removes his coat, then crosses to the shelf*) Do you always eat so late, Marie?

MARIE. I never have time. (*cleans up the books from the couch, quickly hides a notebook*) There is that miserable office all day and then I have to rush to get to the university.

DIAZ. (*crosses to the couch with tea*) Here's your tea.

MARIE. Why are you here?

DIAZ. To find Talvar Singh.

MARIE. Why would I know where he is?

DIAZ. You are very active in our movement, Marie. And our course, I also came tonight to see you before I leave the city.

MARIE. Me? Strange so late at night. (*crosses to center bench*)

DIAZ. (*looks for notebook quickly while her back is turned*) Why is that so strange. I'm leaving the city and I called to see you first.

MARIE. That's good of you considering your opinion of me. And of all women.

DIAZ. You know I don't have the same opinion of you as I have of other women.

MARIE. Perhaps worse.

DIAZ. No, quite the contrary. I know you have worked hard for our cause. That your interest isn't frivolous like so many of the American women. That's why I thought you might know where I could find Talvar Singh. (*comes up behind her, takes hold of her arms, and whispers in her ear*) Are you sure you don't know where he is, Marie? Please, it is very important to our movement.

MARIE. I have told you, I don't know where he is. Leave me alone. Please I am so tired. (*leans back against him*)

DIAZ. Why do you lie to me, Marie. Tell me the truth. Was Talvar here? (*kisses her hair as he slides his arms around her*)

MARIE. No. *(starts to cross to her right but his arms trap her)* Let me go. I have work to do.

DIAZ. Marie, tell me. *(holds her firmly)*

MARIE. *(becoming afraid)* No. Juan, let go of me.

DIAZ. *(turns her to face him)* Marie, you love me, don't you?

MARIE. Don't.

DIAZ. Marie, don't lie to me. I know you love me...

(DIAZ lets go in order to hold her face so he can kiss her. MARIE breaks away. DIAZ grabs her, kisses her passionately, then lowers her to the bed. He climbs on top of her as she continues to struggle. The lights go out, then come up on MARIE lying on the bed. DIAZ is putting on his jacket.)

DIAZ. Why are you crying, Marie. Don't you want me to go?

MARIE. I cannot live through this night. I am afraid.

DIAZ. *(kneeling by the bed)* Don't cry, Marie.

MARIE. Now I know why you came here.

DIAZ. I swear to you, I came to say goodbye. But you lied.about Talvar Singh.

MARIE. I did not lie.

DIAZ. *(rises and starts searching the room)* Forgive me. Promise me you will forget it. That you will tell no one.

MARIE. *(looks up from the pillow)* Why shouldn't I tell. I am not ashamed.

DIAZ. It would ruin me and my work. You know how men regard these things.

MARIE. Yes, only too well. What are you looking for?

DIAZ. My hat.

MARIE. You didn't wear a hat.

DIAZ. I thought I came with a hat. Marie, let me help you. This miserable room. I'll get you a better one.

MARIE. No.

DIAZ. I have more money than you.

MARIE. So you want to make a prostitute of me. I feel like one already.

DIAZ. I want to help you as a comrade.

MARIE. Then you should have offered before. Even then I would have refused.

DIAZ. You have no right to be so bitter. You asked me to stay. You are a strong woman but suddenly you became weak. You could have screamed but suddenly you lost your voice. (*comes over to bed and looks down at her*)

MARIE. That's a lie.

DIAZ. You always boast of being a free woman. Now you act like an innocent little girl who has been wronged.

MARIE. Should I laugh because you attacked me?

DIAZ. It is you who jeer at me. What right have you to offer a challenge and then blame me for taking it up.

MARIE. Keep out of my way if you don't like jeers. Please leave me in peace. I am sick of life and of you. I don't want to live.

DIAZ. I'll leave as soon as you promise to tell no one.

MARIE. If I am to blame, you have nothing to fear.

DIAZ. I do not fear. I only want to prevent this from interfering with my work.

MARIE. Your work? What about my work?

DIAZ. Promise me.

MARIE. All right, I promise then.

DIAZ. No one.

MARIE. Not a living soul.

(*DIAZ looks at her, then crosses to the table and looks at the books again. Not finding the notebook, he tosses money on the table. DIAZ exits. MARIE gets up and staggers to the shelf to get some tea, turns and sees the money. She picks it up and crosses to the platform*)

MARIE. You dare to give me money. You...(*tosses money on the floor*) Oh god, I wish I were dead. (*sinks to the floor*)

Fragment 28: "I Am Not a Spy"

(*The INTERROGATOR, the DETECTIVE, and an ASSISTANT enter quickly as lights come up sharply. The ASSISTANT grabs MARIE'S arm, yanks her to her feet, and pushes her down the stairs. ASSISTANT continues to push her to the bench right. The atmosphere is urgent.*)

INTERROGATOR. Name?

MARIE. Marie Rogers.

INTERROGATOR. Father?

MARIE. John Rogers, a doctor. Mother, Elly Rogers. Dead.

INTERROGATOR. Nationality?

MARIE. American.

INTERROGATOR. (*leans against table and the DETECTIVE lights his cigarette*) Are you sure you're not of German birth?

MARIE. No, I am not of German birth. Nor are my parents.

INTERROGATOR. Are you certain?

MARIE. Yes, I'm certain. My father was of Indian, Native American descent.

INTERROGATOR. Do you know any Indians from India?

MARIE. I don't know any Indians from India except for an old man, an elderly professor and a few students who come to his house. I haven't seen him for many months.

INTERROGATOR. Are you certain you have seen no Indians for several months?

MARIE. Yes.

INTERROGATOR. Not a Talvar Singh by any chance? (*moves toward her, the DETECTIVE at his side like a shadow*)

MARIE. A what?

DETECTIVE. A Talvar Singh. Come, Miss Rogers. We have your things here. We can easily go through them.

MARIE. (*jumping up*) You want to go through my things. Then I demand the right to see a lawyer.

INTERROGATOR. This is just an examination, Miss Rogers. You are not under arrest.

MARIE. By what right do you think you can go through my books?

INTERROGATOR. Just to see what kind of person you are.

MARIE. I demand the right to see a lawyer.

INTERROGATOR. (*takes MARIE'S arm and ushers her to the couch-bed*) Young woman, this is wartime. It is dangerous to play with the United States.

DETECTIVE. (*approaching the bench so that he is on one side while the INTERROGATOR is on the other*) Come, Miss Rogers, it won't go easy with you if you refuse to speak. I know you think you're some grand person protecting these yellow dogs you run around with.

MARIE. Yellow dogs?

INTERROGATOR. Asiatics. You know what I mean.

MARIE. What Asiatics?

DETECTIVE. You have a brother, Dan, in the army? The United States army?

MARIE. I don't know what you're talking about.

DETECTIVE. Yes, you do. And it will not go well with him if his officer learns that his sister is a spy.

MARIE. (*rises and is pushed back down by the ASSISTANT*) You know I am not a spy. And you know if you know anything, that I haven't seen my brother in years. I don't know where he is now. For all I know, he may be dead fighting for your democracy.

INTERROGATOR. We'll find out soon enough.

MARIE. I have told you the truth. I am not a spy. If I were, I would not be poor.

INTERROGATOR. You dirty, lying, little slut. (*to ASSISTANT*) Bring her.

(*INTERROGATOR and DETECTIVE exit. The ASSISTANT shoves MARIE to the platform. She falls to the floor.*)

MARIE. No, it is too cold.

ASSISTANT. You're a Federal Prisoner.

MARIE. Leave the door open.

ASSISTANT. The air will freeze the guards.

MARIE. (*crying out*) Then stay with me. I'll go crazy in here. I am afraid I'll be left here forever.

(*ASSISTANT loosens MARIE'S hold on his arm and exits*)

Fragment 29: "I Tried To See You in Jail"

(Lights lower to blue spot on MARIE upstage center. DAN enters down right and leans against the wall. WOMEN enter in a line and stand in tableau.)

MARIE. The indictment was signed against me and I was put in the Tombs prison, called that by some men of grim humor. It is in the shadow of Wall Street. It is sullen and cynical. It is savage. Inside the odor of carbolic acid penetrates everything and a gray twilight clings like fog to everything. In this prison, women sit for weeks or months waiting the trial that condemns them to servitude in one or another prison of the state or to the freedom that sends them back out into a world that is as pitiless as the prison. Some wait in sickening fear, some in sneaking bravado.

(IRISH PROSTITUTE crosses right and lights a cigarette, ALCIE stands center, and the OLD FORGER stands left)

OLD FORGER. *(takes a photograph out of her pocket and crosses to show it to MARIE)* See this picture. That's my man. I've worked for him for many years. Forging. I went to jail for him. The day they sentenced me to seven years hard labor, he didn't even come. *(crosses right, turns)* Maybe he didn't know I was on trial.

MARIE. Yes. He probably didn't know. How could he? It's not in the papers.

(IRISH PROSTITUTE crosses right and lights a cigarette. ALCIE stands center. The OLD FORGER stands left.)

IRISH PROSTITUTE. So, what are you doing in this here hotel?

MARIE. You wouldn't understand if I told you.

IRISH PROSTITUTE. I coulda' understood once. I was purty once.

ALCIE. I gotta baby.

(WOMEN stare at her)

ALCIE. My parents threw me out when they found out he was illegitimate.

IRISH PROSTITUTE. That won't get you in here.

ALCIE. I stole fifty dollars to feed me and the baby.

MARIE. Won't the father help you?

ALCIE. I won't tell the name of the father. If he knew, he'd never marry me.

IRISH PROSTITUTE. Listen to the angel. She thinks he'll marry her. Why kid, don't you know if he'd wanted to marry you, he'd a done it by now? Chances are that before he's through there won't be a kid in the city he can't slap for fear it's his own.

OLD FORGER. (*comes forward*) There was a woman in here yesterday got three years hard labor for forgery. She stole the money to pay for the hospital. Her two babies was in the hospital with whooping cough. She was sitting right her when they came and told her them two babies was dead. She just sat there, wouldn't move or nothin'. We had to carry her to her bed. She sat on her bed, no tears or nothin'. We all stood around her, even the guards.

IRISH PROSTITUTE. (*after a pause*) Those god damn dirty dogs.

(*Lights change as DAN speaks. WOMEN remain in tableau.*)

DAN. Marie, I tried to see you in jail but they wouldn't let me. They told me you were a spy but I didn't believe a word of it. George is dead, Marie. He was killed working as a day laborer digging a sewer. The walls caved in on him and broke his neck. Company paid Dad fifty dollars.

I was at the front from the time I landed in France. We marched all day through mud and water up to our hips. The water was mixed with blood from the guys dyin'. I watched men torn to pieces right in front of me. Only reason I wasn't killed was luck. We never got any rest. I never knew where we were marching. After, they sent me to New Orleans. I was given land, dry desert land in New Mexico. I got nothin' but my bare hands to work a desert. They never gave me a penny. They put me in the reserves so they can call me back when the next war comes. I don't know how you stand on the war, Marie, but I don't think you were for it or you wouldn't be in jail. I can tell you this, Marie. When the next war comes, I don't fight. They can stand me up against a wall and shoot me, but I won't go.

(*lights fade on DAN, then slowly on the WOMEN in prison as they turn to form a line and exit*)

Fragment 30: Florence and Margaret

(*MARIE rises and comes downstairs to table*)

MARIE. The war came to an end and I found myself free without trial. I went to work for *The Call,* a leading Socialist newspaper. I was the only woman working at *The Call.* I was living at the time with a friend, Florence, and we rented one of the rooms in our apartment to a manicurist named Margaret.

(*FLORENCE enters with a book of poetry and lies on the bed. MARIE joins her on the bed and they read the newspaper. MARGARET enters carrying a pair of stockings, a hairbrush, and nail polish. She gets tea at the shelf.)*

MARGARET. What are you reading over there? One of those magazine stories?

FLORENCE. A newspaper.

MARGARET. A newspaper. Which one?

FLORENCE. *The Call.*

MARGARET. *The Call?* Never heard of it.

MARIE. It's a Socialist paper.

MARGARET. A Socialist paper. Let me see it. *(crosses to bed and pushes her way in to see the paper)* Tell me, Marie, don't those Socialists believe in free love?

MARIE. Yes, some of them do.

MARGARET. *(leering)* Uh huh. I see.

FLORENCE. Marie wrote the story on the front page.

MARGARET. On the front page? My, that's something. Must be hard work doing that. *(sits bench right and begins putting polish on her nails)*

FLORENCE. Marie likes hard work. She never has time for literature, music, love.

(MARIE rises and crosses to table)

MARGARET. You know, Marie, you should work with me in the barber shop. Manicuring's easy if you find the right gentleman. *(crosses to get her stockings left hanging on the shelf)* Today a gentlemen looked at me and said, "It's a shame for a pretty girl like you to wear a cotton blouse."

FLORENCE. Is that what goes on at the barber shop?

MARGARET. Well, it's a damn sight better than having your husband chase you around with a knife. Accusing you of doing it with other men.

FLORENCE. So what did you say to him?

MARGARET. Oh, I didn't say anything. I left him *(crosses back to bench right to get her nail polish)*

FLORENCE. No, I meant the gentlemen at the barber shop.

MARGARET. Oh, I told him it was a shame but that I was always willing to accept silk. See, I wouldn't dream of letting a gentleman know I'm cheap. They have a habit of thinking they can get a girl cheap. But if a girl has the right taste and knows how to wear her clothes right, a gentleman will never make that mistake.

FLORENCE. No?

MARGARET. (*crosses to bed and puts her leg up to put on her stockings*) A nice girl would never let a man fool around with her because he don't respect her after. Now, I got a girl friend who goes out with gentlemen but only if they give her a present of $25 or more. 'Course I don't mean that she does anything for it. No that there's anything wrong with doing just a little bit.

FLORENCE. Especially for a present of $25 or more.

MARGARET. Why sure. I have gentlemen friends in my room. Why just the other night...

MARIE. (*crosses back to the bed*) I thought I heard a man's voice coming from your room.

MARGARET. Well, you don't mind do you? You write for a Socialist paper and all, and believe in free love.

FLORENCE. Oh, Marie doesn't practice free love. She has no time for love.

MARGARET. (*studies MARIE*) You know, Marie, if I was you I'd buy myself a dress, a nice silk dress and get my hair marcelled. You'd look like a million dollars. (*styles MARIE'S hair*) When I first came to New York, I wore cotton stockings and now I wear silk. And gentlemen take me to restaurants where they spend a lot of money on me. If you dressed right, Marie, you could meet a nice gentlemen. How about those Bolsheviks and Mensheviks you're always reading about. What kind of men are they?

MARIE. They're committed revolutionaries in Russia. They're mostly working people.

MARGARET. What's the difference? (*gets her tea and starts off*) Sounds like these Bolsheviks or Mensheviks would treat a girl just about like any other gentlemen. Say, maybe you could introduce me to one of them? (*exits*)

MARIE. Some women will get along well in this life. (*crosses to table*)

FLORENCE. Who knows. Perhaps she'll marry a banker. She's right you know. You should take time from your work.

MARIE. Perhaps, Florence, because you have never worked for a living it makes it hard for you to understand my way of life.

FLORENCE. (*goes to center bench and reclines*) Even so, why pin yourself to a cross? What sin are you trying to wipe off your conscience? You are like the Christians flaying themselves for a sin.

MARIE. Sin. I have never sinned. I am not a Christian.

FLORENCE. You get up at dawn. You work until all hours of the night.

MARIE. You will never understand what it is like to work for freedom. To be part of the struggle for human emancipation.

FLORENCE. But you work for these Indian men. They are all upper class.

MARIE. And the leaders of the Socialist Party are mainly rich intellectuals. I don't want to be led by them. I have no use for leaders.

FLORENCE. But these Indian men. You know their attitudes about women and sex.

MARIE. (*joins her at the bench bringing her notebook with her*) They're no different from the Americans. They both think women are ruined by sex experience while men become men by the same experience.

FLORENCE. But don't you think that all the work you put into their movement would be better spent working for the people of this country?

MARIE. Without the freedom of Asiatic people, European and American workers can not gain emancipation. One of the chief pillars of capitalism is found in the subjection of Asiatic people.

FLORENCE. Most of your friends think you work with these Indians because you are in love with one of them.

MARIE. How could I be? You said yourself that I had no time for love.

FLORENCE. You know what I meant.

MARIE. I do feel a bond with these men in the movement.

FLORENCE. A bond? You mean sex?

MARIE. No. I feel a warmth and affection that perhaps I could never give to my father and my brothers.

FLORENCE. I think if you found a man and lived with him, you would be happier and not live such an insane life.

MARIE. Perhaps I will. (*crosses to bed, then turns to FLORENCE playfully*) Perhaps I have already. Perhaps I have many men friends.

FLORENCE. Why keep it a secret?

MARIE. Because the Indians do not respect women who have independent sex lives.

FLORENCE. Yes, but I think you also are ashamed.

MARIE. In my mind, as an intellectual standard, I do not believe that the sex experience is a shameful thing. But I think that I shall never stop feeling guilty about it. I seem to be in constant conflict with standards that have been ground into my soul. (*sits on the bed*) Now, let me work, Florence, or I won't get any sleep tonight.

FLORENCE. (*crosses to stand over her*) You remind me of those lines of Kabir's about a wild swan that flies from lake to lake and builds a nest in none. Marie, I love you as I have loved no other friend.

MARIE. Love is for weaklings. When one loves, one can be enslaved. I will not be enslaved. Freedom is higher than love, at least today. Perhaps one day the two will be one. You know, Florence, you are the type of woman who will one day fall in love, get married, become a housewife and stay with your husband out of habit.

FLORENCE. (*gets tea*) Well, you are the kind who will fall in love and be simply finished off. I will get my way in life because I don't value men enough to think them worth fighting against all the time. Just wait until you fall in love with a man and wish to be always with him.

(*MARIE laughs*)

I have heard from some of our friends that you have met a man. What's he like?

MARIE. How could they know?

FLORENCE. Then it's true?

MARIE. Well, I have met a man. He's come from India to the conference the Indians are having. He was in prison during the war...

FLORENCE. You see, my prediction is going to come true.

MARIE. He's a friend, Florence. We understand each other. His ideas are very close to mine.

FLORENCE. And his attitude about women?

MARIE. (*smiles*) His revolution extends to women, unlike many of the others. He believes that without the freedom of women, the world will never advance.

FLORENCE. (*goes up the stairs*) With opinions like that, you will be married within a month.

MARIE. I am fairly well insured against marriage, Florence, for I have lived with a number of men. No man would marry me after that.

FLORENCE. Even a man whose revolution extends to women?

MARIE. You write too many lyrical poems.

FLORENCE. And you are afraid of even the word love. We fear things only when we are weak before them.

(*FLORENCE looks at MARIE with deep affection, then exits. Lights change as MARIE sits on the platform and begins working on an article for the newspaper.*)

Fragment 31: "The Silence of Despair"

(*ANAND enters. MARIE looks up from her notebook. ANAND goes to shelf to get tea, then takes a pillow from the couch and joins MARIE on the floor. The scene moves very rapidly pulled along toward its inevitable conclusion.*)

ANAND. We missed you at the meeting today.

MARIE. My article for the newspaper has to be finished.

(*ANAND smiles at her. MARIE leaves her work and ANAND reclines on the pillow. MARIE rests her head in his lap and he strokes her hair.*)

MARIE. I was having trouble finishing my article. I kept thinking about you and our movement. I've often wished that one could just stand in front of the British officials in India, and explain to them very simply that it is not in keeping with the nobility of existence to keep other human beings in subjection. Surely I could creep right down into their hearts and find that one spot of universal consciousness and convince them?

ANAND. (*laughs*) Marie, don't let love destroy your reasoning capacity.

MARIE. (*sits up*) Perhaps love is stronger than the intellect.

ANAND. (*sits up*) That may be, but use it on people who have human traits. The British Empire is a system of iron and steel.

MARIE. But you try and persuade all kinds of people. Yesterday I heard you try to convince a man on the Stock Exchange that he makes his money the wrong way.

ANAND. If someone comes my way, I say what I think.

MARIE. (*sits up on her knees behind him, stokes his hair and his face*) I think love is not just a personal thing. It is like thought. It sweeps in every direction and affects the actions of people.

ANAND. But it must be combined with other things. Love cannot break steel bars.

MARIE. Gandhi believes in the power of love.

ANAND. It may be that we will have to evolve a new weapon of struggle. We have no guns. But Gandhi's philosophy is a philosophy of despair. He preaches personal perfection because he is appalled by terrifying political difficulties. And he is trained in British Constitutional Law. That is always a poison. A terrible poison.

MARIE. But Gandhi is doing more than any other revolutionary has ever done for India.

ANAND. That makes him all the more dangerous.

(*MARIE considers what ANAND has said. ANAND returns to his book. MARIE begins reading through her notebook, leaning against him. ANAND looks up.*)

ANAND. I have often wondered, Marie, why you should work with us. For our movement.

MARIE. I was tired of hunger and poverty and loneliness. I wanted friendship, understanding, and a resting place.

ANAND. You won't find rest in our work.

MARIE. But I find the warmth and the feeling of closeness that gives me rest. The sheer greatness of your movement holds me.

ANAND. But haven't you as a woman and as a human being desired love?

MARIE. Before I met you, Anand, I thought that I did not want love. That there was only sex. The thing I called love did not seem to exist.

ANAND. And what was that?

MARIE. Understanding, tolerance, freedom—all combined.

ANAND. You are wrong, love exists. But it is beyond those things.

(*MARIE puts her arms around him and begins to kiss his neck and his cheeks. ANAND takes her hands in his.*)

ANAND. You say that you did not want love. That you thought there was only sex. Tell me, there have been other men in your life?

MARIE. (*tensing*) Yes.

ANAND. How many?

MARIE. (*tries to keep the mood loving and affectionate*) Anand, don't ask me that. I thought you understood my way of life. I have loved no one but you. I am not a bad woman.

ANAND. I have said nothing about being a bad woman. (*rises and crosses stage right*)

MARIE. Perhaps I believe that I am an evil woman.

ANAND. I hope that one of these men was not one of my countrymen.

MARIE. You hope? (*gets up to go to him, then turns her back*) No, not one of them was your countrymen.

ANAND. I'm glad.

MARIE. Why?

ANAND. Such things should be kept from out movement. Our work is difficult enough without such things confusing it. Don't misunderstand, I believe in the personal freedom of women. You know that. But our comrades do not. They are like most men everywhere.

MARIE. But I know that you have not waited until you met me to live, to love. (*puts her hands on his chest*) What are men and women of the past to you or to me?

ANAND. I am human. I am glad that no man in our movment has come into your life in that intimate way.

MARIE. Your attitude makes me feel guilty. As if I had sinned. (*takes hands away*)

ANAND. Your idea of sin is purely Christian. I only know what is social and what is anti-social.

MARIE. Do you regard a woman who has lived an independent sex life, as I have done, as anti-social?

ANAND. That's purely a private matter, if you have injured no one.

MARIE. Then why should you care if...

ANAND. (gets tea and book and sits) I care only for political reasons. So many western women have an erotic interest in Indians. I haven't married such a woman and I don't want it used against us politically.

MARIE. (squats near ANAND) I don't believe that race has anything to do with men's primitive attitude toward women as purely physical beings.

ANAND. (to shelf) Perhaps not. But you are working with men from India. At the conference the other day when you opposed Juan Diaz and his program, I was watching him and I have never seen such hatred on anyone's face before.

MARIE. Perhaps he does not like a woman who goes her own way, who has her own political ideas. Perhaps he is angry that I spoke against him. You heard what he said, he called me a foreigner and asked that foreigners not be allowed to speak.

ANAND. Yes, and I defended you, as did many others. But later, (to bench right with his book) I heard some of the men in the movement say things about you and Juan.

MARIE. (rises) Things? What things have you heard?

ANAND. Marie, how well do you know this man?

MARIE. We worked together before the war.

ANAND. Marie, did you ever love Juan Diaz?

MARIE. Anand, why do you ask me that?

ANAND. Why don't you answer?

MARIE. You have no business asking me that.

ANAND. Then what I hear is true, that there was something between you long ago?

MARIE. Who told you that?

ANAND. Answer, Marie, yes or no?

MARIE. I can't answer with a yes or no.

ANAND. Then it is true. Now I understand why you act so afraid when I mention his name and when I asked about my countrymen.

MARIE. You must hear me. (comes toward him)

ANAND. I don't want to hear you. After this.

MARIE. I appeal to you in the name of our love.

ANAND. Don't.

MARIE. Then I demand it as a comrade, as a human being.

(*ANAND waits for her to tell her story*)

MARIE. One evening long ago, I came home late. I had just taken Talvar to one of our friends who was going to sneak him out of the country. I found Juan Diaz in my room. He had always treated me with contempt and I was surprised to see him. He said that he was looking for Talvar Singh. I had been warned to confide in no one. When I wouldn't tell him anything, when I pretended I had been out with a friend, he kept trying to get me to tell him. When I wouldn't, he attacked me. After, he made me promise not to tell anyone. He accused me of wanting it. I began to feel that perhaps he was right. I was very lonely at the time. Don't you see, Anand? He tells you about it now to hurt me and to destroy our life together.

ANAND. He did not tell me. Someone else told me that you oppose Juan Diaz because you love him and he would not marry you. That you are a woman of loose character.

MARIE. (*coming down the stairs*) And you? What did you reply?

ANAND. I said I did not believe that. That even if it were true it made no difference to my political decisions.

MARIE. To your political decisions?

ANAND. While he spoke, I believed him.

MARIE. (*goes to him*) Then I will go before these men and tell them my version of what happened. I will prove to them that I am as good as any one of them.

ANAND. (*to shelf*) Don't you know that not one of those men would believe you, even if you are right and Juan Diaz is wrong. He is a man and you are a woman.

MARIE. (*follows him*) Is this the kind of men I'm working with? I went to prison for these men. I helped free many of them from jail.

ANAND. (*gets tea from platform*) They are no better than other men. They don't pose as liberal or modern in such things as American men do.

MARIE. Then Juan Diaz has the right to lie?

ANAND. You must say nothing. Perhaps they will have respect enough for me and my work to let it go no further.

MARIE. Your work? I will not depend on your work or my position as your wife to defend myself from any man.

ANAND. I will defend you. I know how. You don't know men.

MARIE. I will defend myself.

ANAND. If you do, you, with your ideas, will only injure yourself and me. I have suffered enough through you.

MARIE. Suffered through me? What do you mean?

ANAND. You have acted as if I were an ordinary stupid Christian husband to whom you had to lie. I can never forget this.

MARIE. I kept a promise to a man I knew long before I met you. And even if I had told you about him, as I told you of other men friends...

ANAND. Friends? You call them friends?

MARIE. Yes, friends. You would not have understood, as you say. Look how you've reacted.

ANAND. Why did you leave me unprotected before Juan Diaz?

MARIE. I didn't tell you because of my promise to him and my love for you.

ANAND. Now that I know you lied, how do I know you haven't lied about everyone else? Perhaps all of the other men are my countrymen also. Any time I take a stand, one of them will try to break me because of you.

MARIE. You seem to think it is all my fault. As if Juan Diaz were right. (to center bench)

ANAND. What I think of him could best be said with a gun. Except men will say I did it for personal reasons. (comes behind her) I am sorry, Marie, what I say to you is bitter because I love you.

(ANAND reaches out to put his arms around her. MARIE reacts violently.)

ANAND. What is wrong?

MARIE. (moving to avoid him) Don't come up behind me like that, I am afraid.

ANAND. Afraid of what?

MARIE. I am afraid of you.

ANAND. (comes toward her) Of me? Why of me?

MARIE. (backing away) I don't know. I am afraid that you will strike me in the back.

ANAND. Marie!

MARIE. I don't know why. (crosses to table, picks up newspaper in an effort to cover her emotions)

ANAND. What are you doing?

MARIE. I'm going to work. I have to finish my article. (coldly)

ANAND. You ought to stop writing for a time.

MARIE. Stop writing?

ANAND. What you write will have no influence after this. Men will say your ideas are an attempt to justify your kind of life. (*to the bed*) And then that article you wrote last week was not very good.

MARIE. What are you doing to me, Anand?

ANAND. What have you already done to me.

MARIE. What have I done to you? Anand, did you hear yourself. You asked me to stop writing, the one thing I have worked for all these years. Do you really want me to stop writing? (*pauses*) If I give up writing what kind of work should I do, Anand. (*begins to rage, picking up books and throwing them, picking up teapot, cups and slamming them down*) What kind of work would you like me to do, Anand? Perhaps I could go back to taking down the thoughts of men. Of some man, and then I can spend the whole day typing them. Is that what you think I should do? Should I sit at home, a wife, a housewife doing the things I have always hated? Washing? Ironing? A female at last. Why do you do this to me?

ANAND. It is you, Marie, who has done this to both of us.

(*ANAND coldly takes his book and exits. MARIE begins to pick up the mess she's made. She crosses to the platform and sits by the pillow. Gradually she lies down and falls asleep fitfully. ANAND enters quickly and kneels to waken her*)

ANAND. Marie.

MARIE. (*takes his hand*) Anand.

ANAND. A man has arrived from India. He has accused Juan Diaz of being a spy. He was in India during the war. No revolutionary could have gone there and come away again. Yet, he traveled everywhere in safety. Think what he will do to us in the future. He will openly boast of his relationship with you, he will do it to ruin me.

MARIE. No, men don't use such weapons against other men. They use them only against women. It is only of women that they are so physiological. (*rises and crosses to pick up remaining books*) Anand, you must leave me. Say you left me over this affair with Juan Diaz. They will respect you for that.

ANAND. I cannot go. I seem to have waited for your coming for years.

MARIE. Then I will go.

ANAND. What do you mean?

MARIE. I will go away. We are no longer happy. I am tired and my work is ruined. I will go to stay with Karin in Denmark.

ANAND. I thought you loved me.

MARIE. Yes, I loved you. But look at you, look at me. There is not trust or understanding between us. And without these there can be no love.

ANAND. We can change.

MARIE. Change the story of Juan Diaz? It will always be a political weapon against you. I prefer to be alone after this. Juan can hurt you only through me and I refuse to be hurt.

ANAND. Our men will not work with you after this.

MARIE. Then I will work alone.

ANAND. Are you trying to kill me?

MARIE. (*kneels by him*) I am trying to save you.

ANAND. And our love?

MARIE. Surely the blending of all things in two human beings cannot endure for all time. Last night I dreamed I was holding a bowl in my outstretched hand. A beautiful bowl curved gently and about it was painted a wreath of flowers as delicate as all the art of ancient China. So beautiful and delicate it was that I held it far from me to see it shimmer as a ray of sunlight fell on it. And as I stood, wondering at its beauty, a crack crawled down the side, to the bottom, up and around to the top again, and the broken fragment rolled over and lay in my palm. I hadn't broken the bowl. Nobody broke it. But it was broken, irrevocably broken by something I knew not what. I turned and awoke and there was no sound. And the silence of death hung over everything. Worse than death, the silence of despair.

(*Lights out. ANAND exits in the dark.*)

Fragment 32: "We Are of the Earth"

(*MARIE stands center where she began*)

MARIE. Before me stretches a Danish sea. The sky is as gray as my spirit these days. For thirty years I have lived. And for those years I have drunk from the wells of bitterness. I have loved, and bitterness left me for that hour. There were times when love itself was bitter. Now I stand at the end of one life and the beginning of another. I have the knowledge that comes from experience and work that is limitless in its scope and significance. Isn't that enough to weigh against love?

To die would have been beautiful and there were times when my path would better have lead into the sea. But now I choose otherwise. For I belong to those who do not die for the sake of beauty. I belong to those who die from other causes. Exhausted by poverty (*ELLY, ANNIE, GEORGE enter*), victims of power and wealth (*JOHN, HELEN enter*), fighters in a great cause (*ANAND and SARDAR enter*). For we are of the earth and our struggle is a struggle of the earth.

(*lights slowly fade on final tableau*)

Lydia Sargent as Marie Rogers in "Daughter of Earth." Photo: Jim Mullen.

Sweet Marie

CY WARMAN

RAYMOND MOORE

REFRAIN—Slowly

Come to me SWEET MA - RIE, SWEET MA - RIE come to me Not be-cause your face is fair, love to see.____ But your soul so pure and sweet Makes my hap-pi-ness com-plete, Makes me fal-ter at your feet, SWEET MA - RIE.___ Come to -RIE.___

The Harvest Dance Call

(there are three couples who stand stage left, right, and center in an open square)

Circle to the right, hand held high
Circle to the left, now don't be shy.
Swing your partner 'round and
   'round
'Til her feet come off the ground.

Now swing a new gal, pretty little
   maid.
Then grab your gal and promenade.
Promenade around and then
Why promenade back home again.

Gals in the center, lookin' mighty
   sweet
Gents in the middle and move your
   feet.

Face your partner, Grand right and
   left.
Twice 'round the circle, then catch
   your breath.

Now grab hands and form a snake.
Snake, snake, pretty little snake.

(form a line holding hands; the leader goes under the arms of the middle of the line and they wind their way up the platform and back down)

Grab a gal, pretty little thing.
Grab a gal for one last swing.

PRODUCTION NOTES

DIRECTING: It is very important that the director and cast read the novel from which this play was adapted. While much has been left out, much has been adapted word for word. In addition, the beauty and originality of Smedley's writing has been preserved in Marie's narrations at the beginning of many fragments. Marie and characters, events, feelings, and politics she writes about can be better understood through reading and studying the novel itself.

STAGING: *Daughter of Earth* was performed in a rectangular room with a 3 foot high platform at one end. The audience surrounded the stage on 2 sides partly to seat more people and partly to help create a more panoramic environment. Stage directions are based on this partial theater-in-the-round staging. A more orthodox staging would require some adjustments.

SET: Gray flats with brown wood trim form the background on the platform for both Parts I and II. The set change from Part I to II is performed by the actors and involves minimal work. The table in Part I was long a narrow and is replaced by a square table in Part II. The bed in Part I is covered with a faded brown blanket and is moved to center stage in Part II and covered with a red print bedspread and throw pillows. The short and long benches are painted gray with the exception of one long bench which is behind the table in Part I and is moved to down center in Part II. A clothesline stretches across the gray flats from stage left to stage center. Upstage exits in Part I go to the fields and town; downstage exit goes to another part of the cabin. In Part II, upstage and downstage exits are all exterior.

PROPS: As indicated within the script. Cold canned beef stew, baked beans, and french bread were used for food in Part I.

LIGHTING: Blue specials were used for Big Buck's monologue about the cowboy who got up and danced. A flash effect was used for the mine explosion offstage. Blue lighting for the Tombs and for the Dan Rogers monologue were also effective.

TABLEAUX: The end of almost every fragment involves either a freeze in tableau or a moving tableau. In most cases, where time changed or a blackout was felt to be needed the directions read "lights fade out." Where a blackout was felt to be unnecessary, the directions read "lights change." The closing tableaux, whether moving or frozen, should be staged with care and concern for their contribution to the spaciousness of the West, and the epic quality of the portrayal of 30 years of a woman's life.

CASTING: The combining of parts was used to give actors a variety of roles to play and ample stage time. The three Boston productions each combined the parts differently depending on the skills of the particular cast. In one production, 5 men and 5 women were used. In another, musicians played during *The Harvest Dance* and *She Is a Worker*. Big Buck and Jim Watson have been played by the same actor or by different actors. The actor playing John Rogers played Anand in one production, etc. The combinations used in the 1984 production are listed on pages 5 and 6 and worked very successfully. The actors playing Marie, George, Beatrice, and Annie do not necessarily have to look young, they just have to be able to play young.

COSTUMES: Some of the costume changes are extremely fast—particularly Annie who becomes Sally in *The Harvest Dance* and the changes back and forth from Aunt Helen to Beatrice. Also the transition from the Bohemian cocktail party to students at the University. These were all done successfully by keeping them simple. Quick changes in hair and jackets or blouses; or baggy overalls with dresses underneath helped facilitate beautiful changes in a matter of seconds. Also note that the Rogers family are all in barefeet except for John.

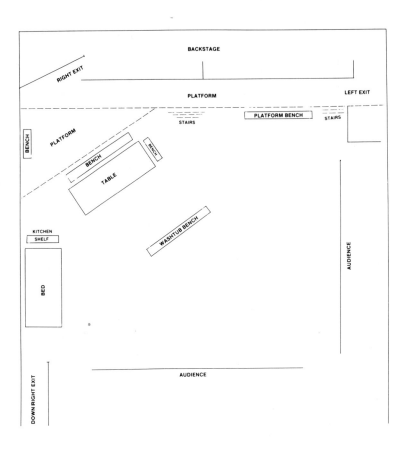

BACKSTAGE

RIGHT EXIT

PLATFORM

LEFT EXIT

PLATFORM

PLATFORM BENCH

STAIRS

STAIRS

BENCH

PLATFORM

BENCH

BENCH

TABLE

WASHTUB BENCH

KITCHEN

SHELF

BED

AUDIENCE

AUDIENCE

DOWN RIGHT EXIT

SET DESIGN
ACT I
DAUGHTER OF EARTH

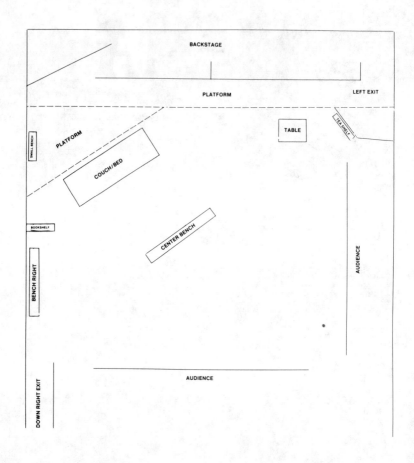

SET DESIGN
ACT II
DAUGHTER OF EARTH

EMMA

by

Howard Zinn

"Emma" first performed in 1976 at Theater for the New City, New York City, produced by Crystal Field and George Barteneiff, directed by Jeff Zinn. (Ran for three weeks.) Next performed in 1977 at the Next Move Theater, Boston, directed by Maxine Klein. (Ran for thirty weeks.)

Cast and Staff for the New York production:

Emma .... *Susan Marshall*

Sasha .... *Stephen Randolph*

Anna .... *Ellen Sherman*

Fedya .... *Jared Sakren*

Vito,
prisoner, ... *Peter Gelblum*
Frick

Father .... *Marc Burd*

Mother,
prostitute .... *Nancy Herman*

Johann Most .... *Ed Shiff*

Mr. Sachs,
President McKinley, ... *David Kabat*
prison guard

Sister,
prostitute .... *Lori Meadows*

prisoner
guard .... *Ed Merullo*

Pianist and music director, Elizabeth Myers; production manager and audio designer, Donna Jacobs; lighting designer, Rick Belzer; set designer, Kenneth Shewer; sound engineer, David Baldwin; light engineer, Anitra Hoffman; stage manager, Linda Miller.

Cast and Staff for the Boston production:

Emma .... *Geraldine Librandi*

Sasha .... *Gil Schwartz*

Anna,
factory worker .... *Lani Zera*

Fedya .... *Steve Warnick*

Vito
Mr. Vogel .... *Brad Jones*

111

Mr. Sachs,
Frick, ... *Martin Anderson*
prisoner

Mother,
prostitute .... *Karen MacDonald*
Lizabeth

Mr. Levine,
Inspector Sullivan, ... *Paul Peeling*

Johann Most,
prisoner .... *Moses E. Wilson*

Sister,
factory worker, ... *Cynthia Caldwell*
prostitute

Sets by Michael Anania; costumes, Nancy Bailey; lighting, John Polglase; musical director, Andy Gaus; choreography, Marilyn Plotkin; historical consultant, Isidore Levitt; lighting and technical crew, Tom Clewell; stage manager, Paul Peeling; house manager, Thalia McMillion.

ACT I

Lower East Side, New York City. Time: 1886-1892.

ACT II

In and out of prison. Organizing and agitating. In and around New York City. Time: 1892-1917.

STORY OF THE PLAY

"Emma" tells the story of Emma Goldman who breaks from her factory job, her family, her husband, in Rochester, and (it is 1887, and the Haymarket Affair anarchists have just been executed) goes to New York, where she meets the group of anarchists who hang out in Sachs' Cafe on the lower East Side. She and Alexander Berkman become lovers, and they form a little commune with Anna Minkin and Fedya. Aroused by the shooting of strikers at the Carnegie steel plant in Homestead, Pennsylvania, they plan the assassination of Carnegie's manager, Henry Clay Frick. Berkman (Sasha) volunteers to do it; but he botches the job and is sentenced to twenty-two years in the Western Pennsylvania State Penitentiary.

The story then weaves back and forth between Sasha in prison, repeatedly beaten and tortured, and Emma, organizing and agitating, being imprisoned herself, becoming involved in a passionate affair with the flamboyant Ben Reitman, learning to be a midwife, and planning with their old comrades the escape of Sasha from prison. The escape plan fails, Emma is arrested as a suspect in the assassination of President McKinley. The play ends with Sasha's release from prison, and a reunion of the old group in Sachs' Cafe, pledging to carry on the struggle.

DESCRIPTION OF CHARACTERS

EMMA GOLDMAN: She is eighteen to twenty-two in Act I, twenty-two to thirty-seven most of Act II, forty-eight at the end. Blue eyes, blonde or brown hair, strong, pleasant features. Her temperament by turns fiery and gentle.

ALEXANDER BERKMAN: Same age as Emma. Powerfully built, strong, bespectacled, scholarly face, serious demeanor.

JOHANN MOST: In his forties, short black beard, short hair, face disfigured around his jaw, a powerful orator, capable of rousing a crowd, biting wit.

EMMA'S FATHER: Overbearing, Act I.

FRICK: In shadows, Act I.

BEN REITMAN: Appears in Act II, twenties or thirties but looks older, handsome, dark hair, mustache, a flamboyant character, a doctor in the Chicago slums who takes care of hobos, beggars, prostitutes, who wears flowing silk ties, a cowboy hat, carries a cane.

ANNA MINKIN: In her twenties in Act I, thirties in Act II. Short, thin, a comic disposition, good singing voice.

DORA: A factory worker, Act I.

TAUBE: Emma's mother. Matronly. Kindly temperament. Act I.

MR. SACHS: Rough, good-humored cafe owner, Act I.

JENNY: A factory worker, Act I.

ALMEDA SPERRY: mid or late thirties, tough, smart, working class woman, drinker, sometime prostitute, Act II.

LIZBETH: A prison nurse, Act II.

HELENA: Emma's sister. A few years older than Emma in Act I

ROSE: A factory worker, Act I.

MAUREEN: A young working class woman, sometime prostitute, good singing voice.

VITO: In twenties and thirties, Act I. Thirties and forties, Act II. Short, thin, a comedian of sorts, good singing voice.

MR. LEVINE: A lecherous friend of the family, Act I.

VOICES: Needed for McKinley, J. Edgar Hoover, Attorney General Thomas Gregory, Monty, Vogel, and Andy.

Act I

Scene 1. The Factory

(Overture "Mein Ruhe Platz," on the piano, or, if taped, sung in chorus. A factory whistle is heard in the dark. As the lights come up, four women, of various ages—EMMA, ROSE, JENNY, DORA—are sitting at their imaginary machines, and go through the motions of sewing, their feet working the treadle, making a steady beat on the floor, their bodies going forward and back from the waist up, one hand working the material through, the other hand turning the wheel, and every few turns, without losing the rhythm, quickly wiping the sweat from their foreheads. They work silently, quickly, with excruciating regularity, and the only sound we hear is the rhythmic sound of feet on the floor, simulating the treadle. Then one of the women begins to sing "Mein Ruhe Platz." She sings two stanzas, and then the foreman, VOGEL, appears, or his voice is heard offstage; an excitable man, not unkind, but fearful and nervous about his responsibility.)

VOGEL. How many times do I have to tell you? No singing on the job. Please!

(the WOMAN stops)

VOGEL. Who wants to sing, get a job with the opera! *(shakes his head, exits)*

(The WOMEN continue working in silence. When they do speak, they do it without breaking the work rhythm.)

JENNY. You remember the fire at Kachinsky's shop last month?

DORA. Eighteen girls died. Some burned to death. Some jumped from windows. Who can forget such a thing?

JENNY. Well, it said in the paper this morning why those girls couldn't get down the back stairs.

DORA. So?

JENNY. The door was locked from the outside. Kachinsky locked it because a few girls were sneaking out on the roof for a little air.

DORA. The dirty bastard! And he calls himself a Jew.

ROSE. Is a Jewish boss any different?

DORA. A Jew is supposed to be different.

ROSE. They're all the same, believe me. I've worked for Jews, gentiles—even Italians.

JENNY. I don't feel good working here on the eighth floor. There's too many fires these days. Did you read what the fire chief of New York said?

ROSE. Who reads all that foolishness?

JENNY. You better read. He says his ladders only reach up to the sixth floor. If you're on the seventh or eighth, like us, pray to God.

(*The WOMEN stop. There is no motion, no sound for a few seconds, then slowly they start up again on the machines.*)

ROSE. (*soberly*) You know, the back door on this floor is locked from the outside too—

JENNY. What are you saying?

ROSE. It's been that way ever since I've been working here.

DORA. That's not right!

ROSE. It's better not to think about it.

JENNY. Someone should tell Vogel to open the door.

DORA. You talk, you get in trouble. Who'll tell Vogel? Not me.

(*the WOMEN work in silence*)

EMMA. (*loudly, startling the others*) Mr. Vogel! Please! Go outside and open the back door. In case of a fire...

VOGEL. (*his voice offstage; a man who gets excited quickly*) Mind your own business! You work on the corsets. It's Mr. Handlin's shop. I have nothing to do with doors. Emma, take my advice. You're the youngest girl here. Learn to mind your own business.

EMMA. (*getting up from machine*) I'm not working if the door is locked.

VOGEL. (*even more excited now*) Good! Good! Leave! Go home right now. Who needs you? (*he is a great gesticulator*) Dora, you stay a little later tonight and do Emma's work. You'll get paid extra. We have to finish this order tonight. Mr. Handlin is waiting for it.

DORA. I can't stay later.

VOGEL. (*pointing*) You, Jenny.

JENNY. I have to be home on time tonight. My children...

VOGEL. (*desperately*) Rose!

(*ROSE shakes her head*)

VOGEL. (*shouts*) What's the matter with all of you?

ROSE. (*quietly*) The door, you have to open the door.

VOGEL. It's not my business.

(*EMMA starts to leave*)

DORA. Emma, wait for me. (*gets up from the machine*) Mr. Vogel, I'm sorry. I'm scared of fires.

JENNY. Me too. (*gets up*)

ROSE. Mr. Vogel, if there's a fire, you won't be able to get down the stairs either.

VOGEL. (*desperately—they've all stopped working*) What are you doing to me? Please girls, I've got a family to support. Please, back to the machines, the order has to get out tonight. You're all *meshugah!*

EMMA. Open the door!

ALL. Open the door!

VOGEL. (*shouting*) All right! Enough! All right! (*goes off, opens the latch opening and shouts*) You're satisfied? I'll lose my job and then you'll be satisfied. All right, back to work!

(*WOMEN go back to the rhythm of the machines, working silently, only the sound of their shoes on the floor*)

DORA. A friend of mine saw the fire at Kachinsky's shop...(*WOMEN keep working in silence*) The girls on the tenth floor came out on the window ledge, the flames all around them. They looked so small up there. And when their clothes began to burn, they jumped. Two of them, three of them, at a time—holding hands...

(*Silence as WOMEN work the machines. Then one of them starts humming "Mein Ruhe Platz" and the others join in, one by one, all humming and working the machines as the scene ends.*)

Scene 2. The Family

(*In the darkness, a happy Yiddish tune. Lights up on the Goldman kitchen. EMMA and her sister HELENA are dancing, HELENA teaching EMMA, both laughing. MOTHER prepares food. FATHER nodding his head to the music. MR. LEVINE enters, a well-off relative in the dress business.*)

FATHER. Hello, Mr. Levine! Emma!

(*EMMA turns*)

FATHER. Stop dancing and say hello to Mr. Levine. Helena, you too!

(their faces show their distaste for LEVINE as they look at one another as if to say "There he is again")

LEVINE. *(embracing the girls a little too tightly)* Ah, your beautiful daughters! Hello, everybody!

FATHER. Sit down, sit down. Girls, go help your mother.

(The GIRLS go off to the side where their MOTHER is, to help her, and to have fun, whispering: "MR. LEVINE is here!" THEY pinch and fondle one another, laughing.)

FATHER. Taube! *(calling his wife)* Taube, where's the soup?

EMMA. *(imitates him for HELENA'S benefit)* "Taube, where's the soup?"

FATHER. What are you talking about there, you two? Come and sit down like people.

(THEY sit at the far end of the table, having brought over the soup)

LEVINE. Mrs. Goldman, how are you liking Rochester?

FATHER. *(answers for her)* It's a thousand times better than New York.

EMMA. *(carries on her own intimate conversation with HELENA at the end of the table)* Our mother cannot speak for herself!

HELENA. Father knows her mind best!

(THEY'VE been through this before)

FATHER. *(continuing)* Here, in Rochester you see a flower, a blade of grass...

EMMA. One flower, one blade of grass...

(HELENA giggles)

FATHER. It's not so crowded here as in New York...

EMMA. *(to HELENA)* Only seven in one room...

FATHER. *(sternly)* No secrets there, girls! Be polite!

LEVINE. Was it hard finding work here?

FATHER. No, not hard at all.

(The GIRLS are making faces like: "No, not hard at all!" FATHER turns to them annoyed.)

FATHER. What are you two making those noises for? Don't you know how to sit at a table? *(to LEVINE)* You know Jacob, Emma's husband. He has a good job. A big factory. They make beds.

EMMA. Six dollars a week. Twelve hours a day. He isn't even home yet.

FATHER. *(ignores that)* Emma has a job, too. They make skirts. Emma, tell Mr. Levine about your job.

EMMA. What's to tell? The place smells bad. (*HELENA giggles*) Two dollars and fifty cents a week. We aren't allowed to sing. We aren't allowed even to talk. The foreman tries to put his hands on the girls. He did it to me, so I gave him a *zetz* in the face. (*demonstrates—HELENA giggles*) Well, (*shrugs*) I'm not allowed to *talk*...

FATHER. What a mouth on her! She goes to these meetings, and she listens to these socialists, communists, anarchists, who knows what they are? She doesn't realize what we all went through in the old country.

EMMA. I worked in a factory there too, Papa. It's no different, except here you have to work faster.

FATHER. (*angrily*) Here they don't kill Jews!

EMMA. They don't have to. The Jews kill themselves, on the machines.

FATHER. Here we have a place to live. Knock wood! (*raps on the table*)

EMMA. Yes, wood. It burns fast. Last week, down the street, a whole family burned to death. You think that happens to Rockefeller in his stone mansion?

FATHER. At least we have firemen here; who knows from firemen in the old country?

EMMA. That's America. Here are the most firemen, and the most fires.

FATHER. (*heatedly*) Where is it better, in New York? Packed into the tenements? The children dying of diphtheria, smallpox...

EMMA. At least in New York, people are protesting...

FATHER. All right! Go to New York, where all those *trumbenicks* are! Lazy slobs! They loaf around and then they scream, "America is no good." They don't appreciate this country. (*Bangs the table. Silence*)

MOTHER. (*heads off an outburst*) Emma, serve the soup.

(*EMMA starts serving*)

LEVINE. (*tries to change the subject*) I brought you the Yiddish paper.

FATHER. Thanks, thanks. So what's news?

LEVINE. You remember that Haymarket business in Chicago? The fellows who threw a bomb in Chicago last year, and killed all those policemen?

EMMA. (*loudly, firmly*) No one ever found out who threw the bomb. So they arrested eight anarchist organizers: Parsons, a printer, Spies, an upholsterer, Lingg, a carpenter...

FATHER. See—everything she knows. All right now. Quiet while Mr. Levine is talking.

LEVINE. I'm just telling what's in the paper. Yesterday, they hanged four of them.

(*EMMA sobs. HELENA puts her arm around her.*)

FATHER. What are you crying for?

LEVINE. They were anarchists. They had it coming to them.

EMMA. (*shouts*) Shut up!

FATHER. (*stands up, threatening*) Respect!

LEVINE. (*not wanting to make trouble, but needing to say something; shrugs*) What's to cry about? They were murderers.

EMMA. (*picks up a plate of soup*) Shut your mouth!

(*EMMA throws the soup into MR. LEVINE'S face. FATHER starts after her, pulling at his strap. Her MOTHER gets between them.*)

MOTHER. She's upset! She's upset!

EMMA. You touch me and you'll get it right back!

FATHER. (*enraged*) What did you say?

EMMA. You heard me!

FATHER. (*lifts the strap*) I'll teach her.

MOTHER. Helena, take her away before her father kills her.

(*HELENA pulls EMMA away. MOTHER hands LEVINE a towel to wipe his face.*)

FATHER. That girl is crazy, out of her mind!

MOTHER. Shhh! Shhh!...

(*lights down, and EMMA and HELENA are sitting on a cot in the corner, a faint light, music barely audible in the background, "Mein Ruhe Platz"*)

EMMA. Sleep with me, Helena.

HELENA. Isn't Jacob going to sleep with you?

EMMA. We don't sleep together. Not since the first night. I should never have married him.

HELENA. Why did you?

EMMA. I was lonely.

HELENA. That's not a good reason.

EMMA. And stupid.

HELENA. That's a good reason.

EMMA. But no more. I have to live my own life. I've made up my mind I'm going to New York.

HELENA. You're leaving Jacob, the family, your job?

EMMA. Everything.

HELENA. I wish I had your nerve.

EMMA. You like your husband. Why should you leave?

HELENA. If I had more nerve I wouldn't like him so much.

(*THEY both laugh, then are quiet; then HELENA starts to laugh again*)

EMMA. What's so funny?

HELENA. The soup! Did you see Papa's face?

EMMA. Did you see Mr. Levine's face?

(*THEY both laugh, then are silent*)

You know, Helena, I love you.

HELENA. (*holds back tears*) You take care of yourself in New York. You heard what Papa said. That's where all the *trumbenicks* are!

(*THEY embrace, laughing, crying, as lights go down, music still faintly heard*)

Scene 3. Sachs' Cafe

(*Lower Manhattan. A piano player. Mood of exuberance. Young people eating, drinking beer. Two tables. A hot August day. Mr. Sachs is playing Morro with the pianist between numbers, throwing fingers in the air, shouting out*)

SACHS. (*shouts*) Uno! Due! Tre! Quattro! Cinque! Seis! Sette! Otto! Nove! Dieci!

(*EMMA enters with VITO. She looks different, at ease, enjoying her freedom, although she is the stranger in this place. VITO is small, thin, smoking.*)

EMMA. It's wonderful here!

VITO. This is where we come after work. How many plans have been made here! How many revolutions have been won here!

FEDYA. (*at a table with ANNA MINKIN, who is smoking*) How much beer has been drunk here! (*they laugh*) Sit down, Vito. Who is your friend?

(*EMMA and VITO sit*)

VITO. (*calls out to SACHS*) Mr. Sachs, two beers! This is Emma Goldman. She's just come from Rochester.

FEDYA. And before that?

EMMA. From Kovno, in Russia.

FEDYA. Ah...Kovno!

ANNA. He has *no* idea where it is. If you said Schmetrogorsk, Fedya would say: Ah, Schmetrogorsk!

FEDYA. So you're from Rochester. I hear it's called the city of flowers.

EMMA. No, the city of flour, like in bread.

FEDYA. Well, welcome to New York, the city of sewers.

VITO. Fedya can't forget that I work in the sewers.

ANNA. Vito, you work in the sewers. But you're really a philosopher.

VITO. Is there a difference? But it's true. Everyone here is really something else. Anna works in a corset factory, but what is she really? An organizer of the corset workers. Fedya is unemployed. But what is he really? An artist.

FEDYA. Really, I'm unemployed.

EMMA. How is it, to work in the sewers?

VITO. First of all, it's temporary work. Just until there's general constipation in New York.

(*ANNA shakes her head. She knows VITO.*)

VITO. According to the Marxian theory of capitalist crisis, the rich will get more and more constipated, and the poor will have less and less to eat, so the sewers will run dry. At which point I and my fellow sewer workers, the true proletariat, will rise up (*gets up dramatically*) out of the *drek*...

SACHS. Enough! People are eating...

VITO. There's no more to say. When that day comes, then you'll see something, Sachs!

SACHS. When you start paying for your beer, then we'll see something.

VITO. Don't worry, I get paid next Friday.

SACHS. My family has to eat (*counts on his fingers*) Monday, Tuesday, Wednesday, Thursday...

VITO. And I don't have to eat?

SACHS. No, you're a revolutionary. You can live on hot air!

(*EVERYONE laughs. SACHS resumes his game of Morro with the pianist: "Quattro! Seis!"*)

FEDYA. Laugh! When the revolution comes we'll collectivize this place, and then we'll have...

ANNA. Free beer!

(*EVERYONE chants: "Free beer! Free beer!" SACHS goes off shaking his head*.)

EMMA. *(smiles, to VITO)* So this is how anarchists in New York plan the revolution.

VITO. *(shrugs)* We work hard all day, and in the evening...

ANNA. Yes, during the day, in the shop, we denounce the capitalists. And in the evening, at Sachs Cafe, we denounce one another. There are the Marxists, and the Bakuninists, and the Kropotkinists, and the DeLeonists.

EMMA. And you?

ANNA. Ah, when I first read Marx! The *Manifesto*! So clear, so glorious! Workers of the World, Unite! The capitalist system has created enormous wealth, but it has done this out of the misery of human beings. It is a sick system. How does it solve the problem of unemployment? By war and preparations for war. It must give way, to a new society, where people share the work and share the wealth and live as human beings should.

(EVERYONE applauds. ANNA bows)

ANNA. But then, I read Bakunin.

(VITO makes a gesture of disgust)

ANNA. At first, I hated him for his attacks on Marx. But I was intrigued. The dictatorship of the proletariat, he said, is like the dictatorship of the bourgeoisie. It will not wither away by itself. It will become a tyranny. There can be no workers' state. The state is an evil in itself. We must have no governments, no gods, no masters.

(EMMA and FEDYA applaud.)

VITO. Bakunin is a dreamer, a romantic. Marx is rooted in history, in reality.

FEDYA. Three cheers for Bakunin!

VITO. Four cheers for Marx!

FEDYA. *(holds up fingers in the Morro spirit)* Bakunin!

VITO. *(follows suit)* Marx!

ANNA. *(laughing)* Kropotkin!

VITO. Engels!

SACHS. *(gives them all the finger)* The revolution!

(A man comes into the cafe. Black hair, spectacles, powerful build. Strong face and jaw. He looks around, is clearly at home here.)

VITO. Hello, Sasha!

(FEDYA and ANNA too: "Hello Sasha!" SASHA BERKMAN nods, sits down at a table. VITO turns to EMMA.)

VITO. His name is Alexander Berkman. He never speaks until he eats.

SASHA. (*calls to SACHS*) Mr. Sachs. A steak, large. And beer, large.

FEDYA. Sasha, who died and left you money?

SASHA. (*ignores this*) Today was payday.

VITO. (*to EMMA*) He works in a cigar factory. Guess his age.

EMMA. Thirty-five?

VITO. Twenty-one.

EMMA. He's no older than me.

VITO. Sasha is older than everyone. (*calls over*) Hey, Sasha, say hello to our new comrade from Rochester, Emma Goldman.

SASHA. (*looks up, nods, and without stopping to eat*) Johann Most is speaking at the Academy of Music tomorrow night. (*reaches into his package of rolled-up newspaper*) I have the leaflets here.

EMMA. Johann Most himself!

SASHA. You've never heard him speak?

EMMA. No, but I read his articles in *Freiheit*.

SASHA. Who will distribute on the West Side?

VITO. (*to EMMA*) Sasha doesn't waste a moment. (*to SASHA*) Okay. I'll do the West Side on my lunch hour.

(*SASHA hands him a bunch of leaflets*)

ANNA. I'll do Union Square, right after work.

FEDYA. I'll help you. I'll see you there at six.

SASHA. I've got a shop meeting at lunch time. I'll distribute down Broome Street an hour before I go to work.

ANNA. Sasha! You'll have to get up before five...

SASHA. So?

ANNA. So nothing. After the revolution we will erect a statue right on Broome Street, (*strikes a pose*) Sasha—distributing leaflets before dawn.

EMMA. I have a room right near Broome Street. I'll help you.

SASHA. At five in the morning?

EMMA. If you'll be there, I'll be there.

VITO. Distributing leaflets with Sasha is an experience. (*takes a bunch of leaflets, stands up, goes into his act, imitating SASHA on a street corner, speaking with gravity*) My good friend, do you realize that Johann Most is speaking tonight? Here is the information. (*hands the leaflet, then switches to the voice of the passerby*) Who? What? I have no time. (*then back to SASHA, speaking with indignation*) You have no time! Ten hours a day you give to the capitalists, and you can't spare one hour for the movement that will end your slavery? Shame on you! (*Rams leaflet into*

FEDYA'S stomach. FEDYA gasps. EVERYONE laughs. SASHA shakes his head and smiles. He can take it. VITO switches.) Fedya is another story. *(assumes a gracious stance)* My dear Madame, I have something for you. Do not fear. It is a free ticket to a concert. A concert of words. A symphony of ideas. The conductor? Johann Most. My pleasure, Madame. *(hands the leaflet to EMMA, dances gracefully around her, humming a tune)*

SASHA. Now let's be serious.

VITO. I'm serious. I'm serious. *(pokes another leaflet into FEDYA'S stomach)*

SASHA. I think it's not correct for Fedya and Anna to go to the same place, and me and our friend Goldman to be at the same place. A waste of people. We could be covering more territory.

EMMA. No, it's not a waste. If a policeman comes along, it's harder for him to arrest two at once.

ANNA. She's right.

EMMA. Besides, it looks better to have two people. It shows we are an organization.

ANNA. She's right.

SASHA. *(annoyed)* She's *not* right. She's just come from Rochester, and she's telling us how to distribute leaflets in New York.

EMMA. *(quietly)* What a petty display of provincialism.

SASHA. *(approaches aggressively)* What was that word?

EMMA. *(rising to face him)* Petty.

SASHA. I mean the other word.

EMMA. Provincialism?

SASHA. I don't know that word. *(there is an embarrassed silence)*

EMMA. *(softly)* You call yourself an anarchist.

SASHA. *(angrily)* Yes!

EMMA. And an internationalist.

SASHA. Of course.

EMMA. Provincialism is the opposite of internationalism.

SASHA. That's an insult.

ANNA. She's right, Sasha.

SASHA. She's right, she's right! Enough already.

VITO. Sasha, it's time you lost an argument.

EMMA. I'll meet you at five, Sasha. On Broome Street, where the street car stops.

(EMMA holds out her hand. SASHA looks at her curiously, and slowly extends his hand. They shake hands, looking at one another, the first trace of a smile in SASHA'S eyes.)

Scene 4. Most Speaks: Emma and Sasha

(A revolutionary song, taped. The Deutschvereins Hall, a spotlight on JOHANN MOST, center stage, coat and tie, crew-cut hair, black-grey beard, tall, a distortion on the left side of his face from a childhood accident. He has force and dignity. A member of the German Reichstag who has been imprisoned, he is a veteran of the revolutionary movement. A dramatic speaker, but able to slow down and almost whisper for effect. He is giving the audience a lesson in anarchism, as he is giving the police the same lesson. There is a POLICEMAN on each side of the stage, holding a club, in darkness. It's a long speech for the stage, and can only work if MOST really grips the audience.)

MOST. Comrades! Friends! And members of the New York City police. *(Laughter. MOST peers into the audience, using his hand to shade his eyes. He points)* Ah, there is Inspector Sullivan in the fourth row, taking notes. *(laughter)* Please, Inspector, write my name correctly—Johann Most! *(laughter. MOST extends his hands, palms up. There is no longer a smile in his eyes. His tone is changing.)* My friends, here we are, at a peaceful meeting. There are women and children in the audience. *(there is now anger in his voice)* Yet the walls are lined with police, carrying clubs, armed with guns. Is this what is meant in America by freedom of speech? *(murmurs in the audience)* New members of the police force, why are you here? Perhaps you have heard that this is a meeting of anarchists. *(laughter)* Yes, we are anarchists. *(applause)* Perhaps you have heard that we believe in disorder. *(claps his hands sharply together like a schoolmaster)* Wrong! We believe in *order*. No, not an artificial order, enforced by the club and the gun, the courts and the prisons; but the natural order of human beings living and working together in harmony. Who says we believe in chaos and disorder? The capitalists and warmakers, the promoters of economic chaos, the architects of world disorder!

Let me explain to you, *(voice softens)* Inspector Sullivan, and to you, members of the police force, how we came to be anarchists. *(pauses)* First, we examined our own lives and found we were living by rules we had not made, in ways we did not want, estranged from our most powerful human desires. Then, we opened our eyes and looked around the city. At five in the morning we could see the workers open their windows to catch a breath of fresh air before going to the factory. In the winter, we saw the corpses of old men and women who froze because they had no fuel. In the summer we saw the babies in the tenements dying of cholera. (*there is total silence, then his voice rises*) And we saw something else. We saw that 700 buildings in this city are owned by one family, the Astors, whose fortune is 100 million dollars. Yes, we saw the rich living from the wealth created by generations of workers. We saw that a party was given at the Waldorf Astoria in honor of a dog. Yes, a dog! Who was dressed in jewels, while mothers on Cherry Street had no milk for their children. (*voice choked with anger, he waits to get control and speaks more quietly*)

We also saw that these same men who own the industries of America pick the presidents, and the congressmen. They appoint the judges, anoint the priests, own the newspapers, endow the universities.

(*The POLICE start smacking their clubs in their hands in unison. MOST'S voice rises above the sound.*)

Every year, 35,000 workers die in their mines and mills. Every generation, the sons of the workers are slaughtered in their wars...and they accuse us of violence! (*pauses*) Let us make our position clear. Violence against innocent people? Never! Violence against the oppressor? Always! Yes, take notes Inspector Sullivan. We expect to hear from you. (*laughter*) But we are taking notes, too. And some day, *some day*, you will hear from us!

(*MOST bows, to signify the end of the speech, and he walks off. Applause. Stamping of feet. Singing "The Internationale" in German. The POLICE are still smacking their clubs into their palms. EMMA and ANNA have been in the audience, applauding. They come up on stage.*)

ANNA. What a meeting!

EMMA. So that is Johann Most. I know now why he is in and out of prison.

SASHA. (*joining them*) Hello, Anna...hello, Emma.

(*FEDYA joins them too. He is wearing a finely embroidered shirt*)

Look at that shirt! You can always tell an artist.

FEDYA. Sasha is annoyed by my shirt.

EMMA. I think it's beautiful.

SASHA. (*wisely*) We all have our tastes. But should we spend money on such things when the movement needs every cent we have?

EMMA. Don't we need beautiful things to remind us of what life can be like someday?

ANNA. Jews, when they talk, everyone asks questions. No one gives answers!

EMMA. Must we give up music and the smell of lilacs to be revolutionaries?

ANNA. (*nudging FEDYA*) See?

SASHA. Who said you have to give up music or lilacs? But shirts like this, yes.

FEDYA. What about art?

SASHA. It's an objective fact; the artist lives on the backs of the poor. Don't take it personally, Fedya.

FEDYA. Why shouldn't I? Am I not a person?

EMMA. Sasha, there is something wrong with the way you think. I can't quite express it...

SASHA. If you were right, you would be able to express it.

EMMA. (*calmly*) You are insufferable.

SASHA. I don't know what that means, but I think I have been insulted again. (*he says this in good humor*)

ANNA. I think, Sasha, it means you want us all to suffer until the revolution comes.

SASHA. You don't understand.

ANNA. I understand, and I'm going home right now—to suffer! Are you coming, Emma?

EMMA. I'll come a little later. I want to change the dates on these posters. Most is speaking again in two weeks.

ANNA. She's staying with me until she finds a job (*starts to leave, nudges FEDYA until he begins to comprehend*)

FEDYA. (*simulating a yawn*) I'm tired. I'll walk home with you, Anna. (*THEY leave*)

SASHA. He's tired! He sleeps all morning. (*hesitates, his voice softens as he turns to EMMA*) How about a little walk?

EMMA. I'm not finished with these posters yet.

SASHA. And let's not argue. After all, we're comrades.

EMMA. Shouldn't comrades argue?

SASHA. Now she wants to argue about arguing! (*silence*) Let's go for a seltzer.

EMMA. (*having fun*) Isn't that a luxury?

SASHA. (*after a second's pause*) A plain seltzer?

EMMA. What if I want a little chocolate syrup in it?

SASHA. (*having fun, too*) I'm not as dogmatic as you think. A *little* chocolate syrup.

EMMA. *(her tone changes)* How did you come to be what you are, Sasha?

SASHA. You mean, insufferable?

EMMA. *(laughing)* Yes. No. I mean, your ideas, our ideas. They tell me you're organizing the cigar workers.

SASHA. In the old country, at the age of 11, I was expelled from school because I gave the wrong answer on an examination.

EMMA. For one wrong answer?

SASHA. The question was: "What are the chief products of Russia?" And I wrote: "Revolutionaries."

(THEY laugh)

EMMA. At 13, I was already working in a factory in St. Petersburg. I did not know words like *capitalism, anti-semitism,* the *state.* But it was all so clear. Who needs the words when you feel it in your bones every day?

SASHA. Didn't you think America would be different?

EMMA. In the factory in Rochester, I could feel no difference. Yes, America had a Constitution. But it meant nothing in the factory.

SASHA. It meant nothing for those executed after Haymarket.

EMMA. So many of us had our eyes opened by Haymarket.

SASHA. I'll never forget the last words of Spies to the jury: "These are my ideas. They constitute a part of myself. I cannot divest myself of them, nor would I if I could...I say, if death is the penalty for proclaiming truth, call your hangman." *(both are moved at hearing those words again)* I hope I will have such courage when the time comes.

EMMA. *(coming forward, grasping his hands)* Sasha! You're too young to talk of dying.

SASHA. One day, the choice will be before us, to bow down, or to risk all. To give our lives if necessary.

EMMA. I am ready to give my life for what I believe in. But I would like to give it over a period of fifty years, not in one heroic moment. The movement needs us to live for it, not to die for it.

SASHA. Perhaps only our grandchildren will be able to live full lives.

EMMA. I don't believe that. We must live ourselves. And beautifully, to show how life can be lived.

(In her fervor, EMMA has held onto his hands, comes closer to him. THEY are suddenly conscious of their closeness and break away.)

SASHA. *(hesitates)* What are you doing tomorrow?

EMMA. I have to go to the baggage room at Grand Central. I left my sewing machine there.

SASHA. You brought it all the way from Rochester?

EMMA. Yes, I'm tired of working in a corset factory. I'd like to work for myself, maybe set up a cooperative shop. Like Vera, in "What Is To Be Done?"

SASHA. Oh, have you read Chernishevsky?

EMMA. Why are you surprised?

SASHA. Well, you're so young.

EMMA. So are you.

SASHA. But I'm a man.

EMMA. *(anger rising)* And I am a woman.

SASHA. You're very sensitive.

EMMA. And *you* are very *insensitive.*

SASHA. *(sighing)* Do you think you and I will ever be good friends?

EMMA. *(softly)* Aren't we? *(a second of silence)* Sasha, let's go for that seltzer some other time. Anna is waiting and she needs her sleep.

SASHA. All right! Tomorrow I'll come with you to Grand Central. I know my way around the city. Afterward, if you like, we can take the El down to the Brooklyn Bridge and walk across. The air is wonderful on the river.

EMMA. *(incredulous)* I didn't ask you to come with me! Don't you have to work?

SASHA. *(a little abashed)* This morning, on the job, I made a tactical mistake. I gave some of our leaflets to the workers. The foreman said "This is your last day." So, I'll come for you tomorrow.

(EMMA starts to respond. SASHA holds up his hand)

I know where Anna Minkin lives. What time?

(EMMA doesn't respond)

What time?

EMMA. Ten o'clock.

SASHA. Good. Before I meet you, I can look for a job.

EMMA. I saw how much you eat. You need a job.

SASHA. Emma, I think you are...insufferable. *(Turns to go, then turns back. THEY both smile. HE turns again and goes.)*

Scene 5. Love scene—Anna's apartment

(*Flute music. ANNA MINKIN'S apartment. EMMA and SASHA tiptoe in. She is wearing a sailor hat.*)

EMMA. Come in, we can talk a while.

SASHA. Will we wake up Anna?

EMMA. Nothing can wake up Anna. (*To prove it, EMMA stamps on the floor, then listens. No reaction. EMMA smiles*) You see...

(*It is dark. THEY are close. They slowly embrace. Then comes ANNA'S delayed reaction.*)

ANNA. (*sleepily*) For God's sake, a little quiet!

(*EMMA and SASHA break off, listen. EMMA shrugs. It is quiet again. THEY slowly embrace once more, and kiss, the music still soft in the background as the scene ends.*)

Scene 6. Forming the Commune

(*Lively piano music, exuberant, befitting a scene of four young, attractive, life-loving, dedicated people. EMMA and SASHA are sitting in ANNA MINKIN'S apartment, having tea in glasses. SASHA is enjoying it, blowing, cooling, sipping. ANNA and FEDYA come in.*)

SASHA. Look, he's wearing that shirt again!

EMMA. (*softly to SASHA*) Who's going to tell Anna, you or me?

SASHA. I'll tell her.

ANNA. Tell what?

EMMA. That girl hears everything.

ANNA. Yes, *everything*. (*laughs and bends over to kiss EMMA*)

EMMA. Anna dear, Toby Golden is moving out of her place on Forsyth Street. It's five dollars a month. Sasha and I are going to take it.

ANNA. So you'd rather live with Sasha than with me. A true friend!

EMMA. Anna, you know this place is just big enough for you. With me here you've had no privacy at all.

ANNA. You mean ever since Sasha started coming around—(*dances around provocatively, groaning and sighing*)—it's been *oy* and *ah* and *ooh* and *mmm*. Yes, (*embraces EMMA*) you need a place! It has three big rooms. It's twice as big as this apartment, isn't it?

SASHA. Yes, twice as big.

ANNA. Good! Then there's room for me.

SASHA. Now look, Anna...

ANNA. Do you believe in collectivity or not?

SASHA. Of course, but...

ANNA. (*orating, imitating SASHA or someone*) Bourgeois individualism corrupts us all! We must begin the new culture right now, comrades! Share and share alike! Break through the prison of monogamy!

EMMA. Of course she's right, Sasha.

SASHA. (*gloomily*) Of course she's right.

(*FEDYA has been walking around, rearranging pictures on the walls, now stops*)

FEDYA. I know Toby Golden's place. There are three big rooms.

ANNA. Yes, you see?

FEDYA. Yes, it's big enough for me too.

ANNA. You too?

FEDYA. (*jumping onto the bed, imitating ANNA*) We must begin the new culture now, comrades. Love thy neighbor, says the Bible. Workers of the world unite, says Marx. Live in free association, says Kropotkin. Make room for Fedya, says Fedya.

ANNA. Fedya, I'm not the same with you as Emma with Sasha. We're just friends.

FEDYA. Yes, and we'll live together as friends. What do we always say? (*orates again*) Between men and women there must be an endless variety of relationships—passion, companionship...

ANNA. Hostility! Murder! (*attacks him*)

EMMA. (*excited*) The four of us together! It *is* big enough. There's a bedroom and we can put a bed in the living room, and a folding bed in the kitchen.

(*SASHA has been gloomy in a corner. Now he is aroused.*)

SASHA. Why stop with four? How about a bed in the bathroom too? Then my friend Yussel Miller can join us. We could put the bed upright and Yussel can sleep standing up. (*a little bitter*)

EMMA. (*disapprovingly*) Sasha!

SASHA. Don't say another word. (*comes over to THEM, puts his arms around them*) You are right. You are all right. When I'm wrong I admit it. We're all friends and comrades. Why can't we live together, live collectively? That's the way of the future. And we have to start the future now. (*doesn't look too happy*)

ANN. (*jumping up, truly happy*) Yes! Yes!

FEDYA. (*producing a bottle of wine from a paper bag*) Let's drink to our little collective.

SASHA. (*shaking his head*) Everytime you see him he has a bottle of wine.

FEDYA. (*uncorking it with a loud noise right in front of SASHA*) Emma, you wash some glasses, and I'll pour the wine.

(*EMMA shrugs and goes to do it*)

SASHA. We'll all contribute equally to the rent and food.

EMMA. We'll all contribute according to our ability. Anna and I are working in the corset shop. You're working in a cigar factory.

SASHA. And Fedya can sell his shirt. We can live on that for a month.

ANNA. Don't laugh. When Fedya sells a painting he makes more than I make in a week.

SASHA. Fedya, when's the last time you sold a painting?

FEDYA. What day is it?

ANNA. Wednesday.

FEDYA. (*counting on his fingers*) About a year ago...

SASHA. Well, I can see we will eat well.

FEDYA. None of us will eat as well as you, Sasha. You eat and drink as much as the three of us.

EMMA. To each according to his need. Sasha needs to eat like a horse. Fedya needs to sleep late in the morning. I need to read without people talking to me. And Anna...(*turns her head mischievously*) Anna needs to spend about an hour in the toilet every morning.

ANNA. A perfect group! We'll never interfere with one another. Fedya will be sleeping. Sasha will be eating. Emma will be reading. And I'll be in the toilet. (*takes their hands to execute a little place-changing routine*) And every hour, we can change places!

FEDYA. Let's drink to our needs!

(*EMMA pours the wine for all of them. SASHA slugs it down with great enjoyment, for one who objected to it.*)

SASHA. We can organize the tenants in Toby's building!

EMMA. Oh, what the four of us can do together!

(*FEDYA pours the wine for all of them. Again SASHA drinks it down in a gulp and FEDYA pours him another. ANNA starts singing a Yiddish tune, "Mein Grune Kuzine." She takes EMMA'S hand and they dance. Then EMMA takes FEDYA'S hand and the three of them dance.*)

SASHA. Each to his need. I'll have more wine. (*pours himself another*

glass as the others spin around him...But then he starts dancing himself.)
To tell you the truth, I think I'm a little drunk! (*smiling happily, he suddenly calls out*) Fedya, I want your shirt!

(FEDYA flamboyantly takes off his shirt, throws it at SASHA. SASHA holds it over his head, dancing. All four dance exuberantly together as the music quickens to "Mein Grune Kuzine," and the scene ends.)

Scene 7. Fedya and Emma

(FEDYA is sketching on the kitchen table. He looks up in surprise. EMMA has just come in, weary. She puts down her workbag.)

EMMA. It's so hot up here, Fedya. How can you work? It's worse than the shop.

FEDYA. You're home so early. Is something wrong?

EMMA. Kargman found out who is organizing the union. Three of us were fired this morning. It was a big commotion. More girls wanted to walk out, but we told them to wait. After work today, there'll be a meeting, and if enough girls come...well, we'll see... Oh, God, it's so hot. (*removes her shirt, is wearing a camisole*)

FEDYA. Emma, what are you doing?

EMMA. (*amused*) Fedya, darling, you've seen me like this before.

FEDYA. Yes, with everybody here. But like this...

EMMA. I'll put my blouse back on, if it makes you nervous.

FEDYA. (*nervous*) Why should I be nervous? After all, I'm an artist. At the Settlement House, we painted women all the time. We had models. Now I can't afford that. I paint nudes from memory. (*smiles*) And my memory is not too good.

EMMA. If you ever want me to pose for you, Fedya, just tell me.

FEDYA. You're serious, Emma?

EMMA. Why not? We're friends and comrades.

(SHE leans over and kisses him on the cheek. HE gets up and paces the floor nervously.)

What's the matter?

FEDYA. I would like you to pose for me Emma. But I don't know...

EMMA. What is it?

FEDYA. (*stops pacing, comes over to her*) I have been so troubled. (*shakes his head*) Sasha is my friend, and yet...I have been longing for you,

Emma. I have, yes. I can't help it.

(*HE takes her hand. With her other hand SHE strokes his hair.*)

EMMA. Sweet Fedya. It's all right. It's all right. We both love Sasha, but Sasha and I don't own one another. Why shouldn't you have feelings for me? Why shouldn't I have feelings for you?

FEDYA. (*taking both her hands*) Emma...do you think...

EMMA. Why are we living? Why are we struggling and organizing? What is all this for? Sometimes in the midst of all the tumult, I think back to the old country. I must have been eight or nine. This peasant boy worked around the farm, and one day he took me out in the meadow. The sun was strong. We sat in the long grass and he played his flute. Then he lifted me in his arms and threw me into the air and caught me. Everything smelled of grass. My soul melted. He threw me and he caught me, again and again. I think that was the very first time I realized that life could be...ecstatic.

(*FEDYA presses his lips to her hair*)

EMMA. Years after that, I was with my aunt in Konigsberg. She took me to the opera, *Il Trovatore*. I had never in my life been to any theater. I sat there in the balcony as in a trance. When it was over and everyone was leaving, I heard my aunt calling me, but I sat there in my seat, the tears streaming down my face. I was young, I knew so little, but at that moment I knew what I wanted life to be...

(*SHE throws her arms around FEDYA, and he around her, in a long embrace. FEDYA sits up, shakes his head in confusion.*)

What's the matter?

FEDYA. I am Sasha's friend.

EMMA. That makes it better.

FEDYA. I feel like a betrayer.

EMMA. You've taken nothing from him. He and I are still as we were.

FEDYA. Will he see it that way?

EMMA. You know Sasha. At first, he will be angry.

FEDYA. Oh, will he be angry!

EMMA. He may smash a piece of furniture.

FEDYA. Maybe two or three.

EMMA. And then he'll say...

FEDYA. (*orating like SASHA*) I was wrong—when I'm wrong I admit it. We must live like free people—we must live as in the future society.

EMMA. Yes, that's exactly what he will say.

FEDYA. I love Sasha.

(*music as scene ends*)

Scene 8. The Strike at Kargman's

(*Opera music. Picket line. Six PEOPLE, including EMMA and ANNA, with signs, walking, shouting. One PICKET has a bandaged head. A POLICEMAN stands by, holding a club.*)

PICKETS. Strike! Strike! Don't work for Kargman, stay out! Strike! Strike! Don't work for Kargman, stay out!

(*another STRIKER comes running up to the line excited*)

STRIKER. Scabs! They're bringing scabs!

(*A small group of GIRLS, WOMEN, led by a well-dressed MAN, arrives. The STRIKER who just spoke picks up a rock. EMMA puts a hand on his arm.*)

EMMA. No, Yankele, wait.

(*The PICKETS mass in front of the shop entrance. The SCABS stop.*)

EMMA. Look at them. They're just off the boat. Look at their faces. They're hungry, just like us!

(*YANKELE moves back. The SCAB LEADER rushes forward, knocking EMMA down. Her FRIENDS rush back. The POLICEMAN moves in, lifts his club threateningly, they move back to the line. EMMA walks back and forth quickly around the SCABS, speaking to them at first haltingly, then louder.*)

EMMA. *Schwester! Bruder! Herr tzu!* Listen to me! They didn't tell you there's a strike here, and you are taking our jobs.

(*the MAN leading the scabs comes up to her threateningly*)

MAN. Get the hell away from here before I break your head.

(*EMMA pulls her arm away angrily*)

EMMA. Keep walking, comrades! (*keeps walking herself, talking loudly, then stops, as someone puts a box before her. She mounts it, at first hesitantly, then lifts her head and addresses the scabs directly, appealing.*) I know you need to work. Your families are hungry. *Azoi vie unzere.* Just like ours! Your houses are cold! *Azoi vie unzere!* Just like ours! Kargman has promised you good wages. But let me tell you something, brothers and sisters. We know Kargman well. He is a liar! *Er iz ah Ligner!* But you know that already, because he didn't tell you there was a strike here! He despises you, just as he despises us. *Er iz dein Sonne!* He is your enemy. Just as he is ours. He will pay you good wages, yes, until the strike is over. But what happens then? Then he will cut your wages, as he cut ours. And you'll go on strike, just like us. And the police will come and smash you with their clubs, just like us! And then Kargman will get others to take your place!

(*The POLICEMAN moves toward her, raises his club. EMMA raises her stick. He steps back. She continues talking.*)

Brothers! Sisters!

(*She is gaining confidence, this is her first speech. The well-dressed MAN calls to the scabs: "Come on, let's go in!" He starts pushing forward. The SCABS seem uncertain. EMMA isn't walking anymore, but is standing speaking with great strength now.*)

Schwester, Bruder! (*the power, urgency in her voice makes them turn*) If you try to go in there'll be a fight. We shouldn't fight one another. Together, we can make our lives better. Listen. We are not alone! All over the country, working people like us are joining together. Right now, in Pennsylvania, 3,000 workers are saying "Enough!" to the richest man in America, Andrew Carnegie. Enough to working twelve hours a day in the steel furnaces. Enough to a heat like in hell. Enough to fourteen cents an hour. Enough! Three thousand workers standing together, saying "Enough!" Let us stand together too! Join us, my brothers and sisters. (*almost a whisper now*) Don't work for Kargman!

(*THEY seem frozen in place by her words. The well-dressed MAN is shouting at them: "Inside! Inside!" But they don't move. Then one of them, a WOMAN, shawl on her head, comes forward to EMMA. She is weeping. She holds out her hands. EMMA grasps them. The picket line continues chanting.*)

PICKETS. Stay out! Stay out! Don't work for Kargman! Strike! Strike!

Scene 9. The Decision to Kill Frick

(*Opera music. SASHA at the kitchen table, writing, intent. EMMA comes in, flushed, holding violets, humming from "Carmen." She puts an arm around SASHA gaily, kisses him on the cheek.*)

EMMA. Oh, what a picket line at Kargman's today!

SASHA. Anna told me. You made your first speech. She said it was good. (*all this without looking up*) You've been away all evening.

EMMA. Yes. (*hums...SASHA does not respond, continues working*) Sasha dear, what are you doing up so late?

SASHA. (*without looking up*) A leaflet on the strike in Pittsburgh. Have you heard the latest news?

EMMA. No.

SASHA. Carnegie has put Frick in charge. You know him. Henry Clay

Frick. A lover of art. A gangster. And Frick has called in the Pinkertons. You know them. The biggest strike-breaking agency in America. Two thousand men with the latest weapons.

EMMA. A private army.

SASHA. And Frick is going to use them to break the strike. The strikers will need money, weapons, support from all over the country, or they are done for. I must finish this leaflet tonight. (*looks up at EMMA*) Where have you been all evening?

EMMA. Johann invited me to go to the Metropolitan Opera House with him. We saw *Carmen.*

SASHA. Johann? (*temper rising*) Johann who?

EMMA. Johann Most.

SASHA. So now it's Johann! The opera! That's how Most uses the Movement's money. (*thinks*) The opera must have ended hours ago.

EMMA. We went to a restaurant afterward.

SASHA. A restaurant! You probably drank wine all evening too.

EMMA. (*heatedly*) Yes, we drank wine!

SASHA. Of course, Most loves expensive wine. That's our great revolutionary leader.

EMMA. Most is a wonderful man. You told me so yourself. He gave up his seat in the German Reichstag. He spent years in prison. He risked his life!

SASHA. (*coldly*) The Movement gives no special benefits for war veterans. The most heroic figures can become corrupt. We see that in history.

EMMA. Then I am corrupt too, by going to the opera, by drinking wine?

SASHA. (*shouting*) Yes! You too! You're worse than Most, you with your pretensions, cuddling up to every leader of the Movement...

EMMA. Shut your mouth!

SASHA. I'm speaking the truth and you know it. What are you holding there?

EMMA. Flowers. (*defiantly*) Yes, I know flowers are an unnecessary expense when people are starving. Well, they are beautiful, and I love them. (*goes to put them in a jar*)

SASHA. It makes me nauseous to see them when the strikers in Pittsburgh are in need of bread.

EMMA. (*angered and hurt*) And what are *you* doing about the families in Pittsburgh? Writing a leaflet!

SASHA. Yes, we need to write leaflets.

EMMA. It will take more than that.

SASHA. (*shouting*) And I'm prepared to do more than that.

EMMA. So am I. And so is Most.

SASHA. We will see.

EMMA. What do you mean?

SASHA. We will see.

EMMA. (*more softly*) Don't you understand, Sasha, we can't all live at the level of the most oppressed. We have to have a little beauty in our lives, even in the midst of struggle.

SASHA. You think Most cares about beauty? What do you think was in Most's mind when he gave you those violets?

EMMA. You're jealous, Sasha. I thought you had overcome that. I thought you believed in my freedom.

SASHA. (*shouting*) Freedom, yes! Decadence, no! With Fedya it is different. Fedya, we both love. But Most! He is not good for you, Emma.

EMMA. (*angrily*) Who is to decide that, you or me?

SASHA. (*a little subdued*) Yes, that's for you to decide. (*suddenly angry at her scoring a point, and he bangs his fist on the table*)

ANNA. (*emerging from her room in her nightgown*) Will you two stop that? You've kept me up for the past half-hour. I've got to be on the picket line early in the morning. You do too, Emma.

(*Another VOICE from the next apartment: "Shut up in there!" Some banging on the walls, general protest over loss of sleep. SOMEONE yells: "Quiet already!"*)

EMMA. Yes, for God's sake, let's go to sleep!

ANNA. (*turning on her*) You don't care. None of you care any more—you and Sasha and Fedya—you're moving to Wor-ces-ter, Massachusetts, so you don't give a damn about anybody.

EMMA. (*correcting her*) Wooster.

ANNA. (*rejecting the criticism*) To Wor-ces-ter. And without me.

EMMA. You said you wanted to have nothing to do with our idea.

ANNA. Such a brilliant idea! An ice cream parlor run by revolutionaries. What kind of revolution will you have today, sir! Vanilla? (*doing her comic routine, pretending to be carrying a tray*) Chocolate? Not strawberry! Not a real *red* revolution. Not in a petty-bourgeois ice cream parlor!

EMMA. It's just for a few months, Anna. We need the money to start our new magazine.

ANNA. (*voice is breaking*) The three of you are leaving me here alone.

SASHA. You want to stay, Anna.

ANNA. I didn't want to go to Wor-ces-ter.

(*SHE bursts out crying. EMMA comforts her.*)

EMMA. (*wearily*) Why are we all fighting? Let's go to sleep.

(*VOICES from the other apartment, shouting: "Go to sleep, you bums!"*)

SASHA. (*replying to the voices*) Go to hell, all of you!

ANNA. You wanted to organize them, now you curse them.

SASHA. Oh, shut up and go back to sleep.

ANNA. (*to EMMA*) How can you put up with that man? (*starts to leave*)

FEDYA. (*arriving*) What's all this noise?

EMMA. Go to sleep!

FEDYA. I'll go to sleep when I feel like it! (*returns to his usual low-key demeanor*) Did you hear about Pittsburgh?

(*ANNA turns back to listen*)

EMMA. Sasha told me. The Pinkertons have been called in.

FEDYA. Well, they started. There was a battle there today.

SASHA. Today?

FEDYA. Frick brought 300 Pinkerton police down the river on a barge. An army of them. Machine guns, rifles. They opened fire on men, women, and children. There are seven dead.

(*EMMA puts her hands to her head as if to shut out the news*)

SASHA. (*looking at EMMA with combined anguish and fury*) While you were at the opera! (*smashes the vase of violets with a sweep of his hand*)

EMMA. (*shouting, weeping*) While you were writing a damn leaflet! Don't talk to me that way, you bastard!

FEDYA. Stop it, you two. What are we going to do?

SASHA. (*to himself, pacing the floor, fists clenched*) What's wrong with me? I must be crazy! Going with you two to Massachusetts to open an ice cream parlor so we can publish some intellectual garbage. I must be out of my mind. I should be in Pittsburgh right now, with the strikers.

EMMA. And what are you going to do in Pittsburgh?

SASHA. It was you who said: "It will take more than leaflets..."

EMMA. Yes, I said it, but...

SASHA. But! But! There is something that must be done in Pittsburgh! (*Speaking calmly, thoughtfully now. The OTHERS watch him as he paces the floor, building up his rationale and his resolve at the same time.*) We must show the world that the Carnegies, the Rockefellers, the Fricks, are not invincible. We see their pictures in the newspapers. The arrogance in their faces. The contempt in their eyes for all who have not succeeded in their game of becoming rich. Yes, the pictures. Frick going to church. Frick in the White House with the President, while his workers fall from exhaustion in the mills. Frick, drinking whiskey at his country club while his detectives shoot down women and children. Frick. Frick. Yes, there is something that must be done in Pittsburgh.

FEDYA. What are you talking about?

SASHA. (*after a few seconds of total silence*) Frick must die.

EMMA. Keep your voice down. Are you crazy?

SASHA. What does your friend Most say: "There are times in history when a bullet speaks louder than a thousand manifestos."

EMMA. (*anguished, fearful*) Yes. Yes. (*thinking, speaking almost to herself*) We have all said to one another, that when the right time came . . .

FEDYA. (*excited*) We would be ready! Yes, we said that. We all did. (*there is anguish in his voice now as it all becomes more real*)

SASHA. I'm going to Pittsburgh...

EMMA. We'll all go. It is the right moment. All through the centuries they have slaughtered the working people. And now once more. But this time, it will be different. We will show everyone: they can die too!

ANNA. (*trembling*) The four of us can do it.

FEDYA. (*very nervous*) It will have to be planned very carefully.

EMMA. But it will go around the world. It is the right time. We can do it.

SASHA. (*quietly*) Who kills Frick surrenders his life.

EMMA. (*crying out*) We said that we are ready. Remember how the four of us said we are ready? How we would stand together when the time came?

SASHA. I will do it alone.

(*a second of silence; astonishment*)

EMMA. You are crazy, Sasha!

SASHA. No, we are not going to give them four lives for one. No.

EMMA. You're not going to do it yourself!

FEDYA. What are we talking about? It takes money to go to Pittsburgh. And what will it be? A bomb? A gun? It takes money.

SASHA. That's right. And we don't have train fare for one.

EMMA. If we can raise the money for one, we can do it for four. I will get the money somehow.

SASHA. (*shaking his head slowly, firmly*) It's not the money.

EMMA. (*almost screaming, but trying to keep her voice down*) Well, what is it then? You want to do it all by yourself? You want to say, to hell with our comradeship, our love? Is that it?

SASHA. You don't understand. If Frick is killed, someone must explain. Someone must know why it was done, and explain. Otherwise they will say, as they always do, that it was the work of a madman.

FEDYA. They will say it anyway.

SASHA. No, Emma can explain it. She has the tongue. She has the gift. She can do it. All of you must stay behind and make it clear to the whole country.

FEDYA. (*almost in tears*) But I'm not needed for that. I'm no speaker. I can help you, Sasha. Together...

SASHA. (*shouting; the word comes out like an explosion*) No! Fedya, we don't have to sacrifice you too!

EMMA. (*she is in despair*) Keep your voices down!

SASHA. You know I'm right. You know it's necessary. A moment comes when someone must act, must point, must say: "Enough!" You know that...

EMMA. (*almost whispering*) Yes, Sasha...

SASHA. (*very calm now*) All right.. Money. A train ticket. A device that will kill...

EMMA. (*becoming calm now, holding back her feelings*) You will need a new suit of clothes...

ANNA. (*almost in tears*) Yes.

SASHA. (*totally calm*) Let's sit down and make plans.

(*With a sudden gesture, HE embraces FEDYA, ANNA, EMMA. THEY hold him tightly. Then, almost in slow motion, they sit down at the table as the lights go down.*)

Scene 10. The Attempt

(*In the darkness, a steady beat. Then an eerie light on the scene, which will take place in semi-darkness. FRICK and another MAN are sitting, talking, on one side of the stage, while SASHA can be seen in the shadows, on the other side, getting dressed.*)

MAN. Is that the American way, to riot in the street when things don't go right?

FRICK. We don't riot when things don't go right. We go through the proper channels.

MAN. We go to the Speaker of the House.

FRICK. We go to the Attorney General.

MAN. We go to the Secretary of the Treasury.

FRICK. And they always respond to us with generosity.

MAN. That is democracy.

(*SASHA stands up*)

SECRETARY'S VOICE. Do you have an appointment? Mr. Frick cannot see you now. You must see Miss O'Neil.

MISS O'NEIL'S VOICE. I'm sorry, but Mr. Frick cannot see you now. (*her voice rises*) Where are you going?

(*SASHA walks toward FRICK*)

SASHA. (*calling out*) Frick!

(*FRICK rises. SASHA fires. Misses. Pandemonium. SASHA is pounced upon, breaks loose, goes at FRICK with a knife, stabs, is knocked down, bodies over him. You see an arm with a hammer rising and falling, and SASHA groaning. Then silence, darkness. Then SASHA'S voice, weak, delirious with pain, almost a whisper.*)

SASHA. My glasses, I can't see! I can't see. Where are my glasses?

(*In the shadows, EMMA is standing, as if watching the scene across 500 miles. She cries out in anguish: "Sa-sha-a-a!"*)

END OF ACT I

Act II

Prologue

TAPED VOICE OF JUDGE. Alexander Berkman, for the attempted murder of Henry Clay Frick, you are sentenced to the Western Pennsylvania State Penitentiary for a period of twenty-two years.

Scene 1. Most is Whipped

(*Lights up on JOHANN MOST, center stage, hand extended toward the audience. The beat of a revolutionary song in the background.*)

MOST. Comrades! Some here are circulating petitions for Alexander Berkman. I have refused to sign. Let me explain: revolutionary violence is one thing—a comic opera is another! (*Applause. MOST holds up his hand. He is serious. His humor is biting. He doesn't mind if people laugh, but his intent is serious. He doesn't smile.*) Comrades! I am not urging anyone here to assassinate the nearest capitalist. But let me say this. If you do decide on it, please do it efficiently. (*laughter*) They tell me that before the shooting, Berkman made a bomb to kill Frick. There was only one thing wrong with Berkman's bomb—it would not explode. (*more laughter*) Now, comrades, you know I would never suggest the making of bombs, (*laughter as everyone knows he has urged the making of bombs*) but it seems to me, there is one essential requirement for a bomb. It should explode! I understand Berkman's trade is cigar-making. Maybe he thought it was like making a cigar. (*laughter*) Well, all right, his cigar—I should say, his bomb—did not work. So he used a gun. (*MOST shakes his head*) When his shots missed, he took out his knife. Now we must admire one thing about Berkman—he was well-armed. (*more laughter*) But what he really needed was a guillotine, and an agreement from Frick to hold his head still.

(*Applause, laughter. A WOMAN has stood up in the audience, not immediately recognizable because she is in the front row facing MOST, or in the aisle.*)

144

Comrades (*getting serious now*) we have a revolution to make, and we will have to do it right! So don't come to me (*showing anger*) with petitions for that fool, Alexander Berkman!

(*Applause. The WOMAN is still standing. MOST peers into the audience to see who it is. Then, graciously___*)

Comrades, I recognize Emma Goldman, who is known to you as an organizer of the cloak and suit workers. I believe she has a question...

EMMA. (*her voice strong and clear*) Shame on you, Johann Most!

MOST. (*straining for humor*) That is not a question..

EMMA. (*her voice shaking with anger*) Shame, shame on you!

(*SHE leaps onto the stage and stands facing MOST. HE is angry, rattled.*

MOST. Do you have a question?

(*EMMA is dressed in a long cloak. She pulls a whip from under cloak and as she strikes MOST with it, she cries out.*)

EMMA. Shame!

(*MOST falls back, covers his face. Four more strokes with the whip.*)

Shame! Shame! Shame! Shame!

(*Several MEN jump on stage to stop her. She flings the whip at MOST, then turns to the audience, standing straight, and says, in a low emotional voice.*)

Shame on all of you!

Scene 2. Sasha in Prison

(*One thin shaft of light illuminates very dimly the FIGURES who call out (the loud clanging of steel doors, the light goes out, and a GUARD'S voice is heard)*

MONTY. Hey Berkman!

SASHA. Hello, hello, who's that?

MONTY. They call me Monty. Hey, Berkman, how much were you promised for killing Frick?

SASHA. How much?

MONTY. Dollars, Berkman. How much?

SASHA. Nothing.

MONTY. I don't get it, Berkman...

FIRST VOICE. Don't you get it? He's a nut!

SASHA. I have to explain to you. There was a strike...

FIRST VOICE. You're crazy, Berkman.

SECOND VOICE. He's one of those anarchist nuts.

THIRD VOICE. Hey, Berkman, ever been in a strait jacket?

FIRST VOICE. Watch out, Berkman! They're comin' down the block with a strait jacket!

SECOND VOICE. Hide, Berkman!

MONTY. Don't mind them, Berkman. Just be my boy and you'll be okay.

SASHA. I'm nobody's boy.

THIRD VOICE. He's Monty's boy. Let him alone.

SASHA. I'm Alexander Berkman. I must explain to you...

FOURTH VOICE. Hey, Berkman. I worked in the Carnegie plant in Pittsburgh.

SASHA. Then you know. Tell them...

FIRST VOICE. Yeah, I know. You're crazy, Berkman!

SASHA. (*anguished*) No! No! You don't understand. I must talk to you.

(*the loud clanging of steel doors, the light goes out, and a GUARD'S voice is heard*)

GUARD. Quiet in cellblock D!

Scene 3. *The Little Group Moves Out*

(*ANNA, EMMA, FEDYA, and VITO in the apartment where ANNA, EMMA, FEDYA, and SASHA lived. They are removing the last of their possessions, into shopping bags and suitcases.*)

ANNA. How I hate to leave.

EMMA. It's better, Anna dear. The newspapers keep coming around. "This is where Berkman lived." The police talk about a conspiracy. They are just waiting for an excuse...

VITO. Yes, better to separate for a while. Fedya, you can stay with me as long as you like. You can have the room with the window.

FEDYA. Yes, there's a wonderful view. It overlooks a stable. And a wonderful smell.

ANNA. I love horses.

FEDYA. It's not horses. It's an elephant stable. For the circus.

VITO. After a day in the sewer I come home, I open the window, and take a deep breath. (*breathes deeply*) How often do you get a chance to smell an elephant?

ANNA. Emma, do you think they will ever give you permission to visit Sasha?

EMMA. (*shaking her head*) They enjoy saying no.

FEDYA. Are you taking Sasha's books? (*hands her several*)

EMMA. Ah, Pushkin! (*reads a line or two*) Sasha loves these poems.

ANNA. (*hugging a painting*) Thank you, Fedya. I always wanted this.

(*faint sound of SOMEONE singing Bizet's "The Pearl Fishers"*)

VITO. Who's that?

ANNA. The man downstairs bought one of those new machines last week. He's a baker. He works nights—twelve hours—and when he comes home he likes to listen to this wax plate on his machine. (*listens, but the music has stopped*) It doesn't always work...

EMMA. (*looking around*) Oh, I can't stand it anymore. It's time to go, dear friends.

FEDYA. Goodbye, our little place.

ANNA. Goodbye. (*pauses*) Goodbye for Sasha, little place. (*brushes her hand over her eye*)

EMMA. It's all right. We will all be together again some day.

ANNA. Yes, some day...

(*ANNA kisses EMMA, then VITO and FEDYA. EVERYONE embraces. They pick up their bags, full of the things they have moved, arms full of paintings. Suddenly the song comes from downstairs loud and clear on the gramophone—the aria from "The Pearl Fishers," as the lights dim, and then go out, with the song continuing in the darkness as EMMA dresses for the next scene.*)

Scene 4. Emma Meets Reitman

(*Ragtime music. FEDYA and EMMA on a station platform.*)

EMMA. How good of you to wait with me, Fedya dear. I know you are late.

FEDYA. A lucky chance that I have an exhibition in the same city where you are giving a lecture. It's been so long since...

EMMA. (*grasps his hand*) Yes.

FEDYA. Who is meeting you?

EMMA. A Dr. Reitman. I don't know anything about him, except he's a doctor, but they say he takes care of prostitutes and hobos; he's not interested in money.

FEDYA. Then he's not a real doctor.

(*A MAN has been standing on the opposite side of the stage. Dark hair falling over his eyes. Tall, mustache, wearing a silk tie and a big hat, carrying a cane. A confident man. EMMA glances over, amused.*)

EMMA. Is that how men dress in Chicago?

FEDYA. A bit odd. But handsome, no?

EMMA. Handsome, yes. But a bit odd.

FEDYA. (*whispering as the MAN walks toward them*) I think...

REITMAN. Miss Emma Goldman?

EMMA. Yes...

REITMAN. (*grandly*) Welcome to Chicago. An honor indeed, Miss Goldman. I am Dr. Ben Reitman.

(*REITMAN bows with a flourish. EMMA and FEDYA exchange glances.*)

EMMA. This is my friend, Fedya.

REITMAN. A friend of Emma Goldman is a person to be cherished.

FEDYA. (*amused*) Well, Emma, I leave you in good hands.

(*THEY embrace. HE goes off.*)

EMMA. You are taking me to the Workers Hall?

REITMAN. Not exactly. In anticipation of your arrival the chief of police has closed it.

EMMA. (*sardonic*) Well, of course...Won't the police close your place too?

REITMAN. I am on good terms with the police.

EMMA. Then you cannot be on good terms with me.

REITMAN. (*amused*) You and I have found, by diligent search, a difference between us. I believe in speaking to everyone.

EMMA. I believe in speaking to almost everyone. But not the police. Surely you know...

REITMAN. I know very well. I was arrested just last week during a march of the unemployed here in Chicago. In the station house, they knocked me around a bit.

EMMA. And you still...

REITMAN. The police are no different than the prostitutes and thieves I work with every day—deprived people, acting out of desperation.

EMMA. There is truth in what you say. And also great innocence.

REITMAN. I believe I can make friends with any human being.

EMMA. You have supreme confidence in yourself.

REITMAN. I know what I can do. Just as you know what you can do.

(*HE takes her arm. SHE withdraws it.*)

EMMA. (*good-naturedly*) I know I can walk very well without support.

REITMAN. My object is not support.

EMMA. No?

REITMAN. No. It is to hold the arm of a woman I have admired for years.

EMMA. You don't know me.

REITMAN. I know your ideas. I know what you think about government, about prisons, about men and women.

EMMA. So, you know all about me.

REITMAN. No, not all. One thing I am curious about.

EMMA. Only one thing?

REITMAN. Yes.

EMMA. What is that?

REITMAN. (*quietly*) I wonder if your body is as beautiful as I imagine it.

EMMA. (*stepping away from him and looking directly into his face, incredulous*)

REITMAN. I said, I wonder if your body is as beautiful as I imagine it.

EMMA. (*amused*) I think you are a bit cracked.

REITMAN. Perhaps, but honest.

EMMA. (*laughing*) Do you know what I am speaking about tonight?

REITMAN. No.

EMMA. (*her laughter turning to anger*) About vulgar men who think of women as nothing but flesh. About arrogant men who think they have but to touch a woman's arm to produce an orgasm of delight. And about women who are stupid enough, slavish enough, to accept that.

REITMAN. (*softly*) Then your speech is not about me. And not about you.

EMMA. I think that we should go.

(*HE takes her arm again. SHE pulls it away firmly.*)

REITMAN. Can we meet again after your lecture?

EMMA. I don't think so.

REITMAN. We could share some wine, talk.

EMMA. Women like me don't trust men like you.

REITMAN. There are no men like me. And no women like you.

EMMA. (*deliberately*) I don't trust you.

REITMAN. Will you have a glass of wine with me after the lecture?

(*HE takes her hand. SHE pulls it away, then turns her head to look intently into his face as the lights go down.*)

Scene 5. Emma with Almeda and Maureen

(*a hot August day, MAUREEN ironing, ALMEDA reading, in a plain room, suggesting a cheap frame house in a small town in western Pennsylvania*)

MAUREEN. Almeda, we're crazy. Taking in laundry for pennies. And in this heat. Those two guys from the South Side came around again this morning. Quick money, sweetheart! I never knew you to be so stubborn about this. You sound like a Sunday School teacher. And here I am, ironing, in this heat...I swear, Almeda...

ALMEDA. Oh, shush! She'll be arriving soon, and how's it gonna look to her? No, we can't now. She's been visiting her boyfriend in the penitentiary in Allegheny City. It's for a night. I promised we'd put her up. God, I know it's hot. Have some lemonade. Here. (*she pours*) All she knows is we're the Socialist local in New Kensington, PA.

MAUREEN. Almeda, what good are we doing in this damn miserable town? I don't know. You got your heart in all that, Almeda, but I don't know. (*she tastes*) You keep calling it lemonade! It's got no lemons in it! No, I don't know what we're doing in this town.

ALMEDA. (*reciting*) "If the sun and the moon should doubt,
              They'd immediately go out."

MAUREEN. Did you make that up?

ALMEDA. William Blake.

MAUREEN. What you remember, I swear! I never heard of him. William Blake. And I'll bet he's famous.

ALMEDA. He is.

MAUREEN. I like C.B. Hawley—you know his latest?

(*ALMEDA shakes her head. MAUREEN sings.*)

"They Kissed, I Saw Them Do It..." (*stops singing*) What do you know about her?

ALMEDA. You'll like her.

MAUREEN. How do you know?

ALMEDA. I know what people say. She's a keg of dynamite. She's been organizing the cloakmakers strike in New York. Very educated.

MAUREEN. (*after a few seconds of silent reading and ironing*) Well, one night is okay. I told those guys to come back some other time.

ALMEDA. Maureen!

MAUREEN. When we're broke, why not? Hell, didn't you go off with that lawyer last month, and did I say a word?

ALMEDA. After that, I swore no more. I was ready to tell him to stick the money you know where.

MAUREEN. But you didn't, you came home with it.

ALMEDA. We ate that week.

MAUREEN. And drank. (*they both laugh*)

ALMEDA. Let's not talk about that.

(*A knocking at the door. ALMEDA goes to it, opens it. EMMA is there wiping sweat off her face, suitcase in hand. ALMEDA extends her hand.*)

Come on in. We didn't know when you'd come. Can't count on the Pennsylvania Railroad. This is Maureen. Here. (*takes her satchel*) Sit down. We've got some lemonade. (*motions to MAUREEN, who looks dubious but brings it*)

EMMA. (*sipping*) Wonderful! (*they look at one another*) Good of you to take me in. Ah, lemonade!

ALMEDA. If you don't mind this little place. There's an extra bed in my room right under the window. It's cool at night. We can use some company.

MAUREEN. Yeh, if not for Almeda, I'd go loony around here. Except, every Saturday night, it's Socialist night. Everyone comes and brings good stuff and we sing and have a great time.

EMMA. The people who come are Socialists?

MAUREEN. Oh, no. But after we decided—well, Almeda decided—this would be Socialist headquarters, we got up our nerve, and one Saturday we put up a sign outside: Socialist Party. That night all of our neighbors showed up. They said, thanks for inviting us to the party. So now every Saturday night we have a Socialist party.

EMMA. (*laughing*) A good idea!

ALMEDA. We made some biscuits this morning. We could have tea. Come on, Maureen, no more ironing. (*explaining to EMMA*) That's our livelihood these days. There's no work no-how in town. We take turns with the old iron.

EMMA. In New York one out of three is out of work. Worst of all, there's been a shortage of water. The pumps are running dry, and all over the city children are dying of cholera.

MAUREEN. (*distraught*) The little kids!

EMMA. Yes, women, are selling their bodies to feed their children.

ALMEDA. In this town, too. Maureen and I...

MAUREEN. Oh shush!

EMMA. Doesn't everyone in this system have to sell something to stay alive?

MAUREEN. I'm going to write my church-going mother back home and tell it to her just like that.

EMMA. (*laughs*) It's so good to be with you both. So good, after being out at the penitentiary.

MAUREEN. Did you see your boyfriend?

(*EMMA puts her head in her hands and starts to cry. ALMEDA comes over embraces her, no one speaking, then.*)

EMMA. They said they would never let me see him.

MAUREEN. You traveled the railroad all the way from New York and they wouldn't let you see him?

(*EMMA sobs, nods her head*)

ALMEDA. Those sons of bitches! Did they make you cry?

EMMA. (*suddenly lifting her head*) Cry? No! Not in front of them! I shouted. I cursed them. I told the warden his time would come. I could have killed him on the spot. No, I'd never cry in front of them. (*starts sobbing again*)

ALMEDA. Maureen, sing us a song.

(*MAUREEN sings a humorous, popular song. EMMA gradually stops crying, begins to smile. Soon ALL are laughing.*)

ALMEDA. Want some more lemonade?

EMMA. Yes, please.

MAUREEN. It's not really lemonade.

EMMA. I know.

(*THEY all laugh together*)

Scene 6. Speech at Union Square

(*EMMA appears center stage, revolutionary music in the background. She gets up on a box to address an enormous crowd of the unemployed. It is the economic crisis of 1893.*)

EMMA. Welcome to Union Square, my friends. (*pauses*) Look around.

Look around. In the richest city in the world, the lines of the unemployed stretch for miles. People want to work, but this system has no jobs for them. Yes, the richest city in the world, and children are dying for lack of food. We ask for work, and they tell us to wait. We ask for medicine for the sick, and they tell us to pray. We ask for food, and they tell us to vote. (*POLICE appear*) We cry out for help, and they send the police! Brothers and sisters! (*up to this point her tone has been strong but restrained, now it rises*) If the children need milk, let us go into the stores and take it! If families need bread, let us find out where the flour is stored, and take it! (*the POLICE move toward her*) Take it! Take it! (*the POLICE grab her roughly and pull her off the platform as the lights go down and revolutionary music is heard louder and louder and louder*)

Scene 7. Emma in Prison with Lizabeth

(*The clanging of steel doors from Scene 2 continues into this scene. But now the figure illumined is a black WOMAN, or else she is a white Southern woman—the language will be similar for both, sitting and sewing her nurse's smock as MATRON brings in EMMA, who can barely walk, and who sits down immediately on a cot.*)

MATRON. Lizabeth, here's a new helper for you. She's just out of the solitary. The warden says to teach her good, keep her out of trouble. (*leaves*)

LIZABETH. (*goes over to EMMA, hunched over*) Now don't sit squinched-ed up like that. You not in solitary any more. You better start using' your legs, else you'll never be able to walk again. Now get up. (*She pulls EMMA up and helps her walk in a tiny circle, while continuing to talk*) What they got you in solitary for? (*looks into EMMA'S face*) No need to tell me. You're that Red Emma they talk about. They say you don't take sass from no one. They say you put in charge of the sewing room and they wanted you to get the girls working faster and you wouldn't no-how. (*laughs*) Yeah, I hear them talk about you. They say you want to change the whole world. Yeah, I hear about you...I hear something else. I hear you got a handsome boyfriend brings you home-baked cookies and you gave them out to everybody. Now see here, Emma, I just love home-baked cookies.

(*LIZABETH laughs. EMMA smiles, beginning to come alive. What happens in this scene is that LIZABETH, by her words, by her physical help, revives EMMA from the half-dead state of solitary.*)

You know me?

(*EMMA shakes her head*)

I'm Lizabeth. I'm the prison nurse. They wants you to help me in the hospital ward. And I'm goin' to teach you all kinds of things. Startin' right now. Lay yourself down. Like this. (*genty pushes EMMA down, massages her legs*) You got to know when to make people walk, when to make them keep still. You got to know when to rub hard, and when to rub gentle. You got to know when to use a cold compress, and when to use a hot one. Hey, why do they call you Red Emma?

EMMA. It's a long story.

LIZABETH. We got lots o' time in here. You tell me about that, and I'll tell you how to do when a woman starts bleeding down there. You ever bring a baby into the world?

EMMA. No.

LIZABETH. Emma, you bring someone's baby into the world, and you can do just about anything. Next week there's a girl up in the ward about to have her birth. And you're goin' to help me. (*takes EMMA'S wrist and puts her fingers on her pulse*) Now first thing, I'm going to teach you to take a pulse. You put your fingers here. (*holds out her wrist*) Feel that? That's my life, beating for you. Won't stop no matter what. Goes on beating, on and on. Isn't that beautiful? (*looks into EMMA'S face*) You want to learn nursing, Emma?

EMMA. I want you to teach me, Lizabeth.

LIZABETH. I will teach you. Now I want you to remember one thing.

EMMA. What?

LIZABETH. I just love home-baked cookies!

(*they laugh*)

Scene 8. Return: Talk to Friends at Thalia Theater

(*Music from Verdi. Shouts: "Welcome home, Emma." EMMA comes on stage to address her friends at the Thalia theater, greeting her return from prison. She is low-key, a little pale.*)

EMMA. It's strange. Do you know, I tried two years ago to investigate prison conditions. They wouldn't let me near a prison. Then, suddenly, a stroke of luck...(*smiles*) I was inside! (*shakes her head*) Oh, I learned so much in that year on Blackwell's Island. And what I learned I'll never forget. (*pauses*) Being there made me think, even more than before, about our comrade Alexander Berkman. (*applause*) And all the others who fill the prisons. (*chokes up a little, remembering*) And I promised myself, day after day inside that hell, listening to the other women, marveling as I took their pulses that their hearts could beat so strongly in defiance of their condition...I promised myself that I would not rest...until the prisons of this country are taken apart, brick by brick, and the iron bars melted down, to make playgrounds for our children in a new society... It's good to be back with you, my brothers and sisters...

(*music rises, then fades*)

Scene 9. The Plan for Escape

(*Reprise, "Mein Ruhe Platz." VITO, ANNA, and FEDYA sitting at a table.*)

VITO. A good idea, Anna, to bring us together again.

ANNA. It was Emma's idea.

FEDYA. It is seven years since Sasha went away.

ANNA. And they have not let her see him in all this time.

FEDYA. Where is she? She should have been here an hour ago.

VITO. You know where she is. She's with Reitman.

(*The OTHERS are silent. They would rather not comment, but VITO is working himself up good.*)

How can she stay with that good-for-nothing?

FEDYA. It's not hard to understand—Reitman worships her. He works hard, organizes her lecture tours, goes everywhere with her. He is her serf.

VITO. And she is his slave. I never dreamed this could happen to her. What is there about him, Anna, maybe you can explain, tell me.

ANNA. (*smiling insinuatingly*) I've only heard what women say...

FEDYA. Heard what?

ANNA. That he makes love like a tiger. (*she growls at FEDYA*)

VITO. Does that make up for the fact that he is a liar and a cheat?

FEDYA. (*wryly*) Of course!

ANNA. He does have courage. Out in San Diego, they threatened to kill him. He went anyway. The mob took him out of the lecture hall and into the countryside at night. Stripped him naked, beat him, burned his flesh with hot irons, covered him with boiling tar and left him to die.

VITO. He has the courage of a circus performer. He is an entertainer. He seeks sensations, no matter how...

FEDYA. Do we have a right to interfere? Emma still carries on as before. She makes me feel ashamed of my inactivity. She's running all the time, here, there, speaking, organizing.

ANNA. I agree with Fedya. What right do we have to tell her who to go with?

VITO. I have my opinion. Reitman...

ANNA. Shhh! I hear someone on the stairs.

(*EMMA enters, embraces everyone, sits down, smoking as she often does. It is winter. She removes her coat.*)

EMMA. Someone just out of the penitentiary today brought me a letter from Sasha. It's not a trick. It's his writing.

VITO. Well?

EMMA. Sasha has been in and out of the basket cell—it is too horrible to talk about. He refuses to bow down and so they punish him, again and again. Someone else would be dead.

FEDYA. You know Sasha. He's a bull.

EMMA. In his heart, yes. But he is flesh and blood. Even with good time, he has eight years left. He has seen his friends die, one by one. Some die of sickness. Some hang themselves in their cells. He says he will not last.

(*FEDYA, agitated, gets up, paces*)

There is a reason he sent this letter with a friend. He has a plan. (*looks around*) Anna, is the door closed?

(*ANNA checks, returns*)

A plan for escape.

(*EVERYONE is listening. EMMA keeps her voice down.*)

He says there is a vacant house one hundred yards outside the prison wall. It can be rented. A tunnel can be dug from the house, under the wall, up into an abandoned washhouse in the yard where he takes his walk.

VITO. A tunnel? Has Sasha gone out of his mind? I know what it takes to dig tunnels. It is impossible.

FEDYA. Poor Sasha. He has lost his senses.

ANNA. Is it so crazy?

VITO. Yes, completely crazy. It is impossible to do without being detected. It is a noisy operation. It takes more equipment than we have. More money than we have. More people than we have. More time than we have. Yes, it is completely crazy.

ANNA. What do think, Emma?

EMMA. I think two things. First, it is, as Vito says, insane. In fact, impossible. And second (*pauses*)

VITO. (*softly*) And second...we must do it.

EMMA. Yes.

FEDYA. Yes.

ANNA. Yes, yes.

(*Lights out. Flashlights turned on by those digging the tunnel.*)

FEDYA. Anna, where are the buckets?

VITO. They're here.

ANNA. Where? Oh, here they are. I've got them.

VITO. We need some rope Fedya.

FEDYA. I'll go get some. I'll be right back. (*leaves*)

VITO. We must remember to shore up as we go along.

ANNA. What will we use?

VITO. I brought some planks. I'll take care of it.

(*footsteps offstage*)

ANNA. Vito, stop, someone's coming!

FEDYA. It's me.

ANNA. It's Fedya.

FEDYA. I had to come back. The digging can be heard out on the road. It won't do.

ANNA. He says he can hear the digging out on the road.

VITO. We need music.

ANNA. He says we need music to drown out the digging!

FEDYA. So?

VITO. I have a friend who plays a tuba.

ANNA. He has a friend who plays the tuba!

FEDYA. He will run out of breath. We are digging ten hours a day.

ANNA. A piano can be played for ten hours. (*excited*) I'll ask Leon Heimer!

(*piano playing begins*)

FEDYA. He's a concert pianist. All we need is noise.

ANNA. But he's trustworthy.

VITO. Do you think I'm going to dig with an ordinary pianist? We'll have concerts. We'll distribute leaflets. A concert pianist or nothing! (*Lights down. In the dark you hear a piano playing. Faint light on the figure of SASHA in his cell. Another figure on the other end of the stage—MONTY.*)

Scene 10. Sasha and Monty—Happy New Year

MONTY. How's it coming, Sasha?

SASHA. What?

MONTY. You know what I mean.

SASHA. So far, good. But no news in a week and I don't know what to think.

(Sirens begin to sound, get louder. SASHA is agitated.)

What's that?

MONTY. Don't know. Do you think...

SASHA. *(anguished)* No! It mustn't be! *(the sirens get louder, are joined by factory whistles)*

MONTY. It's the factory whistles from across the river, Sasha...

SASHA. Yes.

(the noises get louder)

MONTY. It's the New Year, Sasha. It's midnight, 1900, a new century, Sasha! Happy New Year!

SASHA. *(weeping with relief and joy)* Happy New Year! Happy New Year!

(Church bells are joining in now. VOICES from all over the cell block: "Happy New Year, you bastards!" "Happy New Year, everybody!" "Happy New Year!" Lights out, church bells still tolling in the darkness.)

Scene 11. Emma and Maureen

(Music recalls the Almeda-Maureen scene. EMMA comes with a candle into a darkened room.)

EMMA. Maureen? Where are you? Don't you have any light?

MAUREEN. Here, I'm in bed. I ran out of kerosene last week. Emma, I'm so glad you're here. *(they embrace)* We heard you went to Europe.

EMMA. To Vienna. To learn to be a midwife.

MAUREEN. That's what they said. A midwife! So I thought, I want Emma to bring out my baby, no one else. Am I your first?

EMMA. In Vienna, I delivered six babies. No, seven. One woman had twins. And just last week on the East Side. The woman was so sick. It was such a foul and miserable room. And she gave birth to a beautiful black-haired baby. What a fighter!

MAUREEN. A boy?

EMMA. A girl. (*both laugh*) How far along are you?

MAUREEN. Maybe seven months. You can see...

EMMA. Yes... You have good color in your face. (*takes her wrist*) Your pulse is regular. (*touches her*) Does this hurt?

MAUREEN. No, it feels good.

EMMA. Now let me listen. (*places her stethoscope against MAUREEN'S uterus*)

MAUREEN. What are you listening for?

EMMA. Shhh!

MAUREEN. You're listening for the heartbeat. You hear it?

EMMA. Don't talk now. (*listens*)

MAUREEN. Do you hear it? You should hear it!

EMMA. We'll try again in a few minutes. Sometimes it takes a while. Now just relax. Tell me about Almeda...

MAUREEN. Almeda's still in New Kensington. Living with Fred again. Hey, how's your boyfriend, Sasha? Did they ever let you see him?

EMMA. (*shakes her head, then turns her face away*) They found an escape tunnel. It was a crazy idea, but it almost worked. They weren't sure it was for him, but they punished him anyway. (*closes her eyes, then shakes it off*)

MAUREEN. How much longer does he have?

EMMA. Six years. (*takes up the stethoscope again, listens*)

MAUREEN. You hear the heartbeat?

EMMA. Sometimes the stethoscope doesn't work right. Now don't aggravate yourself. I can feel movement down there. You feel good, don't you?

MAUREEN. Yes, but I'm nervous, Emma. You know, I lost the last one. For months after, I cried. Now I want this baby so much. You understand. You love children. Someday you'll have a baby.

EMMA. Last week the doctor told me I'll never be able to have a child— unless I have an operation.

MAUREEN. Then you'll have the operation.

EMMA. (*shakes her head*) A woman has the right to decide not to have children, doesn't she?

MAUREEN. Sure, but...

EMMA. (*placing her stethoscope again*) Shhh! (*hands the stethoscope to MAUREEN, holds it to her ear*)

MAUREEN. I hear something!

EMMA. That's your baby.

MAUREEN. (*throwing her arms around EMMA*) Oh God! (*looks at EMMA*) Why are you crying? (*looks again*) You'll have the operation, Emma, you'll have your own baby.

EMMA. (*recovering*) Come, let's walk. It's good for you. (*THEY start to walk*) You know, Maureen, I'm going to bring a million little babies into the world. And as they come out of their mothers' wombs, I'm going to whisper in their tiny ears: "Rebel! Rebel! Join together! Change the world!" And in one generation...

MAUREEN. Emma! Don't you get arrested before my time comes!

Scene 12. Sasha and Andy: Memorial Service for Monty

(*This scene is played in the semi-darkness before dawn. SASHA is thrown onto his cot by two GUARDS who then remove his strait jacket.*)

ANDY. (*perhaps the voice of a black MAN*) Sasha, are you okay? What they do to you?

SASHA. The stomach pump. Every day. Then, at night, they put me in a strait jacket. Strapped my arms to the bed. Chained my feet to the bedposts. How long have I been gone?

ANDY. Seven days. Seven nights.

SASHA. (*gets up, goes to the tiny window. A stream of sudden sunlight comes through, and a bird begins to sing. He weeps.*) Listen! They failed! I'm alive! (*recovers*) Hey, who are you? You're Andy. What are you doing in Monty's cell. Where's Monty?

ANDY. I have to tell you, Sasha. He kept calling for a doctor, but they paid no attention. Friday they took him to the hospital. It was too late, Sasha. He's dead.

(*SASHA, anguished, utters a cry*)

They're giving a service for him in the chapel on Sunday. I'm in the choir and they want us to sing a hymn for him. (*chokes up in grief and anger*) First they kill him. And now they want us to sing a fuck'n hymn for him!

SASHA. (*standing up suddenly and going to the bars*) Let's have our own service for Monty.

ANDY. What do you mean?

SASHA. Look, Andy, every time we do something for ourselves, against their wishes, we are free.

ANDY. (*quiet for a moment, then suddenly shouts out*) We're gonna have a service for Monty. Everybody, a service for Monty!

FIRST VOICE. Yeah, Sunday.

ANDY. No, to hell with their service. We're having our own. Now. Right now. Say something for Monty!

VOICES. Goodbye, Monty! Monty helped me when I was sick! Good luck, Monty, wherever you are! Goodbye Monty! We miss you, Monty, you son of a bitch!

(*sound of a club on steel bars*)

GUARD'S VOICE. Quiet in cellblock D! (*there is silence for a second, then*)

SASHA. (*cries out*) Quiet yourself! This is a service for Monty!

(*silence, then a PRISONER begins a hymn, as the lights go down*)

Scene 13: Reitman and Emma

(*EMMA is waiting in her room for reporters to arrive. REITMAN bursts in, attired in his usual flamboyant style: large hat, cape, cane, flowing tie. HE tries to embrace her, but SHE turns away.*)

EMMA. Why did you come, Ben? You stayed away six months. And here you are. In a few minutes there are a dozen reporters coming to interview me.

REITMAN. My darling! As soon as I heard about your arrest I knew you would need me. I heard the police beat you.

EMMA. It's an old habit they have when they get someone behind closed doors.

REITMAN. I am worried for you, Emma. You must be careful how you speak to the press. They are vultures. Your words can be used against you. There are new laws. You know that.

EMMA. I don't need your advice.

REITMAN. Why so cold my sweetheart? Why so utterly cold? What is going on? Is it because I cannot join you in all this revolutionary bravado?

"Refuse to fight! Violate the law!" That's not my way. I don't believe in putting our heads into their nooses.

EMMA.   If we persist, there will one day be too many people for their nooses.

REITMAN.   Dreams, dreams, Emma. How I love your dreams. But I am afraid for you. I can't stand the thought of you in prison again. What would I do without you? You, my sweetheart, my mother, my sister, my Venus, my love!

EMMA.   Enough, Ben! Your one concern is: what will *you* do?

REITMAN.   Have I not stood with you? Have I not faced down howling mobs from here to California?

EMMA.   Yes, I never understood why. You were not one of us...

REITMAN.   My God, so cold, Emma, so cold. What is wrong? Why can't we just be happy? McKinley sends soldiers into Cuba, the Philippines. You call for disobedience. Why is that necessary? Let those who don't want to go not go. Why must we stand on platforms and trumpet our defiance? They are setting a trap for you, Emma. Be careful with the press. And think of Sasha. He will need us here when he comes out.

EMMA.   You're not thinking of Sasha. You're thinking of yourself.

REITMAN.   My darling, you're upset for some reason.

(*HE reaches for her. SHE turns away, opens her drawer.*)

EMMA.   I received a letter from Almeda Sperry.

REITMAN.   Almeda Sperry...I'm trying to remember.

EMMA.   What a bad memory my poor Ben has! Almeda Sperry. She met you when you went to speak in Pennsylvania.

REITMAN.   (*measuring his words*) Oh, yes, that drunken Socialist whore in New Kensington.

EMMA.   (*furious*) That drunken Socialist whore! Who single-handedly built a Socialist group in that god-forsaken little town! Who sold herself to men when she had nothing to eat! The most honest, straight-talking person I have ever known.

REITMAN.   (*humorous*) More honest than me?

(*EMMA shakes her head in disbelief*)

Why are we arguing about Almeda Sperry? I agree: an admirable woman. I didn't mean to call her a whore. In fact, she and I understand one another.

EMMA.   Yes, I think so. Listen. (*reads from the letter*) "Darling

Emma. I am amused by Reitman. But don't ever send him to New Kensington again. I have had a deep horror of him ever since he met me at the railroad station. I understood him thoroughly as soon as he took my arm the way he did. Please ask him, for the sake of the Cause—if he ever goes to meet another sinful woman who is beginning to see the glimmer of light—please ask him, for humanities sake, for his own sake and the woman's sake—not to begin *fuck* talk."

REITMAN. She writes vividly...Truth is, I'm not sure what she's talking about.

EMMA. Truth is, you are such a liar!

REITMAN. Have I ever denied it? I would be lying if I did, and why add one more to my long history? But how can one live in this world without lying, Emma?

EMMA. Lying to your enemies, perhaps. To those you love is unpardonable.

REITMAN. But that is what is wonderful about you, Emma. You have always pardoned the unpardonable.

(*EMMA shakes her head and turns her back on him to put the letter away. HE kisses her neck, turns her around. THEY kiss passionately. Then SHE turns away again.*)

EMMA. Oh, that first time you took me by the arm. How you took me by the arm! How angry I was! How thrilled I was!

REITMAN. (*gently*) I was not playing with you, Emma. I have stayed with you, year after year.

EMMA. (*breaks away*) Yes, you have. On and off. Steadfast and deceitful. You made me forget everything else when I was with you. How ridiculous! I speak all over the country about the independence of women and then I rush to you.

REITMAN. My blue-eyed darling.

(*HE embraces her. SHE yields, then breaks away, shaking her head. HE sees she is determined.*)

Please, Emma. Be careful with the press. Let them see that you too condemn Czolgosz, the assassin. You know he's mad. And they will ask you about the explosion in San Francisco Bay. Don't say anything. Save your words for a better time.

EMMA. If we save our words, there will be no better time. Goodbye, dear Ben, terrible Ben.

(*THEY embrace. SHE breaks away, turns her back. HE straightens his tie, picks up his cane, walks off.*)

Scene 14: Emma and Reporters

(REPORTERS come on stage, surrounding EMMA. THEIR backs are to the audience, she is facing the audience.)

REPORTER. Miss Goldman, after President McKinley was shot, why did they arrest you?

EMMA. You are reporters. You know the police don't need evidence to arrest someone. The President was assassinated. A government always goes into a frenzy when someone else uses its own tactic. *(calm, good-humored in all this)*

REPORTER. Its own tactic?

EMMA. Murder.

REPORTER. Radical organizations all over the country have repudiated the assassin. It is said you defend him.

EMMA. I defend not his act, but his anguish.

REPORTER. Don't you believe the assassin is insane?

EMMA. He must be. He killed one man without official permission. If he were the President of the United States, he could do as McKinley did, send an army into the Philippines to kill ten-year old children. That is considered legal. And perfectly sane.

REPORTER. Is it true you offered to nurse McKinley after he was wounded?

EMMA. Yes. But for some reason, my offer was not accepted.

REPORTER. Then you felt compassion for the President?

EMMA. Of course. McKinley did not know where the Philippines were until the merchants and bankers pointed it out to him on the map.

REPORTER. Do you claim that the business interests benefited from the war?

EMMA. I know one thing. The working classes got nothing from it. Their sons die in Cuba from rotten beef supplied by the war contractors.

REPORTER. The United States did liberate Cuba from Spain, did it not?

EMMA. Yes. Because we did not want the Cubans to liberate themselves. Spain is gone. And our marines are there. We have become the bully of the Western Hemisphere.

REPORTER. Do you have no feelings of patriotism?

EMMA. What is patriotism? Is it love of the land? the people? Then I am a patriot. Is it obedience to the *government*, which destroys its own land, robs its own people? True patriotism demands that we denounce what our government does.

REPORTER. Do you have a comment on the recent bomb explosions aimed at the battleships in San Francisco Bay?

EMMA. I would be happy to sink the whole fleet. Yes, all the battle fleets everywhere in the world. But I don't believe in bombs.

REPORTER. Then have you decided that the way to change is through the ballot box, through voting?

EMMA. When Rockefeller wants an oil refinery, does he take a vote? When McKinley wanted the Philippines, did he take a vote? Voting is a game, to keep everyone busy while the rich take what they want.

REPORTER. Then what do you propose?

EMMA. People will organize, wherever they work, wherever they live. And when they are strong enough, they will take back this country from those who have stolen it. That's much simpler than voting.

REPORTERS. (*in disbelief*) Can we quote you on all this?

EMMA. (*smiling*) Will your newspapers print all this?

Scene 15: Sasha is Free

(*No dialogue in this scene. Railroad station. It is May 18, 1906. Spring, dusk. Railroad whistle, sounds of engine starting up as train moves away. A MAN is standing, back to audience, far left, wearing a hat, an oversized coat, carrying a small suitcase. He is motionless. EMMA comes in from the right, stops. She is carrying flowers. She sees the man, from behind, stops. He doesn't move at first, back is to her. Then SASHA turns and looks at her, remains where he is. She takes some steps toward him, stops, then moves toward him. He nods his head. She throws her arms around him, and they embrace. She holds out the flowers, he takes them, closes his eyes, presses his lips against them.*)

Scene 16: Sachs Cafe

(*Sachs Cafe. Music. VITO and ANNA arrive, sit down. They are somewhat better dressed than in the old days.*)

VITO. Mr. Sachs! (*turns to ANNA*) It's still the same service! (*SACHS arrives*)

SACHS. Vito! Anna! After all these years! (*grasps their hands*) Vito, you're still complaining. But it's good to see you back. Do you still work in the sewers?

VITO. Do I look like a man who works in the sewers?

SACHS. (*looks him over carefully*) No, you look like a man who *once* worked in the sewers.

VITO. You are a perceptive man, Mr. Sachs. I have risen in the world. I am a bookkeeper for the Sewer Department.

SACHS. Who would believe that the Sewer Department keeps books? (*muses on that*) And you, Anna?

ANNA. I'm not in the factory any more. I'm an organizer for the garment union.

SACHS. Still tumulting. I knew it. Tell me, have I changed in ten years?

VITO. No. And neither have your tablecloths. Don't you think after ten years, you should change the tablecloths?

SACHS. (*sighs*) The same Vito. A wonderful person. Just a little crazy. How about a little wine to sober you up? I know it's a special day. Where are the others?

ANNA. Here comes the wine!

(*FEDYA arrives, carrying several bottles, dressed elegantly. ANNA and VITO get up and embrace FEDYA. SACHS, standing off, looks at FEDYA.*)

SACHS. Beautiful! Beautiful!

FEDYA. Good to see you, Mr. Sachs (*shakes his hand*) How about some glasses? You'll drink with us.

SACHS. Like old times. You bring your own wine. I supply the glasses. It's a miracle I'm still in business.

ANNA. Fedya, we read about you in the papers. Exhibitions here, exhibitions there. You're well-known!

(*FEDYA shrugs*)

VITO. Look at him. Like a prince. What happened, Fedya? You were going to use your art for the working class.

FEDYA. You were going to organize the working class so they would want my art. What happened, Vito?

ANNA. Don't ask what happened. Ask, what's happening? The IWW is organizing all over the country—men, women, colored, white, immigrants, natives—one big union.

VITO. Yes, Fedya, people are on the move all over the world.

FEDYA. I'm sorry. I don't see it.

ANNA. You're not looking.

FEDYA. I'm looking! I'm looking! (*suddenly*) And guess what I'm seeing!

(*HE rises to greet EMMA. SACHS is arriving with glasses, stops short at the sight.*)

Mr. Sachs, meet my friend, Emma Goldman, from Kovno. (*embraces EMMA*)

SACHS. (*putting down the glasses, embraces EMMA*) My dear girl, I knew you would come back some day.

(*EMMA embraces VITO and ANNA*)

ANNA. Where is he? Did you see him? Did you met him?

EMMA. At the railroad station. I brought flowers for him. There were tears in his eyes. In mine too. We didn't talk at first. I took him to my room. He wanted to be alone for a little while. But he'll be here.

VITO. How does he look?

EMMA. He is fourteen years older. His walk is different.

FEDYA. (*shaking his head*) Sit down, Emma. Drink with us. I hear you were arrested again last month. What was it this time?

EMMA. I was giving a lecture on how to use contraceptives.

FEDYA. Of course...

EMMA. To a meeting of Jewish women on the East Side. It was good speaking Yiddish again. But there was a police spy there. A woman.

VITO. She understood Yiddish?

EMMA. Not a word. But the judge gave me fifteen days anyway.

SACHS. (*calling out*) He's here! He's here!

(*SASHA enters, hat, long coat. ANNA rushes to embrace him, then VITO, then FEDYA, wiping a tear from his eye.*)

SASHA. (*his voice soft*) Dear, dear friends.

SACHS. Sit down, Sasha. (*he pulls over a chair*) Here, let me take your coat.

(*SASHA demurs*)

So many years! Have something to eat. It's my treat.

SASHA. I'm not hungry, Mr. Sachs. I'll just sit for awhile.

SACHS. This is something new. Sasha refusing food! I never though I'd see...

EMMA. Enough, Mr. Sachs.

SACHS. What did I say? Did I say something wrong?

VITO. It's all right. (*turning to SASHA*) Sasha, you should have some food.

EMMA. Don't' tell him what to do, Vito.

VITO. Don't do this, don't do that! Emma, you've become such a big shot!

(*THEY'RE all on edge*)

ANNA. Quiet, all of you! We're here to celebrate Sasha's homecoming.

FEDYA. Yes, let's drink a toast. Come, Mr. Sachs, you too. It's on me. (*fills up EVERYONE'S glasses*) To Sasha's return.

(*THEY all drink. SASHA takes a small sip.*)

SASHA. (*softly*) Thank you, dear friends.

SACHS. Did you hear about Johann Most?

VITO. Yes. He was arrested again, sent to Blackwell's Island. His health has not been good.

SACHS. It was in the papers this morning. He's dead.

(*silence*)

VITO. (*lifting his glass*) To Johann Most, and the revolution for which he fought.

(*THEY drink*)

FEDYA. You still have faith, Vito, after all that has happened? The revolution in Russia, crushed, the workers massacred before the Winter Palace. And everywhere, the state, armed, all-powerful? War, the state nourishes. Revolution it destroys. Ask Sasha about the power of the state.

VITO. Don't speak too soon Fedya. We're only six years into the twentieth century.

FEDYA. Even if a revolution succeeds, my friends, may it not become corrupted?

EMMA. So, we try again. Who says we are limited to one revolution?

VITO and ANNA. (*holding up their fingers in the game of Morro*) Due! Tre! Cuatro! Cinco!

(*Laughter all around, EVERYBODY drinks. THEY'RE interrupted by sounds from the street. Marching, singing. SACHS goes to the window, watches. The singing dies down.)*

EMMA. What is it?

SACHS. It's the painters. They're marching to Union Square. Didn't you hear? All the painters in New York are going on strike tomorrow.

VITO. *(having fun)* What did I tell you? It will all start with the painters. And some day...

FEDYA. It's always: "some day." How many times have I heard that..."some day..."?

ANNA. You may laugh, Fedya, but it's true. Some day, people all over the world will go on strike against their governments—no more war, no more poverty.

FEDYA. But in the meantime...What do we do in the meantime? Must we not live? You always said that, Emma. I admit it, that's what I've decided to do. To escape all the stupidity. I'm ashamed to say this in front of Sasha, after all he's been through, in front of Emma, who does so much.

EMMA. I escape, too, Fedya. For an hour, a day, a week. To walk the beach, to read a novel, to dream, to make love, to eat chocolates. I had some just before I came here. *(smiles)*

FEDYA. But then you always return.

EMMA. Yes. To be with friends, in the midst of struggle, it's such a beautiful way to live.

(ANNA, moved, embraces her. ALL are silent)

SASHA. *(removing his coat)* Mr. Sachs, I would like something to eat. *(voice is firm, he has straightened up)*

SACHS. Aha!

(EVERYONE smiles. A GIRL comes prancing into the cafe. She is overloaded with posters, and she puts them down while she puts one up on the wall. She is dressed dashingly, a red beret, a jacket, stockings.)

GIRL. *(calling out)* Support the painters strike! Everyone to Union Square tomorrow! *(stops)* You're Emma Goldman!

VITO. Maybe *you're* Emma Goldman!

GIRL. I'm with the new theater group on Third Street.

EMMA. The Orlenieff troupe. I know them.

GIRL. Yes, we open a Chekhov play on Sunday. And we support the painters' strike. We want to put up these posters in the dark before the police take them down. Maybe you'll help us? *(happy, as the idea strikes her)*

VITO. My friend do you know how many posters we have put up over the years? We would like to help, but tonight we're celebrating a special homecoming. Perhaps you have heard...

EMMA. Surely we can help in some way. Maybe tomorrow...

ANNA. Yes, it's Sasha's first evening back.

SASHA. (*suddenly*) Where do you want the posters put up tonight?

GIRL. (*happily*) Anywhere downtown.

ANNA. But Sasha...(*then, seeing the expression in his eyes*) I'll take 14th Street! Who will distribute on the West Side?

VITO. I'll do the West Side. Fedya, you come with me.

(*FEDYA shrugs resignedly*)

It's better for you two to go. Don't you think so, Sasha?

EMMA. Sasha and I can take Broome Street. I used to live on Broome Street.

SASHA. I remember. Anna Minkin's place. (*smiles*)

(*THEY all rise, take hands, music*)

END OF PLAY

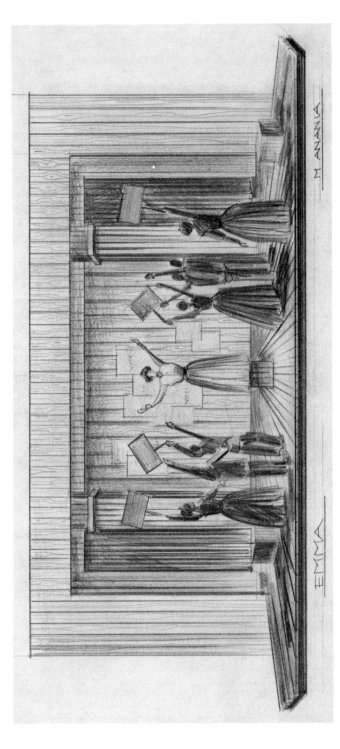

EMMA

M. ANANIA

Bibliography

For background on Emma Goldman, the primary source is her magnificent autobiography, *Living My Life*, which is now available in a one-volume paperback put out by New American Library. There are several good biographies: Richard Drinnon, *Rebel in Paradise*; Alix Kates Shulman, *To the Barricades;* Alice Wexler, *Emma Goldman: An Intimate Life;* Candace Falk, *Love, Anarchy, and Emma Goldman.* Alix Kates Shulman has edited a collection of Goldman writings, *Red Emma Speaks*, and there is Emma Goldman's volume of lectures, *Anarchism and Other Essays.* Richard and Marie Drinnon have edited some of the fascinating correspondence between Emma Goldman and Alexander Berkman after they had been deported to Europe: *Nowhere At Home*. An absolutely essential source, and an epic of prison literature, is Berkman's *Prison Memoirs of an Anarchist.* Paul Avrich's *The Haymarket Affair* is excellent for general background on the anarchist movement. (Historical note from the author of *Emma*: scrupulous readers may see that I have taken some liberties with the chronology of Emma's life.)

THE FURIES OF
MOTHER JONES

by Maxine Klein
Music by James Oestereich

"The Furies of Mother Jones," produced by Little Flags Theatre, written and directed by Maxine Klein with music composed by James Oestereich, premiered in Boston on November 10, 1977.

Mother Jones .... *Ellen Field*

Turn of the century women,
Raleigh Firman .... *Peggy Ings*

Turn of the century men,
Hank Firman ....*Rick McDermott*

Mae Black .... *Anita Barzman*

Pete Black .... *Wiley Moore*

Diller Oden .... *Davis Bate*

Jupie Barnes .... *Andrea Saragov*

Senator Riner,
Turn of the century men,
Frank....................................... *James Oesterich*
Chorus

Bert,
Johnny .... *Allen Oliver*
Senator Scott

Lisa Black .... *Stacy Klein*

Set design by Michael Anania, costumes by Nikki, lights by John Polglase.

PROLOGUE

ACT I

Homes of the miners, deep coal mines.

ACT II

Halls of Congress, homes of miners, and deep coal mines.

TIME: Turn of the century and late 1960s.

175

STORY OF THE PLAY

"The Furies of Mother Jones" is an epic musical drama. Serving as the voice of history, Mother Jones, the great labor organizer, old and bold and battling, strides across our fighting past and into our heroic present.

The play is a rousing musical drama that takes place in turn-of-the-century Appalachia when labor organizing was a matter of life and death, and in the late 60s when the struggle continued at an almost equal risk.

The struggle then and now centers around three major conflicts: the people's struggle to keep their ancestral land, the long battle of the deep pit miners to initiate and enforce life-saving conditions in their work, and the attempt to elect an honest, democratic leadership to the United Mine Workers union. This last conflict centers around the campaign of "Jock" Yablonski to oust the corrupt machine of Tony Boyle, a man subsequently convicted of Yablonski's murder.

The opening scenes, set in the late sixties, focus on the lives of three Appalachian mining families. These people, their way of life, and their involvement in the events of the drama are drawn from oral and written histories, court records, congressional records, newspaper accounts, etc.

Overlooking this present and affirming the indissoluble spirit that binds together generations of laboring men and women is the heroic presence of Mother Jones, a tough and tender militant whose voice is still heard among the miners who, to this day still call themselves "the Jones boys."

The play's action takes place on a wooden structure with two levels. The structure is so designed that there are specific locations for Mother Jones, for the mines and a house for each of the mining families. The rest of the space is open so it can be transformed as the action suggests. The action moves fluidly from one area to another, the only blackout occurs at the end of each act.

DESCRIPTION OF CHARACTERS

DILLER ODEN: A deep-coal miner and union organizer who is dedicated to improving the miners' lot. He has obviously endured much hardship but understates his personal sufferings—he prefers action to complaint. He is determinedly optimistic about improving the union.

JOHNNY TANNER: An adolescent boy whose father was killed in the mines. He worries that Diller, his father's best friend, will share the same fate.

HANK FIRMAN: A deep-coal miner. Paitent, cheerful, and reassuring with his wife, Raleigh, Hank is more somber with the other miners; experience has hardened him.

RALEIGH FIRMAN: A textile worker, Raleigh's energy, sharp wit, and controlled concentration are her most apparent traits. An excitable, forceful woman, her soft playfulness is revealed in her interactions with her husband, Hank.

MAE BLACK: Younger than Raleigh, Mae is both tough and tender. She also works at the textile mill.

LISA BLACK: Mae's daughter, she is young, sprited, and sassy.

PETE BLACK: A deep-coal miner and Mae's husband. Generally good-natured and even-tempered, he can become impatient with those who don't share his pragmatic support of union reform.

MOTHER JONES: A feisty labor organizer with almost supernatural energy. Forceful and unflappable, her strong orations inspire the miners. Witty and warm, she's a tireless defender of miners' rights. She changed the course of American history.

MAN, YOUNG MAN, ANOTHER MAN, QUARTET, WOMAN, AMOS' SISTER, LISBETH: Turn of the century laborers.

JUPIE: A proud, strong mountain woman, she is determined to protect her land from Con El Coal. She's fiercely loyal to the mountain people and contemptuous of "traitors" who side with the company. Her family has died, she now lives alone in the family house.

BERT: A strip miner, he's determined to do his job, right or wrong.

MOLLY, MATTIE, ARVILLA, JANE, BEA: Miners' wives and children.

FRANK: An organizer for Tony Boyle

JOHN HENRY: A guitarist.

TWO THUGS: In the employ of Boyle's campaign.

SHERIFF: Like Bert, just doing his job.

STRIP MINERS: Like Bert, they do their job.

SENATOR SCOTT, SENATOR RINER: Formalistic, concerned with their execution of the law of the land.

RALEIGH'S FATHER: A miner. His spirit has been beaten by the company, but he is filled with concern for his family.

CHORUS: Sings the peoples' soul.

BOY and GIRL: They play an innocent game in a deadly playground

Ellen Field as Mother Jones. Photo: James Oestereich.

Prologue

(The CAST enters and stands proud. They are the voices of history and prophecy. ENSEMBLE sings.)

> *Labor's Story*
> Labor's story's told and told
> Just not so's you can hear
> Labor's story's told and told,
> You believe me, don't you dear?
>
> We don't know their names now,
> Most didn't know them then,
> Those hundreds of thousands
> Of laboring men,
> Working dawn 'til the dusk
> And on through the night,
> Who died far too young,
> And that's never been right.
>
> Strong women beside them
> Who wed them and tried
> To work double shifts in factories
> Where too many of them died.
> It was courage they had then
> That made them struggle on
> Those legions of warriors
> Nameless shadows in the dawn.

SPEAKER. *(over instrumental underscoring)* We sing the story
ENSEMBLE. Appalachia.
SPEAKER. A once beautiful and fertile country now turned into a
ENSEMBLE. Desert

SPEAKER. For the sake of

ENSEMBLE. Profit.

SPEAKER. We sing the

ENSEMBLE. Unborn generations

SPEAKER. Who must someday

ENSEMBLE. Inherit and inhabit this desert.

SPEAKER. We sing the

ENSEMBLE. Mining people

SPEAKER. Whose

ENSEMBLE. Streams

SPEAKER. Whose land, whose

ENSEMBLE. Homes

SPEAKER. Are under seige. We sing the

ENSEMBLE. Laborers

SPEAKER. We sing the

ENSEMBLE. Survivors

SPEAKER. We sing the

ENSEMBLE. People, Appalachia. And we will sing their song

SPEAKER. Until the land they have worked with their hands and

ENSEMBLE. Fertilized with their blood

SPEAKER. Is theirs once again.

ENSEMBLE. (*exits singing*)
> Labor's story's told and told
> Just not so's you can hear.
> Labor's story's told and told
> You believe me, don't you, dear?

Act I

Scene 1: *"Diller and Johnny's House"*

(*It is early morning, not yet light. Leaving for work is DILLER ODEN, a deep-coal miner and union organizer. DILLER is now surrogate father to young JOHNNY TANNER whose father was killed in the mines. The house they live in was built by JOHNNY'S father and DILLER.*)

DILLER. (*waves and starts to exit*) See you at seven, Johnny.

JOHNNY. (*stopping him*) What're you up to today?

DILLER. Thought Pete and I might do a little organizing for Yablonski.

JOHNNY. (*their banter, as has been the case recently, is good-humored but pointed*) Well, at least you got yourself a job with a quick pay-off. Last organizer for Yablonski got hisself killed within six months of the day he declared.

DILLER. Damn! You are just like your dad, always warnin' me of disaster waitin' 'round every corner!

JOHNNY. Does that tell you a little somethin' about yourself?

DILLER. (*lightly, putting JOHNNY'S fears to rest*) No, just tells me about the two of you—worry warts.

JOHNNY. (*not taken in at all*) You worry 'bout something that'll never happen, you're a fool. You worry 'bout a sure thing, you're smart, 'cause you just might get yourself prepared for it.

DILLER. With someone like you 'round frettin' all the time, how could I not be prepared?

JOHNNY. (*shaking his head good-naturedly*) I don't know, but you sure do seem to manage.

DILLER. See you later, Johnny.

(*DILLER exits to the mines as JOHNNY exits to work at the local lumber store*)

Scene 2. "Hank and Raleigh's House"

(In the pre-dawn preparation for the workday is RALEIGH FIRMAN, who works at a textile mill. She moves precisely about her tasks, with energy and concentration. This normally tough and witty woman is obviously upset about something. She is fixing bag lunches, doing up the last of the breakfast dishes and mentally organizing for the day ahead. Her husband, HANK, is a deep-coal miner. With RALEIGH he is patient, reassuring, a foil for her intensity. With the miners, a more somber HANK is apparent. Experience has taught him to expect the worst.)

HANK. *(calling to RALEIGH from the bedroom)* Raleigh, where'd you put my helmet?

RALEIGH. *(preoccupied)* I put it back.

HANK. Back where?

RALEIGH. Where it belongs, on the shelf over the bed. *(picks up a knife the wrong way)* Ouch!

HANK. What's wrong?

RALEIGH. *(clutching her hand and grimacing with pain)* Nothin'. I just cut three fingers off my left hand.

HANK. I found it. *(enters a bit sheepishly)*

RALEIGH. *(obviously upset, she keeps her back to him as she hands him the jacket)* Here's your jacket. Now do you think you can find the mines all right?

HANK. Hey, what's wrong? Did you really hurt yourself?

RALEIGH. I'll be alright.

HANK. You upset about Jupie? *(RALEIGH shakes her head "no")* It's your brother, ain't it? Every fall, regular like clockwork, you start thinkin' about him. *(chucks her under the chin)* Well that ain't gonna happen to me. I'll be careful 'n' everything'll be fine. Hell, us Kentucky miners got more lives than a cat.

RALEIGH. *(sardonically)* Yeah, and you know what happened to our last cat.

HANK. *(as though remembering)* Oh, yeah. *(picking up the bag)* This my lunch?

RALEIGH. What's it look like?

HANK. *(fixing to leave)* How many gonna be over to Jupie's today?

RALEIGH. Enough.

HANK. You be careful, hear? *(beginning what is obviously a friendly ritual with them, she holds out her hand)*

RALEIGH. If you will.

HANK. (*holds out his*) I will if you will.

(*They shake hands and HANK starts out without his helmet. RALEIGH picks it up and runs after him.*)

RALEIGH. Hank, oh Hank!

HANK. What are you doin'?

RALEIGH. (*coquettish*) Wavin' goodbye to you like they do in the movies. (*holds out the helmet*) Did you forget somethin'?

HANK. You hid it on me. You stood yourself in front of it and hid it on me.

RALEIGH. (*playfully pushing it towards him*) If it'd been a rat, it would've bit you. (*starts back toward the kitchen*)

HANK. You takin' Henry junior to school tomorrow?

RALEIGH. I would 'cept he'd be alone. School begins a week from tomorrow.

HANK. Okay, Wise Guy. Whenever it begins, you takin' him?

RALEIGH. Of course. On his first day? 'Course I'm gonna take him.

HANK. Can you get another day off from the mill?

RALEIGH. I got some time comin' to me.

HANK. (*casual, with just a touch of swagger*) How'd you like to get him a new notebook, a new pair of shoes and a new pair of jeans, the whole kit and kaboodle?

RALEIGH. (*she stops, obviously delighted*) Oh God, could we afford it? You said last week we might could get him a new outfit, but I just pushed it from my mind. Oh, it'd really make that first day of his so much better.

HANK. I'm still workin' on it. You didn't mention it to him, did you?

RALEIGH. (*butter would melt*) 'Course not.

(*HANK starts to exit. RALEIGH calls after him*)

Size nine straight-legged jeans and the shoes gotta be Buster Browns, or he told me he wouldn't wear 'em.

HANK. Raleigh, you told him. Damn it, Woman!

(*RALEIGH laughs and exits. HANK shakes his head good-humoredly and exits.*)

Scene 3. "Pete and Mae's House"

(*MAE BLACK is in her kitchen. She steps out of her door and stands a moment savoring the early morning. She is a thoughtful woman, tough, tender. Like RALEIGH, she works at the textile mill. She starts to prepare breakfast and calls to her daughter.)*

MAE. Lisa, you up?

LISA. *(offstage)* Yeah.

MAE. You was up late last night readin' that book I got you, wasn't you?

LISA. Uh huh.

MAE. How'd you like it?

LISA. *(entering)* I didn't like the endin'.

MAE. *(upset)* Why not?

LISA. *(with impish delight)* It was too far from the beginnin'!

MAE. You just ready yourself for school.

LISA. I ain't goin' to school.

(PETE enters)

MAE. Yes you are goin' to school.

LISA. I ain't goin' to no consolidated school.

MAE. Not "ain't" Lisa. "Aren't." You "aren't" goin' to no consolidated school.

LISA. *(sassy)* Right!

(PETE starts laughing as LISA sprints off)

MAE. *(taking hold of PETE'S shirt)* Don't you dare laugh at her jokes, or I'll send you to school right alongside her. *(notices under her hand)* You got a hole in your shirt.

PETE. That's my air-conditionin'.

MAE. You need it to let some of that hot air outta you.

PETE. You are the sassy one today.

MAE. *(in dead earnest)* Pete, Lisa's got to go to school. We got to bring her 'round.

PETE. She'll go, Mae. She's just scared. In them consolidated schools, they put the rich in with the poor, and those brats with pedigrees sewn on their underwear can be real mean on ours.

MAE. *(sewing a button on his shirt)* It's consolidated or nothin'.

PETE. Sometimes I wonder which is better. When I was a kid, all the grades was put together in one room. And we learned a helluva lot from each other...

MAE. *(interrupting him, turning away because he won't deal with the issue)* Will you stop talkin' about your childhood! I'm sick of hearin' about it.

PETE. Now look here... (*points his finger at her and she grabs it*) You gonna break that thing off?

MAE. Maybe I will if you don't listen to me serious for a minute. Consolidated is all there is, and she's got to make the best of what there is.

PETE. Mae, she always has, and I 'spect she always will.

MAE. Not if you keep laughin' at her dumbass jokes.

PETE. I wasn't laughin' at her jokes, I was laughin' at her mother (*she starts to hit him playfully*) Okay, Toughie, gotta go. (*puts on his jacket*) You gonna miss work today and go over t' Jupie's?

MAE. I figure the mill can get along without me for one day.

PETE. Take care, hear?

MAE. It's a habit.

PETE. Uh huh. Just remember when you met up with that bulldozer over t' Thorpe's. Con El can play tough.

MAE. So can Jupie Barnes, Raleigh Firman and Mae Black.

PETE. Remember what I said. (*starts to exit but MAE speaks with sudden urgency*)

MAE. Pete!

PETE. (*stopping*) Gotta get to work.

MAE. (*making it a blunt command to cover her terrible concern*) Now just a damn minute. There's a chill in this fall air. You watch your step down under.

PETE. (*suggestively*) Couldn't you think of somethin' a little more interestin' for me to watch?

MAE. Lemme see. Well, there's Jock Yablonski. Yeah! He's real fine to watch.

PETE. (*shaking his head, exiting*) You're gettin' worse than Diller. Two of you talk like paradise is just around the bend and Yablonski's the only one knows where the road turns.

MAE. (*laughing*) You said it, Honey. (*exits*)

Scene 4. "At the Mines"

(*MEN arrive at the mine. They talk over the sound of the mine in operation. They get their gear ready as they talk.*)

HANK. Mornin', Pete, up to another day are you? (*shivers*) Got us a chill in the air.

PETE. Real fine of you to remind us of that, Hank. Real fine.

DILLER. (*enters with gear*) Gimme a hand, will you, Sunshine?

PETE. (*while HANK helps DILLER*) "Sunshine"—that's a good name for him! (*laughs*)

HANK. (*giving voice to the concern from which he shielded RALEIGH*) If I ain't happy there's a reason. Remember Raleigh's brother was with that first shift over at Hurricane Creek. Buried thirty-three men standing up. Just this kind of weather when the chill starts dryin' up the underground air.

PETE. Federal inspector's been here twice this year; he ain't found nothin' wrong.

HANK. What's that prove, 'cept his pockets is a little fatter.

DILLER. Okay, Chuckles. I been workin' here three years. Every one of those years, soon's a chill sets in, you warn us of disaster, and every one of those years we end up safe and sound.

HANK. (*spokesman for all of their darker thoughts*) Maybe this fall we're due.

DILLER. (*laughing with PETE at HANK'S customary pessimism*) You are somethin'! Only a pessimist like Henry John Lewis Firman could look at four safe years and see disaster. Lemme ask you somethin', Hank— if there was a half a glass of beer in front of you, would you say it was half full or half empty?

HANK. All depends on who was needin' to drink it.

(*ALL three laugh. There is a loud crash.*)

PETE. (*jumping*) What in the hell was that noise?

HANK. Just the first cage hittin' bottom. Now who's jumpy?

(*HANK and PETE rough-house playfully. DILLER breaks them up. They start to pack up their gear when FRANK, one of Tony Boyle's campaign organizers, enters. Boyle is the current President of the United Mine Workers of America. In the upcoming UMWA election, the progressive miners are pulling their support from him and throwing it to Jock Yablonski, a contender for the UMWA presidency whose promise to clean up the union has the ring of truth. The contempt these men feel for Boyle's organizer is palpable.*)

FRANK. Mornin' boys. How's it goin?

DILLER. (*waiting a beat before answering*) Can't complain.

FRANK. Least way's not so's anyone upstairs can hear you, that right, Diller?

DILLER. (*cooly firm*) Oh, I don't mind the people upstairs hearin' from me, Frank, don't mind at all.

FRANK. That's good to know. Like to keep everything in the union open and above board...which brings me to why I'm here. How much you boys plannin' to kick in to see Mr. Boyle gets re-elected.

(*silence*)

Well, you don't have to tell me now. You can send your checks over to the campaign headquarters. Now endorse 'em real clear so's we can read 'em. We like to know everyone who's with us, okay? (*starts to leave, then speaks in a cold threatening tone*) Line's gotta be drawn real clear between us and that piece of red meat, Yablonski.

(*FRANK exits. Men are silent for several beats.*)

HANK. (*bursts out*) God, he makes my skin crawl!

PETE. (*trying to calm everyone*) That's his job.

DILLER. Yeah, he knows we don't support Boyle, so he's tryin' to put a little scare in us.

HANK. (*with his customary dry humor*) By the looks of us, I'd say he done a pretty good job.

PETE. Contribution for Boyle. Should've asked him if he had change for a dime.

(*ALL laugh and start to leave for the elevator except DILLER, who heads off in another direction*)

DILLER. Enough of this early mornin' cheer. See you muskrats later.

PETE. Hey, what's up? You ain't goin' down with us?

DILLER. 'Fraid not. They're makin' me work alone today. Punishment, I guess, for organizin' that grievance committee 'bout the water leak in shaft number four. Company couldn't buy me off, so they're tryin' to scare me off. (*turns to go*)

HANK. (*angrily, knowing the seriousness of the situation*) The *union* mediated that grievance, didn't they? All grievances supposed to be anonymous. That's in our contract. If you ask me, one of Boyle's goons is playin' pattycake with the company to get you silenced permanently.

PETE. One more reason to get Yablonski in.

HANK. (*trying to cool off the tempers that have flared*) God, you two sound like a broken record. Every time I bring up a problem, you say Yablonski can fix it. What about my love life? Can he fix that too?

DILLER. (*relaxing out of his anger*) I don't think even Yablonski would tackle a problem that severe.

(*ALL laugh*)

HANK. Get on with you. (*with deep-felt concern*) But you take care, hear?

DILLER. (*starting to exit*) Always do. Always do.

PETE. (*calling after him*) You'll be all alone down there. No one to help watch out for fallin' rock. You get injured, you could lie there for hours and no one would know.

DILLER. (*stopping and turning*) Look, in my short, beautiful life, company thugs have roughed me up 'til there ain't a smooth part on my body. Even had a few shots whiz by this dimpled cheek and I'm still here. This is one stubborn, donkey-ass miner who can take care of hisself. (*exiting and calling over his shoulder*) So you take the east cage and I'll take the west, and I'll be in hell afore ye!

PETE. (*calling after him*) You just take care.

(*HANK and PETE collect their gear and enter the elevator as the CHORUS sings from offstage*)

> We got heroes in this land,
> Red, black, white, yellow and tan,
> They work in coal and plow the land.
> It's on their backs this country began.

PETE. (*pressing the elevator's start button*) Here we go. (*elevator starts, descends a few feet, then stops suddenly*)

HANK. No we don't. Damn relic stalled again. (*calling up for help*) Hey! We're stuck! Hey!! (*joking with PETE*) You just watch, next time this elevator stalls and keeps us from workin', the company'll dock our pay.

PETE. Or call it a paid vacation and ask for a little kick-back. (*tries in vain to get the elevator moving*)

HANK. (*shouting up*) We're down here!

PETE. Pity I didn't bring my needle point. (*in a whisper*) Now that we got some time to talk, you gonna join up with Yablonski or not?

HANK. Why you whisperin'? You afraid this elevator's got ears?

PETE. You damn right.

HANK. So why should I stick my neck out and get it chopped off? Hell, every time Boyle says "Jump," Yablonski asks, "How high, and should I smile for the TV camera while I'm at it?"

PETE. You wasn't born yesterday. Yablonski had to stick with Boyle 'til he knew he wasn't leadin' a one-man band. And with the pressure the company's been putting on the UMW's membership lately...

HANK. I know all about company pressure. But I also know about rotten union leadership. It wasn't...

PETE. (*infuriated*) No one's denyin'...

HANK. (*warming to his argument*) Shut up, will you? I'm talkin'. It wasn't the company got rid of Big Jim Thornesbury over in District Thirty last year for leadin' those wildcat strikes. It was the union. They got rid of him for good.

PETE. Am I talkin' to a wall? That's one of the reasons why we're throwing our weight behind Yablonski...

HANK. (*going right on*) It was the union again that charged the miners who supported the Black Lung Association with dual unionism. And I ain't heard Yablonski take that one on.

PETE. Give him...

HANK. And you know what that means to a disabled miner, like your own brother. No more medical benefits!

PETE. (*diverting his anger by shouting up to those at ground level*) Hey, we're stuck!

HANK. Damn right we're stuck. They got us in a squeeze play to end 'em all. Coal company's on one side; union thugs on the other. We can't win for losin'.

PETE. I'm through arguing with you. Diller's organizin' the Yablonski rally for this Sunday. Put up or shut up.

HANK. (*Grudgingly. Now that he's blown off steam, he'd just as soon be won over.*) I don't know. All union leaders can't be bad, law of averages says there's gotta be a good one somewhere.

PETE. (*sensing the mood shift*) Talk is Yablonski might be another John L. Lewis.

HANK. Lewis would never have sat still and let Boyle ruin the union. Anyway, you been a miner long enough to know talk is cheap.

(*A jolt is felt and the elevator descends. This phase of the argument ends.*)

PETE. Here we go—on our way to where the sun don't shine. (*HANK starts laughing*) What are you laughin' at? You gone slap-happy on me?

HANK. Speakin' of my namesake, you know that story about John L. and the stooge?

PETE. Even if I did, you'd tell it to me anyhow.

(*The cage continues down the shaft. It will arrive at the bottom and the men will exit. The lights in the mines are blue. There is the sound of water. The space is cramped as the men crawl under the structure.*)

HANK. (*laughing fondly*) It seems whenever a stooge spoke out at a public meetin' against the union, old John L.'d march that burly frame of his right down to the front row, sit hisself down so'd everyone could see him, and then stare at the guy's feet. Lewis'd just sit there starin' 'til everyone else in the hall was starin' at the same place, not hearin' a word the stooge said.

(*HANK crawls through the mine, PETE following*)

PETE. Speakin' of feet, you better get some shoes. Yours got no more tread than the tires on my pick-up.

HANK. That was one great Lewis story, wasn't it?

PETE. 'Stead of listenin' to your stories, I'd like to tighten the headings in this shaft and get the hell outta here. Too many gas pockets.

(*CHORUS singing offstage as men work*)

> Methane gas, sudden rock fall,
> Black dust so thick he hardly breathes at all,
> Sets his fuses, shoots the coal,
> Sucks the dust and powder into his soul.

HANK. I wonder how things are goin' over t' Jupie's?

PETE. I ain't worried. Jupie is one strong mountain woman. And our wives ain't nothin' to sneeze at. Company will be able to budge them 'bout as easy as they used to budge old Mother Jones. (*relishing the name*) Old Mother Jones, you ever heard the one about her at Red Warrior Camp coal strike?

HANK. Now who's tellin' stories?

PETE. (*emphatically*) This ain't a story. It's the truth.

(*HANK and PETE exit to another part of the mine*)

Scene 5. "Turn of the Century Appalachia"

(*Simultaneously the play goes back in time to the turn of the century. Three WOMEN enter the stage, one at a time. They are in a state of awesome expectation, awaiting the arrival of one of the greatest labor organizers this country has ever known: "Mother" Mary Harris Jones.*)

WOMAN 1. She's comin! She's comin!

WOMAN 2. She'll know what to do.

WOMAN 3. Oh my God, look at all them soldiers. I'm gonna run warn her.

WOMAN 2. Not me. I'd rather face the militia than her. She's got no use for cowards.

WOMAN 1. We gotta warn her. She's a battler but she ain't bullet proof!

WOMAN 2. I'm standin' with her. I'd rather be me beside her than those soldiers agin' her.

(*WOMEN sing*)

Patriotic Soldiers

The patriotic soldiers
Came a marchin' down the pike
Prepared to shoot and slaughter
In that coal mining strike.

With whiskey in their bellies
And vengeance in their souls,
They prayed God would help them
Shoot the miners full of holes.

In front of those brave soldiers
Loomed a sight you seldom see:
A white-haired rebel woman
Whose age was eighty-three.

"Charge!" cried the valiant captain
In awful thunder-tones,
And the patriotic soldiers charged
And captured Mother Jones.

(*MOTHER JONES appears in all her feisty glory, challenging the U.S. militia, not depicted on stage. MOTHER JONES looks at the audience as if they were the militia.*)

MOTHER JONES. Stand back, young man! Don't you move another step! You think I've never seen a gun before? I've been fightin' your kind a long time. I'm Mother Jones, from Colorado and Utah, from Idaho and Pennsylvania, from New York and Kentucky, and Virginia and West Virginia. And I remember Tennessee. Yes, I remember Tennessee. (*MOTHER JONES sings*)

Mother Jones Song

Fever took the poor of Memphis,
It killed them day by day.
It took my four young children,
Took my workin' man away.

But I found out in those sad days
And through those nights of grief
The poor folk are my people
From Denver to Tennessee.
A mother's job is fighting for
The human family.

> I was born in 1830,
> So they tell it.
> I died in 1930,
> And I say
> To be born ain't the beginning,
> And to die ain't really the end.
> The struggle goes before winning;
> The straightest of roads has a bend.

They call me Mother and they call me true.
I'm a mother through and through.
I'm a mother to all the poor ones,
The maimed and crippled, too.

Those that need me are the working class,
Of all God's children the best!
Workers, you're my class,
North, south, east and west.

I will be your best friend
'Til they take me to my final rest!

> I was born in 1830,
> So they tell it.
> I died in 1930,
> And I say
> To be born ain't the beginning,
> And to die ain't really the end.
> The struggle goes before winning.
> The straightest of roads has a bend.

This Mother was a rabble-rouser,
A hell-cat organizer.
I liked whiskey and bar room talk.
Spent more nights in jail than out.

They put this old Mother behind bars
To stop her cold,
But they soon found out
When old's not old.

There's enough fight in this old girl
To stop the bosses cold!

> I was born in 1830,
> So they tell it.
> I died in 1930,
> And I say
> To be born ain't the beginning,
> And to die ain't really the end.
> The struggle goes before winning,
> The straightest of roads has an end.

(It is 1886. MOTHER JONES is preparing to speak at a Knights of Labor meeting. She addresses the audience.)

MOTHER JONES. It was back in 1870 when I first joined up strong with labor. I enrolled in the Knights of Labor, and from then on, whenever labor needed me, 'til I was 99 years old, I went. You're thinkin' it was illegal to organize in my day. Sure it was! Everything that benefitted the workin' men and women of this land was illegal. Still is!

CROWD. *(entering the hall and speaking severally)* Hello Mother! Good to see you, Mother Jones!

MOTHER JONES. Hello, Friends! Glad you could make it!

CROWD. *(severally)* So are we, Mother! We wouldn't miss it, Mother.

MOTHER JONES. I guess you all know I just got out of jail...*(pausing, then with wry humor)*...again!

(CROWD laughs)

I asked a man there how he happened to be behind bars. He said, "Mother, I stole a pair of shoes." I told him he should have stolen a railroad. Then he'd be a United States Senator!

(CROWD roars, MOTHER lets her voice soar)

That's why I say to all you assembled in this Knights of Labor hall, 'til we can clean up this country and let the Stars and Stripes wave in all her glory, take her down!

(MOTHER JONES' ferocity terrifies the CROWD. Some start to leave, but one MAN steps forward.)

MAN. I'll do it, Mother!

MOTHER JONES. There's a young man with guts!

MAN. (*going to the flag*) My class wove this flag, we live under this flag and we'll die under this flag. But I'll be damned if we'll *starve* under this flag.

(*The MAN tears the flag down. The CROWD is varied in their responses: some applaud, but most are terrified. A WOMAN steps forward.*)

WOMAN. Me and my daughter want to shake your hand. (*they shake, but don't release the MAN'S hand*)

MAN. Consider it shook.

(*the tension is broken and the CROWD responds with laughter*)

MOTHER JONES. And we're going to shake them at the top; those we work for—ten, twelve, fourteen hours a day and then return to our homes too tired to breathe. Every time we ask 'em for anything, we get beat up; we get thrown in creeks. Well, we've been pushed around long enough. So that's why I say to you on this day, May first, 1886, I want all you men to get your women.

MEN. (*rising*) We'll do it, Mother. We'll sure get 'em!

MOTHER JONES. And I want you women to get your children.

(*WOMEN rise and cheer*)

CHILD. My mom will bring me!

MOTHER JONES. And I want you grandfolks to make certain your families are there. (*CROWD roars in approval*) And then I want you all to go out in the streets and stand there. For how long?

CROWD. Until we get our eight hour day!

MOTHER JONES. And that's just the beginning!

(*CROWD again grows fearful when MOTHER JONES implies there will be more beyond this action. They start talking fearfully among themselves. MOTHER JONES looks around silently assessing the situation.*)

MOTHER JONES. What's wrong?

MAN. (*says something to his neighbor, then steps uncertainly forward*) Some people been talkin', and I may as well ask, ain't there some anarchists mixed up in this?

WOMAN. They gonna turn this eight hour day around to serve their own godlessness?

MAN. *Chicago Tribune* says on May first every lamppost in the city's gonna be decorated with an anarchist carcass!

(*The CROWD starts to leave. MOTHER JONES' ferocity stops them.*)

MOTHER JONES. I'll tell you one thing, young man. They ain't gettin' this carcass! (*slaps her bottom, her courage gives the CROWD courage*)

MAN. You're seventy-three years old and you ain't afraid of them?

MOTHER JONES. (*tough as nails*) I'm seventy-*six* and I ain't afraid of nothin'! (*starting with low, spitting rage and building, carrying the CROWD with her*) But ain't that their same old tricks! First they make sure you worry about everything but your tired backs, and your sick lungs, and your hungry children...

CROWD. (*beginning an angry undercurrent*) That's true. Yes, the children...(*they continue talking, but are barely audible*)

MOTHER JONES. Meantime them Armours, Swifts, Mellons, Fields and McCormacks walk over us with royal strides, being made, they think, of finer clay then us Irish...

CROWD. Irish!

(*each PERSON then, with great pride calls out his or her own nationality, and the CROWD echoes and applauds*)

French! Swedish! Jews! Italians! Welsh! Indian! Negroes!

CHILD. (*doing a little dance*) Russian!

MOTHER JONES. And all the nationalities of working folk, who do their work for them, fatten their bellies, line their pockets and swell their goddamn pride. Well I say, let's show 'em!

CROWD. Say it again, Mother! Say it again, Mother! Say it again!

MOTHER JONES. Alright! I'll say it again! Let's show 'em!

(*ALL laugh and applaud. A YOUNG MAN makes his way through the CROWD.*)

YOUNG MAN. Mother Jones, we got a surprise for you.

ANOTHER MAN. You want to hear it?

MOTHER JONES. Is it a good surprise?

ANOTHER MAN. You damn betcha!

MOTHER JONES. Then you damn betcha I wanna hear it!

MAN. The Mother Jones Organizing Committee down at the Denton Mines has got itself a barbershop quartet, Mother. This here is Cliff Oden, Sam Lucy, Bill Martinson and...

(*AMOS' SISTER comes forward and the MAN is dumbfounded*)

MAN. My, Amos, how you have changed!

AMOS' SISTER. I'm here, Mother. My brother couldn't make it, so I'm here to sing for him.

MOTHER JONES. Here's a sister after my own heart.

AMOS' SISTER. Thank you, Mother.

(*the MEN are obviously skeptical*)

MAN. Well, uh...

AMOS' SISTER. "Well, uh" what?

MAN. How can you barbershop sing, when you can't even shave?

(*MEN in the CROWD laugh and hoot*)

AMOS' SISTER. If I didn't have anything but that soup strainer on my face, I wouldn't say nothin'!

(*WOMEN all cheer*)

MAN. Well, I'll be damned! Come on over here!

AMOS' SISTER. (*joining the men*) Well, damned if I won't!

(*QUARTET tunes up with a pitch pipe and a long hum, begins to sing*)

> *Toiling Millions*
>
> Toiling millions now are walking,
> See them marching on!
> All the tyrants now are shaking
> Ere their power's gone!
>
> Storm the fort, ye Knights of Labor,
> Battle for your cause!
> Equal rights for every neighbor;
> Down with tyrant laws.

(*The CROWD applauds wildly as the QUARTET steps down. Realizing that they are appreciated, they quickly step back up to sing.*)

QUARTET. Working men and working women,
             The end is now in sight!

(*ALL joining the anthem*)

ALL.   Take control of our own labor!
             That is labor's right!

MOTHER JONES. Beautiful! Beautiful! That's the way I like to hear my children sing!

(*LISBETH, a little girl, jumps up onto the speaker's platform*)

WOMAN. Lisbeth, you come back here!

MOTHER JONES. Let her stay. I have a special place in my heart for the children of this land. What did you have to say, dear?

LISBETH. I wanted to give you this scarf I knitted, Mother Jones.

MOTHER JONES. Thank you, child. Now I want to give you

something. Good brings good. (*MOTHER JONES sits with LISBETH at her feet*) I'm gonna tell you a story about when me and a lot of poor children went on a long journey. I took an army of young children, just like you, to see the President. We walked for miles through the mill towns and mining towns that had crippled and maimed these children. And all along the way I told folks, "Our kids are being injured and killed in the name of American progress, and it ain't right!" We marched right up to the company bosses with all the fat of the land in their bank accounts. And one of them looked at my hungry, hollow-eyed, listless little children and said, "Of such is the Kingdom of Heaven." (*rising in rage*) And I said, "If heaven is full of hungry little angel children, I want to go to the other place with the bad little boys and girls." Nobody said nothin'. So I told them, there's a lot of empty cups inside these kids' homes, and their fathers' cups are empty inside their dusty lunch pails. Then I looked them straight in the eye and said, "I've got a question for you, and the question is: 'Who needs to drink the cup?'"

(*the PEOPLE rise as they speak over the guitar introduction to "Who Needs to Drink the Cup?"*)

WOMAN. I joined the march in Montana, Mother.

MAN. So did I.

WOMAN. I walked right beside you.

WOMAN. My brother died on that march.

MAN. We'll never forget that march.

WOMAN. It was the hardest thing I ever did, but I was with you every step of the way.

MAN. We remember that question you asked, and we're still askin' it. 'Til we get the answer we want we're gonna keep on askin' it.

MOTHER JONES. Ask the question, my children.

(*ALL sing*)

> *Who Needs to Drink the Cup?*
>
> Who needs to drink the cup?
> Who needs to drink the cup?
> Those who live high at the top
> Or those who mine the dark, way below
> For need of it?

MAN. (*over the last "For need of it"*) Us coal miners starvin' to death in the company towns got the same question.

MOTHER JONES. Ask the question, my son.

ALL MEN. We go to work when the sun is low,
Dark when we leave, darker where we go,
Through a gash in a mountain, down a three-mile hole
Where drag cable sparks light the thirty-inch coal.

ALL.   Who needs to drink the cup?
Who needs to drink the cup?
Those who live high at the top
Or those who mine the dark, way below,
For need of it?

(*The WOMEN exit as they sing "For need of it." The MEN and MOTHER JONES are left on stage.*)

MAN. (*over the last "for need of it."*) And every time we ask that question, Mother, we know what the coal bosses answer.

MOTHER JONES. Tell us that answer again, so we'll hear it, and hate it, and fight it.

(*lights dim on everyone but the CHORUS*)

CHORUS. Coal bosses say to their millionaire friends,
"Buy off those liberal congressmen.
Their safety rules cut our profits down.
If we lose a hundred men,
There's plenty more in town."

(*MEN going into the mines, turning on their blue helmet lights which become the only illumination on the stage*)

MEN.   Tighten up your headings, set the wedges in.
Crawl on your bellies, your troubles just startin'.
This day that's a night, this pit without sun,
Tomorrow's a long shot that may never come!

(*ALL sing as the scene transforms back into present time with HANK, PETE and DILLER working in the mines. The lights from their mining helmets still the only illumination on the stage. MOTHER JONES speaks the words over the ENSEMBLE'S singing, then disappears.*)

MOTHER   Who needs to drink the cup?
JONES   Who needs to drink the cup?
and ALL.   Those who live high at the top,
Or those who mine the dark, way below,
For need of it?

Scene 6. "Outside the Mines"

(MINERS come out of the mines, their work completed for the day. They are cold. Their muscles are stiff. They cough the coal dust out of their lungs.)

DILLER. (emerging from a different area than HANK and PETE) Another day, another dollar.

PETE. But the same old Diller.

DILLER. What could change me? I been a miner so long my character's ossified.

HANK. (his posture revealing a now-chronic bad back) Maybe that's my problem: ossification.

DILLER. How is that back of yours, Hank.

HANK. Still back there.

DILLER. You been to a doctor?

HANK. Yeah. He said he wasn't worried. I said I didn't 'spect he would be. Wasn't his back.

PETE. (to DILLER) You comin' back down with us tomorrow?

DILLER. Missed your old buddy? Heart ached for him a little, did it?

PETE. It wasn't exactly heartache we felt for you friend, more like heartburn.

DILLER. At my age, I'll settle for what I can get. (THEY start to exit) Wonder if the women are still over t' Jupies's?

HANK. If Con El's still there, the women are.

PETE. I'm bettin' on our side to take the first round.

HANK. Yeah, but there's always a second round.

(MEN exit as WOMEN enter)

Scene 7. "Jupie's Home"

(JUPIE, MAE and RALEIGH appear in front of JUPIE'S house. JUPIE is a proud, strong mountain woman, fierce and immovable. Her family has died, so she now lives alone in the family house. To confront the strip miner, BERT, the WOMEN shout over the sound of the threatening bulldozer.)

BERT. (he has obviously been out in the sun a good, long time and is irritated, hot and tired) I can't stand here all day. You were given a warnin'—now move, Jupie.

JUPIE. (*cool as a cucumber, strong as an ox*) Nope. (*repeating a question she has obviously asked numerous times that day, but asking it as though for the first time*) Did I ask why you got that mask on?

BERT. Yes, and I told you. Company gave it for the dust.

JUPIE. And did I tell you, company'd get that damn bulldozer off my land, wouldn't be no dust?

BERT. (*calling offstage toward the bulldozer*) Wait up, Joe. Hold that dozer a minute more.

(*bulldozer motor is turned off*)

JUPIE. (*calling off in the same direction*) You go on and rest now, Honey. It is a hot day. (*back to BERT*) Now you was sayin'.

BERT. You'll be relocated just thirty-six mile from here. It's for your own good.

JUPIE. I'm real glad you're so interested in my happiness, Bert. And you know what'd make me real happy? To stay in my own home. (*her rage erupts*) So why don't you just skiddaddle?

RALEIGH. Did you hear that, Bert? Skiddaddle!

BERT. Now lookee here, girl—

RALEIGH. Don't "girl" me! You know this is where Jupie's folks is buried. You know this is where she was born and where she wants to die.

JUPIE. (*awesome as she relays her knowledge and her warning*) Listen Bert, I know you take your salary from Con El Coal. And I know you can find a judge who's on their payroll to sign an eviction order. And I know you can find a sheriff who's also on their payroll to carry it out. But you listen to me, Mother Earth ain't on their payroll. This land holds my mama and my papa and four generations behind 'em. You try to push this mountain around, and we'll all get back at you.

(*the WOMEN'S tone is low and ominous, suggesting a mysterious retribution beyond human power.*)

MAE. Yeah, Bert. Like Gus Pynes' mountain over in Leesburg. Strippers dug it up and the rain washed it right down Main street.

RALEIGH. Or what happened over in Huntley where a whole mountain started burnin'. Wiped out every home in the valley.

MAE. You keep diggin' up your neighbors' land, and maybe that new ranch-style home of yours'll end up in the Brandywine River. Never can tell about these things.

JUPIE. Mother Earth's got one way and another of strikin' back. But you know what saddens me, almost as much as losin' my home? It's watchin' neighbors like you turnin' 'gainst their own kind.

BERT. (*this strikes deep*) Now lookee here, Jupie...

JUPIE. Oh, it's bad fightin' the company. But it's worse bein' stabbed in the back by your own. I'm just glad your daddy ain't around to see you...may his soul rest in peace...but I'm happy he ain't alive to see you now.

BERT. (*trying to convince them of their lack of sense*) Look, women. You ain't strong enough to fight Con El Coal. Whole mountain of people ain't that strong. Jupie'll get a place not thirty-six mile down the road—it's a lot better than this shack.

RALEIGH. Oh yeah, a lot better. You put her in a place with eighty other folk that's big enough for eight.

MAE. She'll have to pay for God's water, pay double for sewage, triple for heat...

JUPIE. And be charged a ticket price to visit a holler like the one I grew up in...

RALEIGH. 'Cause now it's a tourist attraction.

MAE. Place the land speculatin' man can rest up after spendin' a day sight-seeing us monkey Appalachians.

JUPIE. (*with the strength of the mountain she is protecting*) You'll have to test your strength, young man, 'cause I ain't leavin' here peaceful. And if you drag me off, I'll come back at you. Mark my words, Bert. I'll get back at you and that goddamned company you sold out to! I ain't sure how I'm gonna do it. But you can be sure; you touch this land, and you'll have a hard time sleepin' from there on out.

(*WOMEN lie down in front of JUPIE'S house*)

BERT. (*exasperated*) Now what are you doin'?

JUPIE. Seems clear enough to me, don't it to you gals? We're sittin' here, front of my house, front of where my kin is buried, front of where my nieces and nephews want to play when they come to visit their aunt. Now in order to get that bulldozer over to my place, you're gonna have to ride on over us. (*laughs a clear, strong laugh*) And I'll tell you, Bartholomain, that'll be some ride over these carcasses. Us mountain gals is built to last!

(*WOMEN join in laughter*)

BERT. (*resigned that the WOMEN have won the day*) I'll just go and get the Sheriff and a court order, Jupie, and we'll be back in a couple of days. (*exits*)

RALEIGH. (*calling after him*) Now don't you hurry none, Bert, 'cause we'll be right here.

JUPIE. (*running in direction of BERT'S exit and shouting her defiance*)

If it takes you two weeks to get that court order, if it takes you two months, if it takes you a lifetime, *we'll be right here!* (*JUPIE sings*)

Rain Fallin' on the Mountain

JUPIE. Rain washed out my fields and valleys.
Rain washed out my barren hills.
Rain washed out my dreams of dying
In my wood shack home in the Cumberland hills.

Sun shinin' on the mountain,
Sun shinin' on my home,
Coal dust settles kinda' heavy
It is the end of the day.
It is the end of the day.

My daddy taught me 'bout these mountains;
I've loved 'em ever since.
He said he needed these mountains,
They gave him somethin' to rest his eyes against.

WOMEN. Now they're tearin' down these mountains.
Now they're rippin' down these hills.
Now there ain't hardly nothin'.

JUPIE. Won't leave me nothin' to rest my eyes against. Ain't gonna leave me nothin' to rest my eyes against.

WOMEN. They came to take her from these mountains,
Move her off her land.
Ain't no one left in this holler;
Just a few of us to make a last-ditch stand.
Just a few of us to make a last-ditch stand.

Now they're tearin' down these mountains,
Now they're rippin' down these hills,
Now there ain't hardly nothin'

JUPIE. (*speaking over the last lines of the song*) Nothin' to rest my eyes against...

(*The WOMEN embrace as MOTHER JONES emerges on the upper platform. The WOMEN return home as the scene slowly dissolves to the past.*)

Scene 8. "Women's Mop Brigade"

MOTHER JONES. (*spoken for healing with great sorrow, great pride and immense rage*) It's been a long, hard struggle for laborin' women. Sure we lost some battles; lost some of our bravest and best women in 'em. Mining mountains are red with their blood. Like the great Fanny Sellins, organizer from St. Louis, shot and killed by a mine guard in Pennsylvania. Or Mary Thomas, who kept our sisters at Ludlow singing union songs 'til the U.S. Militia burnt their tent colony down. 'Course, in our long, fightin' history, we won a few, too. Like that female mop brigade in Arnot, Pennsylvania. It was in 1899.

(*It is Arnot, Pennsylvania in 1899. WOMEN enter one at a time carrying mops and brooms, pots and pans. They are worried but determined as they call to their husbands and families, trying to sound calmer than they feel.*)

MOLLY. No, no, I should take the *tin* pie plate. You keep the *glass* one. And don't ask me no questions, 'Cause you ain't gonna get no answers.

MATTIE. Henry, Henry, you're such a flibberty-jibberty! Listen, I'll be back. Don't worry, I ain't worried, so why should you be?

ARVILLA. Now Mama, don't wait up for me.

MOTHER. (*offstage*) 'N why not?

ARVILLA. (*with saucy pride*) 'Cause I might be spendin' the night in jail!

JANE. I gotta go.

HUSBAND. (*offstage*) When'll you be back?

JANE. Whenever you see me!

MOLLIE. Well, Mother, you told us to be here today and it took a whole lot of doin' but here we are!

MATTIE. None of us dared tell our menfolk that we were on our way to something dangerous as all hell.

(*WOMEN are shocked at MATTIE'S tough language*)

ARVILLA. You swore!

MATTIE. I talk tough when I mean tough! And we gotta be tougher 'n toenails 'cause the company's called in over eighty scabs on donkeys!

MOTHER JONES. And you girls are aware that donkeys can be meaner than the scabs that ride 'em!

MOLLIE. Mother, whatever are we gonna do?

MOTHER JONES. Well, I've been railroaded, run over roughshod and horsewaggled to hell and back. And you wanna know what I always did? Put up my dukes and yelled my lungs out!

(*the WOMEN do exactly that*)

MOTHER JONES. Now we got a hard day ahead of us, and the longer we stand here awhoopin' and awhoopin', the harder it's gonna get! Jeremy heard at the company store they got an injunction against your men. They picket, they land in jail. You picket, you land right aside 'em.

(*WOMEN look at one another, aghast. JANE takes a deep breath and summons up her courage.*)

JANE. Well, suppose we do!

(*WOMEN applaud and give support*)

MOTHER JONES. You're full of spit and vinegar! Ready to risk jail to save your men's jobs!

MOLLIE. That's why we're here, Mother.

MATTIE. (*with triumphant courage*) We're gonna keep them scabs outta the mines!

MOTHER JONES. (*with a twinkle*) How ever could a gaggle of defenseless women keep armed scabs away from the mines?

JANE. You got something up your sleeve, don't you Mother? That's why you had us bring these kitchen utensils and wear our finest hats.

MOTHER JONES. Take a look at yonder scraggly oak over there and tell me what you see.

WOMEN. (*all look long and hard, then answer together*) Nothin'.

MOTHER JONES. That's exactly what you're supposed to see. Bea's up there, lookin' out for scabs. Soon's she sees one coming, she'll whoop a warning.

(*BEA gives the sound of a whippoorwill offstage*)

Mattie, you got a big voice?

MATTIE. Bigger 'n thunder.

MOTHER JONES. When you hear Bea awhippoorwillin', you yell, "Charge!" Yell it for me, Mattie!

MATTIE. Charge!

(*each WOMAN echoes the call*)

MOTHER JONES. When she shouts, you run down the mountain toward the scabs, beatin' out your sweet mountain music and yellin' like crazy. The scabs'll think we're banshees outta hell, and the donkeys won't know what to think.

JANE. (*shouts*) We'll do it, Mother! (*adding in a tiny tremulous voice*) But there's one thing we wanna tell you.

MOTHER JONES. What is it, child?

JANE. (*practically in tears*) We're scared.

MOLLIE. Oh Mother, we are.

MATTIE. Scared stiffer'n a frozen bedsheet in December.

MOTHER JONES. So am I scared! But what difference does that make? We've got work to do!

(*All WOMEN raise their brooms and pots in defiance and sing. Their movements are angular, flat-footed, tough. Pots and brooms are used to accentuate a battling spirit.*)

> *Yahoo*
>
> Women, let's fight! We're tough and we're right!
> Clobber them scabs, show 'em our might!
> Yahoo, ay yoo, yahoo, ay ya!
> Yahoo ay ya, ya, ya, ya, ya!
>
> Scabbin' is bad; give it up, lad!
> You'll have scars like you never had!
> Yahoo, ay yoo, yahoo, ay ya!
> Yahoo ay ya, ya, ya, ya, ya!
>
> Cross that line, you'll never come back!
> That's the life-line of our John, Jim and Jack!
> Do the good deed! Follow our lead!
> Let our men fight for the jobs that they need.
> Yahoo, ay yoo, yahoo, ay ya!
> Yahoo ay ya, ya, ya, ya, ya!
>
> Us women got today! We'll say our say!
> We're strong enough to hold a thousand scabs at bay!
> Yahoo, ay yoo, yahoo, ay ya!
> Yahoo ay ya, ya, ya, ya, ya!
>
> Cross that line, you'll never come back!
> That's the life-line of our John, Jim and Jack!

BEA. (*offstage*) Whippoorwill! Whippoorwill!

WOMEN. (*after a moment of stillness which crystallizes the phrase "scared stiff"*) Charge! (*all WOMEN pause one pregnant second then charge, beating on their pots and pans and yelling like crazy as light fades to black*)

Scene 9. "Deep in the Mines"

(*The scene dissolves back to present time. Only the blue lights on the miner's helmets are visible. The MEN arrive at a designated place deep in the mines.*)

DILLER. (*whispering*) Okay, this looks safe. No one should find us here.

HANK. The question is, can we find our way back?

DILLER. We gotta talk fast. Goddamned foreman's been sniffin' my dust all mornin'.

PETE. You keep on organizing for Yablonski, they're gonna blow you outta this mine like a cannon shot.

DILLER. They better have a double barrel, 'cause you'll be alongside me.

(*A noise in the background. HANK goes quickly to check it out.*)

HANK. I don't know if I'm overhearin' things or things is overhearin' me, but I got a spooky feelin' this coal is alive and watchin' me.

PETE. Relax. The reason you got a feelin' someone's watchin' you is someone usually is.

HANK. That's real relaxin'.

DILLER. It's who's gonna be watchin' us tomorrow that's the important thing. Boyle's goons are sure to be there. What we don't know is if they're gonna try any rough stuff.

HANK. Who's on security?

DILLER. Whatever security we got will be in our numbers.

PETE. Exactly. The only way to make sure us votin' miners don't get singled out and picked off is to get everybody to the rally: every miner, retired miner, woman, child, dog and cat in town. (*turning to HANK*) Now tomorrow's the big one. You're comin' out clear as a bell for Yablonski, right?

HANK. Can beggars be choosey?

DILLER. (*deadpan humor*) That's what I call an inspiring endorsement. Deserves some TV time. I can see it: big picture of Yablonski in front of an American flag. Hank over there to one side sayin': "Can beggars be choosey?"

(*ALL start to return to their places of work*)

Okay, let's get back to work.

PETE. I wasn't planning on goin' swimming.

DILLER. See you tomorrow at nine A.M. And you better bring a gun or two—just in case.

Scene 10. "Yablonski Rally"

(PEOPLE enter from all sides, talking animatedly to each other. Signs and banners, and balloons fill the stage.)

MAE. Hey, Diller, you're gettin' better lookin' every day! Raleigh, is the bus unloaded?

RALEIGH. All set.

JUPIE. Am I late? Good to see you, Hank.

(PETE enters carrying a misspelled sign marked "Miners for Yablonsky")

DILLER. What are you doing here, Johnny?

JOHNNY. Oh, I seen you clowns and thought I'd come check out the funny show.

PETE. *(standing on the speaker's platform)* I want to thank all of you for comin' out today.

RALEIGH. Well, you're mighty welcome.

(ALL laugh, applaud)

PETE. I know you're stickin' your necks out just bein' here. Later on we're gonna show our thanks with a barbeque and some guitar pickin', but first, and the reason you're here, let me present the Yablonski organizer from our district—most of you know him—Diller Oden!

MAE. Pete! Oh, Pete!

PETE. Whoops! I almost forgot. My wife Mae and a carload from the mill come over to help us out. I'd like you to give them all a fightin' Union welcome.

(CROWD cheers enthusiastically. DILLER comes forward applauding the mill workers.)

MAE. We're just here to say whether it's brown lung or black lung, it's all the same fight. Vote for Jock Yablonski!

(CROWD cheers enthusiastically, then quiets as DILLER begins his address)

DILLER. *(starting his address)* Now I'm not sayin' that Jock Yablonski is the answer to all our problems. But he looks like where we gotta go, right now, with this Union. *(reflecting)* You know, with all the big money floatin' around at the head of some unions, it's hard to remember that unions was built with the flesh and blood of workin' men and women, fight for fight, and gain for gain.

CROWD. *(responding with names of places where blood has been shed in the struggle)* Cripple Creek! Ludlow! Haymarket! Harlan County! Pullman! Buck's County!

DILLER. A lot of money has been spent to corrupt our unions. And a lot of good boys have been put into prison, shot, and thrown in creeks to weaken our unions.

CROWD. *(responding with names of martyrs they know)* Jessie Wilson! And Tom Allen! Maggie Sims!

DILLER. That money was spent for a reason!

PETE. You can say that again.

(CROWD responds.)

DILLER. The reason is the bosses know us workin' folk got one organization we can build to get justice and better conditions.

CROWD. *(rising one by one and joining the chant)* The Union! The Union! The Union!

DILLER. That's right! The goddamn union! Now the big power consortiums are takin' more and more coal from non-union areas like Wyoming and Arizona.

CROWD. *(calling out names of other non-union mining areas)* Utah! Colorado! Montana! Iowa! Kentucky!

DILLER. The big railroads are tied in with 'em. The whole national energy policy is geared to movin' away from union coal!

CROWD. *(jumping up)* Bring 'em back!

DILLER. And you know why? *(answering his own question)* They're afraid of the UMW!

CROWD. *(criss-crossing the stage)* The UMW! The UMW! The UMW! The UMW! The UMW!

DILLER. *(riding over the chant)* They want to strip mine cheap coal and pay scab wages to do it!

PETE. The only good scab is a dead scab.

DILLER. So we got to have a union that'll fight like hell to expand the membership and protect our jobs...

CROWD. That's right!

DILLER. Hold the line on safety battles.

CROWD. Firm! Hold it! We need safety!

DILLER. Fight for land reclamation.

CROWD. Our forests! No strip minin'!

DILLER. And unionize those new mines on the far-off hills!

CROWD. Utah! Colorado! Arizona! Wyoming!

DILLER. Now, Jock Yablonski says he wants a democratic union.

CROWD. *(beginning to chant softly)* Yablonski! Yablonski! Yablonski! Yablonski! Yablonski!

DILLER. (*over the chant*) That's a start. We have to open the way for all unions in this country to be democratic, 'cause maybe then we'll all pull together and get some real labor power in this country!

CROWD. (*rising to a crescendo as DILLER concludes his speech*) Yablonski! Yablonski! Yablonski! Yablonski! Yablonski!

HANK. (*to PETE, who is carrying his "Yablonsky" sign*) Hey Pete, you spelled Yablonski's name wrong!

(*CROWD laughs*)

PETE. (*turning sign around to read it*) Who cares how he's spelled, as long as he does a good job?

JOHN HENRY. And he's gonna. But not without some muscle from the rank and file! So I say let's get behind him. (*beginning to play his guitar*) You gonna join me on this one, Diller?

DILLER. Sure. (*sings with JOHN HENRY*)

        Gotta Organize

DILLER   Coal boss got the money, he's got the might.
AND   Won't back down without a fight.
JOHN   No matter how strong, he won't last long
HENRY.   If we get together and organize.

TWO MEN. (*dancing*)
           Laborin' man is built to last
           From Warsaw, Naples and Belfast.
           Workin' all day for a poor man's pay?
           Gotta get together and organize!

ALL.   It's all for one and one for all.
           Organize the workplace, large and small.
           Might be a rocky ride,
           Set our differences aside.
           Get together, organize!

(*instrumental break with dancing*)

MEN.   Murphy, Lewis, John Brophy, too,
           And that is listing just a few
           Each minin' man has lent a hand,
           Built a union rock on which we stand.

WOMEN.   Sell-out bosses been around too long
           Their hold on us is too damn strong!

> Rank and file gotta move 'em along.
> Gotta get together and organize!

ALL.   It's all for one and one for all.
        Organize the workplace, large and small.
        Might be a rocky ride,
        Set our differences aside,
        Get together, organize!

PETE. Who do we support?
CROWD. Yablonski!!

DILLER. Now we got a new good man
         He wants to lend us a helpin' hand.
         If he's got the will, then we'll find a way!
         Gotta get together and organize!

(PETE exits with a whoop. The CROWD follows, leaving DILLER alone on stage.)

ALL..   It's all for one and one for all.
        Organize the workplace, large and small.

(CHORUS offstage, slowly, hauntingly)

> Might be a rocky ride,
> Set our differences aside,
> Get together, organize!

Scene 11. "Diller Alone"

(Scene dissolves, leaving DILLER alone in his house. He starts to get ready for bed, but a noise outside stops him. He locks one door, then a VOICE outside calls to him)

FIRST THUG. Diller, we wanna talk to you.

(DILLER locks the other door)

SECOND THUG. Now you let us come on in. If you don't, we're takin' you out. And we're takin' your queer boyfriend with you.

(*DILLER unlocks the doors. The THUGS take up positions on either side of him.*)

FIRST THUG. We been readin' that grievance petition you wrote and got all them dumb miners to sign.

DILLER. I didn't *get* them to sign nothin'.

SECOND THUG. Well, we read it, and it gave us a grievance.

DILLER. They're old enough to make up their own—

SECOND THUG. (*interrupting*) And you been talkin' up Yablonski to any damn fool who will listen. You botherin' us, Boy. Flauntin' your fag, your petitions, your dumb Polock Yablonski.

FIRST THUG. Get that Yablonski in the union, and he'd just turn it over to the Communists, you know that. (*pulling a club out from behind him*) You gonna quit talkin' him up, Boy?

DILLER. It ain't me that started—

FIRST THUG. We've heard enough!

(*The two MEN beat DILLER to his knees and then they rush away. CHORUS enters the stage and sings as DILLER slowly pulls himself up.*)

This Man is Down

This man is down, like men before,
Losing one battle, knowin' there'll be more.
Harry Sims, he came to educate,
Left bleeding outside the hospital gate,
Robins sang to this man of a boy,
Cottonwoods sighed when he finally died.
He carried our load down a long and lonesome road.

This man is down, like men before,
Losing one battle, knowin' there'll be more.
A boy named Fred and his mother Mae
Were burned alive that Ludlow day.
Wind swept the ashes through the amber glow
Dropped them down on the terrified town.
He carried our load down a long and lonesome road.

This man is down, like men before,
Losing one battle, knowin' there'll be more.

(*DILLER exits. MOTHER JONES enters, her face a mask of sadness as she sees in memory a dead child. CHORUS continues singing.*)

A little girl came to Mother Jones,
"Mother, help me, I'm chilled to the bone."

In that fire-hot night, her mothers knew
Dawn would never come to that hungry little one.
She carried our load down a long and lonesome road.

(*as the CHORUS exits*)

This man is down, like men before,
Losing one battle, knowin' there'll be more.

MOTHER JONES. (*speaks as the chorus sings, not the voice of
mourning, but of record-keeper and prophet*) This man is down like men
before, losing one battle, knowing there'll be more.

Scene 12. *"Rape of the Land"*

(*MOTHER JONES remains on stage overlooking the action as MAE,
RALEIGH, and JUPIE enter one at a time and position themselves in
front of Jupie's house for the final onslaught in the fight to save Jupie's
house from the strip miners. It is night time.*)

MOTHER JONES. (*as WOMEN enter*) I am not blind to the short-
comings of my people. We're divided by selfishness, prejudice, and
sometimes just plain stupidity. But this knowledge does not outweigh the
fact that my class, the working class, is exploited, starved and beaten into
submission. And whenever we strike out against these inhuman conditions, we are judged in the rigged courts of the ruling class.

SHERIFF. (*offstage, through a megaphone*) Jupie, this is Sheriff Zinne-
man, and I got a court order. I'm sorry to tell you this, Girl, but your pa
didn't have no mineral rights to this land. It all belongs to Con El. So
you're gonna have to come down outta there, Girl. Like I said, Jupie, I got
a court order. You all come down, or I'll have to send the boys up to get
you.

(*Strip MINERS in masks enter to take JUPIE from her home. The
WOMEN put up a valiant struggle, but, in the end, the MEN prevail as
they forcibly remove the WOMEN from Jupie's land. During the struggle,
the CHORUS slowly sings.*)

Rain fallin' on the mountain,
Hard rain washin' down the road,
Strip miners didn't leave her nothin'
Didn't leave her nothin' to rest her eyes against.

(*The CHORUS sings until the WOMEN are pushed, dragged, and beaten
offstage. Then there is the sound of rain. BERT returns and prepares his*

crew to demolish Jupie's house and strip mine the land.)

BERT. Damn, it's rainin'. Okay, boys, let's make the first cut up behind the house. Move that dozer up the back driveway.

STRIPPER. *(offstage, with alarm in his voice)* But Bert, that's where...

BERT. I know that's where the cemetery is, but it's also where the goddamned coal is!

STRIPPER. *(offstage)* Hey Boss, I'm havin' trouble gettin' traction here...

BERT. Will you get diggin'? We're a week behind on this job already! *(puts on his mask)*

STRIPPER. *(offstage, with terror still in his voice)* Boss, you better come up here. Something's wrong.

BERT. *(ripping off his mask)* Can't you guys do anything right? *(crosses to look)* Now what is it?

(an eerie, ominous sound fills the stage)

STRIPPER. *(offstage)* Rats!

BERT. Rats! Oh my God, oh my God!

STRIPPER. *(offstage)* There's a million rats up here!

BERT. Get down off that rig fast! Fast! No, don't! That's what they want. Rats'll attack you if you move sudden. Bang that stick you got, and I'll bang mine. The noise'll scare 'em.

(softly, THEY tap the ground with their sticks in a rhythmical beat)
That's it.

STRIPPER. *(offstage)* They're goin' back in the ground.

BERT. *(speaking slowly, ominously, rhythmically)* Now get down, slow like. Real slow. You know, I hear this same thing happened when they was diggin' in Colorado. Unearthed a huge colony of rats. Here they're right where Jupie's dead is, sort of like they're watch dogs, guardin' the dead.

(STRIPPER appears)

But never mind. We'll come back tomorrow night with some dynamite and blast these rodents to kingdom come.

(THEY start to move off slowly as the lights fade)

Move slow and easy. Don't provoke 'em.

STRIPPER. That is what they remind me of.

BERT. What are you talkin' about?

STRIPPER. The rats, they're like watch dogs guarding the dead.

(THEY exit. The strong figure of MOTHER JONES remains as the lights fade to black.)

Act II

Scene 1. "Congressional Hearing"

(*Two SENATORS enter and assemble their materials readying themselves to meet the Kentucky Welfare Rights Committee. RALEIGH, HANK, PETE, MAE, and JUPIE enter the meeting extremely agitated. They have just heard on the radio that Yablonski has been murdered. They whisper, barely audible.*)

MAE. My God, is it true?

PETE. Yablonski, his wife and daughter, all dead.

RALEIGH. Who do you think did it?

JUPIE. I'll give you two guesses.

PETE. Where does that leave us?

HANK. Up death's creek without a paddle.

(*THEY quiet one another down as Congress begins*)

SENATOR SCOTT. These hearings have been called to investigate the operations of public assistance programs in the Appalachian region. We are particularly interested in the counties of Pike, Harlan, and Bell in Kentucky where the percentage of the population receiving federal aid is the highest in the nation. We have already heard testimony from welfare and AFDC administrators. Today we will question citizen's groups. We begin our questions with my colleague, the senior Senator from Pennsylvania, Senator Riner.

SENATOR RINER. Thank you, Senator. Before I begin my direct questions, I have a comment I would like to make. I have just been informed, as I am sure many of you already know, of the tragic death of your UMW presidential candidate, Joseph Yablonski. His death is a great loss to his people, as well as a deep personal loss to me, your representative.

RALEIGH. (*not able to restrain herself any longer, but in a very low tone*) He's full of...

(*HANK quiets her*)

SENATOR RINER. Now, if we could be so mundane as to turn to the business at hand, these hearings have been called to investigate inequities in the distribution of welfare in the Appalachian region, where payments are among the highest in the nation. I understand that several witnesses on the list today are not actually welfare recipients, but are representing local welfare organizations. We will admit their testimony if it is given in an orderly manner, with proper documentation...

RALEIGH. (*interrupting, but with proper respect stemming, in part, from her nervousness*) Excuse me, Sir, we'd like to make a statement. You say our welfare payments in Appalachia are too high. We'd like to explain why that is. I want to read somethin' to you. (*has misplaced the letter she wants to read, and is more nervous than ever*) Hank, where is it?

HANK. I've got it.

RALEIGH. (*agitated, she whispers to HANK a bit too loudly*) Give it to me. (*to the SENATOR, with letter in hand*) The man who said this was my father. He was talkin' to the county judge about why he wasn't sendin' us kids to school.

SENATOR RINER. I don't exactly see the relevance.

RALEIGH. (*again interrupting and answering his concern*) Things haven't changed much since my Pa's day. Poverty breeds poverty. Now the county judge was threatenin' to throw my dad in jail 'cause us kids wasn't in school, and this is what my dad said to that judge: (*the painful memory makes it difficult for her to speak*) "My kids have not been goin' to school, and nobody wants them to go more than I do. I've been out of work for four years. I been all over this coal field and over into...

(*The lights dim slowly on the present and the scene dissolves into the past. Raleigh's FATHER enters and speaks to the county JUDGE.*)

RALEIGH'S FATHER. (*simultaneously with RALEIGH, whose voice dims as the lights dim, leaving only her FATHER speaking*)...I've been out of work for four years. Been all over this coal field and into Virginny and West Virginny lookin' for work. I've made trip after trip to Indianny, Ohio, even Michigan, and I couldn't find a day's work anywhere. I drawed out all my unemployment compensation over three years ago, and the only income I've had since has been just a day's work now and then doin' farm work for somebody. I sold my car and shotgun, my radio, and even my watch to get money to feed my family. And now I don't have a thing left in the world that anybody'd want. I'm dead broke and about to give up. I live over two miles from the schoolhouse, and I simply don't have any money to buy my children shoes or clothes to wear. Last spring, the company that owns the coal rights augered my land and totally destroyed it. I couldn't *give* the land away now. Me and my boy, we got one pair of shoes between us. When he wears 'em, I don't have none; when I wear 'em, he don't have none. I guess if it wasn't for those little rations the government give us, my family would've starved to death long afore now. If you want to fine me, I ain't got a penny to pay it with, and I'll have to lay it out in jail. If you think puttin' me in jail will help my young 'uns any, then go ahead and do it, and I'll be glad of it. If the county attorney or the truant officer...

(*lights gradually dim on the FATHER and the scene returns to the present, illuminating the Congressional hearing*)

RALEIGH. (*her voice joining her FATHER'S and taking over as the memory dissolves into present time*) If the country attorney or the truant officer will find me a job where I can work out somethin' for my kids to wear, I'll be much obliged to 'em as long as I live. (*passionately, sure that the SENATOR has been moved by the ageless plea of poverty*) Does that tell you anything about why we need welfare?

SENATOR RINER. (*absolutely unmoved*) That personal history is very moving, Mrs. Firman. But these hearings have been called to talk about what's happening today in Appalachia, not twenty years ago with your father.

HANK. Like she told you, Sir, the story's the same today, only a little worse, what with pollution and automation...

JUPIE. A lot worse.

SENATOR RINER. How can that be? There are benefits today that did not even exist when Mrs. Firman's father...

PETE. (*interrupting, desperately persuasive*) Oh, sure us UMW miners get medical and disability benefits—when we can get certified sick enough, that is! But fifty-five percent of the coal bein' mined is non-union...

HANK. That's right! Fifty-five percent of the men workin' the mines are scabs. There's hardly a union shop in all East Kentucky.

PETE. And even in the union mines a hundred-fifty-thousand miners are forced to do the job that six hundred thousand used to do...

HANK. Drivin' the death and accident rates sky high...

PETE. Leavin' thousands of widows and disabled miners...

SENATOR RINER. What are you trying to say with all these numbers?

RALEIGH. We are sayin' that Appalachia is a living hell for miners and their families, and the Company don't pay no nevermind. They take the money we earn for them and run.

SENATOR RINER. Our data suggests that the companies are assuming as many responsibilities as they can.

PETE. In West Virginia alone over fifty thousand miners have black lung disease. What does your data say the companies are doing for them?

JUPIE. I can tell you what they're doing. Nothing!

SENATOR RINER. Might I remind you that we are not investigating the policies of the coal companies in these hearings. We are concerned with welfare abuses.

MAE. (*interrupting*) And job lay-offs?

SENATOR RINER. I can understand your concern about job lay-offs. But this Congress has given federal funds to meet the social problems in your area, *and those funds have been abused.*

JUPIE. (*rage finds its voice*) Welfare's nothin' you gave us! Few years back miners' wives planted their behinds on the White House lawn and hollered the day and night out 'til the big man psuhed a little blood money at us for the lives drained out of our men. (*sotto voce*) Gift my ass.

SENATOR RINER. Your men chose to work in the mines.

JUPIE. (*Furious, she starts to leave. HANK pulls her back.*) Now I heard it all.

RALEIGH. Yeah, an all American choice: work in the mines or starve.

(*the MINERS and their WIVES are getting angrier and angrier*)

SENATOR RINER. (*with the cool reason of those in power*) Mining's a risky occupation; it always has been and it probably always will be. But your own UMW representatives have been before this committee and received medical programs for the miners. I know of other institutions in your regions, like the Presbyterian Church, which have built fine hospitals...

RALEIGH. (*outraged*) Hospitals!

(*as RALEIGH shouts, SENATOR SCOTT pounds his gavel to silence her*)

Excuse me, Sir, I'll tell you about those hospitals.

HANK. Raleigh, sit down.

RALEIGH. Leave me alone, Hank. He's gonna hear this. (*to SENATORS*) I wouldn't put a dog in one of your hospitals. Not a dog!

HANK. They close four days after they open.

JUPIE. You have to be certified dead to get in one of those hospitals!

(*SENATOR SCOTT ceases pounding his gavel*)

SENATOR RINER. As I've been trying to say, there are institutions in your area which, unlike many Appalachian recipients of welfare, are operating within the limits of the law to better your conditions.

MAE. (*quietly, but with awesome rage*) Mr. Senator, I'd like to ask you somethin' 'bout your law. Now strip minin's legal, isn't it?

SENATOR RINER. Yes, it is.

MAE. Let me tell you 'bout the floods your legal strip minin' brings. My daddy died in one. Floods lifted our house off its foundations and shoved it into the neighbor's house. We could not see above the top of the water. The only warnin' we had was a shout from the neighbors, and it was a shout I will remember for the rest of my life: "Run, the dam's broke!" I saw a house float by with seven people in it, all dead. My daddy and my brother never got out either. They got me and Mama out safe, and they went back for Tykie, and they never came back. They died a legal American death.

(*JUPIE, RALEIGH, and MAE all speak at once*)

JUPIE. And the company knew that dam wouldn't last.

MAE. They knew it! They knew it!

RALEIGH. It would have cost them two hundred thousand dollars to build a safe one, but they didn't. Instead they drowned eighty-seven miners and their families.

MAE. (*continuing to shout*) They drowned my family. You hear me? They're murderers!

SENATOR RINER. Ladies, please don't yell.

RALEIGH. We're not yellin'. (*huge as God*) We're talkin' loud!

SENATOR SCOTT. Every disruption you cause undermines the democratic principles and proceedings of this Congress.

RALEIGH. (*starts laughing*) If I could find one democratic principle, hell, I wouldn't undermine it. (*turning to MINERS and their WIVES*) You see a democratic principle here? Pete? Hank? (*to world at large*) Has *anybody* seen a democratic principle here?

SENATOR RINER. If you could find a way to control your hysteria, we'd like to move these proceedings along. If you would just give us some orderly answers about welfare abuses...

RALEIGH. (*in her element and far from hysterical, she begins the innocent and builds to a mighty crescendo*) Oh, you want to know about welfare abuses. Why didn't I realize that sooner? Let's take a look at Abron, you know, the Kentucky branch where Abron moved to because there was no unions? Well, Abron just got six million dollars. Now the good old government called it a tax-break for capital improvement, but it's welfare. The people who get the most welfare in this country are the people who get the most of everything else: the rich!

SENATOR RINER. The Abron Corporation provides badly needed jobs in your region.

JUPIE. Abron just closed down two plants, put three thousand people out of work, and moved the entire operation to Taiwan. That's a great way of providin' jobs, isn't it?

RALEIGH. You got a boat?

SENATOR RINER. I can see this isn't getting us anywhere. We are your elected representatives. If we could get your cooperation, we would be glad to help you in any way we can.

RALEIGH. (*mock seriousness*) Oh, you want to help us? Well that's real down-home of you. You got a pencil handy? We'll tell you what we want and you get right on it.

MAE. We want to see a national health care program that includes poor people.

HANK. We want to see the government stop payin' for the coal the TVA strip mines makin' a desert of our mountain land and callin' it progress.

JUPIE. We want safe roads so's we can get someplace in an emergency. Oh, and while you're at it, could you rebuild our forests, stop strip minin' and put some teeth in safety bills for underground minin'?

PETE. That's what we want. Safe underground minin'. They got it in other countries, you know.

(*SENATOR RINER walks out*)

HANK. And we want protection of our rights to organize and bargain collectively without gettin' beat up or shot at every time we try!

RALEIGH. Give us that, Mr. Senator, and you can shove your welfare up to where the sun don't shine!

ALL. That's tellin' 'em! You said it, Raleigh!

SENATOR SCOTT. This meeting is adjourned. (*exits*)

JUPIE. If you don't change things fast, you might have to adjourn the whole damn country!

(*MINERS and their WIVES take over the halls of Congress and sing their hope, if not their reality*)

Big Takeover
Workin' folk gonna rise up strong
Right the wrongs we been under so long,
Gonna be a big takeover in this land.

All the folks good names and faces,
All the colors from all the races,
Gonna be a big takeover in this land.

Scene 2. *"Big Takeover"*

(past and present merge as MOTHER JONES enters and the big takeover is given its history)

MOTHER JONES. It was back in the steel strike of 1919.

ALL. Cold steel.

MOTHER JONES. I was ordered to appear in the court for speakin' out in the street.

ALL. Speak it out!

MOTHER JONES. That cranky old judge asked me...

ALL. He said, "Mother,"

MOTHER JONES. "Do you have a permit for speakin' in the streets, Mother?"

ALL. You need a permit here.

MOTHER JONES. "Yes, Sir," I replied.

ALL. Yes, Sir!

MOTHER JONES. "I have a permit."

ALL. She does!

MOTHER JONES. "Who issued it?" he asked.

ALL. And you said...

MOTHER JONES. "John Adams, Thomas Jefferson, and Patrick Henry."

(ALL sing)

> Sure as lightning cracks a warning,
> Sure as a rainbow clears the sky,
> Sure as sun brings up the morning,
> There'll be a new day a-dawning.
>
> Black and white walking side by side,
> Yellow and red joining in their stride,
> Gonna be a big takeover in this land.
>
> Men and women proving they
> Can work as one this and ev'ry day,
> Gonna be a big takeover in this land.

MOTHER JONES. It was at Red Warrior Camp.

ALL. We remember.

MOTHER JONES. Gunmen came to stop our strike.

ALL. Stop it cold.

MOTHER JONES. I walked up to one of the gunmen and put my hand over the muzzle of his gun.

(*ENSEMBLE* gasps)

Then I just looked at him.

ALL. That was some look!

MOTHER JONES. The young man said:

MAN. Take your hands off my gun, you hellcat!

MOTHER JONES. I kept it there.

ALL. She kept it.

MOTHER JONES. And said:

ALL. She said:

MOTHER JONES. Young man.

ALL. Listen to this.

MOTHER JONES. My class goes down into the mines. They bring up the metal that makes this gun. This is my gun. You take your hands off my gun!

(*ALL sing*)

> Sure as lightning cracks a warning,
> Sure as a rainbow clears the sky,
> Sure as sun brings up the morning,
> There'll be a new day a-dawning.

(*ALL hum as MOTHER JONES speaks*)

MOTHER JONES. (*organizing the audience*) You want to join the Mother Jones Union? I'm lookin' to sign up some good folk. You, over there. Yes, and you too. All of you, right here and now. Here's your obligation. You don't scab, not ever. You don't work for non-union wages. If they fire your brother or sister, you don't take the job. And when you strike, you stay 'til you win it. You don't work, and you man that picket line so no one works. And you never cross a picket line. Never! Are you for that?

ALL. We're for that!

MOTHER JONES. Then sign up with the Mother Jones Union!

(*ALL sing*)

> Working folk gonna rise up strong
> Right the wrongs we've been under so long,

Gonna be a big takeover in this land.
All the folks, good names and faces,
All the colors from all the races,
Gonna be a big takeover in this land.

(*scene dissolves into the present as the ENSEMBLE moves to their present day houses*)

Scene 3. "Night Song"

(*It is evening. The feeling is gentle. The families are in their homes. The CHORUS enters and sits. MOTHER JONES, seated, speaks from out of the past. Lights focus on individual houses as the people in them speak. Lights come up on CHORUS singing.*)

Night Song
Night falls soft down
Easin' country folk and town.
When old night steals in,
You stop to think what might've been.

A pretty dress that's worn,
A friend you need who's gone,
A love you lent,
The life you spent.

(*lights dim on the CHORUS and illuminate JUPIE, seated*)

JUPIE. (*remembering her home and her life*) Lard buckets, scraps of iron, bent wire, torn rope, honeysuckle bushes, old odors, seventeen mason jars filled with food for the fall, the fresh rainwater I catched off my roof and my old wood stove that's older than my grandpa. It is my belief that all these things are very beautiful, and I will honor that beauty 'til I die.

(*CHORUS sings*)

Night's tall enough for mountains,
Deep enough for grief,
But long enough and kind enough
To give a soul relief.

(*Lights dim on JUPIE and illuminate RALEIGH and HANK on their front stoop. She is leaning in his arms.*)

RALEIGH. *(lifting her head)* That Congressman was real sympathetic about the murder of Yablonski.

HANK. Like a spider to a fly.

RALEIGH. *(trying to get those thoughts out of her mind)* Well...your son cried and kicked up a fuss when I took him to his first day of school yesterday. *(starts laughing as she thinks of something else)* You know what he said when the teacher asked his name? "My name is the son of Hank Firman."

HANK. *(laughing)* Just like I taught him. So what'd you do?

RALEIGH. I just acted dumb and asked around to see who he belonged to. No one claimed him so we got him. *(settles back in his arms)*

HANK. *(smiling)* Did the jeans fit?

RALEIGH. Oh, Hank, he was so proud of them jeans that if they was six sizes too small, you'd never hear a peep outta him. His face beamed more than the shine on his shoes.

HANK. What's gonna happen in a couple of years when he gets into Miss Gerlock's class? They say she gives out books full of sex and communism.

RALEIGH. That ain't no bad combination. Oh yeah, and he learned to whistle!

HANK. Really! That's more than his old man can do.

RALEIGH. *(amazed)* You can't whistle?

(HANK tries but can't)

A full-grown mountain man and you never learned to whistle! *(laughs)*

HANK. Can you?

RALEIGH. Sure I can whistle—in and out. *(whistles)*

HANK. Nice!

RALEIGH. Thank you. *(leans in his arms)*

HANK. Now honey, about that Congressional meeting—

RALEIGH. *(breaking away and rising)* I knew it, I knew you'd jump on me 'bout something. You do after every meeting.

HANK. *(raising his voice defensively)* I ain't jumpin'. It's just that you always take over. An idea is better if it comes from more than one person.

RALEIGH. *(whispering)* Don't talk so loud! You'll wake your son up. *(shouting)* And who cares where a good idea come from so long as it's good.

HANK. Now who's gonna wake him up?

RALEIGH. *(shouting louder)* I don't care if he wakes up! You're just afraid your wife'll look stronger'n you!

HANK. (*rising*) Oh Raleigh, I don't care if you grow hair on your chest and eat rocks for breakfast.

RALEIGH. Good. 'Cause I'm thinking of doin' both.

HANK. Come on, we got better things to do with our little time together than argue.

RALEIGH. You're always criticizin' my speeches.

HANK. You called it! You said it yourself: "speeches". You're always makin' speeches. You're supposed to talk with people, not at 'em.

RALEIGH. (*sarcastically*) Oh, is that the way it goes? Okay. I'll listen a little more at meetings if...

HANK. I learn to whistle.

RALEIGH. (*smiling wryly as that was not what her bargain was going to be*) Yeah.

(*HANK puckers his lips to whistle. RALEIGH kisses him.*)

HANK. Now I would have learned to whistle a long time ago if I'd have known this came with it.

RALEIGH. If you'd asked me, I would've told ya.

HANK. Funny the things a man don't know that a woman does.

RALEIGH. That's 'cause a woman keeps her eyes to the main chance.

(*HANK tries to whistle again. RALEIGH kisses him again, then speaks suggestively.*)

RALEIGH. You know, I'm gonna take Hank Junior over to his grandma's for the weekend.

HANK. Now that ain't no ladylike thing to do.

RALEIGH. You ain't got no lady; you got a woman.

(*lights dim on HANK and RALEIGH and illuminate MOTHER JONES*)

MOTHER JONES. It's God Almighty made women. Rockerfeller's gang of thieves made ladies.

(*lights dim on MOTHER JONES and illuminate CHORUS singing*)

> Night's not quick to move,
> Not a thing she's got to prove.
> All that's left us to do
> Old night's been through.
>
> Night has her own way
> To help us meet the day.
> She knows it's always best
> To heal the wounded heart with rest.

(*Lights dim on CHORUS and illuminate MAE and PETE in their house. They are in the middle of an evening's conversation.*)

MAE. Yes, I'm talkin' about cows.

PETE. That's what I thought you said. I just couldn't believe it.

MAE. My daddy strictly taught me not to use cows roughly. Not to kick 'em or yank their udders. And I think Lisa should know that.

PETE. Well sure, Mae, I don't want Lisa kickin' on a cow, but the fact is we ain't got no cow for her to kick on.

MAE. I think Lisa should be told *now* and by her *father* how to treat cows. Your folks had cows when you was growin' up, my folks had cows, and someday we're gonna have a cow and Lisa's gotta know how to treat it once we get it.

PETE. You always have such plans. Last month I had to show her how to call like a whippoorwill. A whippoorwill!

MAE. Whippoorwill's a very important bird to Appalachia.

PETE. (*making a bird call*) Whippoorwill. Whippoorwill...

(*MAE catches herself from laughing. She takes HANK'S hand.*)

MAE. I don't want Lisa growin' up to be a selfish little brat who only cares about herself. Everything we know, she's got to know. It's got to be a part of her so that when we die, she can carry it on...

PETE. (*taking her in his arms and comforting her*) I have never known no one to talk about dyin' the way you do.

MAE. I can't help it. Jock Yablonski and his wife and daughter all killed, and they was doin' just what you're doin'. That scares me. A whole family goin' like that. Makes me scared for our little family. So, like I said, Lisa's got to know everything we know. She's got to know to take just what she needs, never to waste anything, to honor her friends and her neighbors, not power...

PETE. (*interrupting, gently, firmly*) Listen I ain't plannin' on dyin' soon, and I ain't plannin' on you dyin' soon. Okay?

MAE. Okay. (*Leans in his arms, thinking. There is a long pause.*) But, just to be on the safe side, you teach Lisa.

PETE. (*laughing at his wife's typical persistence*) How to treat a goddamn cow.

(*lights dim on PETE and MAE and illuminate MOTHER JONES*)

MOTHER JONES. Judge asked me what to do about Barney Rice who swore every other word. "Why Judge," says I, "That's the way us workin' people pray!" "Do you pray that way, Mother?" "Yes, Judge, when I want an answer quick!"

(Lights dim on MOTHER JONES and illuminate JUPIE. She fights back the tears.)

JUPIE. You know what I'm gonna miss most about my home? It's my old wood stove. It's the smoke in that thing, flavors the food. Bakin' beans in that; there's no comparison. Your bread and biscuits, everything tastes better when it's cooked in that stove. *(almost breaking down)* Course, you cook in cast iron; nothin' else'll do.

(CHORUS sings)

CHORUS.   Night's tall enough for mountains,
           Deep enough for grief,
           But long enough and kind enough
           To give a soul relief.

(lights dim on JUPIE and illuminate DILLER and JOHNNY in their house)

JOHNNY. You wanna talk about Yablonski?

DILLER. *(rubbing two pieces of coal against each other)* No. Not right now, okay? *(juggling the coal chunks)* Look what I worked out today.

JOHNNY. *(catching a piece of the coal)* You like coal so much, you're bringing it home now?

DILLER. Yeah, I like coal. I like coal minin'.

JOHNNY. *(with great fondness)* Only reason you like it so much is that's all you know how to do. You went down into the mines when you was fifteen, and you never made a dime at anything else. That's the reason you like it. You want to know somethin' real dumb? If my spine ever gets back right, I'll probably go down again, too. Now ain't that dumb?

DILLER. They could make 'em safer if they wanted to. They keep cripplin' youngsters like you and killin' people like your dad, I swear to God I'll fight. One thing's for sure, strip minin's got this land so full of holes already, it's a natural place for guerrilla warfare.

(JOHNNY laughs to ease DILLER out of his anger)

You got your daddy's laugh. You got his sense of humor too. He always got his biggest laugh at my expense.

JOHNNY. Tell me a story about my dad.

DILLER. Why? I tell you a story about him 'most every night.

JOHNNY. Then you should be used to it; shouldn't bother you none.

DILLER. *(wanting to tell as much as JOHNNY wants to hear)* Here's one you don't know. When your Daddy'n I moved into this place, all the windows was out. Wind blew straight in one window, through the house, and out the other. So I set out to fix 'em up. One night I was puttyin' one frame of the window, and it was so cold my hands was numb. Well, your dad walks into the house leavin' the door wide open, and I hollers out, "John, close the damned door!" And he says, for Chrissake, what good's it do to close the door when all the windows is out? (*laughs*) Well, he got me laughin' so hard I dropped the window and broke it. I thought he'd be furious. But then he just laughed. Your dad had that big belly laugh that got everybody else laughin' soon's they heard it.

(*there is a moment of stillness*)

JOHNNY. Diller, do you miss my dad?

DILLER. At first I did, after it happened; but it ain't painin' me so much anymore. It's kind of like you're becomin' him.

(*lights dim on DILLER and JOHNNY and illuminate MOTHER JONES*)

MOTHER JONES. Has anyone ever told you, my children about the lives you are living here, so that you may understand how it is you pass your days on earth? Have you told each other about it and thought it over among yourselves so that you might imagine a brighter day, and begin to bring it to pass?

(*lights dim on MOTHER JONES and illuminate JUPIE*)

JUPIE. (*magnificent in her rage and grief*) They came to take me from my home where I thought I could die peaceful. Bulldozer come in, hit the burial ground, and I seen the casket of my mother raised high on the big blade, then shattered. I seen bad, but no worse than that. They say they're gonna reclaim the land and start excavation. But they can't reclaim a fiddle tune; they can't reclaim the sound of the wind rustlin' by my old log shack; they can't reclaim my mother.

(*CHORUS sings*)

> There's a mother in the night,
> And a father too.
> They know all, and they'll share
> When we're strong enough to bear.
>
> They'll show us things by night
> Too dark to see by day.
> We'll learn things by night
> To help us find our way.

(*Lights dim on JUPIE. With the onset of thunder, lightning and rain, the families respectively ready themselves for the big rain. Lightning illuminates DILLER and JOHNNY.*)

JOHNNY. Uh oh, you know what that means.

DILLER. Get down to the Brandywine River and sandbag the banks.

(*THEY exit. Lights dim on DILLER and JOHNNY and illuminate MAE and PETE.*)

MAE. Did you hear somethin'?

PETE. Just the sound of you wakin' me up.

(*Lights dim on PETE and MAE and illuminate RALEIGH and HANK.*)

HANK. You go over t' your ma's, get her to come back here with you. She shouldn't be alone tonight. Get Mae to go with you. Where's my raincoat?

RALEIGH. You ain't got one.

HANK. You know what I mean, wise guy, that old jacket of your pa's.

RALEIGH. On the hook behind you. If it been a rat, it would've bit you.

(*THEY exit. Lights dim on RALEIGH and HANK and illuminate MAE and PETE.*)

MAE. It's been rainin' hard for three nights now, ever since they kicked Jupie off her land. You'd think old Mother Nature was tryin' to tell us somethin'.

PETE. I saw Bert buyin' dynamite down t' the general store. I told him there was no rush, rain's gonna wash away Jupie's land 'fore he gets a chance to strip it.

MAE. You watch out there, Honey, it's real slippery.

(*THEY exit*)

Scene 4. "Jupie's House"

(*BERT, the strip mining boss, enters checking his dynamite plans*)

BERT. Why the hell is it still rainin'? You're sure that damn fool woman didn't sneak back into her shack?

STRIP MINER. (*offstage*) No one's here.

BERT. Okay, then, let's get that dynamite wired. Mr. C. said to dynamite the rats at night, then throw a ton of dirt on 'em. That way no one'll see 'em, no one'll get scared.

STRIP MINER. (*offstage*) The rats are gone!

BERT. (*horrified*) What do you mean they're gone? What do you mean? They gotta be there!

STRIP MINER. (*offstage*) I tell you they ain't here. Take a look for yourself.

BERT. Don't joke with me. If you're jokin' over a thing like this, I swear to God...

STRIP MINER. (*entering and running across the stage*) I'm gettin' outta here!

BERT. Stay the hell there!

(*The ENSEMBLE sings two themes simultaneously as BERT crosses the stage and looks for the rats. Their fugue underscores his words.*)

(*offstage, first line of fugue*)	(*second line of fugue*)
Toiling millions now are walking,	You keep pushing on us real hard.
See them marching on.	There'll be a day of reckoning,
All the tyrants now are shaking,	But be on guard.
E're their power's gone,	There'll be a day of reckoning.
E're their power's gone.	

BERT. My God, they are gone. They could be anyplace. Goddamned things can move fast when they want to. They could be all over the woods. They could be in your house, in my house. They could be in every nook and cranny of this entire county.

STRIP MINER. (*starting off*) I'm gettin' out of here!

(*BERT grabs him*)

BERT. (*exiting slowly with the STRIP MINER*) Where'll you go, you stupid sonofabitch? Where is it safe? Where can anybody go? Where is it safe?

Scene 5. "Deep in the Mines"

(*It is early morning. The MEN appear on their backs working in the mines.*)

DILLER. Hank, come on over here. That heading ain't safe.

(*CHORUS sings offstage*)

> We got heroes in this land,
> Red, black, yellow and tan.
> They take the risk on demand,
> It's on their backs that this country began.

PETE. Talk is Boyle had Yablonski bumped off. What d'you think?

HANK. Too easy. Boyle's the first one everybody'd suspect. He's crooked, but he ain't crazy.

PETE. Who did it then?

DILLER. What I'd ask is, who profits most from Yablonski's death; the current heads of our union suspected of murder and about to be arrested any day now accordin' to the paper—and it's in every paper—and the whole UMW membership at each other's throats? Now you tell me who profits most from all that, and I'll tell you who bumped off Yablonski.

PETE. Well, 'til we find that out, don't forget the UMW's been under it before and we all lived to tell about it.

(*there is an ominous noise*)

Hank, watch out!

DILLER. Man, you gotta keep your eyes open in the mornin'. Should get you a job in a bank so you don't have to open 'em up 'til nine o'clock.

HANK. I'd be glad to open 'em up earlier, 'cept I'd have to look at your ugly mugs.

DILLER. Ugly? I won the most beautiful baby contest in Macon County, and you call me ugly? You got no taste, Boy.

(*CHORUS sings offstage as miners work*)

> Miner's Life
>
> A miner's life is full of grief and pain
> Lyin' on his back in a hard coal vein,
> Livin' on slagpiles that break away,
> Workin' so his kid's gonna see a better day.

DILLER. (*working his way towards another part of the mine*) By the way, you guys set to join that walkout Yablonski's kid and the Miners for Democracy called? We go out tomorrow at three o'clock.

HANK. We're set. Hey Diller, I hear you talkin', but I don't see you. Where are you?

DILLER. (*offstage*) Just around the bend. what's the matter, can't you see in the dark?

HANK. (*smiling*) Just want to know where you're at.

PETE. Maybe you guys didn't notice, but our lamps is hot enough to cook on. And we're comin' up on that gas pocket we passed yesterday.

(*There is an explosion in the distance. Lights black out except for MINER'S helmet lights. The MEN shout at a fever pitch.*)

PETER. What was that? Somethin' blew!

HANK. Pete, you okay?

PETE. Yeah, where's Diller?

DILLER. (*appearing*) I'm, here, comin' toward ya! What happened? I can't see! Too much dust in my eyes. Where are you?

HANK. We're here, not ten feet away!

DILLER. Just keep talkin'! I'll follow your voices. (*He tries to find them*)

HANK. Keep comin', Baby. We're here!

DILLER. I can't find you!

PETE. We're waitin' on you. We're waitin' on you, Friend!

(*DILLER reaches them. THEY continue to yell reassurance, but wild urgency chokes their voices.*)

DILLER. (*he is shouting at a fever pitch*) Okay, let's not panic. One of the shafts collapsed. From the looks of the dust fallin' off these headings, and the gas in the air, it happened close by. Now we gotta move fast. Just don't panic. There's an air shaft about a thousand feet from here. We get there in time, we can breathe 'til we're rescued.

HANK. What if that's the shaft that blew?

DILLER. We gotta try!

PETE. Let's move. This place will be filled with carbon monoxide in no time.

(*the MEN move to another part of the mine*)

PETE. All right. Look around for the self-rescue equipment. We can breathe two hours with it.

DILLER. That's long enough to make it to the air shaft.

PETE. Where the hell is it? I can't find it!

HANK. Here it is! Here it is! Just put it on!

DILLER. Don't panic...just uses up the air faster...only a thousand feet...

PETE. Gas comin' in! (*coughs*) I...can't...breathe...

(*HE chokes. There is a huge explosion in the mines. The helmet lights on the MINER'S hats go off one by one as the explosion stops them forever.*)

Scene 6. *"The Vigil"*

(*Sirens wail. JOHNNY and MAE run to the mines. They are crying, unable to stop. RALEIGH enters, comforts them both. In a tragic revelation, the tableau of mining families begins their silent vigil.*)

RALEIGH. I will sit at this mine and wait for you for eight days as I waited for my brother. If you don't come out, I won't shed a tear. But until I die, I will fight those who killed you. And if I die in my fight, so be it. Hear me. Hear what I say, my Love.

(*SHE sinks slowly to her knees. MOTHER JONES enters above and speaks their history.*)

MOTHER JONES. They go into the mines such young boys, they are hardly children at all. Too many never grow old. Their lives are hard; they are sometimes hungry; their bones hurt from stooping and crawling, and their lungs hurt from gasping for air. And they do not die easy. But remember, you whose greed kills them, their dying does not stop them speaking to us. You'll hear them if you dare listen.

(*CHORUS offstage, singing slowly and softly under the prophetic words of MOTHER JONES*)

> Workin' folk gonna rise up strong,
> Right the wrongs we've been under so long.
> Gonna be a big takeover in this land.

MOTHER JONES. Oh no, their dying does not stop them speaking to us. You can't kill the spirit of workin' folk. We're survivors. We built this country brick by brick and fed it potato by potato. And after all the dust is settled, this land we worked and built and fed will be ours. Oh yes, it will be ours...I know.

(*CHORUS from offstage as the lights slowly fade on the tableau and MOTHER JONES*)

> They carried our load down
> A long and lonesome road.
> These folks are down
> Like folks before,
> Losing one battle,
> Knowing there'll be more.

END OF PLAY

From left to right: Peggy Ings, Christen Bowen, Ellen Field, Susan Davis in "Mother Jones." Photo: James Oestereich.

M. ANANIA

THE FURIES OF MOTHER JONES

SPLIT~SHIFT

by Maxine Klein
Music by James Oestereich

"Split-Shift," written and directed by Maxine Klein with music by James Oestereich was originally produced at Boston University under the title "Brain." It was then optioned for Broadway under the title, "Brainchild." "Splitshift" is a substantially revised edition of these earlier works.

Except for one telephone exchange, the play takes place in the mind of Billie Murphy.

STORY OF THE PLAY

"Split-Shift" is a musical comedy. The action takes place inside the mind of Billie Murphy, a song-writer and a union organizer who works as a waitress in a fast-food chain restaurant called Lowdowns. The character of Billie is played by three women: Billie I is Billie as she appears to the outside world; Billie II is that part of Billie which is positive, rational, generous and forgiving; Billie II is that part which is negative, egotistical, jealous, fearful and fully convinced that she is right at all times—no matter how much the facts of the world may contradict her.

The play takes place during the course of one evening as Billie awaits the arrival of her male friend, Mark, and plans her drive to unionize the fast-food chain restaurant where she works. Fantasies and realities intermingle with a matrix of memories and expectations about fast-food chains, revolution, man-woman problems, media stars and union organizing.

Out of it all emerges a contemporary woman, with a lot of spunk and humor and good working-class roots. This is a woman who does battle with the dehumanizing forces of modern life and who ultimately, all things considered, puts up a good fight.

DESCRIPTION OF CHARACTERS

BILLIE I: Waitress at a fast food restaurant, songwriter, and union organizer who's caught between her urge to do responsible action in the world and her reactive responses to men, ideas of love, jealousy, and vainglorious visions.

BILLIE II: Billie I's rational persona. She is optimistic and reasonably certain that every problem can be solved.

BILLIE III: An ego-maniacal persona of Billie I who is sure that every problem is unsolvable and that in any case of dispute she is right, the other party is wrong.

GUERRILLERO: Billie's dream vision of a "perfect" revolutionary.

MS. GERLOCK: Billie's second-grade techer who classified students as fast or slow learners.

ROSE STARTNER: The hostess at Lowell Downing's. She is a woman who apes the manners of the well-to-do.

TOM: One of Billie's coworkers at Lowell Downing's. His natural sense of humor continually laid seige to by the conditions in which he works.

MARK: Billie's male friend. A lover with a propensity to be late, a roving eye, and who knows what else.

HARRY the HORSE: Veteran union organizer. His kindness, wisdom, and sense of humor make hm a natural father surrogate for Billie.

ORANGE MEN: Rhythmic embodiments of a composer when the mind wanders.

CLOYCE: Attractive, bubbly, a coquette; a clear and present danger to Billie.

RICHARD: Billie's former husband whose image continues to vex her.

MOTHER: A tough, tender working class woman.

SELF-SUFFICIENT CHORUS and BATS OUT OF HELL: Fantasized female trios who belt out Billie's songs.

IRVING: A dogmatic representative of the left.

WEE PERSON: A poetic dream character two feet high.

MINGO MANGO. The media's idea of Third World women.

TELEPHONE OPERATORS: Hard pressed and pressuring AT & T representatives.

Act I

(The entire play takes place in the mind of BILLIE MURPHY. In BILLIE'S mind are always three aspects of her personality: BILLIE I—BILLIE as she seems to the outside world; BILLIE II—rational, optimistic, mature; and BILLIE III—pleasure-seeking, egocentric, insecure, albeit full of false bravura. The play opens to the sound of a Latin singer on the radio.)

BILLIE I. *(offstage)* What's he singing? I can't understand a single word! *(irritation growing)* Where is that Spanish grammar?

BILLIE II. *(appearing in her cubicle)* Look under the bed.

BILLIE III. *(appearing in her cubicle and moving to the rhythm)* Forget the grammar—you learn a language rhythmically. *(moving to rhythm as she sings) Te amo para siempre.* Just like a native, huh.

BILLIE II. A native infant.

BILLIE I. *(enters, still dressed in her waitress uniform, grammar in hand)* I probably know enough to get by anyway. All I really need are a few words of welcome in Spanish.

BILLIE II. Must I remind you that forty-three of those voters tomorrow night are Spanish speaking.

BILLIE I. *(Groans a grudging assent as she turns off the radio and lies down with her book to conjugate the verb dormir. She first recites the verb in Spanish, then in English.) Duermo*—I sleep. *Duermes*—you in the familiar sleep. *Duerme*—he, she, it sleeps.

(She continues conjugating. BILLIE III yawns.)

BILLIE II. I'd better practice on a different verb. This one's *dangerous.*

BILLIE I. Dormir is the only one they give. *(resumes conjugating)*

BILLIE II. *(irritated)* I know the present, it's the subjunctive I always have trouble with.

BILLIE III. *(loudly yawning over BILLIE I'S conjugation)* This stuff is deadly. I'm not going to make it.

(BILLIE I continues conjugating, her eyelids growing heavier, her words beginning to slur)

(*Blackout. Stage fills with jungle sounds. BILLIE I dreams one of her more grandiose dreams. She is deep in the jungles of Central America. From shadows ominous and dense her slight figure emerges dressed in appropriate camouflage with verdue on her head.*)

BILLIE I. *Donde duerme?*

GUERRILLERO. (*from offstage*) *Duermo aqui.*

BILLIE I. (*urgently as she surveys the jungle*) That's the pass word. Where is he?

GUERRILLERO. (*emerging*) *A la derecha de usted.*

BILLIE I. (*trying desperately to remember her Spanish*) Is *derecha* left or... (*Turns to the left then the right. There is the guerrillero. She starts to scream and the guerrillero puts his hand over her mouth.*)

GUERRILLERO. Shh! The jungle has ears, *comprende?*

BILLIE I. (*Nods "Yes." He releases her.*) I'm sorry, I...

GUERRILLERO. (*interrupting*) This is no time for formalities. They could be upon us at any moment. You have the grenades?

BILLIE I. *Los tengo aqui.* (*opens her jacket indicating the hiding place*)

GUERRILLERO. You know Spanish. *Bueno.*

BILLIE I. (*to keep him from expecting too much of her*) I only got as far as the subjunctive...

GUERRILLERO. (*briskly*) *Su Nombre?*

BILLIE I. (*her tension makes her mispronounce*) Millie Burphy. (*corrects herself*) Billie Murphy.

GUERRILLERO. (*on hearing her name, his manner changes forthwith*) The waitress from Boston?

BILLIE I. (*stunned*) Yes, but how...?

GUERRILLERO. Your organizing work is celebrated the world over.

(*in the distance singing is heard*)

The guerrilleros have a song they sing about you.

> *La mujer de la cafeteria*
> *Se pone mas brava dia por dia.*
> *Su curaje es maravillosa.*
> *Su nombre,* Billie Murphy, *por supuesto.*

BILLIE I. (*demurring, speaking over the song*) Anyone could have got that union going at Lowdowns.

GUERRILLERO. The one quality all great leaders share is their modesty.

BILLIE I. You really think so, because I'm so riddled with self-doubt I can barely...

(*a rustle from the underbrush interrupts them and the song*)

GUERRILLERO. Sshhh...(*gets out his binoculars, looks through them speaking with dreadful urgency as he hands BILLIE I a rifle*) You know how to use one of these?

BILLIE I. (*shaking in terror she clumsily accepts the rifle*) Well, I've seen them in movies, but I've never used one up close. I mean, I was hoping there would be some sort of target practice before I would actually have to...(*by this time she is holding the rifle backwards*)

GUERRILLERO. (*as he readies the area*) Hundreds of soldiers heading this way. We make the counteroffensive here.

BILLIE I. Not just you and me?!

GUERRILLERO. (*his command tells all*) The grenades, and quickly, or I cannot answer for the consequences.

BILLIE I. (*holds the rifle between her knees as her terror mounts and she tries to wrest the grenades from their hiding place*) I'll get them...they're in the lining of my...(*having great difficulty*) They must have sewn these in with piano wire. (*goes to more extreme measures to tear them out of the lining*)

GUERRILLERO. *Cuidado!* You'll dislodge the pins!

BILLIE I. I'll what?!

(*A giant explosion blows the GUERRILLERO and BILLIE I offstage. Over the explosion the BILLIES start to awaken.*)

BILLIE III. (*still dreaming and in the throes of terror*) What is it? Help!!! Run!!!

BILLIE II. (*calming herself as she makes her way out of sleep*) Something in the street. Wake up.

BILLIE III. (*almost awake and transferring her dream fear to waking fear*) An earthquake! This place is built on a fault. That's why it's so cheap! Run!!

BILLIE II. Probably a car backfiring. Wake up.

BILLIE I. (*entering*) I don't believe I fell asleep again. Every time I get to the subjunctive I go right out.

(*sound of clock ticking is heard*)

BILLIE III. (*perfectly serious*) Isn't there a theory you can learn a language that way—subliminally? Sleeping on it?

(*BILLIE I is putting book away in the cubicle of BILLIE II*)

BILLIE II. (*dryly*) That's how you learn to be president.

(*Grandfather CLOCK chimes the half hour and appears in BILLIE'S mind. BILLIE I goes for coffee.*)

BILLIE I. That's enough Spanish anyway—what I know, I know. Where's my coffee? What time is it?

BILLIE II. On the dresser. Seven-thirty.

BILLIE I. (*offstage*) Great, I should have been at it a half-hour ago. The most important event of my entire life tomorrow night, and I fall asleep.

BILLIE III. I obviously needed the rest. Changing shifts from late night to early morning is a traumatic blow to the system—like jet lag without any of the fun.

BILLIE I. (*returning, putting coffee down, settling in at the piano and starting to play*) This coffee's vile...well, half past seven...still enough time to work through the song before Mark gets here. (*starts to play "Gotta Organize!" chording and notating. MARK appears in her mind. MARK is her male friend who has, among other vexing attributes, a propensity to be late.*)

BILLIE III. (*over BILLIE I'S playing*) Before he gets here, there's time to dig another Panama canal...single handed...in a monsoon...with a spoon.

BILLIE I. He knows I can only see him for a half-hour tonight, so he won't be late—will he?

BILLIE III. Is the Pope Catholic? Does a bear...?

BILLIE II. (*trying to get herself back on track*) Forget the man, get to the song.

(*MARK and clock disappear*)

BILLIE I. (*remobilized*) Right. (*sings in slow, working, thoughtful manner*)

       It's all for one and one for

(*she erases a note and writes in another*)

       Organize the workplace
       De da de dad
       Might....

(*she tries two different notes and chooses one of them*)

       Be a rocky ride...

BILLIE III. (*tries to get BILLIE I to quit working, but BILLIE I ignores her negative impulses and perseveres*) I cannot compose on an empty stomach. What have I eaten since lunch?

BILLIE I. Dinner.

BILLIE III. You call a few noodles dinner?

BILLIE I. Don't forget the popcorn.

BILLIE III. Popcorn's not food. It's nothing but air—popped air.

BILLIE I. Well there's nothing to eat around here, and I'm not going out.

BILLIE III. Where's all that bologna?

BILLIE I. I don't know, someone must have eaten it.

BILLIE II. Practice. I'll forget I'm hungry.

BILLIE III. Every time I bring something home, someone eats it. If I brought home an orangutang, someone would eat it.

BILLIE I. (*counts measures of chorus as BILLIE II and III argue it out*)
One-two-three-four

two-two-three-four

three-two-three-four

Four-two-three-four, etc.

BILLIE II. Can you complain about anything else?

BILLIE III. Actually I haven't begun to hit my stride. I'm only half trying.

BILLIE II. Very trying.

BILLIE III. (*responding to the pun*) Yuk.

BILLIE I. (*finishing her computation and nervous about the results*) Eleven and a half measures—no one writes an eleven and a half measure chorus.

BILLIE II. I did—so practice it. There's still my introduction to go over after I finish this.

BILLIE III. *If* I finish this.

BILLIE I. (*makes one final correction*) Okay, let's try it on for size.

BILLIE III. (*shrugs her shoulders*) Nothing ventured, nothing lost.

(*BILLIE I, II, III sing*)

> *Gotta Organize*
> Boss got the money, he's got the might.
> Won't back down without a fight.
> No matter how strong he won't last long
> If we get together and organize.
>
> Laborin' class is built to last
> From New York, L.A. and Belfast.
> Working all day for a poor man's pay.
> Get together and organize.

It's all for one and one for all.
Organize the workplace large and small.
Might be a rocky ride.
Set our differences aside.
Get together, and organize.

Haywood, Lewis, Mother Jones too
And that is naming just a few.
Leaders grand have lent a hand.
Built a union rock on which to stand.

Bosses had it down too long.
Their hold on us is too damn strong.
Rank and file gotta move 'em along.
Get together and organize.

It's all for one and one for all.
Organize the work place large and small.
Might be a rocky ride.
Set our differences aside.
Get together and organize.

(*silence as doubt slips in*)

BILLIE III. Well, what do you think?

(*more silence, more doubt*)

What do you think?

(*BILLIE I does not reply but resumes chording the chorus. An eerie tone accompanies her efforts as her doubt grows.*)

BILLIE II. (*to the rescue*) It's not bad—maybe the chorus needs work.

BILLIE I. (*disparaging*) Maybe a desert needs water.

BILLIE II. (*soothing*) You're just afraid a few people won't like it.

BILLIE I. I wouldn't mind negative comments if I ever got a positive one.

BILLIE II. If it's praise you want, change "All for one and one for all" to "I gotta be me."

BILLIE I. (*pounds piano signalling she is through*) I'm a waitress, not a composer.

BILLIE II. (*doing her best to cheer herself up*) Come on. Remember how much everyone liked your song for solidarity day?

BILLIE III. No.

BILLIE II. They gave you a standing ovation.

BILLIE I. I was on their side. They were applauding my sentiment, not my talent.

BILLIE II. You don't have to put yourself down. There are always enough critics around to do that for you.

BILLIE I. True, that's one thing in life I've never wanted for.

BILLIE III. Never. (*Her anxiety about the song and her abilities evokes a memory from BILLIE'S childhood. In second grade, a teacher classified BILLIE as a slow student, a classification which has haunted BILLIE all her life. MS. GERLOCK, a woman with bright red lips, walks on stage into BILLIE'S consciousness. BILLIE I sinks to her knees becoming a child.*)

GERLOCK. (*addressing class*) The fast readers, the rabbits, may go out to recess. The toads will remain inside and do Lesson Three over again. (*spying something that enrages her and pulling a ruler from behind her back*) Billie Murphy! You're writing with your left hand again. It is *illegal* to write back-slant. That's a state law.

BILLIE II. Why in the world am I thinking about her now with all I've got to do?

(*TEACHER backs slowly offstage*)

BILLIE I. (*watching the TEACHER disappear but still in the throes of her power*) Every time I put pen to paper I still expect someone to break down the door and arrest me.

(*a huge pair of red LIPS appear*)

BILLIE III. I'll never forget her lips—like scarlet frosting on a pound cake.

BILLIE I. I thought they were pasted on and would fall off if she talked fast.

BILLIE III. Nothing Chester or I ever did could get her to talk fast.

BILLIE II. Miss Gerlock was twenty-five years ago. The union vote is tomorrow night.

BILLIE III. There's only one other person in the world with lips like hers.

(*ROSE STARTNER, the hostess at Lowell Downing's, now appears inside the red LIPS. She is a woman who apes the manners of the class she considers superior. Her words and tone project the certain wisdom of rules set down from above. She also has a penchant for mispronouncing words.*)

ROSE. Courtesy and cleanliness make good dollars and sense.

BILLIE II. Will you focus on what needs to be done for tomorrow night before it's too late?

(*LIPS with ROSE inside start slowly to disappear*)

BILLIE I. (*obviously unable to follow her own best advice backs slowly offstage staring at the LIPS*) They do have the same lips, don't they? (*disappears*)

BILLIE III. And the same devil's trill.

(*sound of Lowell Downing's at high noon fills the air—dishes clattering, orders being called out, etc.*)

ROSE. (*beginning to emerge, taking over BILLIE'S consciousness*) At Lowell Downing's we...

BILLIE II. You're getting nothing done, which is exactly what they want to happen.

ROSE. At Lowell Downing's we...

BILLIE II. (*disappearing as she laments the inevitable turn her mind is taking*) That place owns my work, not my mind.

BILLIE III. Uh huh. (*disappears*)

ROSE. (*ROSE is now fully in command of BILLIE'S consciousness as BILLIE remembers an event that happened earlier in the day at work. BILLIE and TOM are in their restaurant garb with smiling ice cream logo.*) At Lowell Downing's we arrive on time; so where is your good friend Billie?

TOM. She's here in the...

ROSE. (*interrupting as is her wont*) It is now seven-oh-four and twenty seconds. (*she has been looking at her watch, counting the seconds*)

TOM. Billie's been here since...

ROSE. (*interrupting*) If you don't believe me, take a look at that clock on the wall. (*as ever, full of bird-like gestures to underline her pronouncements*)

TOM. The dishwasher broke down. Billie's helping Mary fix it...

ROSE. (*interrupting as she walks to the door*) Instead of helping Mary in the kitchen... (*through the kitchen door, all sweetness and light*) Billie, honey, could you come out here? (*turning from the kitchen in dismay*) My isn't that kitchen (*mispronouncing*) "Dish—ee—vlid."

BILLIE I. (*entering*) I was helping Mary fix...

ROSE. (*interrupting*) You are not hired to be a mechanic, dear. If you'd been on the floor where you're supposed to be, you might have noticed the party of five from the Marin County Dentist's Convention waiting in Tom's area with an (*spells the word*) E-M-P-T-Y table staring at them. (*letting fly*) A table is bussed immediately after the customer leaves! *Immediately!*

BILLIE I. So we're supposed...

ROSE. (*interrupting*) "Courtesy and cleanliness make good dollars and sense."

BILLIE I. (*riding over ROSE'S last word*) So we're supposed to leave a table we're half through serving in order to bus another one?

ROSE. Don't interrupt, young woman, it's rude.

(*BILLIE is about to explode, so TOM takes over*)

TOM. If Lowdowns would hire...

ROSE. (*interrupting*) Would you please say "Lo-well Down-ing's." (*separates and overpronounces the words*)

TOM. (*carefully mimicking her*) If "Lo-well Down-ing's"...

ROSE. (*interrupting*) That *is* his name after...

TOM. (*riding over ROSE'S last word*) I know what his friggin' name is!

ROSE. (*in loud tones of moral indignation*) Watch your language, young man! Use it on the streets with your friends! At Lowell Downing's you will speak like a gentleman.

TOM. (*scoring one in perfect deadpan*) You know, Rose, if you didn't yell, I think I'd still hear you. My hearing has improved ever since I stopped eating the fried clams.

(*BILLIE and TOM try to hold in laughter, but they can't*)

ROSE. (*smiles vindictively at their laughter*) Your lack of repentance leaves me no "recurse."

TOM. (*turning questioningly to BILLIE*) What?

BILLIE I. (*sotto voce*) "Recourse."

ROSE. The next time I see a customer *waiting* for your table to be *bussed*, I march right over and... (*ROSE pantomimes picking up the tip*)

TOM. (*outraged and incredulous*) You wouldn't do that!

BILLIE I. You know what we make an hour!

ROSE. You don't bus a table *immediately*, I take the tip. (*starts to exit as do TOM and BILLIE, then remembers something*) And while we're at it, there's another little matter we might as well clear up right here and now.

(*surprised, BILLIE and TOM freeze as ROSE flounces out, obviously to get the proof of the pudding*)

TOM. (*fearful of the worst*) She's found out about the union!

BILLIE I. (*shaking her head "no" and saying sotto voce as ROSE re-enters*) Look what she's carrying.

ROSE. (*returning triumphantly with plate and vegetables, miming her actions as she speaks*) You place the parsley sprig and radish rosette garnish on each and every dinner plate or I'm reporting you to the manager. (*exits*)

TOM. And I'm reporting to the board of health that those vegetables are more fit to tie shoes with than eat! They give you fifteen tables to wait. Six of my arms are serving, eight of my arms are clearing, and with what's left over, I'm supposed to stand in front of those dead vegetables, pull them apart, slap them on a plate, while they hang on to each other like they died in each other's arms!

(*TOM and BILLIE speak rapidly over each other*)

BILLIE I. Let her find out about the union and fire us, I don't care anymore.

TOM. Before I work one more day with that woman I'll starve in debtor's prison.

ROSE. (*from offstage*) Billie! Tom!

BOTH. (*completely forgetting their threats*) Coming! (*THEY exit. The memory scene has played itself out. But red LIPS return to BILLIE'S mind.*)

BILLIE II. (*appearing*) Forget about Rose.

BILLIE III. (*appearing*) Forget about her, I'll murder her.

BILLIE II. Drown her in the clam chowder.

BILLIE III. One gurgle and she'd be gone.

BILLIE I. I've got enough evidence to hang that woman. Why didn't I confront her with it?

BILLIE II. I never think fast enough on my feet; that's why.

BILLIE I. If only I'd...(*BILLIE I pulls a stop watch out from her pocket and plays out a fantasy wish-fulfillment. She addresses the LIPS, waving a stopwatch*) Rose, I've been clocking the time you waste in the kitchen nuzzling up to Harry.

ROSE LIPS. How dare you accuse me...

BILLIE III. (*interrupting, waving evidence*) And we have photographs and fingerprints.

BILLIE I. (*continuing her imaginary confrontation, she takes slips out of her pocket*) And might I suggest that before you waltz off to management with any more self-serving accusations, you look these over? (*waves slips in the air*) Falsified petty cash receipts.

ROSE LIPS. Whom are you accusing?

BILLIE I. "Youm!"

BILLIE III. That would have melted her sequins.

(*BILLIE I starts chording on the piano inventing "Don't Interrupt"*)

ROSE. (*putting head through LIPS*) How dare you accuse me of anything underhanded! I will have you fired for this. (*prattles on*)

BILLIE I. (*to BILLIE III as ROSE speaks*) Of course, the hitch is I'd have had to get her to shut up long enough to listen to me. And there's not a person alive who has ever completed a full sentence in her presence.

(*still prattling, ROSE and LIPS disappear*)

Don't Interrupt

BILLIE I.	If you would only listen to me...
ROSE.	(*entering*) I always listen perfectly.
BILLIE I.	It's a real problem when...
ROSE.	Over there, a party of ten.
BILLIE I.	You haven't heard a word that...
ROSE.	You're not wearing a hair net!
BILLIE I.	(*making a fist*) Someday I'm going to...
ROSE.	What a nice ring. Is it new?
BILLIE I.	Will you let me get to the sense...
ROSE.	Billie, you're so terribly tense.
BILLIE I.	Rose you must let me speak...
ROSE.	Is that a mole there on your cheek?

(*BILLIE backs ROSE offstage as they sing chorus*)

ROSE.   You carry that chip
          Around on your shoulder

          Your manner is getting
          Bolder and bolder.

          I don't know what's the
          Matter with you.

          If you don't get control
          You're through

BILLIE I. Don't interrupt
          Let me speak

          Shut up,
          Let me speak

          Don't interrupt
          Let me speak

          Shut up
          Let me speak

(*silence, sound of CLOCK ticking*)

BILLIE II. Daydreaming doesn't get the work done.

BILLIE III. In Japan, daydreaming is considered productive.

BILLIE II. (*wry and dry*) However they're considerably east of here.

(*MARK appears and disappears*)

Try to salvage what is left of the evening.

BILLIE I. (*doing her best*) Maybe if I played the last chorus in half-time.

BILLIE II. It's worth a try. (*plays the chorus in half-time*)

> It's all for one and one for all.
> Organize the work place large and small.
> Might be a rocky ride,
> Set our differences aside.

(*plays a huge dissonant chord signifying her dissatisfaction*)

BILLIE I. I don't like it, period, the end, no more, *finis.* (*goes to get her guitar*)

BILLIE III. (*exasperation is defined*) Now I decide. Why didn't I make up my what-passes-for-a-mind before I worked myself to death on it!

BILLIE I. (*returning with guitar*) Maybe it's my desperation speaking, but what about a little Country Western?

BILLIE II. (*shaken by this turn of mind*) Country Western!

BILLIE I. (*executes a few guitar picks*)

> Driving down the road
> De da da do da
> What I see ahead
> De do da da da da

BILLIE I. Get everyone to laugh away their fear of voting union.

BILLIE III. Can we make it funny enough I can laugh away mine too?

BILLIE II. I don't know about Country though. My guitar isn't that good.

BILLIE I. Tom and Harry can cut it. They grew up on country.

(*BILLIE tries different lyrical phrases*)

BILLIE I.   "Lowdowns, you're too plastic to be true."
BILLIE II.   "Your gravy is glue."
BILLIE III.   "You put oil in your stew."

(as HARRY and TOM enter with guitars)
BILLIE I. Come out with "gitars" blazing!
(BILLIE I sings with TOM and HARRY)

       Lowdowns

       Driving down the road
       Hungry and tired.
       What I see ahead
       Doesn't get me inspired,
       It's Lowdowns.

       I look around me
       The horizon I scan.
       Got to be another place to eat than
       At Lowdowns.

       They got the highways sewed up.
       Lots of cities too.
       A polyvinyl nightmare
       Is waiting for you
       At Lowdowns.

       Pushed out the little,
       And the middle man too.
       Soon they're going to push out
       Me and you,
       At Lowdowns.

       Their plastic lettuce
       And cardboard meat
       Make the act of chewing
       A herculean feat
       At Lowdowns.

       They got the highway sewed up,
       Lots of cities too.
       A polyvinyl nightmare
       Is waiting for you
       At Lowdowns.

(At song's end HARRY and TOM exit. All three BILLIES are euphoric.)
BILLIE I. One Country Western served to order.

BILLIE II. Done!

BILLIE III. (*even when she is ecstatic, she cannot resist the self-denunciatory pin-jab*) Here it is world! Hate it!

(*The grandfather CLOCK appears and chimes eight-thirty. MARK appears in BILLIE'S mind. There is a pause as the time registers on her mind.*)

BILLIE I. (*slowly, determinedly*) Eight-thirty. He said he'd be here by eight.

BILLIE III. So I should expect him about midnight.

(*the clock ticking grows louder*)

BILLIE. If that clock weren't a gift from Mother, I'd smash it in a billion pieces.

BILLIE III. Over his head.

(*CLOCK disappears*)

(*Two ORANGE MEN appear. They are rhythmic embodiments of the riffs a composer does when her/his mind wanders.*)

> Late at night, no Mark in sight
> Silly Billie's perennial plight.
> Wait and wait and wait some more
> Never able to even the score.
>
> Score, boar, mouse will roar
> Roar, tore, same old lore
> Lore, bore, never more.
> Skidillie skidallie, the girl will fall
> Because the boy doesn't care at all.

(*ORANGE MEN disappear*)

BILLIE II. (*thinking hard*) Wait a minute. Maybe he said he wouldn't get here 'til around nine.

BILLIE III. Notice how he always says "around" and "about." Never "at."

BILLIE II. Well, it's hard for him to know when he'll get out of work this time of year. Everything's due.

BILLIE I. That's a real problem for someone who puts everything off.

(*RICHARD appears next to MARK in BILLIE'S mind*)

He's just like Richard. Neither one ever learned to tell time.

BILLIE III. Did they ever meet? Maybe it's contagious.

BILLIE I. And I can't develop an immunity.

BILLIE III. Or else I'm the carrier.

BILLIE II. If you're really serious about Country Western tomorrow night, you better get that flat pick out again.

(*MARK and RICHARD disappear*)

BILLIE I. (*already worrying that the song is wrong*) Let it sit. Make sure it's right before I waste any more time on it.

BILLIE II. Then take another look at the speech.

BILLIE I. (*Starts to look for the speech. At first she is relaxed, but she gets more and more tense as she can't find it.*) Well, it probably wouldn't hurt, even though it's only a few introductory remarks.

BILLIE III. A prelude to disaster.

BILLIE I. (*who has walked to the bookcase and been brought up short*) Where is my speech? I put it on top of the bookcase.

BILLIE II. You're sure that's where you put it?

BILLIE I. I'm positive. I put it right beside Berdell's *Labor History*.

BILLIE III. Someone has taken it.

BILLIE II. Why would anyone take it?

BILLIE III. Ask them!

BILLIE I. I've got to find it. Tom can improvise in front of people. I must know word for word what I'm going to say.

BILLIE III. If I had to improvise, I'd faint dead away.

BILLIE I. (*imagining what would undoubtedly happen*) Remember that story about the woman who fainted and everyone thought she was dead *so they buried her alive!*

BILLIE II. (*starting to fear the worst*) Well, I don't have time to write another one, not on my schedule.

BILLIE III. I'll just stay home and sit out the vote. That's the smart money anyway.

BILLIE I. (*wincing with pain*) There's a sharp pain in my chest. What's a heart attack like?

BILLIE III. A sharp pain in the chest.

BILLIE II. (*trying to regain control*) That speech is here some place. It has to be. Retrace every step.

(*BILLIE I starts to retrace in cold terror*)

BILLIE III. (*with her usual optimism*) It won't do any good. It's gone.

BILLIE I. (*distantly*) I remember taking it out of the typewriter, walking past the piano...

BILLIE III. To the bookcase.

BILLIE I. *(who had stopped by the piano)* Here it is on the piano.

BILLIE III. *(incredulous)* Well, how did it get there!

BILLIE II. *(disdainfully)* I wonder. *(growing irritation)* Well now that I have it...

(Sound of ticking. CLOCK appears. BILLIE I starts to practice her speech. But a few words into it, the CLOCK chimes nine bells.)

BILLIE III. What *(pause)* time *(pause)* is it?

BILLIE I. You'll hear a lot of people these days saying unions are old-fashioned. Well I say, if unions are old-fashioned, so are decency and humanity because that's what unions are really about—the right of every individual to decent, humane working conditions.

(CLOCK disappears. MARK appears in BILLIE'S mind. She confronts him.)

BILLIE I. Where are you? You know how superstitious I am about people wishing me good luck before a performance.

BILLIE III. *(confronting MARK)* I'll forget my speech totally, play the song horribly, make a complete fool of myself, and the union will be voted down—all because of you.

(MARK disappears)

BILLIE II. Stop yammering. Because he's not here on the stroke of nine could mean either that he might arrive late, *or* that he did not arrive early.

BILLIE I. You sound just like a lawyer.

BILLIE II. Look, even if he'd come early, I've so much work to do, I'd have had to send him away.

BILLIE III. *I* know that. *He* doesn't.

BILLIE I. The only reason I'd like to be a man is then I'd never be a woman waiting for one.

(BILLIE I flounces offstage. ORANGE MEN appear.)

> He is late
> She must wait
> Biting, biting, at the bait
> Anger bubbling into hate.
> At this rate
> The ritual date
> Puts so much weight
> On the female mate
> That the only solution
> We can see
> Is to go it alone
> Through eternity

(THEY exit)

BILLIE II. (*trying to go over her speech to divert herself, but is totally unsuccessful as she focuses all her anxieties on the absent MARK*) Go over the speech again.

BILLIE III. (*not interested and in a deadly tone*) I know it.

BILLIE II. You just said you didn't.

3BILLIE III. I lied. (*pause, MARK and RICHARD appear in her mind*)

BILLIE II. A relationship outside marriage is impossible and marriage was worse.

BILLIE III. Men. I should have listened to what my mother told me about them.

BILLIE II. What did she tell you?

BILLIE III. I don't know; I didn't listen.

BILLIE II. Tomorrow night is all that matters.

BILLIE III. (*direly*) What about last night?

(*CLOYCE, an old school friend of Mark's, now appears in BILLIE'S mind. She is attractive, bubbly, a coquette and a clear and present danger to BILLIE. BILLIE starts to remember the one and only time she met CLOYCE. She and MARK had gone shopping for shoes, and lo and behold, whom should they meet.*)

CLOYCE. (*with shoe box in hand*) Can I fit you, Sir?

BILLIE II. (*incredulous*) That was an accidental meeting. You were there. Nothing happened.

BILLIE III. The point is, what would have happened if I hadn't been there?

CLOYCE. Yes, we have a very nice walking shoe. What the policemen wear.

BILLIE II. He wouldn't be interested in a woman like that—empty as a balloon.

BILLIE III. Men today *say* they want a strong woman, but they're lying in their teeth.

CLOYCE. Have a seat right over there. I'll be with you in a moment.

BILLIE II. Even if he is with her now—which he isn't.

BILLIE III. Is.

BILLIE II. (*ignoring her*) You don't want another monogamous relationship anyway.

BILLIE III. Of course I don't want another monogamous relationship. I just don't want him with another woman!

(*BILLIE II and III disappear. The memory scene begins.*)

CLOYCE. What size foot?

MARK. Size ten triple E.

CLOYCE. (*recognizing MARK*) Mark Wazcot! (*she laughs "her" laugh and starts the school pep rally chant*) Cha Cha a boo. Cha Cha a boo.

(*MARK chimes in*)

MARK and CLOYCE. Fairmont High, is the school for you. (*both hug*)

MARK. (*delighted to see her, oblivious to BILLIE'S jealousy*) Cloyce Morrow! Selling shoes!

CLOYCE. (*always seductively "on"*) Well, actually, I'm a gemologist.

BILLIE I. (*in disbelief to herself*) A gemologist.

CLOYCE. But 'til I get my certificate—or a little diamond of my own, I'm peddling Buster Browns. (*laughs that laugh again*) But don't let me go on and on about myself. How are you doing?

MARK. Can't complain.

BILLIE I. Since when?

CLOYCE. (*with double entendre in her voice*) I always knew an old tromboner like you would go far. (*she laughs*)

BILLIE I. I didn't know you played the trombone.

(*a donkey HEAD is placed on BILLIE'S head*)

MARK. I didn't...Oh, I'm sorry? Cloyce Morrow, this is Billie Murphy.

CLOYCE. Hi, Betty!

BILLIE I. Billie.

CLOYCE. (*she is clearly not listening*) Yeah.

MARK. I don't believe it, of all people to bump into.

BILLIE I. Yeah.

MARK. (*to CLOYCE*) You look terrific.

CLOYCE. Thank you, I've lost a little weight over the years. I'm not the roly-poly barrel of fun you used to know. Would you believe I used to be fat?

BILLIE I. Yes.

CLOYCE. (*she has not heard BILLIE'S reply*) Bonnie?

BILLIE I. Billie.

CLOYCE. Yeah. (*to MARK*) Listen, we must get together and talk over old times. I'm in the book. There's nothing I like better than meeting old friends, unless it's "making" new ones. (*laughs*) Bye, Billie.

BILLIE I. Barney.

CLOYCE. Yeah.

(*BILLIE I and MARK leave the store and exit stage*)

CLOYCE. (*to another customer*) I think we do have shoes for squash. (*exits*)

BILLIE II. (*as the memory disappears from her mind*) Chances are he never saw her again.

BILLIE III. Whose chances?

(*RICHARD appears in her mind*)

BILLIE II. I'm just too close to the break up of my marriage to handle another relationship.

BILLIE III. (*a nerve has been touched*) I was not married. An annulment means there was no marriage.

BILLIE II. So what do you call an annulled marriage?

BILLIE III. A mistake.

BILLIE II. (*in total agreement, her frustration growing*) There ought to be a requirement that every man take special classes before he's even allowed to talk to a women, to say nothing about marriage. (*thinking*) "Introduction to Sensitivity."

BILLIE III. "Dishwashing through the Ages."

BILLIE II. "The Time Piece and the Cod Piece."

BILLIE III. "What's Good for the Goose is Good for the Gander."

BILLIE II. I've got no time to think about you, Richard.

BILLIE III. Go fall in a manhole.

BILLIE II. I think that's a sexist term.

BILLIE III. What connected with Richard wasn't?

(*BILLIE II sings*)

> *The Man I Wanted to Marry*
> I had become the man
> I wanted to marry.
> I did all he could have done,
> Lug, load, carry.
>
> I did all the income tax,
> With home repairs never lax.
> I'd shop and cook every meal,
> Forget how rotten that I feel.
>
> By him I'd act beguiled
> In argument always mild.
> I always opened my own door,
> I asked for less when I needed more.

I knew what liberation meant,
I would never cry or lean,
On a strong man no more depend.
I was where the buck ends.

I had only one slight wish.
Please don't think me too contrary,
Why did not my husband become,
The wife he wanted to marry

(RICHARD disappears)

BILLIE II. And Richard wasn't the only one. Even when I was a kid, boys made me miserable. Remember that terror in fifth grade—you know Mary Ann Roerig's brother?

BILLIE III. Peter...he was so mean to me I almost quit school to get away from him.

BILLIE II. Still, you had a crush on him.

BILLIE III. I did not! *(she did)*

(A memory scene begins in which Billie's MOTHER uses loving humor to put the fight back in her daughter. BILLIE I enters the stage. She is eight years old wearing her best coat and hat carrying a suitcase crying her eyes out.)

MOTHER. Where are you going Billie?

YOUNG BILLIE. *(fighting tears)* To Aunt Evelyn's.

MOTHER. When are you coming back?

YOUNG BILLIE. Never!

MOTHER. Never's a long time.

YOUNG BILLIE. *(beginning to cry)* Everybody made fun of me in school again today.

MOTHER. Who's everybody?

YOUNG BILLIE. They made up a poem about me.

MOTHER. What did it say?

YOUNG BILLIE. Look at Billie Murphy
              Look at Billie Murphy
              She got her dress at the Salvation Army.

MOTHER. Who said that?

YOUNG BILLIE. Peter Roerig.

MOTHER. Sometimes little boys put little girls down to build them-selves up. But you can't let it get to you. That's what they want!

YOUNG BILLIE. Yeah, but...

MOTHER. No "Yeah buts." *(with a mother's shining smile)* You can do it all, Billie Boppity Boo. You've got a great musical talent.

YOUNG BILLIE. *(starting to cheer up in spite of herself)* Aw, Mom!

MOTHER. No, I mean it, I could sing your songs all day!

YOUNG BILLIE. Peter Roerig said my songs was nutty, and that I wasn't writing songs anyway, I was just crazy!

MOTHER. *(with humor, teasing BILLIE out of her despair)* Well, take him up on it. Do like your daddy said. Act as crazy as you want all the time. Then, when things really get bad, and you start walking around with bananas in your ears, everybody'll say, "She's not crazy, I've known her a long time and she always carries on like that." And they won't lock you up.

YOUNG BILLIE I. How can I do that when they're always making fun of me?

MOTHER. Whenever anyone talks mean, just sing that song your daddy wrote for you, and the trick is to sing it louder than they're talking.

YOUNG BILLIE. I wish Daddy was here to sing it.

MOTHER. *(with great tenderness)* He's here in our hearts. Want me to sing that song now? *(singing)*

Ten Commandments of Greed

MOTHER. They teach you while you're young
So they'll have you when you're old,
The Ten Commandments of Greed,
By which a sorry tale is told.

A lie in time saves nine,
Touch base, then steal two.
Work hard
'Til you get others
To do the work for you.

(BILLIE joins on chorus)

MOTHER
and
BILLIE

Cheat but don't get caught
Charm will get you by.
Success will cover sin,
What you are is what you buy.

MOTHER. Darling, listen to me,
And listen to me well.
Listen to a different drummer
With a different tale to tell.

(*BILLIE joins*)

> 'Bout folks like you and me,
> Finding a new way.
> About voices of the people,
> Growing stronger day by day.
>
> Let mother teach you while you're young.

(*BILLIE starts to get teary again*)

MOTHER. Now you stop that crying. Remember what your daddy used to say. You cry, the tears will wash your nose away.

YOUNG BILLIE I. Daddy didn't say that, Aunt Evelyn did.

MOTHER. Well, how am I supposed to know who said what? Who am I? I'm just your mother—your friendly, resident workhorse.

(*YOUNG BILLIE and MOTHER exit. Her mother's words and her tears recall to her mind something that made her cry earlier that day at work.*)

BILLIE II. (*appearing*) Workhorse.

MOTHER'S VOICE. Stop crying, Honey.

HARRY'S VOICE. What's with the fountain works?

BILLIE II. Workhorse. Harry the Horse.

MOTHER'S VOICE. Stop crying, Honey.

HARRY'S VOICE. What's with the fountain works?

MOTHER'S VOICE. Workhorse.

BILLIE II. Harry the Horse.

(*The memory scene begins and BILLIE II and BILLIE III disappear. BILLIE I and HARRY THE HORSE are in the kitchen at Lowdowns.*)

HARRY THE HORSE. What's with the fountain works?

BILLIE I. I spilled some soup on that guy out there. He stood up and started screaming. Called me every name in the book. Then the manager came over and *he* started yelling.

HARRY THE HORSE. (*astonished*) Hey, what have they ever done for you that you should cry for them? Law of averages says you work a place like this twenty-five years, bust your ass moonlighting two other jobs so you can make enough to get by. All the time you're working for some guy that spends every Sunday in Bermuda. You talk union, he fires you. You don't go for the union, what do you get come retirement? Maybe a handshake if you happen to go out on a day when he's around. You don't owe none of 'em. They owe you, Kid, they owe you. So if you need a break, take it. They give you any lip, walk away. Now what did you do again?

Spilled some soup on that guy over there? I'll tell you what—take some more. Baptize the Missus!

(*HARRY and BILLIE I exit*)

BILLIE II. Without Harry I wouldn't have made it through today. I scalded my hand, lost my chitbook, Irving stopped by to pick a fight with me...

(*CLOCK interrupts this thought striking the half hour. MARK appears in her mind. BILLIE III explodes.*)

BILLIE III. And I can always count on you for the *coup de grace.*

BILLIE II. (*forcing herself to be calm*) Get back on track. Work through the song, go over the speech, get a good night's sleep, and by this time tomorrow night, the worst will be over.

BILLIE III. The vote will be over. Mark and I already are. We both know why he's not here. We're simply too embarrassed to think about it.

BILLIE II. You really think that's the reason?

BILLIE III. I know it is.

BILLIE II. How do you know?

BILLIE III. I know, that's how I know.

BILLIE II. How dare he be angry about that? He was the one at fault.

BILLIE III. The wronger he is, the angrier he gets. You know that.

(*MARK disappears as BILLIE and MARK appear in bed together. BILLIE remembers what happened the last time they were together.*)

BILLIE I. Mark?

MARK. (*sleepily*) What is it, Toughie?

BILLIE I. I'd like to ask you a question.

MARK. Shoot.

BILLIE I. (*smiling with understanding as she asks*) Why is it you never touch my breasts when we're...you know...why is that?

MARK. (*flustered*) Why didn't I...your what...I thought I...

BILLIE I. It's not that you're disinterested in that area of the female anatomy; you obviously have fixation. I mean I can't help noticing you stare at every other pair that walks by—in supermarkets, at the movies, in church.

MARK. Billie!

BILLIE I. (*sweetly*) I don't want to embarrass you. There's undoubtedly a perfectly good reason for your insensitivity. What is it?

MARK. Billie, I...

BILLIE I. (*again smiling her forgiveness*) Forget I mentioned it.

MARK. (*trying to make amends*) No, if you say I didn't touch...then I guess I didn't, and if I didn't, I'm sorry.

BILLIE I. Uh huh...

MARK. (*apologizing*) No, I really thought I...

BILLIE I. It's fine, really.

MARK. You're sure?

BILLIE I. (*without a shadow of a doubt*) Absolutely. (*pause*) You wish I had *bigger breasts*, don't you?

MARK. Billie!

BILLIE I. (*examining her breasts*) No I like mine just the way they are. Even if they don't *bobble* like Cloyce's.

(*CLOYCE appears*)

MARK. You're not going to bring her up again.

BILLIE I. Aren't I?

(*MARK leaves the bed, but remains on stage. BILLIE wraps the sheet around herself and plays the voyeur in her ensuing fantasy.*)

(*CLOYCE enters, poised on the opposite side of the stage from MARK. They hungrily appraise one another. CLOYCE and MARK start to advance towards each other.*)

BILLIE II. Stop fantasizing your own torture.

BILLIE III. No.

(*CLOYCE sings*)

> *Put Your Mark on Me*
>
> Put your mark on me
> Could you get into it?
> Put your mark on me.
> There's time to do it.
> Put every other consideration aside.
> Let our passion never subside.
> Life's too short for responsibility
> Forget everyone else;
> There's only you and me.
>
> Look at it this way,
> All work and no play,
> Makes Jack a dull boy
> And Jill a decoy
> For the blues.

That ain't news.
So choose
To lose
Your inhibitions.

(*A stuffed ANIMAL—a very sexy, albeit comical, cat with a tail that punctuates her lyrics—enters making the bedroom scene a menage a trois. Sings.*)

Put your hex on me.
Do you get my drift?
Put your hex on me
I can work a split shift.

Lets have fun where we've never been.
Let's skate where the ice is thin.

Two alone is misery,
Add one more, we've got a party.

Look at it this way,
All work and no play
Makes Jack a dull boy
And Jill a decoy for the blues,
That ain't news,
So choose to lose your inhibitions.

(*CLOYCE, MARK and the stuffed ANIMAL are now in a sexual tableau, all of which BILLIE is fantasizing, but none too well since this is beyond her experience*)

BILLIE II. Stop this!

BILLIE III. (*There was never more honesty in the world than at this moment. The three BILLIES have the concentration of a bird dog sighting its prey.*) I can't.

BILLIE I. Is that how they do it?

BILLIE II. I don't know.

BILLIE I. That can't be right. (*adjusts them as carefully as if she were handling a poisonous snake*)

BILLIE III. That's it. That's how they do it.

BILLIE II. Stop it!

BILLIE III. In a minute.

BILLIE II. Now! (*the last exchange is repeated as BILLIE I defensively pushes the lurid image from her mind and takes charge*) I will not waste one more second of my life on a man. I'm through with all of them.

BILLIE III. No more men. I feel better already—like walking out of a dentist's office. I should have made this decision a long time ago. (*an even better idea*) I'll give up sex, too. Why not? Other people have done it. Ghandi, Heloise and Abelard, Jesus, Ralph Nader. I don't need *anyone* or anything.

(*three WOMEN in white tuxedoes enter and sing "Self-Sufficient" song*)

> She's sufficient, not deficient;
> She's efficient and proficient.
> She reads all of Marx in German,
> Chinese for her is easy learnin'.
> She takes charge when it is needed,
> Never gets rushed or over heated.
> She knows just where she is going
> And she'll get there.
>
> Pass the pasta, it doesn't matter to her.
> She always slimmer never fatter
> Life's the student, she the teacher,
> This enchanting creature.
>
> She doesn't gab, she has conversations
> And what she says inspires nations.
> Her every word is a *bon mot*.
> There's nothing she does not know!
>
> She always garners wild ovations
> For her jazz chords and modulations.
> She joins Ella in the tough scats;
> Waller asked her, "Should I be called Fats?"
> She deciphers Martin Buber;
> Kant can't hold a candle to her.
> Music and philosophy are in her right key.
>
> When she's up against a solid wall,
> She might stumble but she'll never fall.
> Beating down the odds is her best game.
> There's no lion she can't tame.

> And though men around her hover,
> They dare not ask too much of her.
> She knows love is relative,
> She knows how to live.

BILLIE I. (*enters costumed as the self-sufficient woman*) Hi, Hi, Hi, I am I and I am what many of you have striven for but few have achieved: a completely self-sufficient woman. Notice the desk, the fork, the metric conversion ruler, the solar-operated sexual regulator, all in one garment making me mentally and physically complete at all times. On the flip side I have inserted a pouch in which I carry a microtape of the complete works of John L. Lewis, Otis Redding, and Florence Nightingale. I am also self-insistent, self-resistant, self-consistent, and water repellant. I can organize a union in three minutes flat, five during a rainstorm, stage a walk-out in a matter of seconds, and that's all before breakfast. After breakfast, I really get down to work. Work, work, work, work, work, it comes so easy to me, and I owe it all to the fact that I am a self-sufficient woman. I am united to I.

(*BILLIE I and the FEMALE CHORUS disappear singing the chorus. BILLIE III appears and sings*)

> Every task finds me deficient,
> I am always inefficient.
> No one loves or listens to me;
> People passing stare right through me.
> I renounce this rotten rat race.
> Where's the next train out of this place?
> But I don't care where I am going,
> So don't hurry.

BILLIE II. (*appearing*) This is like being in a car with no brakes; get my mind off what it's on or I'll crash. Where's that mystery I was reading?

BILLIE III. I can't read now. I'm too wrought up. Is there any ice cream left?

(*MEDIA PERSONALITY appears in BILLIE'S mind, warning against fat*)

MEDIA.   Oh gee, but ain't it grand
           To have a gal so big and fat
           That when you go to hug her
           You don't know where you're at.

BILLIE III. *(confronting MEDIA)* Ice cream's not fattening. It's nothing but hot, popped air.

(MEDIA disappears singing)

> It must be jelly 'cause jam
> Don't shake like that.

BILLIE II. There isn't any ice cream anyway. Read. I'll forget I'm hungry.

BILLIE III. *(outraged)* Why isn't there any?

BILLIE I. *(entering, reading)* Because if I walk out of that place with one more half gallon hidden under my cape, my stomach will turn into an ice block.

BILLIE III. I could always moonlight as a portable freezer.

BILLIE I. *(entering, trying to read the mystery)* Am I going blind, or is the light bad in here?

BILLIE III. It's better in the bedroom, and it wouldn't hurt to get off my feet for a few minutes, either.

BILLIE I. *(getting alarm clock)* If I am going to lie down, I'd better set the alarm.

BILLIE III. *(indignantly)* I won't fall asleep.

BILLIE II. Just in case.

BILLIE III. Have it your way.

BILLIE I. Ten minutes?

BILLIE II. Fifteen.

BILLIE III. Make it twenty.

(blackout)

END OF ACT I

Act II

(BILLIE II is dreaming and BILLIE III is snoring. It is a dream of betrayal and chase. ROSE and HARRY are discovered on stage in two different locales. ROSE is in a negligee, talking into a jeweled phone, pacing like a cat on the scent. HARRY, on the other end of the line, does not act like the chef at Lowdowns, but like Sam Spade of Dash Hammett.)

HARRY THE HORSE. I told you never to call me at work. We'll talk when you get here.

ROSE. I'm sick to death of this hostess/chef charade—stolen whispers behind the frialator.

HARRY THE HORSE. Pull in your thorns, Rose. I'm baiting the trap now. The mouse is a heavy user. She'll bite.

ROSE. You better be right, Harry the Horse, or you're Hank the Has-Been.

HARRY THE HORSE. Relax. Whether they call me Ned the Nasty, Avi the Avenger, or Ike the Ice, I'm Rick the Right! *(noise)* Someone just came in.

ROSE. Be careful! "Au reverse." *(exits)*

DREAM NARRATOR. *(As the narrator speaks, HARRY carefully "baits" the trap placing a large container of Lowdowns ice cream in a place where BILLIE is sure to find it. He then hides himself.)* The coffee stains on his uniform concealed the fact that Harry the Horse was accustomed to a classier wardrobe in his home turf, the docks of 'Frisco, where he hustled small-time dealers as cover for his real job with the Feds—union buster.

(DREAM NARRATOR continues as BILLIE I stealthily enters the room looking over her shoulder on her way to the ice cream)

DREAM NARRATOR. The mouse sneaks into the room, her habit getting in the way of her sense. Spying the ice cream, she snatches it under her cape and is about to make off with it when...

(HARRY appears, camera in hand. Flash bulbs go off. BILLIE shields her eyes from the assault. She does not see HARRY, only the blinding light.)

BILLIE I. Help! What is it? Stop! My eyes!

(*having the evidence he needs, HARRY emerges from behind the flashing bulbs*)

BILLIE I. Harry! What are you...?

HARRY THE HORSE. Nick the Dick's the name.

BILLIE I. (*in horror*) Nick the Dick, the union buster!

HARRY THE HORSE. (*takes hold of her arm to lead her offstage*) With enough evidence to put you away for life.

(*BILLIE I wrests herself free from his grasp and throws the ice cream out of the window*)

BILLIE I. There's no proof. It's your word against mine.

HARRY THE HORSE. (*with a flourish of the camera*) Pictures don't lie.

BILLIE I. You set me up, didn't you, Harry, to destroy the union?

HARRY THE HORSE. Unions are deader than a cemetery in Cleveland. I figured you for enough smarts to know that.

(*BILLIE I cries*)

Sorry it had to turn out this way, Mouse. I was beginning to get a little soft on you...

ROSE. (*appearing to HARRY*) I knew it you two-timing dick. (*lunging at BILLIE*) I'll tear your eyes out, you vixen!

HARRY THE HORSE. Stay out of this, Rose, this is my collar. I'll handle it my way.

(*Alarm goes off. BILLIE incorporates the sound into her dream.*)

HARRY THE HORSE. (*leading BILLIE I offstage*) There's the Feds now with your one-way ticket to nowhere.

BILLIE III. (*dreams on with another explanation for the alarm*) Help! The smoke alarm! Fire!

BILLIE II. (*beginning to come to consciousness and feeling for the alarm*) It's not a fire; I'm sleeping too close to the radiator. (*finding the alarm and turning it off*) What a nightmare, Harry, a mole from 'Frisco. Nothing could be more farfetched.

BILLIE III. Nothing. (*on second thought*) Where is Harry from anyway?

BILLIE II. (*taken in*) I don't think he ever said. (*but not for long*) This is the way to madness. *Relax.*

BILLIE III. (*defensively*) I am relaxed.

(*MARK appears*)

BILLIE III. (*screaming at him*) Why don't you get here so I can tell you to get out!

BILLIE I. (*entering and confronting him*) I don't care what went wrong. You could at least call. How long does it take to dial seven dig...?

BILLIE II. (*just remembering*) He can't. My phone is out of order!

(*MARK disappears*)

BILLIE I. Mark ordered a repair three days ago. You don't pay your bill the minute it's due, they turn it off. You want them to repair it for you, that's another story.

BILLIE II. You're absolutely certain Mark called them?

BILLIE I. I heard him.

BILLIE II. (*fearful*) Could he have called the wrong service?

BILLIE I. (*groaning*) I better check. Who repairs equipment now, the phone company?

BILLIE III. AT&T.

BILLIE II. I think AT&T repairs the phone, but *only* if we're on their long-distance service.

BILLIE III. That doesn't make any difference. It's if they own the phone.

BILLIE I. (*totally confused*) Wait a minute (*sinking fast*) We don't even know if the problem is with the phone. It could be on the line.

BILLIE II. So what do we do?

BILLIE III. Get a pair of cleats and climb the god damn pole!

BILLIE II. (*taking control*) Call emergency repairs. They'll know.

BILLIE III. The phone is dead!

BILLIE II. (*firmly*) Use the one in the hall.

BILLIE I. (*going to the hall*) What's the number for emergency repairs?

BILLIE II. Call information.

(*A phone booth is wheeled on stage. BILLIE steps in.*)

BILLIE I. Information 114?

BILLIE III. Yeah, it's 114.

BILLIE II. No, it's 411.

BILLIE III. (*she is dead certain, as always*) No it isn't.

BILLIE I. (*makes correct decision and dials*) Please let it be a human voice.

(*As telephone rings, three OPERATORS appear on a revolving dais. OPERATOR I has a crossword puzzle in hand, intent on solving it.*)

OPERATOR I. Operator.

BILLIE II. (*relieved*) It's a person not a thing.

BILLIE III. How can you tell?

BILLIE I. (*sweetly*) Hi, my phone is out of order—or there's a problem on the line—and I was wondering if you could...

OPERATOR I. (*interrupting*) Call emergency repairs.

BILLIE I. (*sarcastic*) We're of a remarkably similar mind. Could you give me the number of...

OPERATOR I. That information is available in your directory.

BILLIE I. It's also available in yours.

OPERATOR I. (*faster than the speed of sound*) Eight-seven-five-six-five-seven-five. (*then ponders*) What's a four-letter word for perambulator?

BILLIE I. (*frantically, speaking over the last sentence of the operator*) Where's a pen?

BILLIE II. In your pocket.

BILLIE I. (*frantically*) Paper!

BILLIE II. Use your hand.

BILLIE I. (*dials as dais revolves to reveal OPERATOR II*)

OPERATOR II. (*boredom is defined*) Operator.

BILLIE I. (*a bit flustered*) Hi, my phone is out of order. I mean, it may be the phone. I mean...

OPERATOR II. What's your lata?

BILLIE I. (*exasperation is defined*) My what?

OPERATOR II. Lata, L-a-t-a.

BILLIE III. Don't answer without legal council.

BILLIE I. What's a lata?

OPERATOR II. (*faster than the speed of sound*) Local area and transport. Check page twenty-seven and twenty-nine in your directory for that information.

BILLIE I. But...

(*OPERATOR II hangs up as dias revolves*)

BILLIE I. (*hysterically*) Where's the directory? Here's the cord. Someone's taken the book again.

BILLIE II. There's one on the floor.

(*BILLIE I checks it*)

BILLIE I. My lata is six-one-seven. (*dawning on her as she dials*) That's my area code. Why didn't she just ask the area code in the first place?

OPERATOR III. (*on the aggressive*) Operator.

BILLIE I. Hi, my phone is out of order and...

OPERATOR III. What's your lata?

BILLIE I. (*proudly*) Six-one-seven.

OPERATOR III. Six-one-seven, that's not *my* lata.

BILLIE I. (*slowly and deadly*) Whose lata is it?

OPERATOR III. Call six-seven-five-six-five-seven-five.

BILLIE I. (*relieved*) I'll call right away.

OPERATOR III. They're not open 'til Monday morning, nine o'clock.

BILLIE I. That's another three days from now. Do you have any idea what it's like for someone in my profession to be without a phone?

OPERATOR II. (*sarcastically*) What's your line of business?

BILLIE I. I'm a hired gunman.

OPERATOR III. I'm trembling with fear.

BILLIE I. I'd take my business elsewhere, but there's no where else to take it. You're a friggin' monopoly, that's what you are—a greedy, corrupt, national virus.

OPERATOR III. Look lady, take your complaints upstairs, huh? I just work here.

BILLIE I. Just!!!!

(*WORKERS emerge from everywhere with caps on their heads, tools in their hands, singing "The International" with BILLIES II & III*)

> The International
> Arise ye prisoners of starvation!
> Arise ye wretched of the earth!
> For justice thunders condemnation.
> A better world's in birth.

BILLIE I. (*simultaneously*) No one just "works"! No one is *just* a "worker"! It is by your labor the phone company runs at all! You should help make decisions, reap your *just* share of the profits. Never say you're just a "worker" or just a "housewife."

OPERATOR III. I'm both and if I don't get my ass back to work, I won't be either.

BILLIE I. Wait a minute.

OPERATOR. Look sweety, start the revolution without me, okay?

(*She hangs up. OPERATORS exit.*)

BILLIE I. She hung up. (*checks*) And I didn't get my dime back. (*exits*)

BILLIE II. (*upset with herself*) I shouldn't yell at them. They're workers. They don't make the policy—they carry it out. It's government of, by and for AT&T.

BILLIE III. (*correcting her*) IT&T.

BILLIE II. (*insisting*) AT&T.

BILLIE III. (*agreeing, sort of*) AT&T and IT&T.

TAP DANCER. (*entering*) Tea for two and two for tea. (*exits*)

BILLIE II. (*a possible course of action occurs to her*) Call the president of AT&T. Threaten to sue him.

BILLIE III. I can't. The phone is out of order! (*the only reasonable alternative occurs to her*) I'll kill him instead.

BILLIE II. (*her mind starts to drift*) Damn telephone!

BILLIE III. Damn telephone!

(*BILLIE III fantasizes another installment of her ideal state. The three tuxedoed SELF-SUFFICIENTS reappear singing.*)

> *Self-Sufficient*
>
> When she's up against a solid wall
> She might stumble but she'll never fall
> Beating down the odds is her best game
> There's no lion she can't tame.
>
> And though men around her hover
> They dare not ask too much of her.
> She knows love is relative
> She knows how to live.
>
> She's sufficient not deficient,
> She's efficient and proficient.
> She reads all of Marx in German,
> Chinese for her is easy learnin'.
> She takes charge when it is needed,
> Never gets rushed or overheated.
> She knows just where she is going
> And she'll get there.

(*BILLIE I enters as the self-sufficient woman. She is wearing an elaborate telephone hat and bodice with wires coming out everywhere.*)

BILLIE I. Hi. It's self-sufficient me again. This time with your new no-fail telephone. It's not controlled by AT&T, your local lata, or Lotta Lenya. It is a people's phone run on people's power. What? A demonstration? Of course. It has two plugs. Place one in the positive, one in the negative currents of your own body. No fees, no interference, just plug it in and dial away.

(*Her phone rings. BILLIE I answers.*)

VOICE. (*offstage*) *Bonjour. Comment-allez vous aujourd'hui?*

BILLIE I. *Je vais tres bien.*

VOICE. (*offstage*) *Je vais tres bien aussi. Madame Pompidou est dans la cuisine en faisons les bonbons.*

BILLIE I. *Je suis tres heureux qu'elle travail.* (*hangs up the phone*) The miracle of this is—I don't speak French. The phone does.

(*Exiting, the SELF-SUFFICIENTS hum the song as BILLIE I speaks German, Spanish, Chinese, etc. into her phone. Upon their exit lights dim leaving only a small light in each of the cubicles.*)

BILLIE III. (*frightened*) I don't remember turning out the lights when I went into the hall to use the phone.

BILLIE II. I must have.

BILLIE III. (*the stillness of terror*) Shhh. Did you hear that?

BILLIE II. What?

BILLIE III. There it is again.

BILLIE II. (*equally terrified*) That rattle?

BILLIE III. Yes.

BILLIE II. (*not as convinced as she tries to sound*) It's the heat pushing through the pipes.

BILLIE III. Did they ever find that lunatic who escaped from the asylum three days ago?

BILLIE II. (*taking control, almost*) Turn the light on.

BILLIE III. I'm not moving.

BILLIE II. *Turn it on!*

(*lights come up*)

BILLIE II. (*repeating the only thought that gives her comfort*) Now get a hold of yourself. By this time tomorrow night the worst part will be over.

BILLIE III. Tomorrow night will never come.

(*ROSE appears. BILLIE III eyes her.*)

She's known about the union all along and has watched us walk head-long into an ambush. She's probably closeted with management right now giving them all our names.

BILLIE II. (*exasperated beyond measure*) You're getting neurotic about that woman. She's become a peg for you to hang all your fears on.

BILLIE III. (*flabbergasted at the charge*) She as much as said...

BILLIE II. (*interrupting*) She talks buckshot, you know that. Eventually she hits everything and none of it means anything.

BILLIE III. (*smug and snide*) Uh huh.

BILLIE II. Look, we have the tightest organization possible. Bernice said her own husband doesn't know about the union drive. How could Rose have found out?

(*ROSE disappears, smug smile on her face*)

BILLIE III. We have an informer.

BILLIE II. We do not.

BILLIE III. Everyone else in this country has one. Why not us?

BILLIE II. Because we don't. (*then*) Who?

BILLIE III. Clifford Banks.

(*CLIFFORD BANKS walks into her mind. He is fidgeting with his briefcase which seems to have a thousand compartments. The sound of zippers opening and closing underscores the scene.*)

BILLIE II. (*disbelieving, or at least wanting to*) Be serious.

BILLIE III. Haven't you ever wondered what he puts in that briefcase of his? He opens and closes it a thousand times every meeting.

BILLIE II. Nothing. He is a fidgeter.

BILLIE III. And those little ferret eyes.

BILLIE II. He's nearsighted.

(*CLIFFORD crosses stage*)

BILLIE III. And he is forever slipping out into the hall.

BILLIE II. (*trying to convince herself one last time that CLIFFORD is innocent*) For a cigarette.

(*CLIFFORD picks up phone and dials. ROSE appears, phone in hand.*)

BILLIE III. Or to use the telephone, to call Rose, to report every move we make.

(*CLIFFORD and ROSE disappear*)

BILLIE II. (*starting to be won over to her darker imaginings, she pauses, reflects, then*) What exactly did Rose say?

BILLIE III. (*smug and mysterious*) Well, right before she left today, she "summoned" us. First there was that moment with Harry and then...

(*The two BILLIES disappear as ROSE enters the scene and the memory of what happened earlier today replays itself in BILLIE'S mind.*)

ROSE. Billie, Tom? Could I see you out back?

TOM. (*from offstage*) Where are you, Rose?

ROSE. I'm out back.

(*TOM appears followed by BILLIE*)

Would you mind closing the door? We're not heating the alley.

(*THEY have closed the door. ROSE continues like the cat who has swallowed an aviary.*)

I saw you whispering to Bernice behind the bubbler. Complaining about our wages again, were we? I might have the two of you sued for interfering with Lowell Downing's livelihood.

HARRY THE HORSE. (*entering in time to hear ROSE'S last remark*) Or we might sue him for interfering with ours.

ROSE. (*going to the door to close it tighter*) Harry, shh! The Downing executives are having a dinner discussion, "Fast Food and Cutlery."

HARRY THE HORSE. Why don't they just eat out of the trough with Harry the Horse?

ROSE. (*ever the flirt with HARRY*) "Harry the Horse," such a silly name for a chef. What does it mean anyway?

HARRY THE HORSE. It means I have to work like a horse around here, not like those executive clowns you fawn over.

ROSE. (*offended*) I don't fawn over anyone. It's just that your better class of clientele requires special handling.

HARRY THE HORSE. Better, huh? Well, I'd like to see one of those three-piece suits service the temperature control on a Baine-Marie, take apart a compressor, keep four sauces cooking at the right consistency while you're installing new heating elements in a 2000-watt toaster and trying to straighten out a few vendors about their mistakes on food-order sheets. Fact is, in most work, there's more thinking goes on than muscling. So who's better than who and why?

(*BILLIE and TOM applaud. ROSE fumes.*)

VOICE. (*from offstage*) Harry, the frialator's on the blink again.

HARRY THE HORSE. (*to ROSE*) Want to give Lowell D. a call—have him jet in and fix it? (*exits*)

ROSE. (*screaming after the departing HARRY*) How dare you make fun of Mr. Downing. Without him you wouldn't have a job at all! And try going without your paycheck for awhile. Then you won't act so high and mighty!

TOM. We've been going without our paychecks ever since we started to work here. It's the customers who have to pay our wages in tips because they know we don't get diddly.

ROSE. The customer doesn't have to tip. It's still a free country, despite what all your communist "agitators" are trying to turn it into.

BILLIE III. (*appearing*) We could kill her right now. No jury would ever convict us. (*disappears*)

BILLIE I. Just what are you charging us with now?

ROSE. (*sly and supreme*) Scratch a union, you find a communist. I suggest you "mule" that over before you set up shop again behind the bubbler. (*exits*)

BILLIE I. (*in sotto voce hysterics*) She knows. We'll all be fired!

TOM. (*calming her down*) Accusations run out of her like water out of a pump. Last week she decided everyone was stealing catchup dispensers.

(*LIPS appear*)

Next she'll say the reason we polish the floor is so she'll slip and break her neck.

(*a loud crash and a scream from offstage*)

TOM. (*running off*) Oh my God! Rose was that you!

BILLIE II. Put that woman out of your mind.

(*steaming, BILLIE I goes to piano to play introduction to "Lowdown Hostess Rose"*)

BILLIE I. How can I! I have to work with that sequined squid every day.

BILLIE II. She's not worth wasting one more second on.

BILLIE III. You know what she's like—one of those mercenaries you read about. No allegiance to anyone or anything!

BILLIE I. I only hope I'm around to see the day she finds out that what she's selling out for she'll never get.

(*BILLIE I plays "Lowdown Hostess Rose" as ROSE et. al. enact it*)

> *Lowdown Hostess Rose*
>
> Lowdown Hostess Rose
> Sashaying down the aisle,
> Dressed in silks and such
> Flashing her boss-pleasing smile.
>
> Lowdown Hostess Rose
> Seating them at the table
> Bending over to show
> Her non-union label.
>
> Now Rose, when the morning comes
> Better have no doubt.
> It's gonna matter what you did
> When the lights were out.
>
> Lowdown Hostess Rose
> There's a run in your left stocking.

But it ain't human error
Which we find shocking.

It's casting your pearls before the swine,
It's going to the highest bidder
And selling your own class down
Down, down the river.

(as THEY sing the final chorus, ROSE leaves the stage)

Now Rose, when the morning comes
Better have no doubt
It's gonna matter what you did
When the lights were out.

BILLIE II. *(over end of song)* If I don't get my mind off Rose Startner, I'll have a nervous breakdown.

BILLIE III. How can anyone remain sane with my pressures? Least of all me!

BILLIE II. Relax.

BILLIE III. No.

BILLIE II. Let your mind drift. Breathe in and out.

(sound of deep breathing fills the space)

BILLIE III. Why do I have to remind myself to breathe?

BILLIE II. Sometimes you forget.

BILLIE III. What I really need is a good movie—I mean I really *need* one. I think they're showing *Revenge of the Damned* with Bella Lugosi down the street.

BILLIE II. Breathe in, breathe out.

(Sounds of deep breathing fill the air. She is beginning to relax and her mind drifts. Disconnected images float through her mind. The ORANGE MEN appear.)

ORANGE MEN. Bella Lugosi, Stanislavski, Martin Nagronski, Morris Carnovsky, Dostoevsky, Paddy Chaevsky, Madam Najinsky, Carl Yastremsky.

(a MAN in a trench coat walks out of a movie and into BILLIE'S consciousness)

MAN. Is this the plane to Cairo?

(offstage a Peter Lorre voice answers)

PETER LORRE. Yes it is.

(MAN exits toward voice. Donkey MASK appears. CLOYCE walks across BILLIE'S consciousness, laughing her laugh, with a shoe on her head.)

BILLIE III. *(eyeing CLOYCE)* Is it better to wonder or to know?

BILLIE II. In this case, neither.

(CLOYCE exits. Lowdowns' sign appears.)

BILLIE III. Are you aware of all the things I should be worrying about right now if I weren't worrying about what that place reduces me to worrying about. Central America, the bomb...

BILLIE II. All that will still be there waiting for me day after tomorrow. Breathe in, breathe out.

CONDUCTOR. *(appearing)* The orchestra will now perform the Horn Sonata in F major by Carl Ditter Von Dittersdorf. *(disappears)*

BILLIE II. *(as MARK appears)* Horn! He's probably stuck in traffic.

BILLIE III. Or he doesn't have the down payment for a tank of gas.

BILLIE II. If he is perpetually late, you struggle with him. That's the dialectic of history. Society develops through struggle. Humanity develops through struggle.

BILLIE III. Yeah, but he ain't human.

(MARK disappears. IRVING now attempts to enter BILLIE'S consciousness. IRVING is a friend, albeit a constant irritant; a representative of the dogmatic left who always knows what's right.)

BILLIE III. *(spying IRVING)* Neither are you, Irving.

BILLIE II. *(to IRVING)* I don't have time to think about you now.

(IRVING exits. A voluptuous Central American NATIVE, a la Carmen Miranda, who exists only in the mind of the hard-sell media, now enters BILLIE'S mind. MINGO MANGO sings one of those mindless jingles that are repeated so often by the media they lay siege to our consciousness.)

> Mingo Mango
>
> I am Mingo Mango,
> Picking fruit as I tango.
> Happy, working and able
> To brighten up your table.

(MINGO MANGO freezes as BILLIE II and BILLIE III attack her)

BILLIE II. If I have to have a song in my head, it could at least not be a racist, sexist commercial.

BILLIE III. It could at least be mine.

BILLIE II. It could at least be good.

BILLIE III. Contradiction in terms. I don't have any good ones.

MINGO   Here near the equator,
MANGO.   Fruit blooms always,
             And later, we ship it to United States
             To brighten up your dinner plates.

(*Chorus of NATIVES bearing fruit baskets. MINGO MANGO and CHORUS start a wild Latin dance. BILLIE I enters and pushes them from her mind. During the melee, IRVING enters. MINGO MANGO and her FRUIT PICKERS sing.*)

             When luscious fruit is pink and ripe
             We gently pluck it from the tree.
             So it will not break or bruise
             We treat it like a sweet baby.

(*THEY exit*)

IRVING. (*the perfect irritant*) If you could only write popular songs.

BILLIE I. (*turning, and spying him, she moves in on him to push him away*) Irving!

BILLIE II. I have far more important things to think about than Irving.

MINGO MANGO. (*racing through BILLIE'S mind one more time as BILLIE turns and takes out after her*)

             Ai yi yi yi yi yi yi
             Yi yi yi yi yi yi

BILLIE II. Help!!

(*IRVING is now seated. The rest of the customers do not appear in BILLIE'S mind though she addresses them.*)

IRVING. (*the psychologist*) Billie, the problem with you is you're too moody, too many highs and lows.

BILLIE I. Try waiting on tables for a living.

IRVING. (*the worker*) My brother's a coal miner, big deal.

BILLIE I. Coal miners get better pay, job advancement, retirement plans. They strike, they shut down entire industries. If all the Lowdowns' workers in the country went out, all that would happen would be a decline in the plastic dividends on Wall Street and a drop in antacid sales.

IRVING. (*the sexist*) I thought my mother *kvetched* 'til I met you.

BILLIE I. I thought the president was sexist 'til I met you.

IRVING. (*the dialectician*) You always have to have the last word.

BILLIE I. Who does?

(*IRVING mutters as BILLIE goes off to serve another customer*)

IRVING. Okay, okay, okay.

BILLIE I. (*to customer's request*) Sorry, the breakfast grill is off after eleven-thirty. (*listens to counter suggestion then responds none too hopefully*) I'll put in the order. (*calls order to kitchen*) Give me a toasted egg sandwich. Take the egg out, put the toast on the side, add marmalade. (*returns to IRVING*)

IRVING. You going to the Alliance meeting tonight?

BILLIE I. (*looking around and talking sotto voce out of the side of her mouth*) I am writing a song for a very important event tomorrow night I am not free to talk about *here*. Now, are you planning to eat or just admire the plastic decor?

IRVING. Brahma burger, rare, my usual.

BILLIE I. (*to kitchen*) Bloody brahma. (*goes to another customer*) Yes, sir, you want a clam Jumbowambe? (*pause*) I'm sorry, you have to take it with mayonnaise. They're all made up in advance. (*pause for reply*) I don't know how many weeks. (*to kitchen*) Clam jam. (*returns to IRVING*)

IRVING. So you're not coming to the meeting. (*shaking his head in disappointment*) Billie, you take your little songs so seriously.

BILLIE I. (*interrupts, coming to a slow boil*) "Little" songs?

IRVING. I didn't say your songs were little.

BILLIE I. Then you've got a damn good ventriloquist. Look Irving, if you'd ever get your nose out of your ideology, you might notice that most people, particularly women, don't work in essential industry like coal. They type someone else's letters and sell headache pills and when the rewards are doled out, they get a kick in the ass. So the reason I write "little songs" is to give these people a sense of themselves.

IRVING. Nobody questions your motives, but the time involved! I mean, if you could write like Shostakovitch, or even that barefoot guy in the tuxedo and get recorded, then you'd be reaching people. I mean, if you have to take time away from valuable work to compose, at least make it popular. Get on television.

BILLIE I. Which network first or should I be simulcast on all at once? Come off it, Irving. Even Pete Seeger has never been allowed on commercial television in this country.

IRVING. (*never at a loss for a put-down even if it is a non-sequitur*) You are not Pete Seeger.

BILLIE I. You are not Eugene V. Debs.

IRVING. I never tried to be.

BILLIE I. Pity. (*meaningful pause*) Are you finished with that brahma burger?

IRVING. No.

BILLIE I. Yes you are! (*takes the burger*)

IRVING. Billie, you can be a real castra...

BILLIE I. (*deadly*) Advance one more syllable and you're a dead man.

(*IRVING leaves. All mayhem breaks loose. MINGO MANGO runs across the stage singing "Ai yi yi yi yi." MARK, the LIPS, and the DONKEY HEAD appear and disapper.*)

BILLIE I. That's what gets me. Men in the movement who ought to know better are just as sexist as all the others.

BILLIE III. All men are a less developed species.

BILLIE II. (*thinking hard*) If I were a castrater...

BILLIE I. (*screaming*) That's a vicious, senseless term. It doesn't mean anything.

BILLIE II. I know. But even if it did and I were, what would be the word for what he does to me?

BILLIE I. (*getting what she's driving at*) You mean when he undermines me as a woman?

(*all three BILLIES are deep in thought trying to come up with the answer*)

BILLIE II. Yes. What is the word for what a man does to a woman that's the same as what men *say* women do to them?

(*BILLIES think*)

Ummm.

BILLIE III. Is it...? No.

BILLIE I. (*dawning awareness*) That word doesn't exist in the entire English sexist language!

BILLIE II. (*sly and supreme*) We'll invent it! (*Pause. Then, hitting one into the bleachers.*) "Clitorator"!

BILLIE III. (*looks at audience slit-eyed and belts out another one*) "Tube-tier"!

BILLIE I. (*and yet another one*) "Vulvarizer"!

BILLIE III. (*riffs*) Don't you clitorate and vulvarize and tube-tie me. Just let me be. Let me be.

(*BILLIE I starts intro to "Dynamite Eatin' Baby"*)

Dynamite Eatin' Baby

BILLIE I.   Who said words don't hurt
            It was not a woman
            They cut hard and deep.
            They are no fun

(*BATS OUT OF HELL, a female rock group, appears*)

            Battles with words
            Are a one way street
            Cause men made the words
            Women take the heat

(*as a smoke bomb goes off, BATS OUT OF HELL circle and prepare to perform*)

BILLIE III. Think of all the vicious, sexist tripe heaped on us everyday!

BILLIE II.   I'm thinkin'.

(*rock GROUP launches into chorus of song*)

BATS   Bitch, nag, whine,
OUT OF   You can take those words and shove 'em
HELL.   Where the sun don't shine
            'Cause I'm sick and tired of 'em.
            Bitch, nag, whine.

LEAD.   I'm a dynamite eatin' baby.
CHORUS.   She's a dynamite eatin' baby
            Oooo, ooo, gonna explode.
LEAD.   I'm a dynamite eatin' baby.
CHORUS.   She's a dynamite eatin' baby
            Oooo, ooo gotta unload.
LEAD.   I've read your dictionary
            Each and every line
            And turned the other cheek
            One too many times.

            I'm getting ready
            To turn the tables.
            Just watch the lady
            Shred the labels.

CHORUS.   Bitch, nag, whine
            You can take those words and shove 'em
            Where the sun don't shine

                    'Cause I'm sick and tired of 'em
                    Bitch, nag, whine

LEAD.   I'm a dynamite eatin' baby
CHORUS.   She's a dynamite eatin' baby
LEAD.   I'm a dynamite eatin' baby

LEAD and   Gonna explode.
CHORUS.

(*BATS OUT OF HELL exit*)

BILLIE I. (*continuing to play piano, on fire with creative energy*) This rhythm is cooking!

BILLIE II. Hot as a pistol!

BILLIE I. (*changes rhythm to swing and riffs "Won't It Be Fine"*) And the temperature is rising. Remember that little swing-time Harry and I fiddled around with for solidarity day? (*plays introduction to "Won't It Be Fine" and sings*)

> One of us alone
> Can be beat of course
> Everyone together
> An unbeatable force

BILLIE I. (*continuing to play song*) This has the right feel for tomorrow night. It's so right I can touch it. Why didn't I think of it before? Swing takes us back to the time when unions were on the move in this country.

BILLIE II. Make us feel we'll rise again.

BILLIE III. The South never did.

BILLIE I and II. Shut up.

(*BILLIE I, II, and III sing*)

> *Won't It Be Fine*
>
> Listen to me brothers and sisters mine
> Gonna unionize and won't it be fine.
> One of us alone can be beat of course.
> Everyone together an unbeatable force.
>
> Soon there'll be so many of us
> We'll take over what's ours because
> The time is right, the place is here
> Union is the word, is our meaning clear?

> We don't want more than the right
> To work an honest day and rest a tired night.
> Over our blue collars to hold our head high.
> We're gonna win won't settle for tie.
>
> Now all of you tell me loud and clear
> That all we have to fear is fear.
> All join together, one by one,
> 'Til the race is over and the battle won.
>
> Let one of us join while the iron is hot.
> The rest will join up like as not.
> That will end in a victory
> For working folk, that's you and me!

(*the BILLIES are euphoric*)

BILLIE II. We're smoking.

BILLIE I. (*continuing to riff at the piano*) Indubitably.

BILLIE III. Are you listening Mrs. Kalabash, wherever you are?

(*in high spirits they do a reprise in half-time*)

> We don't want more than the right
> To work an honest day and rest a tired night.
> Over our blue collars to hold our head high.
> We're gonna win, won't settle for tie.

(*BILLIE I continues at the piano*)

BILLIE II. Wait 'til Irving hears this one.

BILLIE I. It'll make him change his tune.

(*THEY do another reprise*)

> We're gonna win, Won't settle for tie.
> Boo ba ba ba ba bee ba ba da.
> Bee da ba ba ba da ba da ba
> Make my day.

BILLIE I. Done!

BILLIE II. That's it!

BILLIE III. Here it is, world. Hate it!

(*CLOCK appears and striked twelve and BILLIE'S mood changes forthwith*)

BILLIE I. Midnight and no Prince Charming. (*exits*)

BILLIE III. Just a pumpkin and a rat.

BILLIE II. (*trying to come up with a palatable explanation*) Maybe he stopped off at Bob's and the time got by him.

BILLIE III. Bob's still in Chicago. It's more serious than that.

BILLIE II. Maybe he had to work all night.

BILLIE III. (*disgusted with her own gullibility*) Even Teleset wouldn't work him twenty-four hours.

BILLIE II. He stopped off to get something to eat.

BILLIE III. The bastard's broke. He'd eat here.

BILLIE II. That means...(*CLOCK diappears*)

BILLIE III. That means...(*disappears*)

BILLIE II. It's serious. (*Disappears. BILLIE now fantasizes her most delicious fantasy to date. CLOYCE, clothed in a most provocative negligee is discovered in a passionate embrace with MARK.*)

CLOYCE. Are you sure there's nothing between you and Becky?

MARK. Billie.

CLOYCE. Yeah. You two seemed kind of lovey-dovey to me.

MARK. (*kisses her*) You don't have a thing to be jealous about. She was like a mother figure to me.

BILLIE I. (*appears in the bedroom*) Hi! (*Whips out a gun and shoots them. THEY fall.*) Bye. (*walks away, suddenly stops short*) I couldn't kill him. He wouldn't live to regret it.

BILLIE II. (*appearing in the garb of an angel*) Let him suffer the way I have. (*disappears*)

(*MARK and CLOYCE resume their embrace. BILLIE I knocks on the door, opens it.*)

BILLIE I. Hi. (*then with the noble suffering of an MGM heroine*) Bye! (*walks away*)

MARK. (*Leaving CLOYCE who scampers off. He follows BILLIE.*) Billie, please open the door!

BILLIE I. (*standing with a revolver poised at her temple*) You're making this more difficult for me than it has to be.

MARK. (*uncontrollable fear*) Let me explain!

BILLIE I. (*savoring the drama every bit as much Joan d'Arc*) It's far too late for explanations. (*shoots herself*)

MARK. Billie! Billie!

BILLIE I. (*coming back to life, reconsiders*) Wait, I can't see him suffer if I'm dead.

BILLIE III. (*appearing in a devil mask*) There is another device devious, delicious, definitive.

(*BILLIE III disappears. BILLIE I lies down seductively. MARK appears.*)

BILLIE I. Hi.

MARK. (*entering her room*) Hi. I thought I'd never get here. Sorry I'm late. (*MARK lies down with her*)

BILLIE I. (*unconcerned*) It doesn't matter.

MARK. (*spying with jealous horror*) Whose hair is that?

BILLIE I. Oh, I don't know. Harry's or Pete's or Steve's...(*a home run*) Or Eileen's.

(*SHE exits. MARK, appalled, crushed, exits.*)

BILLIE II. Why do I persist in torturing myself?

BILLIE III. It's the only thing I'm any good at.

(*CLOYCE appears in a different more provocative negligee*)

BILLIE II. (*furious with herself*) Stop this. Sex is not the shape and purpose of my life!

(*CLOYCE disappears*)

Can you imagine the makers of history wasting one second of their valuable time in the absurd antics of a love triangle?

BILLIE III. Yes.

BILLIE II. (*disparaging*) Who?

BILLIE III. Cleopatra, Mark Antony, John Kennedy, Robert Kennedy, Franklin Delano Roosevelt, Eleanor Roosevelt, Karl Marx.

BILLIE II. Marx was a happily married man who never...

BILLIE III. Marx had an affair with a cook. Engels claimed what came out of the oven.

BILLIE I. That's a vulgar, bourgeois lie.

BILLIE III. (*going on with the list*) Lenin, Emma Goldman...

BILLIE II. Stop it!

BILLIE III. Eisenhower.

BILLIE II. (*having to find additional ammunition*) Well it certainly was not because of their affairs but in spite of them that they made an indelible imprint on history.

BILLIE III. (*seems chastized*) You're absolutely right. (*then*) Queen Elizabeth, Mary Magdalene...

BILLIE II. That's enough.

BILLIE III. George Washington.

BILLIE II. Go to bed! (*MARK appears in her mind*)

BILLIE I. *(entering, scheming)* That's not a bad idea because then were Mark to show up...

BILLIE III. He won't.

BILLIE II. He might.

BILLIE I. But if he should and I'm asleep, it won't look as if I've been waiting up for him.

BILLIE III. Of course.

(MARK disappears)

BILLIE II. *(angry with herself)* It's counterproductive to lay little traps for him; I should clearly and patiently explain how his behavior upsets me.

BILLIE III. That's all I ever do—explain, explain, explain. I can tell you right now he'll never find anyone else with half my patience.

BILLIE II. *(back to present time)* Well, I'm going to need every ounce of it I can muster tomorrow night.

(MARK disappears. CLOCK strikes the half-hour.)

BILLIE I. Oh God! Sixteen more hours and it's on us; months of planning could go down the drain with one show of hands. *(plays "Won't It Be Fine" very slowly)*

BILLIE II. Even if they vote yes...

BILLIE III. They won't.

BILLIE I. They might.

BILLIE II. But if they do and management doesn't accept the union...

BILLIE III. Which they won't.

BILLIE I. Then we strike...

BILLIE III. *(like Jimmy Durante)* Out, 'cause we don't got the clout.

BILLIE I. *(picks up the tempo of the song)* Unless other unions were to give us a hand.

BILLIE II. With everything that's going down now in this country, I wouldn't count on that.

BILLIE I. But a lot of unions helped out the J.P. Stevens boycott, the Stearns strike, the farmworkers campaign, the Greyhound bus driver's strike...

BILLIE III. The unions united, blew their trumpet and the walls began to crack.

BILLIE II. *(grudgingly)* Well, it *has* happened before.

BILLIE I. *(defiant)* So it *can* happen again. *(sings)*

Won't It Be Fine

BILLIE I.   Listen to me brothers and sisters mine
             Might have us a strike
             cross the union line.
             One union alone can be beat of course
             Everyone together an unbeatable force.

(*ENSEMBLE enters*)

ENSEMBLE. First from the teamsters you're gonna hear.
             We won't truck to Lowdowns is that clear?
             We'll shutdown, closeout, stand still every day
             'Til you get union benefits and pay.

             Now a sister tale we're gonna tell
             And when it comes to fighting garment workers do it well.
             We'll sit it out, won't sew another stitch
             'Til Lowdown's listens to the union pitch.

             If one of us joins while the strike is hot
             The rest will join in like as not.
             That will end in a victory
             For workin' folks, that's you and me.

(*ENSEMBLE exits as they sing*)

             We're gonna win, won't settle for tie
             Ba ba ba ba ba bee doo ba 'n ba
             Bee da ba ba bee da be da ba
             Make my day.

(*the rhythm changes to a night-time blues feel*)

BILLIE III. Well, what do you think?

BILLIE II. (*cautioning*) One step at a time. Go for the edge tomorrow night, and if we get a union, we'll take it from there, but if we get trouble, I still wouldn't hope for any massive union support.

(*BILLIE I stops playing*)

BILLIE I. Hope doesn't cost anything.

BILLIE III. (*grandiose hope as she settles down to go to sleep*) And with a charismatic person leading the charge...

BILLIE I. (*as though she is really figuring this out one step at a time*) A waitress, with moral daring, courage...

BILLIE III. Irish.

BILLIE II. Go to bed, Mother Jones.

BILLIE III. I can't sleep now. I'm too wrought up.

BILLIE II. Close your eyes—you'll sleep.

BILLIE III. No I won't.

BILLIE II. Shhh.

BILLIE III. Maybe if I had something to eat first.

BILLIE I. Shhh.

BILLIE III. *(eyes get heavier as she speaks)* Even if I sleep, I won't sleep. I won't. I'll just...

(Light changes to a mood indigo. BILLIE I falls asleep.)

Clams...

(BILLIE I is in that twilight zone between waking and light sleep. BILLIE II appears and disappears every time BILLIE I speaks)

MARK. *(knocking at door offstage)* Billie?

BILLIE I. *(half-awake, half asleep)* I don't know if I'm dreaming or awake.

MARK. *(more knocking)* Billie! Let me in!

BILLIE I. *(convincing herself not to wake up)* I need my rest. Tomorrow comes so early.

MARK. *(still knocking)* It's me, Mark! Open the door! I've been out canvassing with Harry. I called, but your phone is still out of order.

BILLIE I. *(more asleep than awake)* If I get up now, I won't have a bit of energy left for tomorrow night. *(Sound asleep, dreaming. Dream sequence starts.)*

A WEE PERSON.   Hey diddle diddle
                 The union's in a fiddle.
                 Rose jumped over the moon.
                 Harry laughed to see such sport
                 And the pig ran away with the spoon.

(Dreams on. The ORANGE MEN appear)

ORANGE MEN. United union, union united, unionited ironizers, ironited unionizers, affiliated underwriters, underwriting alligators. Alligating strike breakers. *(exit)*

(CLOYCE dances across the stage whirling a nine foot diamond RING)

CLOYCE. A little diamond of my own.

(ORANGE MEN appear again)

ORANGE MEN. Jimes Jayce, Rills Race, Secal chace, Mirk and Clace. Niw perk, an the dirk, un a lerk, Clace and Mirk.

(*ORANGE MEN disappear. BILLIE I enters dressed in fatigues with a rifle slung casually over her shoulder. She discovers MARK and CLOYCE in an embrace inside the diamond RING.*)

BILLIE I. (*nonplussed*) Hi.

CLOYCE. (*startled*) Bonnie! I didn't expect to see you in my bedroom.

BILLIE I. (*matter of fact*) You two go right on with what you're doing. I'm on my way to Central America.

CLOYCE. You're going to Brazil?

BILLIE I. (*patiently*) *Central* America.

CLOYCE. Yeah.

(*BILLIE starts to leave*)

CLOYCE. (*in a turn-around to end them all*) Wait, I know this is going to sound crazy but I have a lot of respect for you!

BILLIE I. Then join me! Fight with us!

(*CLOYCE leaves MARK who is dumbfounded. BILLIE tosses her another set of fatigues she happens to have with her.*)

CLOYCE. (*putting on fatigues*) Me!! Silly little Me!!! Fight with you!!!

BILLIE I. (*glorious at the barricades*) Yes. We're worth more than a life of subjugation to a man. Let's be women, sisters, comrades, courageous together in the jungle.

CLOYCE. (*convinced and transformed*) Yeah, you're right! I don't know why we wasted so much time on him anyway, Barbie.

BILLIE I. Billie.

CLOYCE. Yeah. He really is a schmuck!

(*MARK disappears. BILLIE and CLOYCE enter the jungles of Central America.*)

BILLIE I. You know how dangerous it is in the jungles.

CLOYCE. (*aware*) I know!

BILLIE I. Can I trust you?

CLOYCE. To the death.

BILLIE I. (*BILLIE gets quickly down to the business at hand*) Repeat the plan.

CLOYCE. The rebels are somewhere north of the Mendez plantation. They need these fried clams immediately. I'm to take the path the people call El Rio Norte. I'm to travel day and night until I reach them. Billie, thank you for having so much faith in me.

BILLIE I. Be careful! (*CLOYCE starts off*) Cloyce, I can't let you do this!

CLOYCE. Billie!

BILLIE I. It's my responsibility. I'll go. Give me those clams.

CLOYCE. You're too courageous for your own good. If anything should happen to you, the movement would die. Be careful!

(*BILLIE starts off and is shot. MARK, BILLIE'S MOTHER, HARRY and CLOYCE appear at the funeral. MARK picks up BILLIE'S dead body and carries her from eulogy to eulogy.*)

MARK. (*his voice choked with grief*) There was never anyone else while you were alive. And there can be no other now that you're gone.

MOTHER. Somewhere in the jungle my brave little girl lies dead.

IRVING. I challenged her only to learn from her. She had the correct position, always.

CLOYCE. (*barely holding back tears*) You changed my life, Bertha.

MARK. Billie.

CLOYCE. (*weeping openly*) Yeah.

HARRY THE HORSE. I just want you to know they voted union and we named it the Billie Murphy Memorial, Local 502.

ROSE. Guess who's union steward. And I owe it all to you.

(*MARK, carrying the dead BILLIE, exits. Alarm goes off. The dream disappears.*)

BILLIE III. (*incorporating the sound of it in her dream*) It's a siren. Rush me to the hospital, Doctor, I'm dying.

BILLIE II. The alarm. Time to get up.

BILLIE III. It's still dark out.

BILLIE II. Five-thirty, time to get up.

BILLIE I. (*entering smiling*) No, it's only five-fifteen. I set the alarm fifteen minutes early.

(*THEY all settle in for fifteen more delicious minutes of sleep*)

BILLIE II. (*falling asleep*) What a resourceful creature I can be.

BILLIE III. Fifteen minutes, I could use an hour.

BILLIE II. Use what you got.

(*lights turn to blue and the WEE DREAM PERSON appears again, singing*)

> Time is passing, slipping, dancing,
> Sailing as she sailed.
> Down and over, round and yonder
> Sailing as she ever sailed.
> Once and ever, so again

Sailing as she sailed.
She dared to follow where she lead,
Sailing as she sailed.
She dared to follow where she lead.

END OF PLAY

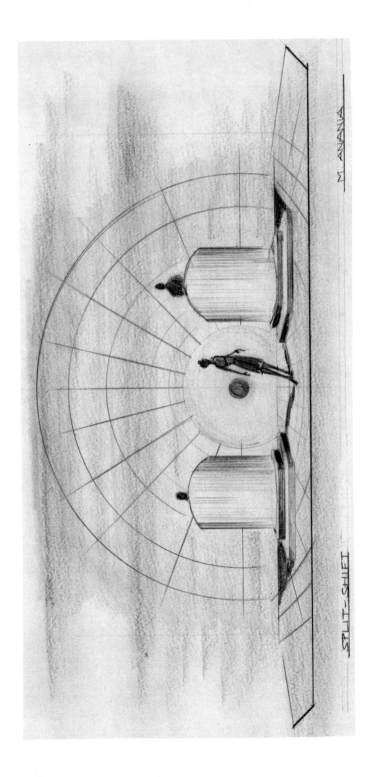

SPLIT-SHIFT

M. ANANIA

I READ ABOUT
MY DEATH IN

VOGUE
MAGAZINE

by Lydia Sargent

"I Read About my Death in *Vogue* Magazine" was first produced in Boston by The Newbury Street Theater in March 1985. It was revised and reopened in February 1986. Both productions were directed by Lydia Sargent. The cast for the second production was as follows:

Woman who writes plays.
Writer.. *Lydia Sargent*
Bugger 7

Woman who is a single mother
Wife/Mother.. *Almayvonne*
Bugger 2

Woman who works for a populist environmental research organization
Secretary .... *Eva Eckles*
Bugger 1

Woman who teaches women's studies
Waitress.. *Phyllis Leach*
Bugger 8

Woman who is an anarchist
Bride.. *Patricia Beatson*
Bugger 6

Woman who has engaged in anti-imperialist activities
Athlete ....*Jane Evans*
Bugger 5

Woman who is a nun
Nurse .... *Peg Flaherty*
Bugger 4

Woman who is an activist
Student ....*Shelley Kooris*
Bugger 3

Lighting by Peter McNeff. Sets by Justin Kaan and Lydia Sargent.

ACT I

Scene 1—Morning in the women's movement. Back and forth between the present and the 1950s.
Scene 2—Somewhere between morning and noon in the women's movement.
Scene 3—Noon in the women's movement. Back and forth between the present and the 1960s.

ACT II

Scene 4—Twilight in the women's movement. Back and forth between the present and the 1970s.
Scene 5—Somewhere between twilight and midnight in the women's movement.
Scene 6—Midnight in the women's movement. Present time.

STORY OF THE PLAY

"I Read About My Death in *Vogue* Magazine" is a comic recounting of and response to the endless insidious creating and recreating of women's images by so-called women's magazines. Eight women participants in the women's movement and other social movements of the 1960s tell the tongue-in-cheek story of how they sat down one fateful day, not long ago, and read about their deaths in *Vogue* magazine. It surprised them really because, until then, they had thought they were alive. And so, they tell the story behind their death beginning over morning coffee brewed according to their personalities and politics. Morning coincides with the early years of the women's movement when they lived over in their own minds not only the image of women in the 1950s but the lives of women who had gone before them and their own upbringings. Morning creeps toward noon. Noon corresponds with the 1960s and the women tell of their struggles to develop a new feminist theory and practice; their struggles with men in the movement, and the magazine image of 1960s women. Meanwhile, the opposition is heating up and, as the first half ends, many men and some women have planted makeup kits in the movement to lure these disgusting feminists back to being "normal" women again.

And so noon creeps toward twilight. Twilight in the women's movement corresponds to the 1970s image of women in fashion magazines, in the news media, in the movies, and in the distortions of feminism by television. It doesn't seem to matter what they do, they are what these images say they are. Finally, at the midnight hour, tired and depressed, feeling they should give up, they recall how their demands to control their own bodies have become a way to sell products in an ad campaign called "Our Bodies, Our Smells." And so they open their *Vogues* and realize that the women's movement is dead, that the new woman has arrived and that she is the 1980s woman, she is the *Vogue* woman who "dares to be feminine."

DESCRIPTION OF CHARACTERS

PLAYWRIGHT: A woman who is writing this play as we speak. She is the primary narrator of the story behind the events leading up to that fateful day, not long ago, when "I read about my death etc." She is energetic, strong, athletic, tongue-in-cheek with a strong sense of humor. She pulls the action along from the morning when they wake and have coffee to the midnight hour when they sit down and read about their death.

SINGLE: A construction worker and single mother who is bitter in her telling of the story because she feels that everyone has just let us die without a murmur. She finds the women's movement important but bourgeois and she argues for class consciousness.

POPULIST: A woman who believes in the power of the people. While she is part of the women's movement, she finds it a little too radical at times. A little irrelevant. She is sometimes hopeful, sometimes depressed about the potential for change. But basically she is a very kind, gentle and nice person.

STUDIES: A woman who is a very optimistic, cheerful person who sees all problems as having positive solutions through analysis and study. She finds the best in people and situations and thinks they can all learn from reading reading about their own deaths.

ANARCHIST: Basically a laid back person with little formal structure to her life. And an athlete as well. She can become very militant when authoritarianism raises its ugly head. She is not intimidated by reading about her death.

ANTI: Incognito after engaging in illegal actions against the U.S. government. She is brisk, blunt, militant. She understands how difficult it is to be a revolutionary and is hopeful and pleasantly surprised that the audience has remained to see the play. While she suggests burning the magazines instead of reading them, she is also ready to find positive surprises inside.

NUN: Very militant, always on the edge of frenzied agitation about the Pope and his patriarchal activities. She is caustic and biting about their "death." While she is eager to tell the other women about the Pope, she sees how equally eager they are not to hear about him and so she begins to tease them, threatening to occupy their entire day with stories of the Pope's activities.

ACTIVIST: Organizes and inspires people. Since she is always busy marching, organizing, and getting arrested she is always rushing to be on time. She is a woman of action, energetic and enthusiastic. She becomes impatient with the stalling and story telling and just wants to read the darn magazine.

BUGGER 1: A right winger concerned with feminist politics as disseminated through books—which he searches for pictures of nude feminists.

BUGGER 2: A designer eager to co-opt the movement by selling revolutionary clothes, bras that aren't bras, etc.

BUGGER 3: A right winger concerned with the "new feminist" sexuality and with their lifestyle.

BUGGER 4: A right wing religious fanatic who is willing to reinstitute laws concerning the burning of witches.

BUGGER 5: A hard hat who wants to burn and bomb birth control clinics.

BUGGER 6: An FBI type looking for subversive activity and eager to play "dirty tricks" which will lure feminists back to being "normal" women.

BUGGER 7: A liberal who's totally excited by the possibility of getting all the sex he wants with no obligations. He's making the most of women's lib.

BUGGER 8: A woman who is not a feminist. Although she believes in some of the things feminists have demanded, she thinks they go too far. Women should be women.

Back row from left to right: Lydia Sargent, Almayvonne, Patricia Beatson, Peg Flaherty. Middle row: Phyllis Leach, Eva Eckles. Front row: Jane Evans, Shelley Kooris. From "I _____ (the sixteen fifties)." Photo: Justin Kaan.

Act I

Scene 1. Morning in the Women's Movement

PLAYWRIGHT. (*enters left on upper ramp and crosses center as she puts on her bathrobe and speaks to the audience*) Hello. (*yawns and makes a fist with her right hand in the air*) It's morning in the movement.

(*EVERYONE pops out from behind large upstage screens, yawns, then disappears*

PLAYWRIGHT. I'm on coffee rotation this month (*crosses to bookshelf right and picks up coffee pot, then starts down right ramp to coffee shelf*) That's why I'm up so early. I don't usually get up this early because I clean other people's houses for money so I make my own hours. And I often sleep a little later. (*starts pouring coffee into her cup*) I also write plays when I'm not cleaning other people's houses for money. I'm working on one right now. This one that you're watching? I'm writing it as we speak. (*crosses to center ramp*) And frankly, I'm also up early because I wanted— well, we decided that I should speak to you first, before the others become conscious.

(*EVERYONE pops up from behind upstage screens and looks unconscious, then pops back*)

PLAYWRIGHT. To tell you our story. You see, it's very important that you're here. (*confidentially to the audience*) I told the others you'd come. They didn't think you would. So when they come out just kind of look like you're here, would you? (*smiles, then backs away from them a few steps*) The point is, something terrible has happened. At least I think it's terrible. So do the others. (*picks up a long green "death cloth"*) Can you imagine my surprise when the other day

EVERYONE. (*rushes out from behind screens with death cloths around neck strangling them and says in surprise*) I read about my death. In *Vogue* magazine. (*exits*)

PLAYWRIGHT. It surprised me really because, until then, I had thought that I was alive. Well, perhaps alive isn't the right word. Living. That's more like it. (*crosses down center ramp, gets coffee and sips*) I can remember the first moment I started living. It was May. May 22, 1969. I was a housewife with three children and I sat down and read *The Golden Notebook* by Doris Lessing—as so many of us did. (*a few WOMEN pop out in solidarity, then pop back*) Now, it's true that to many I had been dead for years. My parents, for instance. I had been dead to them long before 1969. And I was dead to most of the men I had met since 1969. I saw that look in their eyes, "She's death," it said. (*rises and crosses to bookshelf on middle ramp*) And I was dead to many women too—all those who still believed in the American Dream of womenhood, which for many achieved its perfection in the image of women in

EVERYONE. (*popping, prancing, and perking out from behind screens wearing pink and white curtains and high heels, carrying small pocketbooks and speaking in Marilyn Monroe voices*) The nineteen fifties.

(*WOMEN disappear behind screens. "Chantilly Lace" by the Big Bopper comes on and WOMEN reappear in fifties outfits walking on high heels with mincing steps from right to left on upper ramp. WOMEN stop as music stops*)

WIFE/MOTHER. Pretty in pale gray over pretty pink.

(*THEY squeal and wiggle. Music starts and WOMEN continue down right ramp to lower ramp, across lower ramp to left ramp. THEY stop with music.*)

BRIDE. Pretty in white organdy.

(*THEY squeal and wiggle. WOMEN continue down right ramp to lower ramp and across lower ramp to left ramp. THEY stop as music stops.*)

WAITRESS. Pretty in chiffon and taffeta.

(*Music starts and WOMEN walk up left ramp to middle ramp; cross middle ramp to center ramp. WOMEN stop as music stops.*)

SECRETARY. Pretty in soft tweeds.

(*THEY really squeal. Music starts and WOMEN head down and around center ramp out into audience. WOMEN stop as music stops.*)

NURSE. Pretty in pale pink cardigans. (*Music starts again and WOMEN head up center ramp splitting into two group—one goes right, one left. WOMEN stop as music stops.*)

WRITER. Pretty, pretty.

(*squeals as music starts again and stops quickly*)

STUDENT. Pretty little.

(*Intense squealing as music starts again, then stops quickly*)

ATHLETE. Pretty thing.

(*oohing as music starts, then stops quickly*)

EVERYONE. Pretty pretty little thing.

(*WOMEN are in place sticking out from behind their screens showing an arm, a leg, a head, or an ass. The SPEAKER models from the center screen.*)

BRIDE. (*models up and down center ramp*) The fifties woman is a bride in pretty white pique. Ethereal nylon with appliqued pearls. Demure shy veil. Delicate lace. Tiny, tiny shoes. Quiet hair. White cascading drifts of delicate lace. Plunge bra. Little pointed raised pretty little bosom. (*finishes posing and stands posed at screen for a comment*) "Until death do us part."

(*little pretty sighs as EVERYONE moves clockwise one screen*)

SECRETARY. (*models up and down center ramp*) The fifties woman is a secretary in crisp little suit. Well put together look. Tapered cardigan. Soft little walk with teeny tiny tight skirt. Pretty little typing fingers. Longline bra boned from her small pointed bosom to her tiny tiny waist. Soft curls around her outrageously pretty face. A rush of bangs. Pretty way of perching on the edge of her chair. Pretty way of holding her steno pad. (*returns to screen for comment*) "Are you ready for your coffee, Mr. Finkel?"

(*WOMEN squeal and move clockwise one screen*)

STUDENT. (*models up and down center ramp*) The fifties woman is a student in pretty shirtwaist dresses. Pretty little hoop skirts twinkling around her tiny little calves. Tiny tiny pumps with teeny pointy toes. Peppermint pinks. Tied up hair. A quiet tiny brain. Sensible elastic panty girdle designed with a lady in mind. (*poses at her screen for a comment*) "I'm pledging Sigma Kai Alpha Omega."

(*WOMEN make cute noises and move clockwise one screen*)

WAITRESS. (*models up and down center ramp*) The fifties woman is a waitress in pretty white over pink confection uniform. With soft white hat. Perky little pretty waitress pad. Tiny white sensible shoes with perky bows. Tiny tiny voice. Long tiny torso girdle for eased waistline. No stabbing bones or bulging seams over her tiny pretty little hips. (*returns to screen for comment*) "You take your hands off me, buster, or I'll show you well done meat."

(*WOMEN ooh and move clockwise*)

ATHLETE. (*models up and down center ramp*) The fifties woman is a tennis player in pretty white linen resort clothes that sparkle. A skirt that swirls prettily. Soft frilly panties that flirt when she moves. Tiny tiny thighs. A pretty pony tail that bounces prettily. Pretty bows. Running prettily for the ball. Hitting softly, quietly, prettily. (*returns to screen for comment*) "Even my perspiration is pretty."

(*WOMEN make pretty noises and move clockwise one screen*)

NURSE. (*models up and down center ramp*) The fifties woman is a nurse. Smiling prettily as she changes the bedpans. Pretty white frock. Little cherry red cheeks. Cheerful tiny cap. Teeny fingers soothe where it hurts. Little bitty dark curls bounce merrily as she happily cleans up mess from the floor. Crisply she crinkles helpfully to feed her many sick charges as she bestows a smile and a helpful word on each one. (*returns to screen for comment*) "Yes, Doctor, I'll be happy to unwrap bandages while you perform open heart surgery."

(*WOMEN make cheerful noises and move clockwise one screen*)

WRITER. (*modeling up and down center ramp*) The fifties woman is a writer of an advice column for pretty young women in her pretty housecoat, over pretty tweed skirt. Over pretty nylon lace girdle made without a single bone accentuating her pretty little hips and slim tiny thighs. Pink and gray work room writing pretty little columns. Hair soft but efficient. Pretty little smile. Pretty little hat. Pretty little teensy roses on pretty little hat. Pretty little romantic hands. Pretty little mouth. Pretty little miniscule little teeny brain. (*returns to screen for comment*) "Dear fifties young woman, my advice to you is don't give anything away until you get a ring on your finger. After that, girls, you must give it all up and stand by your man."

(*WOMEN shriek with delight and move clockwise*)

WIFE/MOTHER. (*modeling up and down center ramp*) The fifties woman is a wife and mother. Pale with excitement. Pale and pretty. Glowing and pretty. Quiet and pretty. Private and pretty. Purring prettily like a cat with her kittens. Pretty hands with pretty little smiles in the kitchen for her husband. Overflowing big pretty belly over tiny tiny feet wearing bright little slippers. Longline bra. Tiny waist nipper. Tummy slimming girdle for tiny little thighs. (*back at screen for comment*) "Why don't you rest after a hard day, Honey, and I'll bring your pipe and slippers."

(*A chorus of sympathy noises as music returns and WOMEN tap dance to a V-formation in the Busby Berkeley extravaganza tradition with the point of the V center and the ends upstage. WOMEN turn slowly in place, first to the right, then to the left as the music stops.*)

WIFE/MOTHER. Flirting is to a fifties woman

BRIDE. What experimentation is

EVERYONE. To electricity. (*flirting noises and tap dance step a la Rockettes into a long line upstage with arms around each other as they do a crossover step during the following lines*)

WAITRESS. She follows fashion in everything

WRITER. She flows along masked and concealed

STUDENT. *(peels off and tap dances to right middle ramp)* If a man responds to beautiful blonds

EVERYONE. Then be one.

ATHLETE. *(peeling off right)* In her Merry Widow corset

EVERYONE. She's wanted for manslaughter.

SECRETARY. *(peeling off right)* Wearing Roman Holiday perfume

EVERYONE. He came, he saw, she conquered. *(The remaining "Rockettes" peel off and join the line. Facing right with hands on the waist of the Rockette in front of them they choo choo step backwards until they are center. On each of the following lines they move their downstage leg.)*

WIFE/MOTHER. She appears to be

(legs go forward toes pointed)

NURSE. A pretty little saint

(legs go forward, toes pointed)

WAITRESS. Because she needs a man

(toes forward)

WRITER. To bring out

(toes back)

STUDENT. The whirlwind in her.

(arms come up and over in sequence like windmills beginning at the left end of the line, ending at right, then going back back again in sequence)

BRIDE. *(runs to lower ramp and tap dances)* She likes a father figure who can release her captive libido. *(makes yearning noises)*

WRITER. *(runs to lower ramp, tap dances)* She wants a literary lion to fulfill her intellectual itch. *(longing noises and some scratching)*

STUDENT. *(runs to lower ramp and tap dances)* A rolling stone for the woman who likes the constant excitement of being left behind.

(sounds of pain)

WAITRESS. *(runs to lower ramp and tap dances)* The bullfighter for the sensation-loving lady who wants an aphrodisiac.

SECRETARY. *(runs to lower ramp and tap dances)* The beautiful primitive for the lady who wants to take off with the international playboy who enslaves women.

NURSE. *(runs to lower ramp and tap dances)* The boy/man for the older woman who longs to be the eternal nurturer.

(WOMEN who have come to lower ramp rush to middle ramp and join the OTHERS)

WIFE/MOTHER. The newsman, a laconic cavalier who brings the world to the stay-at-home awash in the soap opera.

(*WOMEN groan and rush to lower ramp*)

ATHLETE. The heavy, grinding a grapefruit in a girl's face.

(*Music as WOMEN do a ROCKETTE kick number on lower ramp. Then WOMEN high-heel their way in a line up the right ramp to the middle ramp; across to the left ramp and then to upper ramp. They pause in their path on each of the following lines and turn their heads back toward the audience.*)

EVERYONE. Pretty little.

EVERYONE. Pretty thing. (walks in a line to upper ramp)

EVERYONE. Pretty little thing. (*squeals and exits singing "Chantilly Lace." PLAYWRIGHT crosses to coffee shelf as music fades.*)

PLAYWRIGHT. So, although to many I was dead already, I certainly thought I was alive. (*getting rid of fifties outfit and crossing center to her screen*) So it is terribly important that you're here because if I'm dead then, quite frankly, many of you are dead too. I don't know about you, but I don't like being dead. Neither do the others. So we've come to tell you our story. The story behind our

EVERYONE. (*walk out from behind screens with death cloths dragging behind them, dejected*) Death in *Vogue* magazine. (*exits*)

PLAYWRIGHT. As I was saying, I'm on coffee rotation this month. (*crosses to left ramp tidying up as she goes*) I know that probably sounds like an easy job compared to shopping or cleaning this place, (*goes across lower ramp to coffee shelf*) but you'd be surprised. In the movement, we all have our differences, our individualities, our priories. For instance, this woman...

(*SINGLE mother enters upper ramp carrying a laundry basket piled high with clothes and heads for right ramp*)

PLAYWRIGHT. Who is a single mother and who was very active in the civil rights movement and who is now a construction worker and an apprentice in the construction workers union

SINGLE. Good morning. (*to audience*) So you've come. I told her you wouldn't. Everyone seems so passive lately. No fight. Just watch ourselves die without a murmur.

PLAYWRIGHT. Don't be bitter.

SINGLE. Sorry. Laundry this month for me. (*puts basket down at the end of center ramp*) Coffee ready? (*returns to center*)

PLAYWRIGHT. (*crossing center to meet her with cup of coffee*) Of course.

SINGLE. My aggressive brand? (*takes coffee and smells it*)

PLAYWRIGHT. Very strong and a touch bitter.

SINGLE. Doesn't look like it.

PLAYWRIGHT. Would I make anything else for you?

SINGLE. You never know, the way things have been going lately. *(takes a newspaper from down center and crosses to her own screen)*

PLAYWRIGHT. Anything interesting in your newspaper?

SINGLE. No.

PLAYWRIGHT. Oh. And this woman

(Woman who is a POPULIST enters right carrying check book and a file of bills. She crosses to left ramp and heads down)

PLAYWRIGHT. Who works with a populist environmental research organization and who belongs to a grassroots disarmament group...

POPULIST. *(to audience fairly cheerfully)* Look who's here. It's about time. I knew some of you would come. You can't fool all of the people all of the time. *(puts check book at end of center ramp)* I collect the money to pay the bills. For part of the year. I see you've made coffee? *(joins PLAYWRIGHT center)*

PLAYWRIGHT. *(coming to meet her center)* Your own popular brand.

POPULIST. Looks and smells like toxic waste. I'm switching to the popular brand of herbal tea.

PLAYWRIGHT. Oh well, that's what I said. Here's your tea. *(hands POPULIST the same cup)*

POPULIST. Smells like coffee to me.

PLAYWRIGHT. Would I try and fool you?

POPULIST. Got any half and half?

PLAYWRIGHT. Right here. *(pours it)*

POPULIST. Let's see what's in the news today. *(gets her popular paper from end of center ramp and crosses to her screen)*

PLAYWRIGHT. How's the struggle to clean up the environment going?

POPULIST. Partly good, partly not so good.

PLAYWRIGHT. Hmm. And this woman...

(woman who teaches women's STUDIES enters upper ramp with shopping bags, crosses right and heads down)

PLAYWRIGHT. Who teaches women's studies at the university and who is currently working on a book on feminist theory...

STUDIES. *(cheerily)* Hello, hello, hello. I knew you'd come. And even though there aren't that many of you, it's quality that counts. Shopping this week for me. I like shopping but then I like all the jobs. *(puts bags down at end of center ramp)* Coffee's ready, I see. *(heads center)*

PLAYWRIGHT. Quality brewing for you. *(hands STUDIES coffee at center)*

STUDIES. My obscure brand. So thoughtful.

PLAYWRIGHT. Of course.

STUDIES. (*gets academic journal from end of center ramp and crosses to screen*) Let's see what wonderfully obscure things we can read today.

PLAYWRIGHT. Yes. (*exchanges smiles with POPULIST*) And this woman...

(*woman who is an ANARCHIST enters upper ramp with mop and pail, crosses center and heads down*)

PLAYWRIGHT. Who is an anarchist and who freelances for a newspaper in the day time and who jams with an all women's band in the evenings, playing whatever she feels like.

ANARCHIST. Hello. Frankly, I wasn't sure I wanted you to come. A play is such an elitist experience—you sitting there passively listening to us as we bring you our opinions...

PLAYWRIGHT. Blame it on me. I can't stop myself from putting it down as we speak.

ANARCHIST. Whatever feels good. And of course, (*to audience*) you don't have to pay any attention. Or you can take what you want from it. After all it's only the opinion of a few people. (*puts mop and pail at end of center ramp*)

PLAYWRIGHT. Would you like coffee?

ANARCHIST. (*comes to lower center ramp*) I'm not sure. You make those elitist brands.

PLAYWRIGHT. Never. Your generic brand. (*hands her coffee*)

ANARCHIST. (*sniffing*) Hey. This has an aroma of authority to it. (*getting newspaper at end of center ramp*)

PLAYWRIGHT. Not a chance. What's in the news today?

ANARCHIST. (*crossing to screen*) Hey, I question the authority of all newspapers even the one I write for—especially the one I write for.

PLAYWRIGHT. Sorry, I forgot. (*exchanges smiles with STUDIES*) And this woman...

(*woman who is ANTI-imperialist enters cautiously with garbage bags, pauses to check for FBI*)

PLAYWRIGHT. Who works at a battered women's shelter, and who is not really who she seems to be since she went underground after engaging in some rather militant activities against the United States' imperialist policies.

ANTI. (*briskly*) Hi. You're here. Shows guts.

PLAYWRIGHT. Told you.

ANTI. Yes. Garbage. Hate it. Coffee? (*crossing center*)

PLAYWRIGHT. Ready.

ANTI. Surprising.

PLAYWRIGHT. For you. (*holding out cup at center*)

ANTI. (*coming center but hesitating*) Exploiting?

PLAYWRIGHT. Not today.

ANTI. Revolutionary coffee?

PLAYWRIGHT. From Nicaragua.

ANTI. Love ya. (*takes coffee*)

PLAYWRIGHT. 'Swat it's all about.

ANTI. (*getting newspaper from end of center ramp*) What a pleasant surprise.

PLAYWRIGHT. Good news?

ANTI. Revolution. (*crosses to screen*)

PLAYWRIGHT. Where?

ANTI. All over.

PLAYWRIGHT. Oh? And this woman...

(*women who is a NUN enters upper ramp, crosses center*)

PLAYWRIGHT. Who is a nun and who has served time in prison for her militant and illegal actions against the Vietnam War and who has come out...against the pope and God as patriarchal concepts and who is working for the ordination of women and for a new language and a new religion.

NUN. Blessings on all of you (*mockingly as she looks out over the crowd*) except for maybe a few of you in the back row there. I'm cooking the meals this week. And I don't want any comments.

(*WOMEN at screens look up and groan*)

NUN. (*puts cooking things at the end of center ramp and gets newspaper*) Oh, good goddess, look at this. Let me just read to you a few of the latest words from that idiot pope of ours.

PLAYWRIGHT. Don't you want your coffee?

NUN. (*unable to take her eyes off the newspaper*) Give it to me quick. You must hear this. (*comes center*)

PLAYWRIGHT. Here you are. (*hands coffee to NUN*)

NUN. (*sniffs*) Chock Full of Nuts?

PLAYWRIGHT. Your heavenly brand.

NUN. (*starts for her screen, sips and makes face*) Tastes like sh...

PLAYWRIGHT. And this woman...

(*woman who is a radical ACTIVIST enters upper ramp on the run and comes center, carrying dishwashing liquid and bottle brush*)

PLAYWRIGHT. Who works at a birth control clinic and who is an activist in many women's organizations, a veteran of many teach ins, sit downs, sit ins, speak outs, takeovers, zap actions.

ACTIVIST. *(surveying the audience in solidarity)* Look what we have here. *(to PLAYWRIGHT)* I told you women were still active, still concerned. And there are actually some men out there. *(opening her robe and revealing her body)* Come to look at the women, have you?

(WOMEN look up from newspapers and watch ACTIVIST with amusement)

PLAYWRIGHT. Be polite.

ACTIVIST. Why?

PLAYWRIGHT. Because I'm writing it that way. And we agreed.

ACTIVIST. Yea, but I figured you were just holding yourself back, so I thought I'd throw in something of my own. *(smiling at PLAYWRIGHT)* Oh, all right. *(to audience with exaggerated politeness as she comes down center)* Dishes this week for me. I hate dishes, but then I hate all the jobs. Let men do them for a couple of thousand years, okay? *(putting liquid at end of center ramp)* You didn't make my coffee, did you?

PLAYWRIGHT. I wouldn't think of it.

ACTIVIST. *(to audience)* I like to make my own.

PLAYWRIGHT. Your active brand is over there.

ACTIVIST. *(quickly making her own coffee)* So how is everybody today? Ready to get out there and struggle?

(WOMEN fold and put newspapers down on screens and look various stages of ready)

STUDIES. Always...

SINGLE. You bet.

ANTI. I'm there.

ANARCHIST. Hey, are you giving orders?

POPULIST. Let's not go overboard here.

NUN. If I could just read a few words of inspiration from the Vatican. *(getting her glasses ready)*

PLAYWRIGHT. *(comes center with her coffee cup)* Didn't I tell you? Coffee rotation is not as easy as it looks here in the movement. Everyone has different needs. But we're all equally *(gets newspaper)*

EVERYONE. Incredible.

(PLAYWRIGHT takes coffee and newspaper to screen)

ACTIVIST. *(crosses to visit ANTI at her screen)* You better believe it.

ANTI. No surprise to me.

STUDIES. In theory, anyway. (*joins PLAYWRIGHT at center screen*)

POPULIST. Some of us are incredible, I'm not so sure about the others. (*visits with ANARCHIST*)

ANARCHIST. Are you suggesting we're an elite group?

SINGLE. (*visits NUN*) If we're so incredible, how come everything's so bad?

ACTIVIST. Just a second here. Are you including men in that statement?

NUN. She better not be. And I'd like to read this.

PLAYWRIGHT. Now, let's be clear, while we're all in the movement we don't all live together.

ACTIVIST. (*crossing to her screen*) I live with my lover. (*sits*)

STUDIES. (*crossing toward screen up left*) I'm in between living arrangements. (*sits*)

POPULIST. (*crossing to screen*) I live in a mixed collective household. (*sits*)

ANARCHIST. (*crossing from screen to screen ending at her own*) I come and go as I please. (*sits*)

SINGLE. (*returns to her screen*) I live with my kid and two other single mothers. (*sits*)

ANTI. I can't say, I'm underground.

NUN. With 20 other women on a farm.

PLAYWRIGHT. And let's also be clear, although we're all in the women's movement, we don't really know each other although we...(*darts behind her screen to pop out on*)

EVERYONE. (*poking heads out*) Know (*heads back*)

PLAYWRIGHT. (*stands*) Each other. We...(*darts behind screen to poke head out on...*)

EVERYONE. *poking heads out again*) Know...(*heads back*)

PLAYWRIGHT. Each other because we shared that moment together, that moment sometime before or after 1960 when we all started living. That moment when we each sat down and read

(*EVERYONE pops up ready to mention what they read in that initial moment but STUDIES beats them to it*)

STUDIES. (*pops up excitedly with The Second Sex by Simone de Beauvior*) *The Second Sex.* If I may begin our morning reading? (*looks around at them as if at a women's studies class and so WOMEN sit and listen with interest to reading*) "But first we must ask what is a woman? To state the question is, to me, to suggest at once a preliminary answer...it amounts to this...just as for the ancients there was an absolute vertical with reference to which the oblique was defined, so there is an absolute human type, the masculine.

ACTIVIST. (*pops up and crosses to STUDIES*) Excuse me, but isn't that my copy? Yes, see where I've underlined. If I may refresh your memories..."Woman has ovaries, (*WOMEN pop out, pointing to ovaries, then pop back*) a uterus, (*WOMEN pop out pointing to uterus, then pop back*) and these particularities imprison her in her own subjectivity, (*WOMEN pop out looking imprisoned, then pop back*) circumscribe her within the limits of her own nature."

POPULIST. (*pops up and crosses to ACTIVIST*) Hey, that sounds like my copy. Do you mind? (*takes copy from ACTIVIST*) Let me continue. "It is often said that she thinks with her glands. (*WOMEN pop out pointing to breasts, then back*) Man simply ignores the fact that his anatomy also includes glands, such as the testicles (*WOMEN poke out fists, one on either side of their screens, and hold them there*) and that they secrete hormones." (*WOMEN open and close fists three times, then pop fists back*).

ANTI. (*pops up and crosses to POPULIST to get book*) I'm surprised. My copy. Thank you. Now where were we? Oh, yes. "He thinks of his body as a direct and normal connection with the world, which he believes he apprehends objectively, whereas he regards the body of a woman as a hindrance, a prison (*WOMEN pop out weighed down by large breasts, circle their screens*) weighed down by everything peculiar to it." (*WOMEN sit*)

SINGLE. (*pops up and crosses to ANTI*) Could I take a look at that? I thought so. Typical. This is my copy and I was rereading it just yesterday. "Thus humanity is male (*WOMEN poke fists out on either side and open and close them three times, then bring them back behind screens*) and man defines woman not in herself but relative to him; she is not regarded as an autonomous being."

ANARCHIST. (*popping out from behind screen and crossing to SINGLE*) I don't mean to be possessive or authoritarian about this but you have the copy that I was looking at so if you don't mind I will continue where I left off..."Man can think of himself without woman; (*THEY pop out as statue of THE THINKER, then pop back*) she cannot think of herself without man. (*WOMEN wander confused*)

WOMEN. I have a man, therefore I am. (*pop back*)

NUN. (*pops up and crosses to ANARCHIST*) I am just so certain that this is my copy. Yes. You see. Simone autographed it for me. "She is simply what man decrees. Thus, she is called the sex (*pop out pointing to crotches, then pop back*) by which is meant that she appears essentially to the male as a sexual being. (*lie back on crates and spread their legs, then pop back*)

STUDIES. (*popping out and crossing to ANARCHIST*) I am happy that everyone has a copy of this book, but this copy really is mine. As I was saying..."For him she is sex (*WOMEN lie back again, then pop behind screens*), absolute sex, no less. (*THEY lie back again, then pop back behind screens*) She is defined and differentiated with reference to man (*fists out again*) and not he with reference to her; (*lie back again*) she is the incidental, (*WOMEN rise meekly and stand on crates*) the inessential as opposed to the essential. (*WOMEN begin to shrivel*) He is the Subject, he is the Absolute, she is

EVERYONE. The Other. (*slowly shrivel into little things and disappear behind screens with only eyes peering over the tops*)

STUDIES. (*returns coffee and newspaper to nearest shelf*) That's a classic.

ANTI. (*returns coffee and newspaper to nearest shelf*) It's publication was revolutionary, although there is little discussion of the third world.

ANARCHIST. It's good, as far as it goes. (*returns coffee and newspaper to nearest shelf*)

POPULIST. (*returns coffee and newspaper to nearest shelf*) I like some of it but there are parts that are just too radical, too obscure.

ACTIVIST. (*returns coffee and newspaper to shelf*) Too theoretical, too male oriented.

SINGLE. (*returns coffee and newspaper to nearest shelf*) Bourgeois feminism.

NUN. (*returns coffee and newspaper to nearest shelf*) It's a start. But I'd like to read from this book called *God the Father*. (*putting her glasses on*)

STUDIES. I repeat, it's a classic.

PLAYWRIGHT. Goes without saying. (*returns coffee and newspaper to nearest shelf and comes center as WOMEN return to their screens*) So in those early years, if you remember and I'm sure many of you do, but it bears repeating again and again, given what's happened, this terrible thing, this

EVERYONE. (*popping out from behind screens, speaking in very low voices*) Death.

PLAYWRIGHT. In those early years of the movement we lived over in our minds the lives of women who had gone before us and our own pasts.

EVERYONE. (*rising*) Morning for our mothers.

(*Two WOMEN sit at lower ramp screens for this fast-paced unpunctuated segment. Three WOMEN make pink cloths from crates into aprons; three WOMEN make blue cloths into neckties and mime MOTHERS and HUSBANDS/KIDS. Middle left screen is moved to upper ramp. Center screen to middle left ramp.*)

MOTHER. So here I am up at the crack of dawn (*MOTHERS yawn*) after two hours sleep, up all night with the baby (*MOTHERS hold baby in arms with bottle*) so I'll rush and get breakfast (*MOTHERS rush to get breakfast. HUSBANDS/KIDS rush around looking for clothes*) for husband and four other kids who will be down in a minute after they fumble around and can't find anything for their day and so we'll cook the eggs just right (*MOTHERS break eggs into pan*) so husband will love me (*HUSBANDS rise and throw kiss to MOTHERS*) for serving him (*MOTHERS curtsey*) and quick iron a shirt (*MOTHERS iron*) because he's all out of them because he changes them every twenty seconds so that I can serve him (*MOTHERS hold serving trays*) more often (*more serving*) and husband can then love me (*HUSBANDS kiss*) but also the kids can't find anything for school...

KIDS. (*peer out*) Ma!

MOTHER. So while the bacon is cooking (*MOTHERS cook bacon*) I'll do a load of laundry (*MOTHERS throw clothes in washer while cooking bacon*) because the kids never have any clothes because they throw (*KIDS sit at screens and toss clothes from right to left*) them on the floor and sometimes they just take the clean clothes and throw them on the floor without even wearing them and then put them directly in the laundry basket (*MOTHERS are exhausted from picking up clothes*) and so now the eggs are done just right (*MOTHERS spatula eggs onto plate*) but he wants me to bake a cake (*MOTHERS stir batter*) and serve dinner to his boss tonight (*MOTHERS serve*) for which his boss will love him and husband will then love me. (*HUSBANDS kiss*)

HUSBAND. (*shouting*) Where is my shirt, dearest? (*HUSBANDS stand on crates, shakes fists, and look down at MOTHERS*) Where is my breakfast? Is dinner for my boss ready?

MOTHER. So I throw up his shirt (*tosses shirt to HUSBAND who catches it and disappears*) which I have just ironed (*MOTHERS iron*) while cooking breakfast for five people (*MOTHERS cook for five*) not including me since I don't need to eat since all I do is sit around all day.

KID. (*peering out and pouting*) Ma, where are my socks?

MOTHER. So I toss up the socks (*tosses socks which KIDS catch*) which I have just laundered while ironing husband's shirt and cooking breakfast and also waxing the floor (*MOTHERS bend over and wax*) so they can run their toys over it (*KIDS run toys over floor*) and it must be time to feed the baby (*KIDS become babies and cry for food; MOTHERS feed babies while waxing*) while cooking for five people who will not like what I have cooked and who will shower me with criticism and abuse.

KID. (*KIDS turn sideways and pick at food finding strange things and looking ill*) Ma, the eggs have that slimy white stuff on top that looks like nose pick, and the cereal tastes like the cardboard that Daddy makes you put in the shirts, and the orange juice has funny things in it that look like nose pick; and she breathed her germs on it; and the milk has a crust on it like nose pick.

MOTHER. And I have not served them (*MOTHERS bow and serve*) in order for them to love me (*KIDS screw up faces to get kiss from MOTHERS*) and so today I bake some brownies (*MOTHERS put brownies in oven*) and drive them someplace (*MOTHERS and KIDS sit sideways at screens while MOTHERS drive and KIDS fight*) and then maybe I will have done enough for them to like me at least. (*MOTHERS look at KIDS hopefully*)

KID. (*rising and pouting*) Thanks for taking us to see that movie that scared us to death and thanks for not buying us ten candy bars and five huge vats of popcorn. Thanks a lot, mom, you're such a meany and we hate you for life. Just wait 'til Dad comes home and we tell him.

MOTHER. And then when husband comes home I get to let him enjoy sex (*MOTHERS lie back at screens; FATHERS lean over screens*) after a hard day at work and I am all rested because I had such a fun day shopping (*MOTHERS call out items while still in sex position*) and what fun doing the laundry and cleaning was fun too since all of it will become dirty or eaten as soon as I do them and of course if I had a job, it would be mostly the same because I would be doing

EVERYONE. (*rising wearily*) Double duty.

(*Two other WOMEN come forward and take their places at lower ramp for this next series. One is the MOTHER, the other the HUSBAND and KID. OTHERS mime. WOMEN in pink, MEN in blue.*)

MOTHER. Hi, everyone. I'm home. (*MOTHERS wave*)

KIDS. Where's dinner, ma, I'm hungry. (*KIDS bang table for dinner*)

MOTHER. Let me cook the dinner (*MOTHERS take off coats and put on aprons*) even though I worked all day and you're just lying around doing nothing I'll get dinner don't get up (*MOTHERS motion KIDS to stay sitting down*) and help me with an extra wash (*MOTHERS throw clothes in washer*) and I'll bake a pie (*MOTHERS crimp edges of pie*) and entertain husband's boss and nine other guests (*MOTHERS sing beginning of "My Favorite Things" while HUSBANDS play the piano*)

MOTHERS 1. (*walks center, hands clasped before her as she sings romantically*) "Raindrops on roses and whiskers on kittens."

MOTHER 2. (*same as MOTHER 1*) "Bright copper kettles and warm woolen mittens."

MOTHER 3. (*the same as above*) "Brown paper packages tied up with strings."

MOTHERS. (*shouting and returning to screens*) "These are a few of my favorite things."

MOTHER. So that husband's boss will give him a raise and so husband will find me attractive (*HUSBANDS find her attractive*) even though I look like a dog (*MOTHERS pant like dogs*) because I work like one.

HUSBAND. What's the matter, honey? (*HUSBANDS rise and step toward MOTHERS, gesturing*) You look tired is that why the meat is overdone and the string beans soggy (*HUSBANDS pick food*) don't worry if you serve me (*holds out hand for beer which MOTHERS bring*) I will love you (*HUSBANDS kiss*) and maybe give you extra money (*MOTHERS hold out hands while HUSBANDS deliberate*) at the end of the week. My money is yours after all they pay me for you to serve (*MOTHERS serve*) me by the way how was your day although I'm not that interested in what you do. (*HUSBANDS yawn*)

MOTHER. I typed for eight hours (*MOTHERS sit sideways on crates and type*) so that my boss could do important things which he couldn't do if I didn't type for eight hours and I talked to my friend and co-worker, Mary, (*MOTHERS rise off crates and wave*) for about ten seconds which was fun and I also spent the entire day trying to keep my boss's hands off me. (*MOTHERS remove hands from hips and thighs*)

HUSBAND. I don't really want to hear about your day (*HUSBANDS step forward, looking disapprovingly at MOTHERS*) having all the fun talking with your friends while I slave away, taking time away from the kids just to earn a little pin money. Don't you have enough pins by now and I am angry with you for seducing your boss but let me tell you about my day which is the day that really counts...(*HUSBANDS fold newspapers and prepare to make a speech. MOTHERS try to look really interested.*)

MOTHER. Yes, tell me about your day while you relax and I cook dinner (*HUSBANDS sit and read paper. MOTHERS stir pot on stove*) and play with the kids and help them with their homework and feed the baby.

MOTHERS. (*feeding baby while turning jump rope, in fast jump rope rhythm*) If a train is going 57 miles an hour how many oranges can the passengers eat in 8 hours?

MOTHER. Yes, let me hear about your day you poor thing (*MOTHERS bring dinner*) and then after dinner you can help instruct our sons and daughters in their...

EVERYONE. (*rising*) Upbringing.

(*Two other WOMEN become father and mother and come to lower ramp screens. The other WOMEN cross upstage divided into three girls stage right and three boys stage left. GIRLS tie pink bows around heads. BOYS make blue loincloths. Upper and middle ramp screens are moved to the sides.*)

FATHER. Now sons.

(*BOYS look alert*)

MOTHER. And daughters.

(*DAUGHTERS look pretty*)

FATHER. It's upbringing time and we will review our lessons. First, boys *(BOYS look alert)* since you are boy persons who have a penis *(BOYS check under loincloths)* you will do things like lift heavy objects *(BOYS lift with sweating and groaning and biting bullets)* and put them down *(BOYS put down heavy objects)*

MOTHER. Daughters *(DAUGHTERS are busy fixing bows and don't notice)*Daughters! you stand and watch them lift. *(DAUGHTERS stare at BOYS)* You will occasionally lift babies and groceries which are not heavy but be sure you do it gently and look pretty while you do it *(DAUGH-TERS look pretty holding babies)* and of course you may need help putting them down.

GIRLS. *(calling with tiny voices)* Help?

BOYS. *(crossing middle ramp, taking babies, and tossing them)* No problem.

FATHER. Next, boys having a penis *(BOYS check under loincloths)* means you will walk a certain way *(BOYS walk in a way to focus their penis, loincloths flapping)*

MOTHER. Girls, since you don't have a penis *(GIRLS check for penis)* you will walk a certain other way *(GIRLS do "girlie" walk)*

FATHER. Boys, you will wear pants and sit accordingly. *(BOYS sit with legs spread, looking manly)*

MOTHER. Girls, you will wear frilly dresses and sit so that we can't see underneath them *(GIRLS sit like little ladies, teasing BOYS with a quick look under dresses)*

FATHERS. Boys, you will lead the way, helping the girls over obstacles and through doors *(BOYS try to lead but girls are busy giggling, fixing hair, etc.)*

MOTHER. Girls, you will let the boys lead and help you over obstacles and don't let them see under your dresses. *(GIRLS let boys help them across middle ramp to upper ramp and back to where they began)*

FATHER. Boys will have low voices and do math and scientific things *(BOYS do experiments stepping to middle ramp)*

BOYS. E=MC cubed. 12 times 12 is 134.

MOTHER. Girls, you will carry dolls and talk a lot, incessantly, in fact, in shrill voices, about stupid little things.

GIRLS. (*giggling and shrieking incessantly as they cross upper ramp and then cross back again*) I've got a Barbie Doll, and three Frank Sinatra records. Do you want to borrow my velvet dress? I got these socks at Saks. See my bracelet. Stupid little things. More stupid little things. Incessant stupid little things.

FATHER. And boys, you will lead in all things, even dancing which you aren't supposed to be good at so you just stand there flexing your muscles. (*BOYS try to get GIRLS to dance but GIRLS are talking incessantly*)

MOTHER. Girls, oh girls. (*yelling*) Girls, you will let the boys lead you even though you are good at dancing because you don't have a penis.

(*BOYS ask GIRLS to dance. COUPLE 1 does the jitterbug down right ramp singing "At the Hop." BOY manipulates girl, twisting and twirling her until she ends up on right lower ramp floor. COUPLE 2 does ballet dance down left ramp singing "Nutcracker Suite." BOY manipulates girl until she does the dying swan on lower left ramp. COUPLE 3 dance "Cheek to Cheek" as Fred Astaire and Ginger Rogers. BOY manipulates GIRL until she ends on lower ramp floor. BOYS return to middle ramp.*)

FATHER. And boys you will grow up to be anything you want.

BOY 1. I'm gonna be a brain surgeon. Or Tarzan.

BOY 2. I can't decide between being a lawyer or...Genghis Khan. (*thinking over*)

BOY 3. I'm gonna be a hairdresser. (*starts shaping hair*)

FATHER. Except you can't be things that girls are.

BOY 3. Oh. Then I'll be a barber. (*cuts hair manfully*)

MOTHER. And girls, you can grow up to be

GIRLS. (*excited*) Yes?

MOTHER. Married to a man who can be anything he wants.

(*GIRLS eye BOYS viciously and sink to floor*)

FATHER. And boys, you will feel contempt for the girls (*BOYS walk to lower ramp with contempt*) until you grow up and then because you have a penis (*BOYS check for penis*) you will need them to help you and keep you in line and control those aggressive tendencies that have brought this world to the edge of destruction. (*BOYS walk to upper ramp looking maniacal and powerful, checking under loincloths*)

MOTHER. And girls you will feel upset about their contempt and envious of their penises and you will cry a lot (*GIRLS cry and envy*) until one day you will realize that you have something they want (*GIRLS rise to knees and flash breasts*) and that you can catch one of them through the process of

EVERYONE. Dating.

(EVERYONE lines up across upper ramp as if standing in front of a big mirror getting ready for the Prom, tying pink and blue cloths into bows. SPEAKERS sit at upper ramp screens, facing audience. OTHERS hover helping with makeup.)

GIRL 1. I have squeezed my body into a girdle even though I only weigh 75 pounds and I've stuffed my size triple A bra with tissue paper so my breast will look like Sophia Loren's, and I've squeezed my feet into shoes that are three sizes too small for me even though I am six feet tall and wear a size 12 shoe so that I can look petite and the boys will like me.

EVERYONE. *(Marilyn Monroe voices and sticking out chests)* Because of my personality.

GIRL 2. I've covered my face with makeup so no one can see the slightest blotch, and I've made my lips look like cherries, and my cheeks like roses, and my eyes like stars so that I'll look pretty but not so pretty that the boys will want to have sex with me. I've accented my fingernails, my hips and my breasts so that the boys will fight over me.

EVERYONE. *(Marilyn Monroe voices and sticking out chests)* Because of my personality.

GIRL 3. I have shaved every single hair off my body and sprayed every single hair on my head so it won't get out of place and then I won't look pretty so the boys will ask me for a date.

EVERYONE. *(Marilyn Monroe voices and sticking out chests)* Because of my personality.

GIRL 4. And not my looks and I can hardly breathe, smile, stand up, sit down or talk which ought to really make me able to catch some pimply smelly, clammy, disgusting boy whose idea of conversation consists of grunting and whose head comes up to my waist.

EVERYONE. *(Marilyn Monroe voices and sticking out chests)* Because of my personality.

GIRL 5. And we are all best friends and inseparable from each other. We spend our days and nights laughing and studying together, going to the movies, hanging out. *(GIRLS hug and kiss and be friends)* But in a few minutes we're going to leave this powder room and join the prom where we will have to try to get one of those boys without a brain in their heads to want to dance with us because we can promise to have sex with them in about seven years from now AFTER we get them to ask us to marry them.

EVERYONE. *(pissed)* Because of my personality.

GIRL 6. Even though we know nothing about sex and aren't supposed to and aren't even supposed to enjoy it even though we are the ones who get pregnant we aren't supposed to know about birth control or even be able to get it let alone an abortion which is unheard of and is a sin.

GIRL 7. So let's hug and kiss and be friends and share our clothes and records (*THEY hug and kiss and talk about how you can get pregnant from French Kissing, sitting on the toilet, touching*) and then go out there and lie, cheat, steal, even kill in order to get all of them to like one of us better than the others.

GIRL 1. (*pushing past the others to come downstage*) They have syphilis and I have bigger breasts.

GIRL 2. (*pushing past the others and shoving GIRL 1 to the floor*) She picks her nose and I'm blond.

GIRL 3. (*pushing past the others and knocking GIRL 2 to the ground*) She's flatchested and I can do your homework for you.

GIRL 4. (*pushing and shoving*) She has pit odor, and I have access to money.

GIRL 5. (*pushing and shoving*) She picks her nose and I have access to liquor.

GIRL 6. (*pushing and shoving*) She has dandruff and I'll let you touch me above the waist.

GIRL 7. (*pushing and shoving*) She has bad breath and I have access to a car.

GIRL 8. (*pushiest of them all*) They're all lesbians, and I've got a car, access to liquor, I'll do your homework, plus I have money, plus I'll let you touch me above the waist, plus, plus, super plus, if you promise to respect me and not tell anyone I'll let you go all the way.

EVERYONE. (*angrily clambering over each other to get up*) Pick me, damn it.

PLAYWRIGHT. (*narrating*) And the prize for winning the dating competition and the culmination of our upbringing was to be

EVERYONE. (*eyes misting, rising to knees*) The engagement ring.

ENGAGED GIRL. (*rising like Venus on the halfshell*) I'm so proud.

(*EVERYONE makes sounds of awe*)

ENGAGED GIRL. (*walking on clouds*) Look at my ring.

(*WOMEN cluster on right and left ramps, oohing and aahing, commenting on the size and beauty of the diamond and how much he must love her*)

GIRL 3. A diamond is

EVERYONE. Forever. (*sighs*)

(*THEY break out of religious mood. ANTI comes forward to narrate*)

ANTI. But none of that really mattered. Well, it did. But somewhere deep in our souls we knew with incredible certainty that one day, when we turned twenty-one—earlier for some, later for others—we would have the kind of lives that men and women had in the novels we read late at night or in the movies we saw every week. It went something like this.

(*Three women become MEN making blue neckties and standing middle ramp left; three become WOMEN wrapping pink cloths around breasts and sitting middle ramp right. ANTI and NUN become speakers and sit on lower ramp screens which are flush right and left.*)

MAN. He was working late one night at the club. Sophisticated

MEN. (*looking sophisticated*) Good evening.

MAN. Yet humane.

MEN. (*looking humane*) So, hi.

MAN. Handsome

MEN (*looking handsome*) Can I borrow your mirror? (*to each other*)

MAN. Yet beautiful.

MEN. (*clasping hands in front of them and lifting a leg behind them a la Charlie Chaplin's TRAMP*)

MAN. Strong

MEN. (*looking tough*) Yo.

MAN. Yet sensitive.

MEN. (*looking sensitive*) Be gentle.

MAN. Shy

MEN. (*looking shy*) Uh, would you?

MAN. Yet bold.

MEN. (*looking bold*) How's about it?

MAN. Tall and lean.

MEN. (*looking tall and lean*)

MAN. But not bony...never gaunt.

MEN. (*looking pudgy and bloated*)

MAN. Serious

MEN. (*looking serious*) The deal is off, Mister.

MAN. But with a sense of humor.

MEN. (*looking witty*)

MAN. Intelligent

MEN. (*looking intelligent*) E equals MC squared.

MAN. But not domineering.

MEN. (*looking less intelligent*) Duh.

MAN. Commanding.

MEN. (*looking commanding by drawing six guns*) Reach!

MAN. But capable of being commanded.

MEN. (*looking wimpy and in bondage*) Hit me.

MAN. Wild

MEN. (*looking wild by bringing out whips*) Submit!

MAN. Yet tameable.

MEN. (*looking submissive by offering whips*) Beat me.

MAN. He went about his business as usual, talking wittily with the customers, smiling at the regulars.

MEN. (*smiling wittily*) Everything all right here?

WOMEN. Sure, Rick.

MAN. But he sensed something (*MEN sniff the air*)

WOMAN. And then she walked in.

(*WOMEN rise, walk seductively past MEN, then return to middle ramp*)

WOMAN. She was beautiful

WOMEN. (*looking beautiful by batting eyes*)

WOMAN. Yet modest.

WOMEN. (*looking modest and demure and wimpy*)

WOMAN. Pure

WOMEN. (*looking like Madonnas and singing*) Ave Maria.

WOMAN. Yet passions burned within.

WOMEN. (*looking like tigers in heat*) Take me.

WOMAN. Witty

WOMEN. (*looking like Lucille Ball*) Did ya hear the one about?

WOMAN. But not raucous...

WOMEN. (*toning it down*) Did ya hear the one about?

WOMAN. Spunky

WOMEN (*looking aggressively Gidget*)

WOMAN. Yet statuesque.

WOMEN. (*becoming elegant statues*)

WOMAN. Perky

WOMEN. (*looking like Connie Stevens*)

WOMAN. Yet lyrical.

WOMEN. (*looking like ballet dancer*)

WOMAN. Intelligent

WOMEN. (*looking as if having a deep discussion*)

WOMAN. Yet able to hide it.

WOMEN. (*looking incredibly stupid and incapable of having deep conversation*)

WOMAN. Proud

WOMEN. (*looking snooty*)

WOMAN. Yet humble

WOMEN. (*looking pathetic*)

WOMAN. Wild

WOMEN. (*crazed*)

WOMAN. Yet tameable.

WOMEN. (*hands tied*) Get the whip.

WOMAN. Demanding

WOMEN. (*putting foot down and having tantrum*) Listen fool, I told you...

WOMAN. Yet caring

WOMEN. (*reaching out with love*) Have it your way.

WOMAN. They saw each other from across the room. (*MEN and WOMEN cross to face each on lower right and left; middle right and left, and upper right and left ramps.*

MAN. Their eyes met and locked.

(*WOMEN and MEN lock eyes across the room*)

MAN. Their loins began to quiver.

(*THEIR loins quiver*)

WOMAN. He said sensitively

MEN. Hello.

WOMAN. She pouted back

WOMEN. I detest you.

MAN. He returned forcefully

MEN. God, you've got spunk. I like that.

WOMEN. You're overbearing.

WOMAN. She whined.

MAN. He answered masterfully

MEN. Yes. You're eyes are like fire.

MAN. She shrieked bitchily

WOMEN. You have a wife who's insane and so you can never divorce.

MEN. Yes, but I'm handsome and I love you.

MAN. He said tenderly.

WOMEN. I'm the only woman reporter in New York City. I'm well-paid and well-respected

WOMAN. She responded shrewishly.

MEN. Yes. I love you for your mind.

MAN. He said generously.

WOMEN. I'm also a singer at an expensive night club. I've got the world at my feet

WOMAN. She snipped.

MEN. I look great in three piece suits and I adore you.

WOMEN. I have my own apartment, a personal maid, money.

MEN. I'm Cary Grant.

WOMEN. I'll do anything you say. I'm putty in your hands. (*WOMEN cross to lower ramp right, center and left singing "Falling in love again, never wanted to, what am I to do, can't help it" in their best Marlene Dietrich voices. MEN cross to middle right, center, and left and face the WOMEN who face the audience.*)

MEN. Can you cook?

WOMEN. Yes.

WOMAN. She lied.

MEN. And clean?

MAN. He said, taking command.

WOMEN. Yes.

WOMAN. She twittered passively.

MEN. Come here.

(*WOMEN come rushing*)

MAN. He pulled her to him, hot loins pressed against hot loins.

(*MEN pull WOMEN up close, nostrils flaring, MEN'S heads facing the audience, WOMEN'S heads resting on MEN'S shoulders*)

MEN. Put your arms around me.

WOMEN. Yes. Well?

WOMAN. She begged shamelessly.

MEN. Well, kid (*chuck WOMEN under the chin*) I guess this is it. Let's get married. (*step off middle ramp*)

WOMEN. (*shouting*) I thought you'd never ask.

WOMAN. She shouted victoriously.

(*WOMEN leap into MEN'S arms and they walk forward. PLAYWRIGHT continues narration.*)

PLAYWRIGHT. Our fantasies always ended there. On the threshold.

(*MEN put WOMEN down*) And, of course, our lives didn't turn out like that because around the time we were finished with our upbringing and ready to become our mothers, something happened. (*WOMEN start for middle ramp*) Earlier for some, later for others. But around 1969 we became part of the

EVERYONE. (*tentatively as they remove robes and pink and blue cloths*) Women's movement?

PLAYWRIGHT. We don't want to give the wrong impression, we're not all of the

EVERYONE. (*bolder, putting robes and cloths on their screens*) Women's movement.

PLAYWRIGHT. (*rushing to upper ramp with the OTHERS*) But we were definitely in the

EVERYONE. (*definite and turning full front*) Women's movement.

(*WOMEN turn away as "For a Few Dollars More" music plays. WOMEN turn front, mock heroic; stare at horizon, turn away; then repeat. Two WOMEN step to middle ramp right and left, face each other. As two WOMEN pass each other, all WOMEN stare at horizon, then turn away. Two more WOMEN walk down center ramp, turn right and left, pass first two WOMEN who have come down right and left ramps; all WOMEN stare at horizon. Third TWOSOME step to middle ramp, pass each other; ALL stare at horizon. WOMEN on lower ramp walk up right, center, and left ramp as last two WOMEN walk down center ramp, and are joined by third set of WOMEN at lower ramp. All stare horizon. WOMEN form clump on middle right ramp; stare at horizon, turn away, repeat. WOMEN break from clump in twos, exploring women's movement. Then form phalanx across lower ramp. Stare horizon, walk to middle ramp, stare horizon, walk to lower ramp, run to upper ramp for last look. WOMEN snap out of it, ad lib "Mystical," "Incredible," "Wow," etc.*)

SINGLE. (*checks watch, heads center shelf*) Can we continue this later? I gotta get to work.

ACTIVIST. Look at the time. (*gets backpack at center shelf*)

POPULIST. (*heads to center shelf for backpack*) I missed my bus.

ANARCHIST. I'll get there when I get there. (*heads center shelf*)

STUDIES. (heads center shelf for briefcase) I loved re-living those early years but I have to get to class.

NUN. (*gets work things center shelf*) I had hoped to enlighten you on the Pope and his latest position on women.

(*WOMEN pause, alarmed*)

NUN. But I've got work to do.

ANTI. (*heading downstage for backpack*) Airport for me. Brigades. Nicaragua.

(*WOMEN have collected work things and some of them are offstage. Slowly THEY return and speak quietly, controlling their emotions.*)

PLAYWRIGHT. What's the matter? I thought you were late for work.

ACTIVIST. There were things we didn't tell about. Things that happened when we were growing up. When our mothers were growing up.

SINGLE. They made me

ANARCHIST. They used to

STUDIES. I've read about things

ANTI. I've seen things

POPULIST. It's hard to leave this place

NUN. I'm not sure I want to go out there today

SINGLE. It's not perfect here

ACTIVIST. But it's close.

STUDIES. Tell them what happened. About the effect we were having. (*exits*)

POPULIST. Yes. Continue our story. You remember? The attitudes and reactions. (*exits*)

ANTI. Let's tell them about the strange distortions we began noticing. (*exits*)

ANARCHIST. The outright attacks from people in power in corporations, in the government. (*exits*)

SINGLE. Tell them about the opposition. (*exits*)

ACTIVIST. The men in power. Let's be clear we're talking about men. Mostly. (*exits*)

NUN. How they seemed to be crawling all over the movement, twisting our ideas around, figuring out ways to use feminism for their own purposes. (*exits*)

PLAYWRIGHT. Yes, it seems that even as we began living, others were planning our death. Let us tell you about that curious incident. It must have happened as we approached high noon in the movement, probably while we were too busy to notice. Let us tell you about the time when many men and some women came sneaking in here and began

EVERYONE. (*sneaking around behind upstage screens in men's hats and coats—some corporate, some hardhats. THEY whisper "watch out," "be quiet," "Jesus." Then THEY pop out*) Bugging the women's movement.

(*lights out*)

Scene 2. Bugging the Women's Movement

(*BUGGERS 1-7 enter one at a time to "Diamonds Are a Girl's Best Friend" sung by T-Bone Burnett. THEY walk center ramp splitting right and left to pose at screens along sides. The music fades when BUGGERS 1-7 are in place.*)

BUGGER 1. (*walking down center ramp, posing*) Wearing an expensive manly dark suit, brown shoes, and looking every inch the important man that I am, I have come to investigate the kinds of books they are reading and their politics here in the women's movement. (*crosses to lower right ramp as the others move up*)

BUGGER 2. (*crossing down center ramp, posing*) In my new designer look, I am here to investigate the fashion possibilities for my new line of clothes and fashion accessories for the new woman. (*crosses to lower left ramp as the others move up*)

BUGGER 3. (*crossing down center ramp, posing*) I'm on top of the cohabiting arrangements here in the movement in my dark suit, conservative overcoat and hat that says no to sexual liberation. (*crosses to lower right ramp as the others move up*)

BUGGER 4. (*crossing down center ramp, posing*) In my long black blessed-by-God somber outfit with white collar and correct brain, I am here to investigate their practice of witchcraft and other man-hating rituals. (*crosses lower left ramp as the others move up*)

BUGGER 5. Manfully dressed in t-shirt, tough boots, and hardhat, I am here to kick some ass and put a stop to these clinics where they murder babies and castrate men. (*crosses to lower right ramp as the others move up*)

BUGGER 6. (*crossing down center ramp, posing*) Sporting a trench coat and shoes that say FBI and CIA all over them, I'm here to counter their subversive activities and to plant a few dirty tricks of my own.

BUGGER 7. (*crossing down center ramp*) Guys, let's lighten up here. In my funky shirt and get-down pants, reeking of opportunism and liberalness, I am here because I heard these women will have sex any time, any place. Just what I've always wanted. I'm looking for action. So where are they? Bring on the chicks, the babes, the libbers.

BUGGER 8. (*who is a woman enters*) So this is it. (*BUGGERS 1-7 take off hats and kneel. As SHE moves down center ramp, they replace their hats*) I'm really here in the women's movement wearing my white gloves and tasteful suit. I've very much a woman but every inch a lady. This place is making my flesh crawl. (*to audience*) Doesn't it make your flesh crawl? Look at all these

BUGGERS. (*hold up pink and blue cloths and bathrobes distastefully*) Women's things.

(Music begins again and BUGGERS 1-7 form a clump of "men on a street corner" and they strut to left middle ramp making manly comments, strut left, then step kick "sneak" step down and back center ramp, ending middle ramp center in manly clump. As BUGGERS 1-7 dance, BUGGER 8 cleans shelf right.)

BUGGER 1. *(walks center through clump of BUGGERS)* Look what we have here. *The Feminine Mystique.* Weird. *(tosses each book to BUG-GERS after comment) The Female Eunuch.* Very weird. *Gyn Ecology.* I wonder what that's about? *The Dialectics of Sex.* I'm for sex. *A Room of One's Own.* What for? *Our Bodies Ourselves.* Check for pictures, Guys.

BUGGER 2. *(walks center through clump of BUGGERS showing fashion possibilities with a bathrobe)* This will make a nice combat line of clothes for the new woman. And this can be made into a high heel shoe that looks like a boot. And this can be a backpack that is really a purse. And this we can make into a bra that isn't a bra, maybe an undershirt that's a bra. There is money to be made here.

BUGGER 8. *(crossing through the clump, touching them, as they take off their hats, kneel, then replace hats)* So this is it. Understand I am not a feminist. Sure I think women should have jobs, but I don't think they should be construction workers or in the army. How would we fight a war with pregnant women? I want it made perfectly clear, I am not a feminist. After all, what's wrong with having a man hold the door for you?

BUGGERS. Women's things. *(BUGGERS 1-7 strut to music across middle ramp, then "sneak" down center, then back to middle right ramp. commenting as they dance. BUGGER 8 cleans shelf. Music stops.)*

BUGGER 3. *(crosses down center and back up to clump of speech)* Look at this. *Lesbian Nation.* I guess we know what kind of cohabiting is going on here.

BUGGER 4. *(crosses down center and back up to clump during speech)* Didn't I tell you? *Witches, Midwives and Nurses.* Uh, huh. No respect for the Bible. It's time to burn all of these...

BUGGER 7. *(crosses down center, patting BUGGERS on the back and under the chin on the way)* God, you guys are so dumb. All the sex we want with no strings attached. Don't have to marry them, don't have to pay for their dinner, don't have to carry their lugguage. Jeez, I used to break my goddamn back.

BUGGER 8. So this is really it. *(passes through clump of BUGGERS who take off their hats, kneel, then replace hats)* I am standing here in the women's movement. Understand me well, I am not a feminist. Never have been, never will be. Sure I think bosses should get their own coffee, and take their shirts to the cleaners but I wouldn't want my husband picking out the furniture in our living room. Would you? Of course you wouldn't.

BUGGERS. Women's things. (*Music comes on and BUGGERS 1-7 chase BUGGER 8 down right ramp, across lower ramp. BUGGER 8 turns and chases BUGGERS 1-7 back across lower ramp. Then THEY turn and chase her to middle left ramp. Music fades.*)

BUGGER 5. (*crosses down left ramp to lower ramp then back around to join clump*) Look at this. All kinds of stuff about abortion. I'm blowing these places up. I don't want my wife deciding when to have sex. I don't want her enjoying sex. I don't want to do the dishes or take care of the kids. There's nothing in the Bill of Rights that says a guy has to do those things, is there? Well, is there. (*CHORUS of no's*)

BUGGER 6. (*crossing sneakily down left ramp*) Guys, I'm gonna plant these cute little makeup kits and plant them all over the place. We'll see how feminist these women really are. I bet we have them back to normal in a year or two.

BUGGER 7. (*crossing down left ramp*) Guys, you are so dumb. Just go with this thing. We have total freedom from responsibility, free ass, and all they ask in return is an occasional orgasm of their own. I can swing that. Can you swing that? I am definitely making it here in the...

BUGGER 8. (*crosses down center through the clump, touching them as she goes. BUGGERS kneel and take of hats, then replace them*) So this is really it. This is the women's movement. Understand I am not a feminist. Sure I agree we should have birth control but I won't be forced to have an abortion just because some bra-burning harpies say I should. What's wrong with wearing a bra anyway. I wear a bra. I need to wear a bra. Don't you? (*poses among BUGGERS*)

BUGGERS. Women's things.

(*BUGGERS 1-7 dance up and down the ramps like Fred Astaire on the stairway to heaven. BUGGER 8 moves among them like Marilyn Monroe in "Gentlemen Prefer Blondes." The music stops.*)

(*BUGGERS rush manfully across middle ramp on these speeches*)

BUGGER 1. I am definitely taking these

BUGGERS. (*whispering*) Women's things.

BUGGER 2. I'm using these

BUGGERS. Women's things.

BUGGER 3. I'm repressing these

BUGGERS. Women's things.

BUGGER 4. I'm burning these

BUGGERS. Women's things.

BUGGER 5. I'm bombing these

BUGGERS. Women's things.

BUGGER 6. I'm sabotaging these

BUGGERS. Women's things.

BUGGER 7. I'm getting off on these

BUGGERS. Women's things.

BUGGER 8. (*plants makeup kits on side shelves as BUGGER 6 follows with suitcase*) Understand I am not a feminist. Sure I think we should call women "Ms." but I don't need to go around using words like chairpeople and herstory and fireperson to feel liberated.

BUGGERS. Hey, Ms. Are you coming?

BUGGER 8. Just a second. (*long suffering look at audience*) Sure I think women should have equal rights but not if they're going to use them all the time. I mean if there was a fire and a man said, "Get out of here," you'd obey him wouldn't you? Of course, you would. No sir. I want no part of these

(*BUGGERS dance up and down upper and middle ramp, then "sneak" to form clump around BUGGER 8. THEY kneel as one, hats off.*)

BUGGERS. Women's things.

(*lights out*)

Scene 3. Noon in the Women's Movement

PLAYWRIGHT. (*enters up center*) Well, it's noon in the movement. I'm still here because I'm writing about this terrible thing that has happened, I'm writing about the events that led up to the moment when...

EVERYONE. (*enters with death cloths briskly*) I read about my death in (*snapping*) *Vogue* Magazine (*pops behind screens*).

PLAYWRIGHT. Of course, in those early years, we were dazzled by the light of our own potential. We thought anything was possible. After all, times they had already been a-changing. Not the kind of *fundamental* changes we were talking about but changes had been made in the image of women in...

EVERYONE. (*pops out wearing India print spreads, carrying flowers*) The nineteen sixties.

(*"Visions of Johanna" by Bob Dylan comes on. WOMEN walk upper ramp staring stoned at the ceiling. WOMEN stop as music stops.*)

WIFE. Actively pretty in pant suits.

EVERYONE. Peace.

(*Music. WOMEN walk middle ramp, stop when music stops.*)

STUDENT. Worldbeatingly pretty in mini-skirts.

EVERYONE. Love.

(*Music. WOMEN walk fixated on floor down right ramp, across lower ramp. THEY stop as music stops.*)

NURSE. Naturally pretty in capes and boots.

EVERYONE. Kick some ass, Sisters.

(*Music. WOMEN dance across middle ramp. THEY stop when music stops.*)

WAITRESS. Revolutionary pretty in swirls and whirls of the tent dress.

EVERYONE. Right on, sisters.

(*Music and dancing to middle ramp fixated on a fascinating spot on their own bodies. WOMEN stop when music stops.*)

BRIDE. Combat pretty in safari mess jacket for eluding the police.

EVERYONE. Off the pig.

(*Music and WOMEN wander like flower children down to lower ramp and out center. WOMEN stop as music stops.*)

SECRETARY. A riot of pretty accessories for tear gas, sit ins, takeovers.

(*music as WOMEN wander from screen to screen*)

EVERYONE. Want to buy a flower, Mister.

(*Music. WOMEN dance. Music stops*)

NURSE. Active pretty.

ANARCHIST. Active little.

WRITER. Active thing.

(*Music. WOMEN move screens to original places. Music stops.*)

EVERYONE. Active pretty little thing. (*stands on crates*) Like let's give peace a chance, okay?

STUDENT. (*at center screen modeling up and down center ramp*) The sixties woman is a student. Naturally curly hair. Complexion adventurer. Revolutionary glow. All day eye care for the demonstration. Active pretty boots for marching. Mister pants for those times in jail. Indian print scarves to keep out the tear gas during those riots in Harvard Square. Becomes attractive head gear for nighttime rock party. Designer backpack from army navy for street fighting needs. (*ends up at screen for comment*) Like boycott lettuce, okay?

(*WOMEN make supportive noises and comments as they move clockwise one screen*)

WAITRESS. The sixties woman is a waitress. Nutrition addict. Honest skin. Raw carrots in handbag. Yogurt makeup. Rosemary soap. Lotus powder perfume. Natural beauty. Astrological jewelry as she demands equal rights. (*ends up at screen for personal comment*) "Hey, like do you want your sprouts with cr without wheatgerm, buddy?"

(*WOMEN make comments as they move clockwise one screen*)

SECRETARY. The sixties woman is a secretary. Actively pretty in industrial zippers. Coatdresses. Creating her own odyssey in rayon nylon acrylics. Art of the real. Wicked knits. Powerful prints for office activism. (*ends up at screen for comment*) "Hey, like you pinch my ass one more time, Mr. Finkel, and I'll cut your balls off."

(*WOMEN make appropriate noises and move clockwise to next screen*)

NURSE. The sixties woman is a para-medic. Antiseptically pretty wearing makeup by Fritz she bandages heads after street fighting. Forcefully pretty in comfortable pant suit and no bra as she demands a woman's right to control her own body. Dedicatedly pretty with her gold watch bracelet by Seiko as she stays up all night studying to be a doctor. (*returns to screen for comment*) "Hey, doc. You pinch my ass one more time and I'm scheduling you for unnecessary surgery."

(*WOMEN make noises and move clockwise to next screen*)

ATHLETE. The sixties woman is a weight lifter, football player, marathon runner, boxer, karate expert. Strong in practical clothes for self-defense. Sailcloth top over parachute pants as she tones her muscles. Arm wrestling wearing rope bracelets by Calvin Klein. The no-bra look. A riot of hair. Militant makeup. Militant sweat. (*ends up at screen for comments*) "Like wow, like all I need is like a jock strap."

(*WOMEN make sympathetic noises and move clockwise to next screen*)

WRITER. The sixties woman is a writer of an advice column for active young women. Steely gray streaks through her active hair. Riot of robe for at-home writing. Forceful hands. Masses of bracelets. Fearless attack on the typewriter as she types out advice for the lovelorn. Tiny active brain. Weeny miniscule little mouth. Little bitty feet. (*ends at screen for comment*) "Dear sixties young woman, my advice to you is that it is okay to give it away (*pointing to crotch*) before you get that ring on finger, but honey, eventually you're gonna have to get a man. Any man. Or two, or half a dozen. I don't care just get one."

(*WOMEN move clockwise to next screen*)

BRIDE. The sixties woman is a bride who makes her own wedding in her own time and space. In a riot of colors and fabrics, she creates her own wedding gown from a bedspread. Eastern music. Incense. Barefeet. Nudity. Dancing our vows. Revolutionary jewelry from Cuba. A wedding ring made of daisies. (*ends up at screen*) "We made a commitment in a field of grass. Wow."

(*WOMEN move clockwise to next screen*)

WIFE/MOTHER. The sixties woman is a wife and mother cum civic worker. Helping her husband campaign for political office she tours the slums in a riot of color. Fashion pioneering from South Africa. Bracelets by Monet as she loads the washer. Demandingly pretty as she fights for abortion rights. Assertively pretty as she fights for equal rights in the bedroom. (*ends up at screen for comment*) "Can you believe my husband? The sucker actually told me when we were gonna have sex."

EVERYONE. Right on, Sisters.

(*Music. WOMEN dance to upper ramp and have love in. Music stops.*)

BRIDE. When being blond isn't fun anymore

WIFE. The sixties woman can go back to being natural.

STUDENT. She can look like herself

EVERYONE. Only prettier. (*fists in the air*)

(*Music plays as WOMEN form line on upper ramp, cross hands and join them. Sway until music stops.*)

SECRETARY. She could have danced all night

WRITER. With tampons.

EVERYONE. For the active feminine way. (*fists in air*)

(*EVERYONE marches down right, left, and center ramps to music, arms around each other. Music stops. WOMEN sway.*)

WAITRESS. Change has come through the power of the pill.

NURSE. She can have her cake and eat it too.

ATHLETE. Liberation will come, Sisters. It will all come.

(*Music. WOMEN sing along as they move to middle ramp. Music stops. WOMEN turn.*)

EVERYONE. Active pretty little thing. (*do karate moves, backing offstage*) Like, take that. And like that. And take that. (*exits*)

PLAYWRIGHT. (*crosses to kitchen shelf*) As I was saying, it was noon in the movement and we thought anything was possible. I'm the first one here because I'm one of the organizers for this women's conference we're having. Now, I bet you think that's an easy job compared to marching in the streets, or commiting civil disobedience, or getting arrested but it isn't so easy. We all have our individual politics, our theories and strategies for how to change society. For instance, this woman...

SINGLE. (*enters left with union related banners and book, papers for speech*) Hello. (*to audience*) So you're still here? I told her that you'd have left by now. Nobody seems to care that a woman with a high school diploma and two kids to support can't make it on what they pay for so-called women's jobs. (*crosses down center ramp*)

PLAYWRIGHT. Let's not be bitter.

SINGLE. I'm trying. (*holding up signs*) I've been picketing. (*puts signs down center and starts for right middle ramp screen, then pauses to talk to the audience*) You see, I always wanted to do construction work until I grew up and was told that construction work wasn't a job for women. Then when the women's movement got going, I said, why not?

PLAYWRIGHT. Your strong speech ready?

SINGLE. You bet. Where is everybody?

PLAYWRIGHT. We're running late.

SINGLE. Typical of these bourgeois women's conferences. (*goes to screen to study speech*)

PLAYWRIGHT. And this woman...

STUDIES. (*enters with fat manuscript, books under arm, and walks down center ramp*) Hello, hello, hello. I knew you'd still be here. We're getting to the important part. (*alluding to manuscript and books which she puts down center, then turns to head for center upper ramp screen but turns back to talk to audience*) Education is the most important thing to me. You see, I've always loved reading and learning. But I didn't want to participate in the study of MAN or teach kindergarten so I was contemplating a career as a permanent graduate student when I learned about the women's movement.

PLAYWRIGHT. Your obscure speech ready?

STUDIES. (*holds up fat manuscript*) All 100 pages. (*goes to screen to study manuscript*) How much time do I have to prepare?

PLAYWRIGHT. I don't know. We're running late.

STUDIES. Oh, well, women are busy.

PLAYWRIGHT. Yes, and this woman...

ANTI. (*enters in fatigues, carrying book about Che Guevara*) Hi. (*to audience*) Still here. Brave. Seize the time. A strong wind is blowing.

PLAYWRIGHT. Told you.

ANTI. Love ya'. (*puts book down center, heads for lower left screen, pauses to talk to audience*) Now, I grew up in a very rich family, father one of most powerful men in the country. I was slated for a career as a rich and powerful man's wife. Then, the anti war movement came along. And black power. And the women's movement. So I made my choice.

PLAYWRIGHT. Speaking today?

ANTI. Not me. Just back. Cuba. Brigades. (*heads for screen*)

PLAYWRIGHT. And this woman...

POPULIST. (*enters with stack of books on nuclear power, crosses down center ramp, then pauses on lower ramp*) Well, look who's still here. I wasn't sure about some of you. Sorry I'm late but I was passing out leaflets about the proposed toxic waste dump. When I was younger, I was going to be a legal secretary. You know, the woman from a small town who goes to the big city to work for some big shot and who does all the work while he gets all the credit? But, they built a nuclear power plant near our town and then I read about the women's movement and I changed my mind...

PLAYWRIGHT. Your popular speech ready?

POPULIST. I'm not speaking today. This is a conference on theory. (*crosses to screen*)

PLAYWRIGHT. Oh. And this woman...

ANARCHIST. (*enters carrying book by Emma Goldman*) Hello. Frankly I'm still not sure I like this experience. You sitting there passively. And I'm not sure that this conference is a good idea either. (*hesitates on middle ramp*)

PLAYWRIGHT. Why's that?

ANARCHIST. Well, I spent the first twenty years of my life being bossed, ordered around, coerced, and manipulated by someone who had authority over me. Then, I read Emma Goldman and it changed my life.

PLAYWRIGHT. Are you speaking today?

ANARCHIST. (*puts book on center shelf*) Only informally. (*goes to screen*)

PLAYWRIGHT. Of course. And this woman...

NUN. (*enters with appropriate books and papers flying*) I've got some new information. (*sees audience*) Oh, hello. Nobody move. This information is incredible. Wait 'til you hear.

PLAYWRIGHT. You're speaking?

(*WOMEN stand up concerned that NUN will be giving one of those long speeches*)

NUN. Actually no. (*WOMEN sit, relieved*) I'm running a workshop. (*to audience*) You see, I always wanted to be nun. I thought it was the most beautiful thing to be the bride of Christ. To give up worldly things. To help the poor. I'd still be on my knees praying if things hadn't changed, well around 1965 or so. But that's past. Now I have information about the Pope that is incredibly important.

(*WOMEN rise again, concerned*)

PLAYWRIGHT. We'll be starting soon. (*hoping NUN can wait*)

NUN. Oh, well then. (*goes to screen as others sit relieved*)

PLAYWRIGHT. And this woman who is the last to arrive as usual. I said, and this woman...

(*EVERYONE starts rustling papers, adjusting screens*)

PLAYWRIGHT. And this woman...

ACTIVIST. (*enters with signs, leaflets, petitions, bandana over mouth for tear gas, crosses center*) Hi. Look what we have here. I just came from a reproductive rights demonstration. I think I saw some of you there. (*WOMEN peer out to check the audience as she moves down center*) I got involved in this because the dream of my youth was to be a modern day Florence Nightingale. I pictured myself bandaging the wounded in the next World War. And then, I read *Our Bodies Ourselves* and I began to change my point of view about the world and women. (*looks around at WOMEN studying papers*) What's the delay? Why's everyone sitting around? Let's get started.

PLAYWRIGHT. So you see, everyone was working on something different. Everyone had become involved for a different reason. But we had all been changed in some way. And we were busy. We were raising consciousness and

ANARCHIST & STUDIES. (*rising*) Meeting. (*sitting*)

PLAYWRIGHT. Organizing and

POPULIST & SINGLE. (*rising*) Meeting. (*sitting*)

PLAYWRIGHT. Changing our sexual preference and

NUN. (*rising*) Meeting. (*sitting*)

PLAYWRIGHT. Getting arrested and

ACTIVIST & ANTI. (*rising*) Meeting. (*sitting*)

PLAYWRIGHT. And we looked further into (*WOMEN rise looking studious*) into the nature of our oppression, struggling (*WOMEN struggle*) with that curious disjuncture between theory and practice at the

EVERYONE. Women's conference. (*WOMEN sit*)

SINGLE. (*rises to speak to the conference*) I feel that capital and private property are the cause of women's particular oppression just as capital is the cause of the exploitation of workers in general and I would like to quote if I may from a few woman and many men who had much to say on this topic,

EVERYONE. (*rises quickly and shouts*) I hate them. (*sits*)

SINGLE. So in conclusion let me state that women's participation in the labor force is the key to our emancipation. Thank you.

EVERYONE. (*pops out and shouts*) I'm sick of them. (*popping back*)

ACTIVIST. (*rises*) I feel that there is no private domain that is not political, and no political issue that is not ultimately personal, and that the original and basic class division is between the sexes, and that the motive force in history is the striving of men for power and domination over women, the dialectic of sex. And I would like to quote from many women and no men on this topic.

EVERYONE. (*rises sharply and shouts*) I hate them. (*sits back down*)

ACTIVIST. So in conclusion, the key to women's liberation lies in the elimination of the traffic in women and of obligatory sexualities and sex roles. Thank you.

EVERYONE. (*pops up and shouts*) What's wrong with them?

STUDIES. (*rises*) I feel that the oppression of women is a result of the partnership of patriarchy and capital: patriarchy being defined as a set of social relations which has a material base and in which there are hierarchical relations between men and solidarity among them to enable them to dominate women. And I would like to quote from some women and some men on this topic.

EVERYONE. (*rises and shouts*) I hate them.

STUDIES. So in conclusion let me say that the liberation of women will require an overthrow of capitalism and patriarchy. Thank you.

EVERYONE. (*pops up*) Up to here with them.

ACTIVIST. (*rises to narrate*) And there was a great deal of disagreement during noon in the movement because we were not one group of Amazonian women united against men. We had our differences. (*sits*)

PLAYWRIGHT. (*rises*) I would like to ask why this conference seems to assume that all women are heterosexual.

ANARCHIST. Why are we sitting in this hierarchical fashion?

NUN. You're all missing the point here.

STUDIES. This movement is anti-intellectual.

ANTI. This is a white middle class movement. Where is the analysis of racism? Black women are oppressed as blacks first, women second. Look around. There are no women of color here.

(*Women of color rise to be noticed and are told to sit down*)

ACTIVIST. Theory is too male identified.

POPULIST. I resent the implication that all women must be lesbian to be feminist.

SINGLE. If we don't recognize that not all men are the enemy, I'm out of here.

POPULIST. We have no grassroots support.

ANARCHIST. Why are we arguing? We're not the enemy.

PLAYWRIGHT. Let's not gloss over our differences in some kind of false unity here.

(*WOMEN look at each other, then sit*)

POPULIST. (*rises to narrate*) While expanding our analysis and theory, we were also developing a curious emotional theory. A theory of

EVERYONE. (*pokes heads out to the left*) Them.

POPULIST. Which we couldn't shake off, this mysterious

EVERYONE. (*pokes heads out to the right*) Them.

POPULIST. As in

EVERYONE. (*rises*) I can't stand them. (*sits down*)

POPULIST. Or

EVERYONE. (*rising*) Do something about them. (*sitting back down*)

POPULIST. Because we had almost all been involved in relationships with

EVERYONE. (*rising*) Men in the movement.

(*WOMEN playing MEN put on black headbands. WOMEN playing WOMEN put on purple headbands. FIRST WOMAN stands on screen on upper ramp, miming passing out leaflets. MAN brings screen from middle left ramp to join her. PLAYWRIGHT moves center screen to middle left position. OTHERS disappear behind screens. Scene is fast-paced.*)

MAN. Hi. I'm a man in the movement and I'm a feminist.

FIRST WOMAN. Hi. I'm a woman in the movement.

MAN. Yes, I know. You're new aren't you?

FIRST WOMAN. Been here for about a year. Wouldn't call that new. You just haven't noticed.

MAN. Oh, well I'm noticing you now. Where have you been keeping yourself?

FIRST WOMAN. In the background mostly, typing leaflets, running the mimeo machine. Answering the phone. Cleaning the office. It's wonderful to be a part of this.

MAN. I can't help thinking that you should be part of the leadership. The steering committee.

FIRST WOMAN. I'd like that.

(*first LEAFLETER passes by, mimes taking a leaflet, makes comment, returns to screen*)

MAN. As I said, I am a feminist and I believe women should be in leadership positions as long as they're capable.

FIRST WOMAN. I notice there are some women on the steering committee.

MAN. If you mean Sally, forget it, she'll be leaving because Frank—you know Frank don't you?

FIRST WOMAN. Frank? The one that talks a lot in meetings?

MAN. Yea, Frank is no longer interested in Sally. I mean now that she's shown a lack of commitment and has decided to become a separatist.

FIRST WOMAN. That's too bad. She seemed to do a lot of work around the office. She seemed committed. What about Judith? She's on the steering committee.

MAN. Haven't you heard about Judith. The word is she's just here because she's looking for sex.

FIRST WOMAN. Oh. She always says good things at the meetings.

MAN. You're not one of those women who defends other women just because you think you're all sisters, are you?

FIRST WOMAN. Well, I...

MAN. I didn't think so.

(second LEAFLETER passes, mimes taking leaflet, makes comment, returns to screen)

MAN. Now why don't we finish this leafleting and go over to my place, and we'll smoke some dope, discuss your leadership potential and see what develops.

FIRST WOMAN. What's wrong with discussing it now.

MAN. Too public, too formal. We need a more relaxed environment. Let's go to my place and struggle around sexism.

FIRST WOMAN. I have to be back at the office by three o'clock. Why don't we do it there?

MAN. Hey, I'm against the war, you're against the war. *(FIRST WOMAN not impressed)* Look, since you're new here you probably haven't heard that girls say yes to guys who say no. Look, I got to run. I forgot I have an important meeting to get to.

FIRST WOMAN. What about my leadership potential?

MAN. I don't think you're ready. We'll talk about it later. *(crosses to next screen where SECOND WOMAN pops up and starts leafleting. FIRST WOMAN disappears.)*

MAN. Hi. I'm a man in the movement and I'm a feminist.

SECOND WOMAN. Hi.

MAN. So, I've been watching you lately and I think you've got leadership potential so what do ya say we go to my place, put on some *Doors* records and smoke some dope and talk about your leadership potential.

SECOND WOMAN. I'm ready now. Talk to me while I pass out leaflets.

MAN. Too public. Too formal. We need to be relaxed. Horizontal. I think better then.

SECOND WOMAN. I've noticed. No can do. Too busy passing out leaflets, answering phones, running the mimeo.

MAN. Why are you so uptight? I thought you women were liberated. (*checks watch*) I forgot, I have a meeting to get too. Talk to you later.

SECOND WOMAN. What about my potential?

MAN. I must have confused you with someone else. (*goes to next WOMAN*) Hi, I'm a man and I'm a feminist

ANARCHIST. (*interrupts and pops up to take over narrative*) And many of us were also experiencing

EVERYONE. (*pops up*) Movement men in meetings.

(*EVERYONE forms semi-circle. MEN are on upper and middle ramps facing out. WOMEN are on right and left ramps facing center.*)

MAN 1. Can we start the meeting. As I was saying, as relates to this demonstration, I think that the contradictions are problematic.

MAN 2. Well said, bro.

MAN 3. Important, man, bro.

MAN 4. Heavy, man. So heavy.

WOMAN 1. (*to WOMAN 2*) Did you understand what he said?

WOMAN 2. Not really. But it sounded good.

WOMAN 3. (*quickly and apologetically*) Excuse me, I beg your pardon, sorry for taking even a second of your time but just a quick comment, not really a comment, more like a question? If you're talking about...

(*MEN start to cough, rattle papers, chat with each other*)

MAN 1. Could you speak up? You're talking too softly.

WOMAN 3. I just wanted to sneak in a comment. Really a question?

(*MEN start to get up*)

WOMAN 4. Where are they going?

MAN 2. Go on, I just have to take a piss.

MAN 3. Yea, me too, don't let me disturb the meeting.

MAN 4. Gotta take a leak, back in a minute, don't mind me.

(*MEN exit. WOMEN are left there.*)

WOMAN 1. Is this an example of sexism, do you think?

WOMAN 2. Are you serious? I'm ready to walk out.

WOMAN 3. Well, I mean maybe they had to go to the bathroom.

WOMAN 4. Why don't we have a women's caucus and talk about this and figure out just what is going on here?

WOMAN 2. Let's just go join them in the bathroom.

MAN 1. (*returns with the other MEN*) Okay, where were we?

MAN 2. You were talking about the contradictions being problematic. (*MEN sit*)

WOMAN 3. Excuse me, if I might interject a question here

MAN 3. Is it important? I think women should be allowed to speak if it's something important.

MAN 4. Go ahead but let's keep our comments short.

WOMAN 3. *(as fast as she can because MEN are stirring restlessly and whispering and coughing)* I just wanted to mention that I thought we were having this meeting in order to decide whether we need an office to organize the next demonstration and I wanted to say that the student government has offered us theirs if we want it.

MAN 1. I'd like to remind people to keep their comments short so we can all speak.

MAN 3. If I may address the previous speaker. While I agree, bro, man, man, bro, that the contradictions are problemmatic, I think it goes a lot further than that. If I may quote extensively from Lenin's *Imperialism Is the Highest Stage of Capitalism* on page 53

MAN 2. Please do. I've got time on my hands.

MAN 4. Before you do, bro, and may I say that I want to hear your very important analysis of the situation as interpreted by Lenin, let me say first that with respect to office space I have located the student government office and they have allowed us to use it.

MAN 1. What initiative, man, bro. There's no end to the contributions you keep making to this movement.

MAN 3. Now if I may read from Lenin...

EVERYONE. *(rises and yells)* Please do. All afternoon. *(sits)*

SINGLE. *(rising)* And many of us were living for the first time with

EVERYONE. *(rising)* Men in collectives.

(WOMEN collect cleaning implements from down ramp and go to left and right ramps; MEN hang out on upper ramp)

MAN 1. Is there anything else on the collective meeting agenda?

MAN 2. I think that's it.

MAN 3. Let's go discuss the political situation in South Africa.

MAN 4. Right.

(MEN start out)

WOMAN 1. Aren't you forgetting something?

MAN 1. Yea, my copy of *The Wretched of the Earth*.

WOMAN 2. There's something else on the collective agenda.

MAN 2. What?

WOMAN 3. Cleaning.

MAN 3. What about it?

MAN 4. What is it?

WOMAN 4. None of you has cleaned in the last six months.

MAN 1. It doesn't need it.

MAN 2. I didn't join this collective to be reminded of my mother.

MAN 3. I think we should struggle around our sexism, bros, by remembering what's on the collective agenda.

MAN 4. I personally never mess up the kitchen.

WOMAN 1. You never go in the kitchen.

MAN 1. I personally want to clean but whenever the issue comes up, you women lop all men together and do this knee jerk feminist thing about cleaning...

MAN 2. I personally think we should analyze for long periods of time just what we mean by the word clean.

WOMAN 2. We've done that. Often.

MAN 3. Oh, we'll how about you women write a 35 page paper on the topic in which you outline just what it means to clean. What implements we use. What gets cleaned in each room..

WOMAN 3. We did that.

MAN 4. I personally feel that the place is clean. I think you women have a hidden agenda here. You're sublimating your hostility about other more important things and letting them come out around this petty topic of cleaning.

MAN 1. I think this is just not an issue for the left. It's your hang up not ours. I don't object to you women doing your feminism thing. But let us alone so we can go out and make the revolution. (*MEN head offstage*)

WOMEN. (*yell*) I hate them. (*with suppressed anger*) Who's going to do the cleaning this week?

MAN 1. This emotionality.

MAN 2. All right. We'll clean. Jeez.

MAN 3. Gimme that thing. (*takes mop from WOMAN*) What is this?

(*MEN move center stage. MAN 2 gets pail.*)

MAN 4. I think it's a vacuum.

MAN 1. Hey, bro, toss me a sponge. I'll wash this thing here. Okay I'm done.

MAN 2. I think you have to use water.

MAN 3. Good idea. Water. Bro, toss sponge over here. (*MAN 1 tosses sponge to MAN 3, who tosses sponge to MAN 2 who dunks it in the pail and sets off an impromptu basketball game)*

MAN 4. *(after short game)* I think we're finished.

MAN 1. I know I'm finished with the vacuuming.

MAN 2. Wait. Don't you have to plug it in?

MAN 3. Yea, plug it in.

MAN 4. Where's the plug.

MAN 1. I'll just sweep the stuff under the thing here. I'm finished with the dishes. What's next?

MAN 2. Do we have to do the bathrooms?

MAN 3. Nah. Skip it. There's water running over everything in there.

MAN 4. Yea. It's gotta be clean.

MAN 1. Okay, I know what let's do. Let's wash all the windows in the entire place.

MAN 2. A mansize job.

MAN 3. Sweat.

(MEN rush to do windows grunting and sweating)

MAN 1. Wow. We're better at this than they are.

MAN 2. For sure.

MAN 3. Say, toss sponge.

MAN 4. Tossing sponge. *(prepares to toss to MAN 3)*

MAN 1. And he comes in for an interception. Laterals off.

(MAN 3 fades down center for a long pass. MAN 1 moves to intercept and laterals to MAN 2. MAN 3 tries to prevent touchdown.)

MAN 1. *(after short game)* Aren't we done?

MAN 2. You bet.

(MEN toss cleaning implements on floor)

MAN 3. *(to WOMEN)* I just remembered something. Can you chicks finish up? We have a phone call to make on which they entire future of the world depends.

(MEN start off. WOMEN begin picking up debris, then cross to left and right ramps, cleaning as THEY go.)

WOMAN 1. Do you think this is an example of sexist behavior? I mean my ex-husband cleaned better than this.

WOMAN 2. That does it. Tomorrow I am becoming a separatist.

WOMAN 3. Put them on an island.

WOMAN 4. Did I join the movement to be a maid? Huh?

MAN 4. *(returns with other MEN wanting approval)* How's it look, Womens? We did the windows and everything.

WOMEN. (*yell*) Great. That was very good.

MAN 1. Jeez. What's wrong with them?

MAN 3. On the rag, bros, mans.

MAN 4. Happens every month. Mans. Mens. Bros.

WOMEN. (*yell*) I'm going to kill them!

(*MEN have a moment of solidarity, then EVERYONE breaks out of it, removing headbands*)

ANTI. (*comes forward to narrate*) But none of that really mattered. Well, it did. But somewhere deep in our souls we felt that we had a new understanding of ourselves, our history, and what our future would bring. We had rewritten that novel that we used to read late at night. It went something like this:

(*NUN and ANTI sit. OTHERS play MEN and WOMEN exchanging headbands if needed.*)

ANTI. She was at a sit in protesting university complicity in the war, looking busy, dedicated.

ANTI. She was strong

WOMEN. (*flex and grunt as they pick up heavy objects*) Grunt, sweat.

ANTI. And ready to use it.

WOMEN. Here catch, Macho man. (*mime tossing heavy object to imaginary man*)

ANTI. Built like a tank

(*two women form pyramid*)

ANTI. And still growing.

(*third WOMAN climbs on top*)

ANTI. Intelligent.

WOMEN. (*intellectual*) On the subject of the inferiority of the male of the species.

ANTI. And not to be denied.

WOMEN. You got a question, Sucker? (*ready to take all comers*)

ANTI. Radical

WOMEN. Revolution now, for the sisters.

ANTI. But not sectarian

WOMEN. (*reluctantly*) Okay, for a few of the brothers too.

ANTI. Aggressive

(*WOMEN look aggressive by stepping forward*)

WOMEN. About my salary?

ANTI. Not just assertive.

WOMEN. I said, about my salary. (*karate moves*)

ANTI. Passionate

(*WOMEN pant*)

ANTI. And able to get satisfaction.

(*WOMEN turn backs, throw a kiss to each other and grab each others asses*)

ANTI. She sat there, talking with friends, discussing the situation in the Vietnam, the Pentagon, Africa. And she sensed something. (*sniff*)

NUN. Then HE walked in.

(*MEN walk by WOMEN and stand right middle ramp*)

NUN. He was intelligent

(*MEN look intelligent*)

NUN. But not about anything that mattered.

(*MEN look irrelevant*)

NUN. Strong

(*MEN look strong*)

NUN. But who cared?

MEN. Where is everybody?

NUN. Radical

MEN. The people.

NUN. But sectarian.

MEN. Chapter 7, column 3.

NUN. Aggressive

MEN. (*aggressive*) Hey, babe.

NUN. But able to hide it.

MEN. (*looking wimpy*) Whatever.

NUN. Passionate

(*MEN look passionate*)

NUN. But incapable of satisfying her.

MEN. (*checking for penises*) Where'd it go. What happened? What the...?

NUN. They eyed each other from across the crowded demonstration.

(*WOMEN cross to left ramp, MEN to right ramp and eye each other*)

ANTI. She saw he was carrying a copy of Simone de Beauvoir's *The Second Sex*, Doris Lessing's *Four-Gated City* and the essay "The Myth of the Vaginal Orgasm," and her loins began to quiver. She approached him boldly. (*WOMEN step forward*)

NUN. He correctly waited for her to speak.

WOMEN. What do you think of those books you've got there?

ANTI. She said boldly checking out his...politics.

MEN. I think they are some of the important writings in the last 30 years.

NUN. He said opportunistically.

WOMEN. Of the last 30 years?

ANTI. She asked on the verge of losing interest.

MEN. Of all time.

NUN. He hastened, willing to compromise...for now.

WOMEN. God, I love your politics.

ANTI. She said passionately, knowing her priorities.

MEN. I still have a lot to learn, but I'm open to it.

NUN. He said cunningly.

WOMEN. That's all I ask.

ANTI. She slung back, knowing he was full of shit.

NUN. He waited, looking sincere and dedicated, knowing that showing any interest in her body would be the kiss of death.

WOMEN. Can you cook?

ANTI. She said, willing to give him a try.

MEN. Yes.

NUN. He said, lying through his teeth.

WOMEN. Can you clean?

MEN. Sure.

NUN. He choked, wishing he had learned.

WOMEN. Come here.

ANTI. She said, taking command.

MEN. Okay.

NUN. He said, excited but able to hide it.

(*MEN stumble to lower ramp. WOMEN to middle ramp*)

WOMEN. How about it?

ANTI. She said briskly, willing to take it or leave it.

MEN. Yes.

(*MEN simper to middle ramp*)

NUN. He said, feigning passivity.

WOMEN. Fine.

ANTI. She said, turning to go back to the sit in.

(*WOMEN turn away*)

MEN. Tonight?

NUN. He called after her pathetically, almost blowing it.

WOMEN. No. Not tonight.

ANTI. She said angrily.

MEN. Why not?

NUN. He whined.

WOMEN. Because I see other people.

ANTI. She said making clear he couldn't fill all her needs.

MEN. That's cool.

NUN. He said gazing around the sit in to see who this other guy was.

WOMEN. (*turn back*) Tonight is my study group.

ANTI. She said, her eyes misting over.

WOMEN. (*frenzied*) Only my study group can fulfill my all consuming lust.

MEN. (*excited and hopeful, rushing to middle ramp*) Yes?

WOMEN. (*grab books from MEN*) For theory. (*clumping in orgiastic study group, making noises building to crescendo*) Yes!

ANTI. She shouted victoriously.

PLAYWRIGHT. Yes, well time passed and we got down to the business of day to day life. A new kind of life to be sure, because it was noon, and we were dazzling. There was important work to be done in the...

EVERYONE. (*removes headbands*) Women's movement.

STUDIES. We were out to change the world in the...

EVERYONE. (*energetically*) Women's movement.

(*JAMES BOND theme comes on and they repeat Women's movement dance but more excited now, more active, more dazzling. WOMEN end on upper ramp where they snap out of it. WOMEN start out, checking watches. Then return.*)

PLAYWRIGHT. What's the matter?

ANTI. Hard to leave.

SINGLE. I've learned a great deal.

POPULIST. I liked some things, but I didn't like others.

ANARCHIST. It's a beginning.

ANTI. Brave.

NUN. Spiritual.

STUDIES. I love it here. There's so much to read, to study.

ACTIVIST. It's the most important thing I've ever done.

PLAYWRIGHT. Goes without saying.

(*WOMEN allude to makeup kits, then exit after their speeches*)

SINGLE. Go on, tell them what happened. (*exits*)

POPULIST. You remember (*exits*)

STUDIES. Those strangenesses (*exits*)

ANARCHIST. Those distortions (*exits*)

NUN. The ridiculing, name calling. (*exits*)

ANTI. The manipulating. The subverting. (*exits*)

ACTIVIST. So that we wouldn't know ourselves. We would forget our goals and long to become their image of women, again.(*exits*)

PLAYWRIGHT. Yes. Well, time passed and as that initial excitement disappeared, as noon crept toward twilight, the opposition began heating up. And we began to sense something. There was the incident of the makeup kits. And I guess we should have realized then that we were getting closer to that fateful day, not long ago, when...

(*WOMEN pop out with death cloths and makeup kits, snapping fingers in blues rhythm*) I read about my death. In *Vogue* magazine. I read about my death. In *Vogue* magazine. (*turns and faces left*)

PLAYWRIGHT & SINGLE. (*talking blues*) I walked into the room.

OTHERS. I read about my death.

PLAYWRIGHT & SINGLE. On that fateful day.

OTHERS. In *Vogue* magazine.

PLAYWRIGHT & SINGLE. Not so long ago.

OTHERS. I read about my death.

PLAYWRIGHT & SINGLE. I didn't want to read it.

OTHERS. In *Vogue* magazine.

PLAYWRIGHT & SINGLE. Death was all around me.

OTHERS. I read about my death.

PLAYWRIGHT & SINGLE. Starin' me in the face.

OTHERS. In *Vogue* magazine.

PLAYWRIGHT & SINGLE. (*shouting desperately*) I couldn't help myself.

(*WOMEN face right*)

ANTI & ANARCHIST. (*deep voiced blues*) I read about my death. In *Vogue* magazine.

ACTIVIST & NUN. (*high shrill blues*) I read about my death. In *Vogue* magazine.

POPULIST & STUDIES. (*slow weeping blues*) I read about my death. In *Vogue* magazine.

EVERYONE. (*turning to face left, slow breathy blues, as they apply makeup like war paint*) I...read....about....my....death....in....*Vogue* ...magazine. Ooooooh.

(*lights out*)

END OF ACT I

Act II

Scene 4. Twilight in the Women's Movement

PLAYWRIGHT. (*enters left, crosses down center ramp*) Well, it's twilight in the movement. (*crosses to "bar" left ramp and gets a drink*) Another day gone.

(*WOMEN pop out, looking exhausted, then pop back*)

PLAYWRIGHT. I'm usually the first one home for the evening so I fix the drinks. And we're going to need them because we're getting close to the time when

EVERYONE. (*pops out from behind screens, nervously*) I read. About my. Death in. *Vogue* Magazine. (*look around nervously, pop off*)

PLAYWRIGHT. (*crosses center, then up right ramp*) Don't get the idea that we were totally oblivious or waiting passively for the coming twilight. We were beginning to feel a little chill as the sun went down. After all, we had just lived through the image of women in

EVERYONE. (*popping out, aggressively*) The nineteen seventies.

(*Music "She's the Boss" by Mick Jagger comes on and WOMEN come out with briefcases and newspapers under their arms and cigarettes hanging out of their mouths. THEY charge down the ramps competing for buses and taxis, trying to get to work on time, to make a deal, to get more money. THEY are nasty and competitive muttering "Out of my way, Bitch"; "watch it, Sister."; "Up yours, Bitch" etc. THEY wear purple and orange curtains.*)

SECRETARY. Independently pretty in pinks and reds.

(*Music as WOMEN charge around ramps. Music stops*)

ATHLETE. Pretty career look in extra pretty prints.

(*Music as WOMEN charge around ramps. Music stops*)

NURSE. Assertively pretty because she makes fashion investments.

(*Music as WOMEN charge around ramps. Music stops*)

STUDENT. Believably pretty because she's intelligent.

(*Music as WOMEN charge around ramps. Music stops*)

BRIDE. Uncomplicatedly pretty in clothes she's sews herself.

EVERYONE. Single, sensational, satisfied.

(*Music as WOMEN charge around ramps. Music stops*)

WAITRESS. Independent pretty pretty.

WRITER. Independent pretty little

WIFE. Independent pretty little thing.

(*WOMEN end up at screens for fashion show*)

SECRETARY. (*moves up and down center ramp, showing her outfit as she speaks, cigarette never leaving her mouth*) The seventies woman is a secretary cum office manager. Casual T-shirt dresses. Unstructured weightlessness. Easy. Intelligent makeup. Fashion investments. Wonderful cottony things. Getting tough with those frail nails. Independent hair. Strong typing fingers. (*at screen for comment*) "Listen, Mr. Finkel, I can handle the board meeting without you. And on your way out bring me some strong black coffee—with sweet and low."

(*WOMEN move clockwise one screen*)

WAITRESS. (*moves up and down center ramp, showing her outfit as she speaks, cigarette never leaving her mouth*) The seventies woman is a waitress cum entrepreneur. Simple. Natural. Vegetarian. Fragrance that says ME. Camelia petaled skin. Simplicity is complex. Environmental makeup. Vitamins for pollution control. Practical clothes. Coat becomes sweater becomes pants. (*at screen for comment*) "I own a chain of bookstore cafes called Feed and Read."

(*WOMEN move clockwise one screen*)

STUDENT. (*moves up and down center ramp, showing her outfit as she speaks, cigarette never leaving her mouth*) The seventies woman is a Harvard Business School student. Pretty in her career search. Haircutting with a conscience. Hands in pockets for new undershape. Homework for your hair. Suede and trenchcoats over pretty hardworking feet. (*at screen for comment*) "Gucci, Gucci, Gucci. I love it."

(*WOMEN move clockwise one screen*)

NURSE. (*moves up and down center ramp, showing her outfit as she speaks, cigarette never leaving her mouth*) The seventies woman is a Harvard Medical School graduate. Independent hair. French twists. Pretty independent hands perform delicate neurosurgery. Independent little voice that doesn't have to shout to be noticed. She's forty if she's a day. She doesn't have to experiment because she already knows what works. (*at screen for comment*) "Tomorrow, I'm buying a set of golf clubs."

(*WOMEN move clockwise one screen*)

ATHLETE. (*moves up and down center ramp, showing her outfit as she speaks, cigarette never leaving her mouth*) The seventies woman is a yoga instructor. A gymnastics fanatic. An early morning jogger. Independent little stretches. Lunchtime squash games. Aroma therapy. Forceful relaxation in the hot tub. Comfortable clothes. Sweat pants become evening clothes. (*at screen for comment*) "I'm no fool, I bought up all the stock I could in Danskins."

(*WOMEN move clockwise one screen*)

BRIDE. (*moves up and down center ramp, showing her outfit as she speaks, cigarette never leaving her mouth*) The seventies woman is an independent bride who makes a commitment without needing a piece of paper. She marries whoever she pleases as often as she pleases by simply committing in off-white sensible pants suit. No veil. Honest independent hair. Vows she wrote herself. Alternative wedding, alternative lifestyles. (*at screen for comment*) "Her ex-husband was our best man."

(*WOMEN move clockwise one screen*)

WRITER. (*moves up and down center ramp, showing her outfit as she speaks, cigarette never leaving her mouth*) The seventies woman is a writer of an advice column for independent young women. Reds and purples. Steely gray eyes. Independent pretty little fingers write out pretty independent advice in her independent little home. Tiny, teeny weeny independent hair, teeny weeny minuscule independent feet. Independent little teeny weeny brain. (*at screen for comment*) "Dear seventies young women, my advice to you is to give up men altogether and stand by your goddamn American Express card."

(*WOMEN move clockwise one screen*)

WIFE/MOTHER. (*moves up and down center ramp, showing her outfit as she speaks, cigarette never leaving her mouth*) The seventies young woman is a divorced wife, a working mother and a home manager. Independent as she prowls the bars seeking new relationships. Independent as she takes home a pretty $100,000 a year. Pretty independent hands bring home the bacon. Independent hands fry it up in a pan. And when the kids are in bed, she independently never lets you forget you're a man.

(*Music. WOMEN rush to upper ramp as if they were catching a subway or a bus, jostling each other, grabbing for straps, cursing and lurching into each other. Music stops. THEY keep lurching.*)

SECRETARY. She demands more out of life.

WAITRESS. If her guy is giving out pearls, she asks for a triple strand.

STUDENT. She wears clothes that are what she wants.

EVERYONE. When she wants it.

(Music plays as WOMEN cross to lower left ramp, fighting to get to the office or to buy stocks, cursing and swearing. Music stops.)

SINGLE. She's your friend.

ATHLETE. You share your secrets,

WRITER. Your Saturdays,

WIFE. Your Bill Blass,

EVERYONE. And your Salems. *(lights each others cigarettes)*

(Music plays as WOMEN move center, cursing and swearing their way to a crowded disco. Music stops. WOMEN push and shove to say speeches.)

NURSE. She keeps a balance between her career and her love life.

BRIDE. Careful not to let success be away to express hostility and contempt.

STUDENT. She knows there's a little Eve in every woman.

EVERYONE. Flowers on the outside, flavor on the inside.

(Music as WOMEN jostle their way upstage, then turn as music stops)

EVERYONE. Independent pretty little thing.

(music as WOMEN exit shoving, except for PLAYWRIGHT)

PLAYWRIGHT. *(crosses to bookshelf middle ramp right, leaves outfit as music stops)* As I was saying, I'm home early so I fix the drinks. *(crosses to left ramp and down to cocktail shelf)* It sounds easy, I know, but it isn't. We all have our individual needs. For instance, this woman returning from a hard day at the construction sight...

SINGLE. *(enters left with work stuff, walks down center, deposits it)* I made it back. *(to audience)* You still here?

PLAYWRIGHT. Cut the bitter.

SINGLE. *(comes center)* Sure, sure. My strong drink?

PLAYWRIGHT. *(meets SINGLE center and hands her a drink)* One hundred proof. Have a good day?

SINGLE. Are you kidding? *(goes to right middle ramp screen)*

PLAYWRIGHT. And this woman returning from a day teaching women's studies

STUDIES. *(enters with work things, walks down center, deposits them)* Hello, hello, hello. I'm glad to be home. *(to audience)* Nice to see you again. *(to PLAYWRIGHT)* My obscure drink?

PLAYWRIGHT. *(meets STUDIES center and hands her a drink)* An original.

SINGLE. I suppose you had a nice day.

STUDIES. Always. *(joins SINGLE at screen)*

PLAYWRIGHT. And this woman returning from a day working to clean up the environment...

POPULIST. *(enters with work things, walks center, deposits them)* I almost didn't get here. *(to audience)* I thought some of you would stay but I wasn't sure about the others. *(to PLAYWRIGHT)* My popular drink?

PLAYWRIGHT. Miller Lite.

STUDIES. Was your day as good as mine?

POPULIST. It was so so.

PLAYWRIGHT. And this woman returning from a hard day at the newspaper.

ANARCHIST. *(enters with work things, walks center and deposits them)* Hello. Listen, I still don't like this hierarchical differentiation between performers and audience. *(to PLAYWRIGHT)* My non-elitist drink?

PLAYWRIGHT. Generic brand whiskey.

POPULIST. Did you enjoy your entire day?

ANARCHIST. Eight hours of subservience to authority.

PLAYWRIGHT. And this woman returning from a day at the battered women's shelter.

ANTI. *(enters with work things)* Hi. Home. Still here? Brave. *(to PLAYWRIGHT)* Exploiting?

PLAYWRIGHT. Nope. Rum.

ANTI. Cuban?

PLAYWRIGHT. Right.

ANTI. Love you.

PLAYWRIGHT. 'Swat it's all about.

ANARCHIST. What compromises did you make today?

ANTI. Surprisingly few.

PLAYWRIGHT. And this woman...

(NUN enters up center, crosses downstage with workday things)

PLAYWRIGHT. Returning from a hard day working on her manuscript on a new language, and also collecting money and food and clothes for Central America, as well as...

NUN. Where's the wine. *(notices audience)* Oh, wait 'til I tell you about my day.

ANTI. What happened?

NUN. Well, first I read this incredible thing.

(WOMEN tense)

PLAYWRIGHT. We really want to hear all about the Pope but some of us are in a rush.

(NUN joins OTHERS at screen)

PLAYWRIGHT. And this woman...and this woman...and this woman returning from a hard day at the birth control clinic.

ACTIVIST. (enters with work things, walks down center and deposits them) Together again. And will you look at this, there are still some men out there.

PLAYWRIGHT. Be polite.

ACTIVIST. Hey, goes without saying. And I'll fix my own drink.

PLAYWRIGHT. Your active ingredients are over there.

ANTI. What kind of day did you have?

ACTIVIST. Let me put it this way...

PLAYWRIGHT. And so it was twilight in the movement. We had all arrived for dinner and we were sipping our drinks and

STUDIES. (crosses to her screen) I suggested reading from that wonderful book Capitalist Patriarchy and the Case for Socialist Feminism.

SINGLE. And we said

EVERYONE. We'd love to but we're in a rush.

POPULIST. You see the evening was often when we did our real work. Our important work.

ANARCHIST. So we sipped our drinks rather hurriedly.

ANTI. I finished mine first and put my glass away. (crosses to cocktail shelf and leaves glass there).

ANARCHIST. I was late for an informal women's basketball league. (crosses to cocktail shelf)

POPULIST. I said I had to go to an important meeting. And you all agreed that you had to go back out into the world too.

NUN. I was the last to finish because I was reading the latest statement from the Holy Fathers.

STUDIES. And suddenly a strange mood came over us. (crosses to cocktail shelf)

SINGLE. A chilliness as we stood there in the twilight. (crosses to cocktail shelf)

ACTIVIST. (crosses to cocktail shelf) We began to feel that the opposition was too strong for us.

PLAYWRIGHT. And then someone said

SINGLE. I said, has anyone read the newspaper lately?

PLAYWRIGHT. Yes, you said that. And we started remembering things. Portrayals of the women's movement, of the goals of feminism. Changing images and concerns that were supposed to represent us...We remembered

EVERYONE. Women in the news media.

(*WOMEN grab reporter's vests, cigarettes and ashtrays from shelves, and wear purple and pink cloths as neckties. Screens are moved to face each other across center ramp with CHIEF on the upper ramp at the head. Pace is rapid fire.*)

CHIEF. All right gentlemen and lady, let's see what we've got for our top story today.

(*EVERYONE sits*)

CHIEF. City desk.

CITY. Here, Chief.

CHIEF. What's your top story?

CITY. Reported incidents of rape are up. Domestic violence a major problem in this city.

CHIEF. Serves 'em right. Don't we have anything on a local football player?

CITY. Not this week, Chief.

CHIEF. Bury that story on the obituary page.

CITY. Right.

WOMEN'S PAGE. Excuse me, Chief.

CHIEF. Let's hear from the little lady from the

EVERYONE. (*pops up and then down*) Women's page.

WOMEN'S PAGE. I think women are interested in those figures what with the new consciousness from the women's movement and all.

CHIEF. That's why rape is up, because of the women's movement.

WOMEN'S PAGE. The incidents being reported are up, Chief.

CHIEF. Ah, what's the difference. All right, cutie, I like your style. Put it on page 10. National?

NATIONAL. Chief.

CHIEF. What's you got?

NATIONAL. Number of working women almost 50 percent. And we have some incredible statistics on number of single mothers living under the poverty level.

CHIEF. Serves them right. Should have stayed with their husbands.

NATIONAL. You bet.

CHIEF. Don't we have something on a local football player being invited to the White House?

NATIONAL. That was last week.

CHIEF. So what. Bury those statistics. Run the White House story again.

WOMEN'S PAGE. Chief.

CHIEF. Let's hear again from the little lady from the

EVERYONE. (*pops up and then down*) Women's page.

WOMEN'S PAGE. Those statistics are significant. Let's find out why.

CHIEF. We know why, don't we guys?

(*guffaws from the REPORTERS*)

CHIEF. Foreign Policy?

FOREIGN POLICY. Yep.

CHIEF. What d'ya got?

FOREIGN POLICY. I got a couple of wars here.

CHIEF. Nothing on a local football player freeing hostages or something like that?

FOREIGN POLICY. Nah. I got a personal interest story on that chick head of state. What's her name? Maggie.

CHIEF. Use it. That ought to satisfy the little lady from the

EVERYONE. (*pops up and then sits again*) Women's page.

WOMEN'S PAGE. I don't think that feminists or the women's movement are primarily interested in women becoming prime ministers.

CHIEF. Sure they are. Finally we have the little lady from the

EVERYONE. Women's page.

WOMEN'S PAGE. I have something on the ERA.

CHIEF. Nah, something cuter for the

FVFRYONE. (*pops up and down*) Women's page.

WOMEN'S PAGE. I have a feature here on women who have made it in the new feminist world.

CHIEF. Don't you have something on the wife of a famous local football player...or at least the girl friend?

WOMEN'S PAGE. Not this week.

CHIEF. All right. Who are these feminists? Gloria Stein...Ham no doubt?

WOMEN'S PAGE. Well, yes. Gloria Steinam and

CHIEF. Nah, something sexy for the

EVERYONE. (*pops up and then sits*) Women's page.

CHIEF. Get Joan Collins and Princess Di.

WOMEN'S PAGE. But they're not feminists.

CHIEF. Sure they are, they're women aren't they. Sounds cute. Run that story on the

EVERYONE. Women's page.

CHIEF. That's our paper for tomorrow (*rises*). Thank you guys. And the little lady from the

EVERYONE. (*rises and starts for upper ramp*) Women's page.

(*WOMEN break from news media scene*)

POPULIST. (*stepping forward to narrate*) Well, now that we had started remembering, now that we began to find reasons for this restless uneasy feeling we were having, we started to remember lots of other things.

PLAYWRIGHT. Yes, and I remember someone said

SINGLE. I said, Let's watch television.

PLAYWRIGHT. Yes, you said that. And it began to dawn on us that some strange things had happened since the sixties to

EVERYONE. Women on television.

(*WOMEN clear screens to right and left ramps and exit to prepare for women on television. Purple and pink cloths become bows, headgear, bras, etc. depending on the scene. One person becomes NARRATOR.*)

NARRATOR. Changes in the family. Take 1: the fifties: "Father Knows Best."

(*WOMEN form a family; father, mother, and three kids*)

FATHER. I'm white, a college graduate, earning a good living and I'm the father and I head the household using a firm hand because I know best.

(*FAMILY looks at father*)

MOTHER. I'm white and I take care of the household, and the college graduate, and disciplinarian, and good father because he knows best.

(*FAMILY looks at father*)

KID 1. I'm a teenage boy who gets into trouble but I turn out to be a good kid and I respect Father because he knows best.

(*FAMILY looks at father*)

KID 2. I'm a teenage girl who talks incessantly on the phone and is constantly having boy problems and needing to be disciplined by father who knows best.

(*FAMILY looks at father*)

KID 3. I'm a little girl who is sometimes a tomboy and sometimes a sweet little girl and I can get away with murder because father is busy with the others but in the end

EVERYONE. *(looking at father)* Father knows best.

NARRATOR. Changes in the family. Take 2: the sixties. "The Brady Bunch."

(FAMILY rearranges itself to pose as Brady Bunch)

FATHER. I'm the father. I'm white. I'm a liberal. I make money but I understand that father doesn't always know best.

((FAMILY looks at each other)

MOTHER. I'm white and I help him be liberal and I get to help him understand that sometimes father doesn't know best.

(FAMILY looks from one to the other)

KID 1. We're the kids. Even though father's confused

KID 2. We know when we've done wrong

KID 3. And we voluntarily punish ourselves

KID 4. By going to our rooms for a week at a time

KID 5. And by having sensitive interchanges with our parents.

(FAMILY looks from one to the other)

ALICE. I'm the maid and for some reason, I know best.

EVERYONE. She knows best.

(FAMILY looks from one to the other endlessly)

NARRATOR. Changes in the family. Take 3: the seventies. "One Day at a Time."

(FAMILY rearranges itself)

MOTHER. I'm a white single mother and I bungle about, dealing with raising kids without a man. I'm not sure but I think that finally Mother is supposed to know best.

DAUGHTERS. She's our mom, and sometimes we let her know best.

JANITOR. I'm the janitor and I wander into their apartment and since they can't have Mother know best ever, for some reason I get to know best.

EVERYONE. The janitor knows best?

NARRATOR. Changes in female role models. Take 1: "The Mod Squad."

(Two MEN and a WOMAN appear. MEN are arm in arm with the WOMAN.)

MAN 1. I'm a white street guy who's sensitive and I realize that being radical is about helping the police make this a better world.

MAN 2. I'm a black ex-criminal and dope fiend who realizes that black power is about helping the police by uttering words of one syllable and saving this white guy's ass.

WOMAN. I'm a hippie white girl who realizes that the way to do good in the world is by helping the police by being pretty and blond and loving babies and crying.

MAN 1. Let's go catch some hippies who are criminals.

MAN 2. Ugh. Solid, thinking white man.

WOMAN. Help me down this step. Now help me walk. I can't see the crime, my long blond hair is in the way.

MAN 1. I'll wait here with blond hair while you go in and get shot up.

MAN 2. Solid.

WOMAN. No. This is mine. There's a baby in there. I'm going to cry. Help me get the baby. Now help me up. Now help me walk. Help me with my knee. Help me get the hair out of my face. Help me breathe.

(*MEN assist her and are practically carrying WOMAN off*)

NARRATOR. Changes in female role models. Take 2: "Charley's Angels."

(*enter three WOMEN in high heels, backing into pose together, looking stunning, never moving a facial muscle. WOMEN turn and point guns at audience.*)

ANGELS. All right. Come out of there.

ANGEL 1. Wait, We've got to

ANGEL 2. Get into

ANGEL 3. A new outfit.

(*ANGELS run to the sides, change, and start again, backing to the center*)

ANGELS. Get your

ANGEL 1. Wait. We've got to

ANGEL 2. Get into

ANGEL 3. The pink outfit.

(*ANGELS run off and start over, backing out as before*)

ANGELS. Get your hands up. (*point guns then break and start jumping up and down*) We got him, we got him. And wearing high heels, too. (*exit*)

NARRATOR. Changes in lifestyles and relationships. Take 1: "Three's Company."

(*GIRLS enter giggling. JACK enters*)

JACK. Gosh, girls. Isn't this fun living together. (*winking and insinu-*

ating) Come on, Chrissie, and Jackie, and Debbie, and Susie, how about it. Let's go to my room and look at my etchings.

GIRLS. (*shriek and giggle*) Ooh, Jack. No Jack. We love you, Jack but no. Bad Jack. Down Jack. No.

(*JACK chases them around screens and off, then back on again, then off, then on again, then off.*)

NARRATOR. Changes in women's career and life goals, the new sisterhood. Take 1: "Dallas."

WOMAN 1. (*enters*) Pick me, JR, or I'll cut your balls off.

WOMAN 2. (*enters and steps on WOMAN 1*) Forget that slut, pick me, PJ, or I'll tell about the illegitimate child.

WOMAN 3. (*enters and steps over WOMAN 2*) Pick me, BVD, or I'll sleep with your rival and help him steal your empire.

WOMAN 4. (*enters and steps over WOMAN 2*) Pick me, VD, or I'll have my ex-husband rape your current wife.

WOMAN 5. (*enters and steps over WOMAN 4*) Pick me, TV, because I have a body that won't quit and a bank account the size of the state of Texas and I'd just as soon shoot you dead as look at you.

WOMAN 6. (*enters and steps over WOMAN 5*) Pick me, BO, or I will tell all of Texas that you had homosexual relations with my brother Bobby's ex-wife's first husband.

WOMAN 7.(*enters and steps over WOMAN 6*) Pick me, BS. I'm a total bitch and I'll dig rivets the size of the grand canyon in your back with my nails.

WOMAN 8. (*enters and steps over WOMAN 7*) Pick me, T—U—R—D, or I'll shoot you dead and have your body stuffed and hung over the fireplace in your mansion which will be all mine, mine, mine.

EVERYONE. (*clambering to rise, but looking beautiful*) Pick me, damn it.

STUDIES. Now, let's be fair. I'm sure there were a few people in the television world who searched for the true meaning of feminism.

(*WOMEN in Lesbian Story exit. STUDIES crosses to middle right ramp and sits at screen. OTHERS sit on middle ramp.*)

STUDIES. All right. Changes in the way women relate to each other. Sisterhood. Take 1: "The Lesbian Story." Camera focuses on two women athletes coming out.

(*two WOMEN come out*)

STUDIES. They approach each other. They admire each others bodies. They fall in love.

WOMAN 1. I love your body.

WOMAN 2. Me too. (*WOMEN try to touch*)

EVERYONE. No touching.

STUDIES. A man walks by. (MAN enters, walks between the WOMEN) He drops something. (*MAN drops something*)

WOMAN 1. You dropped this. (*picks it up, hands it to MAN*)

MAN. Thanks. (*Their fingers touch. He exits.*)

WOMAN 2. (*livid with jealousy*) You touched him. You spoke to him.

WOMAN 1. I can't stand your possessiveness. Your jealousy. It's driving me crazy. (*WOMAN 1 backs away. WOMAN 2 is a mess, begging*)

WOMAN 2. Oh, please. I can't live if you leave me. (*grabs her leg*)

EVERYONE. (*sings out*) No touching.

WOMAN 1. No. You're driving me crazy. (*drags WOMAN 2 off*)

STUDIES. Sisterhood. Take 2: "Another Lesbian Story." Camera zooms in on two women coming out. (*2 WOMEN enter*) They look depressed.

WOMAN 1. I love you. I'm dying.

(*THEY attempt frantically to touch but WOMEN prevent them by continuously calling out "No touching" every time they get near each other*)

WOMAN 2. I'm dying too.

WOMAN 1. You're dying?

WOMAN 2. Yes.

(*WOMAN 1 and 2 keep trying to touch as they slowly die. Other WOMEN keep calling out "no touching." WOMAN 1 and 2 die, then come alive for one last hug but they are shouting down. THEY die again.*)

STUDIES. Good. That's a take.

(*WOMEN are quiet for a few seconds*)

ACTIVIST. Well, naturally we were a little depressed as we remembered these things. Women cops as heroes and women fighting for power in the corporation wasn't exactly what we had in mind for ourselves. We felt we couldn't hold off that inevitable moment any longer.

ANTI. We were tired, you see. And felt perhaps we should give up.

STUDIES. One of my students asked me today if my women's studies course would help her get into business school.

POPULIST. Maybe that's a good idea. I'm still doing typing and filing at my office.

ANARCHIST. What I write for the newspaper gets changed around. Rewritten. Edited.

NUN. I was walking with my lover today and someone threw stones at us.

ANTI. A woman called the battered women's shelter today and said she was going to commit herself to a mental institution so her husband wouldn't kill her.

ACTIVIST. They bombed the clinic today.

SINGLE. When I came off the construction site, I found that some of the men had set fire to my car.

PLAYWRIGHT. It doesn't seem to matter what we do, we are what they say we are. Well, what can you expect. Look at what's happened since the 1960s to

EVERYONE. *(rising slowly)* Women in the movies.

(WOMEN group together on the center middle and lower ramps and act out the descriptions of women in the movies)

PLAYWRIGHT. *(crosses down center ramp and sits)* The bouncing nymphet. *(WOMEN bounce)* Whores *(WOMEN turn to left and grab for a man five times)* and quasi whores. *(WOMEN grab once)* Jilted mistresses. *(WOMEN soundlessly weep and tear hair as one of them vocalizes being jilted)* Emotional cripples. *(WOMEN say "I'm needy" in unison)* Drunks. *(a series of burps)* Daffy ingenues. *(WOMEN smile stupidly)* Maudlin matrons suffering from sexual malnutrition. *(WOMEN turn right and bite hands while one of them frantically paws at her body)* Psychotics. *(WOMEN stare ahead blankly while one of them says "I'm a nothing. I'm astro turf.")* Ball breakers. *(WOMEN break balls like breaking an egg over their knees. THEY repeat it)* Zombies. *(WOMEN stare into space and hum)* Breasts. *(WOMEN shimmy and sing "Let Me Entertain You")* Nymphomaniacs never leaving a guy alone. *(WOMEN pant)* Kooks. *(WOMEN look kooky)* Groupies. *(WOMEN reach soundlessly for a superstar while one of them yells out "Spit on me, Mick, I'm in the third row)* Female superstuds: all crotch and thighs killing at whim. *(WOMEN fire guns in a circle as they say "Take that, Big Guy")* Just plain hags. *(WOMEN become witches from Macbeth, cackling in a circle and then slowly turn heads toward the audience)*

PLAYWRIGHT. And these women in the movies get to watch men in the movies challenge macho sex...And as these men in the movies become more sensitive, they turn in their tenderness not toward women but toward their own mirror images.

(WOMEN become MEN and walk sensitively to stand on screens facing each other across the stage)

THREE MEN. Newman

FOUR MEN. Redford

THREE MEN. Hoffman

FOUR MEN. Redford

THREE MEN. Clint

FOUR MEN. Burt

THREE MEN. Voight

FOUR MEN. Burt

THREE MEN. Marvin

FOUR MEN. Coburn

THREE MEN. Pacino

FOUR MEN. Hoffman

THREE MEN. Redford

FOUR MEN. Newman

THREE MEN. Hey, guy, pal, chum. Come here.

FOUR MEN. Chum, pal, guy, best friend, only person that matters to me. Come here.

THREE MEN. No, you come here.

FOUR MEN. Nah, pal, you come here.

THREE MEN. I got it. Let's both come here at the same time.

FOUR MEN. Great idea, chum.

(*MEN approach each other like manly version of romantic couple running toward each other in a field of flowers as they sing "Raindrops Keep Falling On My Head." MEN meet and pat each other on the back*)

MAN 1. Pal, chum, guy, have a cigar.

MAN 2. Guy, buddie, share my beer.

MAN 4. Brother, pal, buddie, share my money.

MAN 5. Chum, guy, pal, share all my possessions. My saddle.

MAN 6. My girl.

MAN 7. My horse.

MAN 6. My girl.

MAN 8. My campfire.

MAN 6. My girl.

MAN 1. My beef jerky.

MAN 6. My wife.

ALL MEN. My dawg.

ALL MEN. Hey, hey, guy. Hey, hey hey hey. Hey. Hey hey. Hey. (*MEN punch and pat each other affectionately, then hug manfully*)

PLAYWRIGHT. (*narrates*) After remembering these things, it was difficult to go out into the world for our evening meetings and all the other things we were doing.

(WOMEN head to upper ramp. WOMEN pause)

ACTIVIST. I'm afraid to go out there.

SINGLE. Just watch ourselves die without a murmur.

NUN. I'm not letting this happen.

STUDIES. Maybe it won't be so bad.

ANTI. Perhaps it's time to leave the country permanently.

ANARCHIST. If it happens, it happens. It's not the end of the world.

POPULIST. For some of us it us.

PLAYWRIGHT. And so in the chill of the twilight

ACTIVIST. We took a restless walk around the

EVERYONE. Women's movement. *(removes cloths, hangs upper ramp screens, moves center with backs to audience)*

(WOMEN shiver and turn away as music "Chariots of Fire" theme comes on. WOMEN turn and scan the horizon but can't find it. They turn away and then look again. They back up toward the middle ramp, alienated and confused. They move as a clump to right middle ramp, then burst out in twos wandering cold and lonely around ramps. They join together on center ramp, scan the horizon nervously, then break away and walk alone to the corners. The music stops.)

PLAYWRIGHT. You see while we were gone, the opposition returned. And our fate was sealed. They set the bait for the moment when

EVERYONE. *(sinks dramatically to knees)* I read about my death in *Vogue* magazine.

(lights out)

Scene 5. Really Bugging the Women's Movement

("Diamonds Are a Girl's Best Friend" begins. BUGGERS 1-7 jog down fashion ramps, posing. THEY split to sides, then move to upper ramp grabbing pink and purple cloths. THEY form line across middle ramp and dance up and down 4 times. Then shimmy right and left. Then "sneak" step kick to left middle ramp. Music fades. BUGGER 1 leads other BUGGERS across middle ramp in rhythmic crossover step which they continue doing in place.)

BUGGER 1. *(examining books)* Look, more books than last time. *Sisterhood is Powerful.* Don't make me laugh. *(leafs through)* *Women and Male Violence.* This looks good. Aw, no pictures.

BUGGER 2. (*crossover step left*) Hey, Guys, look at this. A scarf that could be a turban, a chador, a choker, a waist cincher, a big floppy bow. Listen, working women make money. All women spend money. We want that money.

BUGGER 8. (*enters*) So this is it. (*BUGGERS 1-7 hold out hands for her. SHE takes hands and pulls herself through the clump.*) Understand I am not a feminist. (*crosses to cocktail shelf*) Sure women should have power. But in the background. (*BUGGERS 1-7 hold out hands again. SHE serves drinks*) On the little things. Think of the outfits you'd have to buy. The ulcers. I don't want to get lung cancer. Do you? And how would you complain to your husband or your boss about your workday? Or have fun at company picnics?

BUGGERS. (*holding up items*) Women's lib.

BUGGER 5. (*leading crossover step to right middle ramp*) Look at this place. These women are destroying everything. I'm gonna fix them. Marriage is the most important thing that ever happened to a woman. It's in the constitution. That's why husbands get better tax deals. Isn't it? Well isn't it?

(*BUGGERS crossover step to left middle ramp during next speech*)

BUGGER 3. How about we make a movie to deal with this whole anti-motherhood trend where the mother walks off and leaves her kid and the father takes over her role—even though he only spoke two words to the kid and even though he makes over $100,000 a year. That'll put the fear of god in these women. Show 'em we can be better mothers than they can.

(*BUGGERS head down left ramp behind BUGGER 7*)

BUGGER 7. Yea, let's call it Kramer versus Kramer. Gosh, you guys are dumb. I have it all. I have one woman who pays for my meals with her American Express card and five other women who give me unlimited sex, free of obligation, after a good game of squash.

BUGGER 8. (*collecting glasses from the BUGGERS*) So this is finally it. Understand me well. I am not a feminist. Oh sure, if a woman is raped she should be able to get an abortion but I'm not gonna let a bunch of women have control over my reproductive organs. What's wrong with mother-hood anyway?

BUGGERS. (*holding up items*) Women's Lib.

(*BUGGERS 1-7 dance up and down middle ramp, shimmy, making manly comments, then sneak down right ramp behind BUGGER 4*)

BUGGER 4. All right. These women are definitely witches. That explains it. We have rules about that. We have commandments. We have papal encyclicals. These things have to be burned. These women have to be....

(BUGGERS follow BUGGER 5 doing crossover step across lower ramp)

BUGGER 5.   Hey, I don't want my wife making decisions. Okay? There's nothing about that in the Declaration of Independence, is there? Well, is there?

BUGGER 3.   How about a movie where a man dresses up as a woman so he can get acting jobs because women are getting all the jobs...and we make it so everybody thinks the man is learning how to be a better man by being a woman but what we're really saying in the movie is that a man is a better woman than a woman.

(BUGGERS follow BUGGER 7 doing crossover step across lower ramp)

BUGGER 7.   Yea. Let's call it *Tootsie.* Guys, guys, guys. You are a bunch of dum-dums. I can live with a woman or ask her to leave if I don't like it. No problem. All you have to do is agree to share the housework. I boil the Bird's eye veggies in a plastic bag and she does everything else.

(BUGGERS crossover step up center ramp)

BUGGER 6.   Out of the question, Mr. Liberal. Sabotage. Works every time. We know what women really want. This is just a phase. Last time we left those cute little makeup kits, this time we leave

BUGGERS.   *Vogue* magazines.

(BUGGER 6 follows BUGGER 8 as she places magazines on every screen)

BUGGER 8.   Understand. I am not a feminist. Never will be. Sure I think women should have women friends but not on Friday and Saturday nights. I refuse to hate men. I love men. What would we do without them? This lesbian thing? Makes my flesh crawl. What do they do together? Do you know?

BUGGER 7.   No, but I'd like to watch.

BUGGER 8.   How would anyone have babies? I like babies. There'd be no babies with

BUGGERS.   Women's lib.

(BUGGERS snap fingers and sneak step down center ramp, then back up)

BUGGER 1.   I'm censoring this

BUGGER 2.   I'm ripping off this

BUGGERS.   Women's lib

BUGGER 3.   I'm condemning this

BUGGER 4.   I'm excommunicating

BUGGERS.   Women's lib

BUGGER 5.   I'm kicking ass

BUGGER 6.   I'm subverting

BUGGER 7.   I'm getting it

BUGGERS. Women's lib

BUGGER 8. Understand I am not a feminist. I like pretty things. And makeup.

BUGGERS. (*rising and heading to upper ramp as a clump*) Are you coming, Ms?

BUGGER 8. (*yelling*) Hey, just wait a goddamn second. (*to audience*) Men! I like to wear makeup. (*backs up to BUGGER clump*) I don't feel right without my face on. Nothing elaborate. Just a little eyeshadow, a little blush, a touch of lip gloss. I mean it, I want no part of this...

(*BUGGER 8 squeals and rushes through line of BUGGERS dancing while they oogle her. SHE run between the rows of BUGGERS to upper ramp. THEY join hands across the aisle and BUGGER 8 falls across their arms. Music stops.*)

BUGGERS. Women's lib.

(*Music. Buggers dance off, smacking lips, making comments. Music and lights fade out.*)

Scene 6. Midnight in the Women's Movement

PLAYWRIGHT. (*enters upper ramp*) Well, it's midnight in the movement. (*WOMEN pop out looking frazzled*) I'm usually here in the evenings working on my plays. In fact, I'm finishing a play right now, this one that you've been watching? We're getting to the end of it as we speak. The rest of them should be arriving home, straggling in after their evenings activities. This is the day and we are moments away from that fateful time when

EVERYONE. (*pops in, snaps*) I read about my death in *Vogue* Magazine. (*continues onstage, muttering, wrapping death cloths around necks as chokers*)

PLAYWRIGHT. How was the union meeting?

SINGLE. Don't ask. (*to POPULIST*) Anti-nuke meeting?

POPULIST. Not many people came. (*to ANTI*) What about your evening?

ANTI. Can't tell you.

ACTIVIST. I enjoyed my karate class.

ANARCHIST. I'm tired.

STUDIES. What did you do this evening?

ANARCHIST. Me? Oh I played non-competitive women's basketball. And you? (*to NUN*)

NUN. I was administering the last rites.

(*WOMEN have all gotten a drink of some kind from the bar or the kitchen shelf. They get into robes. WOMEN look at each other sadly after NUN speaks*)

PLAYWRIGHT. And so it was that very evening, we had all arrived home sometime before midnight and we were having a nightcap when we read about

STUDIES. No, that's not how it happened. First I suggested a bedtime reading from that feminist visionary novel called *Herland*.

SINGLE. And we said

EVERYONE. No, no reading tonight.

SINGLE. We were tired, you see, and wanted to relax in the quiet of the midnight hour.

ANARCHIST. We all started for our beds, didn't we?

ANTI. Yes. (*WOMEN head for screens*) I remember. We sat down with our nightcaps. (*WOMEN sit*) One of our arms was resting lazily next to us. (*WOMEN let arm rest lazily*)

POPULIST. Idly we began playing with the thing laying there where our hands were resting lazily. (*WOMEN begin playing with Vogues lying on floor next to screens*)

ACTIVIST. We looked down somewhat absentmindedly and saw, instead of our usual bedtime reading

STUDIES. Obscure theory

SINGLE. Novels by that working class writer.

ANARCHIST. Science fiction.

ACTIVIST. Adventure novels.

POPULIST. Toxic waste reports.

NUN. A murder mystery.

ANTI. Underground newspapers

PLAYWRIGHT. The collected plays of...

ACTIVIST. We saw instead that it was a copy of

EVERYONE. *Vogue* magazine.

STUDIES. In shock we pulled our hands away. (*WOMEN remove hands in shock*)

SINGLE. We stared, as if at some dead animal by the side of the road. (*WOMEN stare*)

ANTI. We sipped, hoping for strength. (*WOMEN sip*)

NUN. We muttered a prayer (*WOMEN pray*) or two (*WOMEN pray again*) and then

ANARCHIST. We sipped again (*WOMEN sip again*), but it was no use.

POPULIST. Our eyes were drawn to the articles listed on the front cover. (*WOMEN let eyes be sucked down toward magazines*)

ACTIVIST. We felt our hands, the hand not holding the drink, be pulled down toward the

EVERYONE. *Vogue* Magazine.

SINGLE. We picked it up. (*WOMEN do*)

ANTI. We looked at it. (*WOMEN*)

STUDIES. We put it down. (*WOMEN do*)

POPULIST. We picked it up again. (*WOMEN do*)

ANARCHIST. We put it down. (*WOMEN do*)

ACTIVIST. I got up and put my glass away. (*rises and goes to shelf stage left*)

ANTI. I followed, surprised at myself.

STUDIES. We all put our glasses away. I think I yawned. Said I was tired.

POPULIST. We started for our beds

NUN. Wondering if we'd make it through the night.

ANTI. Avoiding our

EVERYONE. *Vogue* magazines

ANARCHIST. We lay down in the

EVERYONE. Women's movement. (*WOMEN lay down*)

SINGLE. Thinking about our day. Tossing and turning (*THEY toss and turn*) and continually rolling over onto our

EVERYONE. *Vogue* magazines.

POPULIST. Our hands went to the cover and we started to open the cover

ANTI. To see what was inside.

ACTIVIST. Our hands were on the cover, ready to turn the page.

STUDIES. Come on, reading is important. (*WOMEN start to open*)

SINGLE. Right. Sure. (*WOMEN take hands away*)

ANTI. We might be pleasantly surprised. (WOMEN start to open)

ANARCHIST. I don't think so. (*WOMEN put Vogues down*)

NUN. And so we put off the moment. We stalled for time here at the midnight hour.

POPULIST. *(to audience)* I know what some of you are saying. You're saying that it was obvious. We should have seen the trap and avoided it. ANARCHIST. After all the signs were all around us. Look at commercials like...

(WOMEN stand and turn backs to audience)

STUDIES. According to the theory of evolution, men evolved with stubby fingers and women evolved with long slim fingers. Therefore, according to the theory of logic, women shoud smoke the long, slim cigarettes designed for them. And that's the theory of slimness.

POPULIST & ACTIVIST & NUN. *(stepping to the side)* Slimmer than the fat cigarettes men smoke.

SINGLE & ANARCHIST. Virginia Slims.

EVERYONE. *(turning forward)* You've come a long way baby.

ANARCHIST. And we know you're thinking that we should have been a little more suspicious. We should have known that death was imminent when we saw a huge fashion spread called

EVERYONE. A Boss of One's Own.

(WOMEN grab pink and white curtains used in fifties fashion show and pose on upper ramp. After each of the following speeches, WOMEN shift into three fashion poses while saying in unison "Shift, shift, shift.")

STUDIES. *(narrating while ANTI and ANARCHIST act out what she's saying as a fashion layout)* Today's woman is a boss lady. Her career has moved her to the top and she's loving it. Going to work she steps into her Jaguar, showing off her shoes by Gloria. She settles back for her ride on the freeway in a black and white camisole from Neiman Marcus. Antique excessories by Fritz of Rome glitter in the sun as she reaches for her morning coffee.

ANTI. *(while STUDIES and ANARCHIST act out words)* Arriving at work in a crisp gray fortrel twopiece from Lord and Taylor she makes deals over the phone wearing bracelets by Simon. Perfume by Dior.

ANARCHIST. *(while STUDIES and other WOMEN act out)* She inspects the factory in a red jacket over dark suit from from Bergdorfs. She admonishes a worker in gloves by St. Laurent, purple hat by Susie, shoes stepping aggressively over dirt and debris. Beige makeup.

ACTIVIST. *(while SINGLE acts out with other WOMEN)* She pitches right in on the factory floor, rolling up the sleeves of her silk blouse by Saks Fifth Ave. and opening lines of communication in a casual crepe shirt dress by Ann.

SINGLE. *(while PLAYWRIGHT acts out with POPULIST)* In her pretty office, pinks and browns, she softly but with assurance tells employees they can't all be promoted in striped dress for the sensible budget, draped waist from Bonwits. With a smile and good sense she fires workers as she changes into her Celanese sports outfit. Shoes by Nike. Bracelets by Monet as she hands out pink slips.

PLAYWRIGHT. (*while ACTIVIST acts out*) She dashes to workout class in a pink sweats outfit with matching jacket, headband, wristband and shoes. Breezing through the aerobics class, she dries herself off with hand towels from Jordan Marsh collection.

POPULIST. (*NUN acts out with ACTIVIST*) On her way back to the office, she stops for cocktails with friends in a black with white overdrape from the Bill Blass collection. Hat by Lulu of Paris. Guatemalan earrings by Dior. Perfume by Gloria.

NUN. (*while POPULIST acts out with OTHERS*) Entertaining clients in the evening, she uses her American Express card with assurance in a sheer off-green acrylic that she can later fold into her purse. Bag by Harold of London. Rings by Lloyds.

ANARCHIST. (*while POPULIST acts out with NUN*) And on weekend trips to lure clients, she asks for a room in a clear firm voice wearing a blue brushed cotton dress with glass beads, off the shoulder wrap.

ACTIVIST. (*WOMEN go to screens and act out*) And late in the evening she sits quietly in her white on white living room with sprays of rose and orange writing memos, planning corporate take overs, in her long white lounge dress, underthings by Mark of Paris. Truly

EVERYONE. A boss of one's own.

SINGLE. All right, I know that we probably should have just rolled over and died without even reading the damn magazine and seeing that huge ad spread, which stressed the importance of women controlling their own bodies called

EVERYONE. Our Bodies, Our Smells.

(*WOMEN takes screens to upper ramp to form a long line in front of imaginary mirror. THEY tie pink and white curtains around necks like beauty parlor bibs.*)

ANTI. The women's movement demanded that women control their own bodies and

EVERYONE. We say yes to that.

(*TWO WOMEN sit*)

ANARCHIST. Today's woman wants control over her own body and she should have it.

(*TWO WOMEN sit*)

STUDIES. Hey, nobody's perfect, but we can help you come close.

(remaining WOMEN sit)

POPULIST. Master the skin game with our new high-tech protection against toxic waste and nuclear fall out in the air.

(WOMEN put on base makeup with sound effects)

SINGLE. Control your eyes, with new soft lenses that can change your eye color with your mood.

WOMEN. *(rising)* It's not how good you look but how long you look good. *(sitting)*

PLAYWRIGHT. Control those lashes with mascara that you put on the way you like it, take off the way you like it.

(WOMEN put on mascara)

NUN. Control your lips with lip brushes that let you say what you want when you want.

(WOMEN put on lipstick)

ANTI. Control your entire face with Rene's feathery new powder for a complete madeover you. Evolution means the survival of the prettiest.

(WOMEN pat on powder)

ANARCHIST. Control those nails with the Aziza polishing pen, stunning colors with a few strokes. Its the ultimate.

(WOMEN put on nail polish: fingers and toes)

STUDIES. At last. Hair liberation with mousse. Personal cuts at Sebastian artistic centers. Gives you control over what you look like and when you want to change what you look like.

(WOMEN fix hair)

SINGLE. Shape and control those breasts with our new all natural looking bras. One bra fits all. It breathes with you. Let's moisture evaporate. You'll never know it's there.

(WOMEN reach inside leotards and yank at bra strap)

ACTIVIST. Control that body at Pretty Body Exercise Centers. By controlling the shape of your body, you'll control the shape of your mind.

(WOMEN remove hands from bra straps and smile brainlessly)

WOMEN. *(rising)* Sometimes I think my period doesn't know when a busy week is coming up. *(sitting)*

POPULIST. Control your monthly flow with new shaped to your body, scented, flow through, stay free protection. It's your period. Who's going to make the decision, you or your Mom?

(WOMEN shove pad into place)

PLAYWRIGHT. Control your in between monthly flow with lighter days protection, drier is worth it. Assure.

(WOMEN shove tiny tampon)

NUN. Why be a victim of your own smells in exercise class or on a date? Control your crotch odor with new raspberry douche.

(WOMEN do massive shoving of toilet plungers in crotch with appropriate sound effects)

ANTI. Why let odor down there dominate your life in the office. Use our new perfume by Antoine: Crotch.

(WOMEN shake can and spray)

FOUR WOMEN. *(rising)* Part of the art of being a woman

REMAINING WOMEN. *(rising)* Is knowing when not to be too much of a lady. *(ALL sit)*

ANARCHIST. Don't let smells from your underarm control your love life. Lady Speed stick protects you like a man, treats you like a woman.

(WOMEN shove armpits)

STUDIES. Are you a victim of menstrual cramps when you're making an important presentation to a client? Get control of those cramps with new pre pills, during pills, and after pills.

(WOMEN control cramps)

POPULIST. When you're beginning a flirtation with your fellow vice president do you worry about your birth control? In 1960, the pill gave women a new freedom. In 1986, the sponge gives you a new choice. *(going beserk, rising and having to be restrained by SINGLE and STUDIES)* Control that sperm, Women, with the sponge. Just shove it up for twenty-four hour use.

(WOMEN shove it up three times)

ANTI. *(rises)* Looking great.

ANARCHIST *(rises)* Feeling great.

STUDIES. *(rises)* Smelling great.

POPULIST. *(rises)* Body by Pretty Body Centers.

SINGLE. *(rises)* Hair by Sebastian.

ACTIVIST. *(rises)* Face by Revlon.

NUN. *(rises)* Mouth by Roger.

PLAYWRIGHT. *(rises)* Odors by Chuck.

EVERYONE. The new women control our bodies, our smells.

(WOMEN sit with Vogue on their laps, contemplating them sadly, resignedly)

POPULIST. Well, it's getting late. Why don't we just take a quick look at these things. Just real quick, like this. *(opens quickly and shuts Vogue without looking at it)*

ANTI. I suggest we burn them.

STUDIES. No, they may not be as bad as they look. We could study them. Analyze them.

ANARCHIST. I'm not going to be intimidated by this, this piece of paper.

ACTIVIST. Let's get on with it. I hate this sitting around. Let's read 'em or let's put 'em away. Now which is it?

SINGLE. Come on. Let's read the damn thing.

NUN. It could be a very spiritual experience.

PLAYWRIGHT. And so we turned the pages of our

EVERYONE. *Vogues (WOMEN turn page)*

POPULIST. On that fateful day

(WOMEN turn pages)

SINGLE. Not long ago

(WOMEN turn page)

STUDIES. Look at this

(WOMEN turn page)

STUDIES. I went to school with this woman.

ACTIVIST. *(turn page)* I like this outfit.

(WOMEN turn page)

ANTI. If I saved my salary for ten years I could buy this.

(WOMEN turn page)

SINGLE. Why would you want to buy that?

ANARCHIST. It's for the new woman.

SINGLE. Oh.

NUN. I'm in heaven.

(WOMEN turn more pages in rhythm, reacting to each one with a sound, a look. Then WOMEN stop turning, close the cover, and look up. Each WOMAN returns her screen to its place on her speech.)

POPULIST. Well, that's that. I guess.

SINGLE. Typical. Just typical.

STUDIES. I had hoped.

ANTI. It looks bad.

ANARCHIST. We're done for.

NUN. I'm not giving up.

ACTIVIST. They finally did it.

PLAYWRIGHT. Goes without saying. And so it happened. We had opened our *Vogues* and turned the pages and finally, finally, finally...

EVERYONE. *(rises with disbelief)* I read about my death. I read about my death. I read about my death in *Vogue* Magazine.

PLAYWRIGHT. Well, what else can we expect. Why not, after all this is the

EVERYONE. Nineteen eighties.

(WOMEN form pink and white curtains into babies cradled in their left arms. THEY tuck Vogues under right arms and head for the upper ramp, cooing and commenting on their own and each others babies.)

EVERYONE. *(coming to edge of upper ramp)* Dare to be pretty.

(WOMEN float to middle ramp, cooing to babies)

EVERYONE. Dare to be little.

(WOMEN walk to lower ramp, shoving each other sweetly)

EVERYONE. Dare to be a thing.

(WOMEN float down center ramp)

EVERYONE. Dare to be the Other.

(WOMEN float to screens)

EVERYONE. Dare to be feminine.

WAITRESS. *(moves to center screen as other WOMEN move clockwise one screen)* Today's woman dares to be financially dependent even though she makes more that he does. She dares to squash union drives *(WOMEN squash union drives under right foot)* without losing her femininity. Dares to get out there and be a waitress again if she has to. She dares to wear pink and carry a perky pad. Dares to use her emotions as part of her new femininity, emotions can help her solve problems on the job.

(WOMEN move clockwise one screen)

SECRETARY. Today's woman dares to be a secretary. Complaining to the boss is as American as apple pie. Why give it up? Dares to do the typing. Dares to make the coffee. Dares to ask for a teensy raise and be able to make it on what she makes. Dares to live with making 64% of what he makes. Dares to wear clothes that flirt in the office. Dares to let a man pinch her *(WOMEN react pleasantly to pinching)* and dares to know the difference between fun flirting and sexual harassment.

(WOMEN move clockwise one screen)

STUDENT. Today's woman dares to be an intelligent educated woman who finds happiness as a full time homemaker and mother. She dares to leave her lucrative job with a Wall Street firm. She dares to admit that its wrong to throw out the baby with the bathwater. *(WOMEN pretend to toss babies, then hug them to breasts)* She dares to admit that a career isn't enough.

(WOMEN move clockwise one screen)

NURSE. Today's woman dares to admit that she doesn't need to be a famous surgeon to be fulfilled. She dares to be feminine by being happy as a nurse. She dares to understand that they also serve who only stand and wait. *(WOMEN wait, whistling and humming)* She dares to know that changing the bedpans is just as important work as performing a heart transplant.

(WOMEN move clockwise one screen)

ATHLETE. Today's woman dares to be obsessed with her looks. She dares to occupy her entire day with health programs, exercise regimes. She dares to show her body to MEN as she dares to twist and shake and bounce *(WOMEN twist and shake as they count sexily "One and two and three and four")* in front of him in the erotic atmosphere of the aerobics dance class.

(WOMEN move clockwise one screen)

WRITER. Today's woman dares to advise women that it's okay to be feminine. That no matter how emancipated she is, deep down her essential femininity is stirring. *(WOMEN stir)* Dares to tell women to throw out that American Express card and let him use his. Dares to advise women to stand by, behind, and underneath her man.

(WOMEN move clockwise one screen)

BRIDE. Today's woman dares to marry. She dares to marry a man. She dares to marry in a church. In white. With pearls. And a long veil. In June. She dares to trap him into it. *(WOMEN hold up babies and say "It's yours")* 'Til death. Or someone better comes along.

(WOMEN move clockwise one screen)

WIFE/MOTHER. Todays woman dares to say as she makes the

(WOMEN move clockwise one screen on each line)

EVERYONE. Beds.

WIFE. Shops for

EVERYONE. Groceries.

WIFE. Matches

EVERYONE. Slipcovers

WIFE. Chauffeurs kids to the

EVERYONE. Brownies.

(WOMEN stop moving)

WIFE. And lies beside her husband at night that

EVERYONE. (*in ecstacy*) Yes!

WIFE. This is really all there is and I love it.

EVERYONE. Pregnant!

WIFE. Is what your mother was.

EVERYONE. Glorious!

WIFE. Is what you are.

(*WOMEN rush to upper ramp cooing to babies who are mostly little girls and calling them things like "angel, cupcake, princess, honeybunch, snookems, muffin, buttercup, sweet pea*)

2 WOMEN. Sure it's wrong to exploit women.

2 WOMEN. Sure it's wrong to ignore and dismiss women in political and commercial areas.

2 WOMEN. Sure it's wrong to treat women as secondary.

2 WOMEN. But it is not

2 WOMEN. (*rushing to lower ramp*) No it's never wrong.

2 WOMEN. (*rushing to lower ramp*) It couldn't possibly be wrong.

2 WOMEN. (*rushing to lower ramp*) It shouldn't be wrong.

2 WOMEN. (*rushing to lower ramp*) Feminists were wrong.

4 WOMEN. It is never never never wrong to

EVERYONE. Dare to be feminine.

(*WOMEN pause for a moment, then coo softly to babies as they walk upstage, then pause*)

PLAYWRIGHT. I feel so fulfilled. I've given birth to a curtain. Well, that's our story. We opened the covers of our *Vogues* on that fateful day not long ago. And as I said earlier, it surprised me really. As it did the others. Imagine our surprise, when we're sitting there in the women's movement after a hard day at work, a hard day trying to live a different way.

SINGLE. (*crosses to her screen*) We didn't think we were asking for that much after all. Just the complete elimination of class differences which would necessarily include getting rid of capitalism. And I was only asking for the right for women to work at any job for equal pay. Was that so much to ask?

STUDIES. (*crosses to her screen*) I certainly didn't think so. All we were asking was a chance to become the subject of history, of daily life, instead of the object. And to eliminate male domination, structural and psychological. Which would of course mean a complete end to patriarchy.

POPULIST. (*crosses to her screen*) Just a basic right really...to control your environment. To demand an end to pollution and to nuclear power and nuclear weapons.

ANTI. (*crosses to her screen*) I certainly was surprised to see the kind of response I was getting. I mean, I was only helping countries overthrow United States imperialism.

ANARCHIST. (*crosses to her screen*) What was the problem here? I only wanted to eliminate any form of authority...by the state, by classes, by gender and by race.

NUN. (*crosses to her screen*) Makes no sense to me. After all, was I asking for that much? Just that women be able to be priests, we get rid of the pope, and patriarchal religion in spirit or in institutions. And we have a new language.

ACTIVIST. (*crosses to her screen*) Just a simple thing really. Seems like common sense. After all I was only asking for a complete restructuring of sex roles, sexuality, sexual preference, and the entire sex gender system. And of course control over our own bodies.

PLAYWRIGHT. (*crosses to her screen*) There's just no accounting for some people. I just wanted to change the entire cultural system. Develop a completely new vision of how people would live their daily lives. Of work and play. But that's all over now. Because we're dead. It says so right here in

EVERYONE. *Vogue* magazine.

PLAYWRIGHT. Yes, there's no getting around it. It says it right here. Feminism is here. Liberation has been achieved. Oh sure, there are a few kinks to be worked out later, but the new woman has arrived and she is the

EVERYONE. *Vogue*

PLAYWRIGHT. Woman. And we're so very sorry but there has been a death in the

EVERYONE. (*sadly*) Women's movement.

(*Theme from "2000!" comes on. WOMEN sink slowly behind screens putting curtains and Vogues down on crates. THEY rise slowly to music, taking the ends of their death cloths and unwrapping them slowly as they turn in place. On a crescendo in the music THEY step out from behind screens, holding up cloths. THEY march forward, then turn and hang cloths on screens so that the dates "196? to 1986" are showing and the screens now look like tombstones. WOMEN look over their shoulders at the audience, then step out from infront on screens and march behind them. THEY pause, then sink down behind screens grabbing Vogues in right hand, curtains in left hand. On crescendo in music, they fling curtains high in the air and rise from behind screens. Then THEY fling curtains in the air one at a time beginning with PLAYWRIGHT. Then*

THEY *fling curtains in unison. THEY turn and run to upper ramp, switching curtains to right hand. Facing left THEY fling curtains out and lay them on middle ramp. THEY lift Vogues high in the air, drop them in unison, then step forward and straddle them. The lights fade as WOMEN look quizzically out at audience. "Diamonds Are a Girl's Best Friend" comes on in the dark. As lights come up WOMEN take curtain call, then pick up Vogues and curtains reprising BUGGERS dance. THEY sneak step to their screens, sitting in unison. Lights go out. Lights come up. WOMEN stand on crates and take three poses as they say "Shift, shift, shift." Lights out, then up. WOMEN bow and sneak step out center ramp.)*

END OF PLAY

PRODUCTION NOTES

STAGING: A fast pace, ensemble rhythm, and aggressive athletic movement are crucial to "I Read About My Death..." Choral phrases, vignettes, interwoven sentences must be sharp and fast. Particularly rapid-fire are "Morning for Our Mothers," "Double Duty," "Women in the News Media," "Women on Television," "Men in the Movement," "Movement Men in Meetings," "Men in Collectives," "A Boss of One's Own," and "Our Bodies Our Smells."

SET: The back and side drops are black. The large upper ramp screens measure 6 ft. 5 inches high by 48 inches wide. They are black draped with pink curtains. The smaller individual screens are built from boards attached to a milk carton. They measure 18 inches across and should be higher than the tallest actors head as she sits on the crate. The screens and crates are painted anemone (purple). Boards across stacked milk cartons form shelves stage right and left. Also painted anemone. The lower, right, left and center ramps are 4 inches high; the middle ramp is 15 inches high; the upper ramp is 25 inches high. The center ramp extends out part 3 rows of the audience.

COSTUMES: Basic costume consists of matching sweat pants and leotards or t-shirts in either black, purple, or gray. Sneakers on the feet. Bathrobes are worn during Scene 1. Long green and black "death cloths" are used for "strangling" in scenes 1, 3, and 4. In scene 6 they are wraped around the neck through the scene, unwrapped during "2001" theme and hung over screens. The dates 196? to 1986 are painted in white on the death cloths.

Morning in the movement vignettes: Long pink cloths for girls, long blue cloths for boys. They are preset on the crates and worn as aprons, neckties, bows, loincloths, bras, and sashes for the various vignettes. They are made from table cloths.

Noon in the movement vignettes: Purple and white print headbands for women; black and white print headbands for men. Made from bedspreads.

Twilight in the movement vignettes: Long purple and pink (same as morning cloths) cloths with no sex differentiation. Made from bedspreads and worn as headband, bows, shashes, neckties.

Nineteen fifties: Pink and white curtains with high heel shoes and small handbags.

Nineteen sixties: India print bedspreads, flowers.

Nineteen seventies: Purple and orange bedspreads, briefcases or newspapers under arms, cigarettes in mouths.

Nineteen eighties: Pink and white curtains (from fifties) carried in left arm as babies, *Vogues* under right arm.

Buggers: men's jackets and business hats, fedoras, hardhats, safari hats etc. worn over sweats and sneakers.

DANCES: The "Women's Movement" dances are a series of tongue-in-cheek heroic walks, then stopping to stare at the horizon. When they end, women have to snap out of them as if they have been having a pleasant dream. The Buggers dances involve strutting, step kicking, clicking of fingers all designed to look manly and cool as they "check out the action," "look for 'chicks,'" and generally show off. Contact the publisher if more specific help is needed with choreography.

387

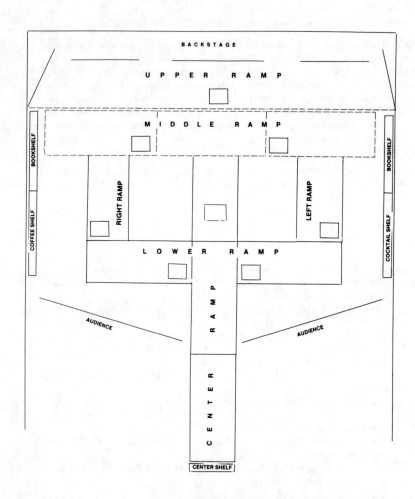

SET DESIGN
ACT 1-2
I READ ABOUT MY DEATH IN VOGUE MAGAZINE

BY MAXINE KLEIN
MUSIC BY JAMES OESTEREICH

"New Rise of The Master Race," produced by Little Flags Theatre, written and directed by Maxine Klein with music composed by James Oestereich, premiered in Boston on February 28, 1979.

Colonel Blakely .... *James Oestereich*

Captain Hertz.. *Peter Schwartz*

Major Cauldwell,
Dragon .... *Gerard Hirsch*

Eleanor Roosevelt,
Mrs. Beidoff .... *Ellen Field*
Margaret Mellon DuPont

Mr. Taft,
Guard .... *David Jernigan*
Crisis Management Actor

Bobby,
Guard,
Crisis Management Director .... *David Carl Olson*
Contact

Ms. Zimmerman,
Lorraine .... *Christine Bowen*
Crisis Management Actor

Corporal Dixon,
Crisis Management Actor .... *Cynthia Fellows*

Carmensita,
Crisis Management Actor........................... *Dee Marie Philips*

Ms. Wazgot,
Crisis Management Actor,........................... *Margaret Dexter*
Ms. Pearson, Crisis Management

Set design by Michael Anania, costumes by David Carl Olson, lights by Elisa Rivers.

ACT I

A checkpoint, Crisis Management Center, The Club, a Bus Stop.

ACT II

Crisis Management Center, General Duallin's office.

PLACE: Washington DC

TIME: Day after tomorrow

STORY OF THE PLAY

"New Rise of the Master Race" is a play with music.

The power play is set! The protagonists collide! Sparks fly! Between the briefing rooms of the Pentagon and the unemployment lines in Detroit, the battle lines are drawn.

But this is no ordinary war. It is fought not to the sound of bombs bursting in air, but to the glitz and jazz of "Stock Market Rag," with the Breadline Blues a persistent underscore. It is fought to the sound of street corner Mozart, while the bag lady at the keyboard punctuates her performance with some classical observations on the state of the Union.

Nuclear disarmament, spies, secret meetings, the moral majority on the rampage, and the military in control of the media all add up to a losing strategy to keep the lid on mounting tension and excitement.

This is a theatrical explosion in which you have a vested interest.

DESCRIPTION OF CHARACTERS

COLONEL BLAKELY: Director of The Crisis Management Bureau—a West Pointer who is essentially ethical within the limits of his military perspective. He is intelligent, a good officer, but increasingly out of his element as his duties change from traditional military matters to civilian control, propaganda, and counter-espionage.

CAPTAIN HERTZ: In charge of Crisis Management's programming, which he handles well for he is entirely competent within his milieu; but he has no vision beyond the next military command, and therein lies his flaw. He is also a worrier who can come apart in a crisis.

MAJOR CAULDWELL: Aggressive, challenging, apparently pushing for tougher military intervention, but a certain watchfulness makes his character enigmatic. Later, we learn he has joined forces with the Detroit takeover.

CORPORAL DIXON: A corporal who efficiently and correctly follows order.

TAFT: A young graduate from an Ivy League School on loan to Crisis Management from the National Security Council. He is smart, sophisticated with an entree into the boardrooms and hallways of the power brokers in Washington, D.C. He is loyal to Blakely and an invaluable informational weathervane who reads the way the corporate wind is blowing.

MS. ZIMMERMAN: Blakely's secretary. Cool and correct in manner, capable and efficient. But, like Major Cauldwell, she leads a double life.

ELEANOR R.: A bag lady. She is a street person: quick, tough, and feisty. She is against the injustice that is her portion. She carries a goodly store of weapons: sharp and mocking wit and a verbal feint.

RALPH: He is the leader of the College Kill Game and heir apparent to the New Master Race. Behind the mask his tone is menacing. He derives sensual pleasure from the cruel, manipulative game he plays.

PLAYERS: College students looking for a thrill.

CARMENSITA: A waitress in the Officer's Bar. In addition, she is a courier for the Detroit Take-over.

MRS. BEIDOFF: A rich woman and an unexpected challenge to her class.

REYNOLDS: Artistic Director of the Crisis Management Programming. He is sharp-tongued, impatient, and in-charge. His manner is phrenetic and crude. He has neither time nor imagination to question his values. If it doesn't sell, eliminate it.

LORRAINE: An exquisite, authentic oriental dancer. Necessity forces her to let Reynolds call the tune in a degrading commercial for Crisis Management Network.

BOBBY: Another Reynolds slave. He is a fine photographer working at Crisis Management Network, forced to do commercial stills in a disappearing job market.

THE REVEREND: A fire-and-brimstone preacher of the New Right who sees every possible benefit to the workers as emanating from the devil, and every country where such benefits abound as slated for hell-fire.

THE DRAGON: High commander of the Ku Klux Klan. He advocates the training of an army to carry out his explicitly violent solutions to the problems created by the Reverend's transgressors, among whom, of course, are all non-whites.

M. M. DUPONT: Upper class lady who has never worked a day in her life. She appears in Crisis Management's filmed advice to the unemployed.

THE BRIDES: Young, unemployed women desperate enough to answer General Duallin's newspaper ad for a wife, in exchange for his promise of security and travel.

NUCLEAR NIGHTMARE MASK: Embodiment of our worst fear.

CONTACT: A member of the Detroit Take-over.

NATIONAL GUARDSMEN: Patrolling checkpoint.

DRIVERS: Stopped at checkpoint.

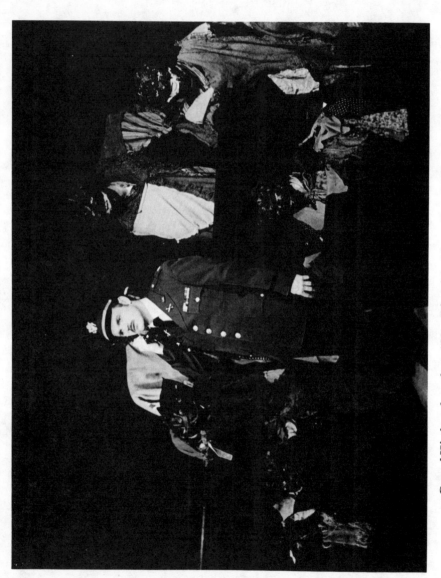

Gerard Hirsh and cast from "New Rise of the Master Race." Photo: James Oestreich.

Act I

(A bag lady, ELEANOR ROOSEVELT, enters and sings "New Rise of the Master Race." ELEANOR is dressed in several layers of an outrageous combination of rags. She carries a shopping bag and has a second bag, with a tin cup attached, slung over one shoulder. Street PEOPLE enter and sing with her.)

> *"New Rise of the Master Race"*
> To be poor was once human;
> Now it's passe, has been.
> It's the day of the rich, pay as you go,
> To the victor the spoils, reap what you sow.
>
> It's a time for gold, a season for glitz,
> The only room left is a suite at the Ritz.
> It's the law of survival, dog eat dog.
> If you don't like chitlin', eat high off the hog.
>
> It's the right time,
> The right place
> For a new rise of the master race.
>
> They have nothing against the poor,
> They don't want us to suffer,
> But inflation is rising,
> And we must provide the buffer.
>
> So they cut all services
> Not essential,
> And their plan for dismantling
> Is democratic and impartial.

They determine whose needs are greatest
And for them they will provide;
Absolute truth is their inspiration,
Their motto, and their guide.

Now the truth of the matter is,
And truth is stranger than fiction,
That money for the rich
Is an absolute addiction.

Yes, those who have the most
Still have the greatest need.
It takes billions to begin
To sate their greed.

Now you have the reason why
The administration
Tells the poor to go it alone
In the richest of all nations.

The slums are dirty and crowded
Too many behind shovel and mop.
But don't think about them anymore
There's always room at the top.

A new spirit runs the country
Hard, ruthless and mean,
It may be beyond your vision;
It's something Germany has seen.

It's the right time,
The right place,
For a new rise of the master race.

(*street PEOPLE exit on last lines of song*)

ELEANOR. Gotta run. If I make it through the check point, I'll see you
on Twelfth Street—if not—(*a whistle sounds offstage*) Gotta run! (*exits*)

Scene 2. *CHECKPOINT OUTSIDE WASHINGTON, D.C.*

(*Night. Flashing lights. NATIONAL GUARDSMEN are stopping PEOPLE at checkpoint. Hubbub of pressured activity. The MILITARY bark commands at PEOPLE who are frantic and confused. Flashing lights pick out faces as PEOPLE speak.*)

TROOPER I. (*offstage, shouting through a megaphone at the PEOPLE and policing a line of cars*) Sergeant, get your people over here. You over there, hold it! Come on, lady, hurry it up. You! (*enters along with other TROOPERS*) Out of your truck! Would you pull over there, Sir?

TROOPER II. Drivers with Michigan plates over here.

DRIVER II. (*in line of drivers waiting instructions to proceed*) Michigan plates in which line?

TROOPER II. Over here, please.

TROOPER I. Would you please come over here, Sir? This is a routine checkpoint. License, registration, employee identification card.

DRIVER I. (*to TROOPER I, indignant*) What do you mean 'routine?' State troopers flashing me down in the middle of the night. National Guard called out...

TROOPER II. All vehicles with Michigan plates are being checked this evening.

DRIVER II. (*wildly to TROOPER I*) This isn't even my car. It belongs to my brother-in-law.

TROOPER III. (*to BAG LADY*) Where do you work?

ELEANOR. Huh? (*pointing to her ears*) I don't hear so good.

TROOPER I. (*examining driver's billfold*) That's a pretty fancy billfold.

DRIVER I. I'm a pretty fancy guy.

TROOPER II. I told you, all vehicles with Michigan plates are being checked this evening.

DRIVER II. What's going on in Michigan, anyway? My brother-in-law says the only radio frequency he can get is some emergency network.

TROOPER II. Something serious is happening in Detroit, Miss. That's all we know.

DRIVER II. But this is Washington, D.C. Why are *we* being stopped? It's like an armed camp.

TROOPER I. Nice ring you got. Georgetown University. You don't look Georgetown.

DRIVER I. Neither do you!

TROOPER I. You're free to go!

(There is a scream, scuffle and voices somewhere in the darkness. DRIVER I returns to his car as TROOPER I runs offstage to quell the scuffle.)

TROOPER II. What's your destination?

DRIVER II. What did you say?

TROOPER II. Your destination!

DRIVER II. *The Washington Post.*

TROOPER II.. *(ushering her out)* Step this way.

DRIVER II. *(in a wail)* What?

TROOPER II. This way!

DRIVER II. Why? My God why? Can you tell me that? *(THEY exit)*

TROOPER III. Where do you work?

ELEANOR. Corner Twelfth and Salem.

TROOPER III. Get out of here. *(goes to exit)*

ELEANOR. Huh?

TROOPER III. *(exasperated)* You're free to go! *(exits)*

Scene 3. ELEANOR'S STREET CORNER

(ELEANOR runs from check point as lights gradually illuminate street corner somewhere beyond the checkpoint)

ELEANOR. Whew! What are they bothering with an old bundle of rags like me for? Questions comin' at me ratatatat, like bullets to the stomach. It's getting tougher than toenails to work the streets without some military type sneakin' up behind you. *(taking the lid off an imaginary can)* Sometimes I no sooner get the lid off the can to rummage for my supper and...*(indrawn gasp as she shifts around to look over shoulder)* ...there's another uniform! *(mimicking soldier's bark)* "License! Employee identification number!" I turn on the radio and "Hroom! Hroom! Hroom!" announcing some general. I tell you that business in Detroit has got 'em all strung out tighter than a circus high wire. *(a whistle blows)* See what I mean? Gotta' get a-move on. Like my mother always said, "Head for the round house, Eleanor. They'll never corner you there." *(exits)*

Scene 4. *CRISIS MANAGEMENT BUREAU*

(*Viewing room within the Bureau. OFFICERS enter from rear of house and sit in the audience. CORPORAL DIXON sets lectern as COLONEL ROBERT BLAKELY walks onstage to lectern.*)

BLAKELY. Corporal Dixon, are all requested personnel present and accounted for?

DIXON. Yes, Sir, and I-corps has completed an electronic sweep of the immediate area.

BLAKELY. (*at lectern, tensely*) As you know, Gentlemen, with the recent events in Detroit, it has become increasingly necessary for the government to gain complete control of the media so we can impose a total news blackout on Detroit and prevent other cities from following their rebellious example. I can now announce that negotiations with the major networks are complete. Tomorrow at eighteen hundred all commercial television and radio stations will go off the air, leaving only the Pentagon's Crisis Management frequency. (*OFFICERS applaud*) This station will carry out the full program devised by our Crisis Control Committee. Government bulletins and programs will be supplemented with classical music and classical theater. As you know, for over a year, Captain Hertz...(*HERTZ rises in acknowledgment; then sits*) ...has been preparing programming for the eventuality of such a national emergency. This programming is designed to maximize the dangerous nature of our society, thereby encouraging people to stay at home behind locked doors, rather than riot in the streets and take over cities.

CAULDWELL. Understood, Sir.

HERTZ. Very good, Sir.

BLAKELY. (*motioning to DIXON*) Corporal Dixon.

(*DIXON walks to the lectern. BLAKELY sits with the other OFFICERS in the darkened auditorium.*)

DIXON. Gentlemen, each day we will be reviewing films from our Crisis Management Series. Today we will be previewing a film that will be shown twelve times weekly on our Crisis Management network. It is entitled "Danger in the Streets," archive number 241.

(*DIXON takes lectern to stage right and stands beside it. A Crisis Management television production "Danger in the Streets" begins with a MIDDLE CLASS COUPLE fearfully making their way on dangerous city streets. During this sequence, the voice of the SAFETY INSTRUCTOR addresses the COUPLE who do precisely what the voice bids.*)

ANNOUNCER. The Pentagon's Crisis Management Network presents a dramatization from its public service series "Danger in the Streets."

SAFETY INSTRUCTOR. Never wear valuable rings. They might cut your fingers off. (*MUGGER reaches from behind door and mimes cutting off MAN'S fingers*) Never wear necklaces. They could choke you. (*another MUGGER reaches in and pulls necklace and the VICTIM responds*) The same goes for ties. (*MUGGER pulls tie*) Also...(*MUGGER enters and attacks the WOMAN, stealing her purse, and then exits*) ...we don't advise prolonged struggle with the attacker unless... (*second MUGGER enters to attack the MAN, but is repelled by a karate defense*) ...you are a karate expert. Instead, it's always best to walk with a police whistle in your mouth...(*COUPLE place whistle into mouth*) ...and carry keys in your hand...(*COUPLE displays keys and fist*)...and use your metal enforced fist as a weapon. (*MUGGERS enter to attack and are struck down by the COUPLE, who then run away*) Then strike and run. Of course, you must know where to run.

BLAKELY. (*speaking over the following televised sequence*) I think you'll all agree with me, Gentlemen, that this type of programming will convince the public that no matter where they are, when they are outside their homes, they are in danger.

HERTZ. I'm glad you like it, Sir.

CAULDWELL. Excellent footage, Sir.

SAFETY INSTRUCTOR. When you're out on the streets, keep a continuous lookout for the least dangerous place to run toward, should danger strike. (*MUGGERS appear ominously onstage*) If you run out into the street, you might be struck by a car. (*MAN mimes being struck by a car*) If you run toward a door to ask for help, the people might not let you in. (*WOMAN knocks in vain*) Or they might think you are an intruder and shoot you. (*WOMAN falls as if dead*) It is estimated that one third...(*MUGGER lunges with weapon aimed*)...of all drivers now carry handguns, and one half...(*second MUGGER does likewise*)...of all homeowners are prepared to defend their homes with firearms. (*MUGGERS exit*) And please remember, when you arrive home... (*MAN and WOMAN rise and cross to center and walk arm in arm*) ...don't think you are safe and let your guard down. (*COUPLE stops walking*) Home is where the real danger begins. (*COUPLE makes fists. Vegetation is carried on and COUPLE hides behind it.*) Hide in a bush or behind a thick tree while you carefully survey the area around your home. (*the COUPLE does*) Once you feel reasonably safe outside your home, communicate with your spouse to ascertain the safety of the situation inside. Use your beeper. (*COUPLE buzzes their beeper*) If your housemate does not answer his beeper immediately...(*COUPLE holds beeper to ears*)...he might be in danger, or dead...(*COUPLE grimaces*)...or in the thrall of something like Detroit where entire neighborhoods of private housing have been confiscated. (*VEGETATION exits*) As defense against the roving bands of the out-of-work who are rendering life and property unsafe across the nation...(*COUPLE marches upstage. A uniformed GUARD enters and distributes handguns*)...our President has ordered the Crisis Management Bureau to set up distribution points in all our major cities. Upon presentation of proper credentials—bank statements, credit references, and proofs of property ownership—applicants will be issued free handguns. (*COUPLE exits with their guns as GUARD marches offstage. Lights fade as film concludes.*)

ANNOUNCER. This has been a message from the Crisis Management Bureau.

BLAKELY. (*crossing onto stage*) Thank you. Please restore the lights. (*DIXON replaces the lectern*) The man responsible for that film is Captain Hertz—

TAFT. (*entering*) He had to step out for a moment, Sir. (*sits*)

BLAKELY. Well, then, let me introduce the new man on our committee, Mr. Taft...(*TAFT rises, then sits*) ...on loan to us from the National Security Council. He will be watching and interpreting the economy for us, as well as being liaison to the Joint Chiefs.

HERTZ. (*re-entering and sitting*) Excuse the interruption, Sir, I just received a report on some of the commercials we're accepting for Crisis Management.

(*BLAKELY, TAFT and CAULDWELL speak simultaneously*)

BLAKELY. Excellent film. Captain.

CAULDWELL. Well done, Captain.

TAFT. Fine effort, Captain Hertz.

HERTZ. (*rising*) Thank you. I'm preparing additional footage on the Klan, the Moral Majority, and several other...

CAULDWELL. (*rising and speaking over HERTZ'S last words. HERTZ sits.*) Excuse me, Sir.

BLAKELY. Major Cauldwell.

CAULDWELL. (*with an ominous tone*) While I appreciate the importance of Crisis Management Programming in controlling the public during this emergency, my superiors are more concerned with the actual events in Detroit. The Sixth Army in Illinois is boiling over with questions about the take-over. They want to know why the Army has not been sent in.

(*CAULDWELL sits. A deafening silence meets this bold challenge to BLAKELY. Finally TAFT speaks to BLAKELY.*)

TAFT. Sir?

BLAKELY. Mr. Taft.

TAFT. (*rising*) The National Security Council has been wondering the same thing. (*sits*)

CAULDWELL. (*rising*) Sir, they understand that a plan has been initiated here at the Crisis Management Center delaying military action. (*sits*)

HERTZ. Is this true, Sir?

TAFT. (*over HERTZ'S words*) Sir?

BLAKELY. Mr. Taft.

TAFT. (*rising*) For the Army not to be sent in when a city has been taken over by rebels is without precedent in our military history. (*sits*)

HERTZ. (*rising*) Colonel?

BLAKELY. Captain Hertz.

HERTZ. Ah, Sir, in the sixties we sent entire battalions to handle college kids, and all they were doing was throwing a few beer cans and bitching about the war.

(*HERTZ continues to argue that the army be sent into this dilemma. TAFT and CAULDWELL talk simultaneously with him.*)

TAFT. (*rising*) Sir, wouldn't non-intervention set a very dangerous precedent?

CAULDWELL. (*rising*) Sir, when is the Army going to be allowed to...

BLAKELY. (*rising over all three and snapping them to attention*) You're minimizing the current crisis, Gentlemen. Those college kids in the sixties posed a *philosophical* threat to the government. Detroit is another matter.

(*TAFT and CAULDWELL sit. BLAKELY looks at HERTZ who has remained standing.*)

BLAKELY. Captain Hertz, something still on your mind?

HERTZ. Well, yes, Sir. We have the most powerful and sophisticated military communications center in the world located just a few miles north of Detroit. Couldn't they assist us?

TAFT. (*rising and riding over HERTZ'S words*) I have corroborative data from the NSC which...

BLAKELY. (*dropping a bomb*) That center has been *jammed* for three days.

HERTZ. (*dumbfounded*) What?

BLAKELY. We don't know how they did it, but the Detroit take-over has managed to jam the primary communications center for all United States military operations...

TAFT. Not possible. (*sits*)

HERTZ. Jesus God! (*sits*)

BLAKELY. ...a center which, I might remind you, has control of a large percentage of our land-based nuclear missiles. Now without access to highly classified codes, they will never be able to operate that center, but if they can figure out how to jam it, they can figure out how to dismantle it...

HERTZ. Jesus God!

BLAKELY. ...and leave us as vulnerable to the Soviets as a newborn babe.

TAFT. (*after a short silence*) Sir, the enormity of risk notwithstanding, I still submit that the Army must be sent into Detroit immediately, or we might have hundreds of rebellious cities on our hands.

HERTZ. (*other OFFICERS respond simultaneously*) I hesitate to say it, Sir, but I concur. (*standing*) Those missiles are our first line of defense.

CAULDWELL. (*standing and riding over HERTZ*) Sir, the same conditions that made Detroit blow sky high—unemployment, detention centers, bread lines—already exist in Boston, Minneapolis, Pittsburgh, seven of...

BLAKELY. (*crossing around to the front of the lectern and snapping to attention, silencing the OTHERS*) I was going to wait until after lunch for this.

(*all OFFICERS sit*)

BLAKELY. The Detroit rebels have taken control of all the automobile factories in and around Detroit, suspended manufacture of the internal combustion engine and are attempting to produce their own electric cars and sell them on the world market...

(*HERTZ, CAULDWELL and TAFT speak the following simultaneously in an undertone of agreement*)

HERTZ. That squares with the data I have received.

TAFT. Yes, Sir, that was covered in my briefing with NSC.

CAULDWELL. There is no doubt the take-over is now in control and transforming Detroit's auto industry.

BLAKELY. ...to finance their take-over. You already know this information. What you do not know is that the take-over has also *wired those plants with high explosives*. We send the Army in, they detonate, blowing the major industry in this country to smithereens. (*crosses back to lectern*)

CAULDWELL. Colonel Blakely, I don't think they'd do it.

BLAKELY. (*very angry and commanding, slamming files onto lectern*) It is inconsequential what you think! We do not precipitate a move that would undermine the economic base of this country. That is an order from the Commander-in-Chief.

CAULDWELL. Which one?

BLAKELY. It's not easy to tell. They all use the same letterhead and signature. But it is official, I can assure you.

HERTZ. (*rising*) Sir, I agree that we don't question whether or not the Detroit take-over *would* destroy the auto industry. But militarily, can they do it? Do they have the weaponry?

BLAKELY. (*calmly, deadly*) Yes.

(*HERTZ sits as though the wind has been knocked out of him*)

BLAKELY. Our intelligence has all but conclusive evidence that the Soviets are daily transporting massive quantities of armaments to the Detroit take-over, travelling in unmarked fishing vessels up the St. Lawrence Seaway.

(*BLAKELY has stunned the listening OFFICERS. HERTZ breaks the silence and signals that all OFFICERS are behind BLAKELY.*)

HERTZ. (*rising*) Do you have a plan?

BLAKELY. Yes again.

(*HERTZ sits. BLAKELY takes files from his lectern and hands them to DIXON.*)

BLAKELY. Gentlemen, not one word of what I am about to say may be mentioned outside this briefing room. Is that completely understood?

OFFICERS. (*all rising*) Yes, Sir. (*the OFFICERS sit as CORPORAL DIXON hands out files to them*)

BLAKELY. (*crossing stage right*) After exhausting every standard avenue of counterinsurgency for over a month, my office has finally made contact with a group inside the city of Detroit ideologically opposed to the take over.

TAFT. Excellent. Fifth column!

HERTZ. Counterinsurgency!

BLAKELY. This counterrevolutionary organization is code-named "Walnut."

CAULDWELL. (*standing*) Sir, could we have the crypto-system equivalent to Walnut, please?

BLAKELY. (*crossing back to lectern and opening file*) Crypto-system equivalent to Walnut is 55-314, to be used in all communiques regarding Walnut. With the assistance of General Hoffman...

TAFT. (*clearly impressed*) Hoffman!

BLAKELY. ...we are supplying Walnut with substantial military hard-ware in order to convert their ideological opposition into the most powerful counterrevolutionary army this nation has ever seen.

HERTZ. Excellent, Sir!

TAFT. Brilliant!

CAULDWELL. (*over HERTZ'S words*) What does General Duallin think of this plan?

BLAKELY. General Duallin is reviewing the plan at this very moment. When he gives the go-ahead, the Army will *move*. We will coordinate efforts with Walnut and retake Detroit.

(*the OFFICERS rise and applaud then snap to attention*)

BLAKELY. Now, Gentlemen, I don't need to remind you that we are in a race with time. The country needs a strong central force to keep the lid on this crisis. That's what our Crisis Management media programming is all about. If we do not do our job well, the vigilantes and the increasingly well-armed citizenry may take matters into their own hands. (*coming to attention*) Now I suggest we break for lunch and resume our discussion at fourteen hundred, at which time we will review Walnut's request for additional supplies and personnel.

(*OFFICERS salute, BLAKELY returns salute, TAFT exits. HERTZ walks up to congratulate BLAKELY.*)

CAULDWELL. (*rising*) Sir, I thought you said General Duallin had to approve Walnut as a legitimate counterrevolutionary force before we could proceed with arming them.

BLAKELY. Naturally I have General Duallin's provisional okay until final approval is given...

CAULDWELL. Sir, if General Duallin's approval to arm Walnut means further delay, I don't think the Sixth Army will stand for it. They want the military in Detroit *now*.

(*BLAKELY gives CAULDWELL a long, hard look*)

HERTZ. (*interrupting this tense moment*) If I may interrupt, Sir, I have a press conference going worldwide via satellite tomorrow, and the world press will be asking questions about Detroit, to say nothing of the mounting pressure to get more information about our absentee President. It would help me enormously if I could be appraised of Walnut's timetable for retaking Detroit.

BLAKELY. (*writing memo at a furious pace as he speaks at an equally rapid rate*) As you know, Gentlemen, domestic counterinsurgency is the most precarious of occupations. A single breach of security could destroy the entire operation, so you will understand why I am not at liberty to share, even with you, all the information available to me at this time concerning Walnut's timetable. (*hands DIXON the memo, who looks at it and glances inadvertently at CAULDWELL, the subject of the note*)

HERTZ. I understand fully, Sir, but what about the press conference?

BLAKELY. Cancel it.

HERTZ. Yes, Sir.

BLAKELY. Don't you have some other program you could do in its stead?

HERTZ. Yes, Sir, I could do another program on the current status of the president with his humorous quote of the week.

BLAKELY. Do it.

HERTZ. Yes, Sir. By the way, I am preparing to view the next installment of Crisis Management's "Danger in the Streets" series: "College Killing Game." Would you be interested in assessing its scare value?

BLAKELY. I'll trust your judgment.

(*buzzer sounds*)

BLAKELY. Dismissed.

HERTZ. Thank you, Sir.

(*CAULDWELL prepares to leave*)

BLAKELY. Corporal Dixon, will you get that please?

DIXON. (*gets communique, hands it to BLAKELY who quickly reads it*) It's from General Duallin, Sir.

(*CAULDWELL stops in his tracks*)

BLAKELY. (*in controlled triumph*) General Duallin has given his unconditional approval to our plan to equip Walnut with all the supplies, personnel and weaponry they need.

(*BLAKELY leaves as OFFICERS applaud. CAULDWELL exits.*)

HERTZ. Dixon, I'm going to the booth. Please run the killing game footage. (*exits*)

DIXON. (*removes lectern as he speaks*) Yes, Sir. Projectionist, ready to run "College Killing Game," archive number eight-seven. (*exits*)

Scene 5. COLLEGE KILLING GAME

(*Another Crisis Management Network segment begins as killing game INSTRUCTOR enters through the center door carrying pistols. He stops and faces front. Like all game participants, he is masked in a ritualistic hood. Two other PLAYERS pull modules onto the stage, as two more*

PARTICIPANTS arrive and cross downstage to the modules. Here, and throughout the scene, their movements are perfectly synchronized. An aura of horror pervades the entire scene.)

ANNOUNCER. *(speaking as participants enter the scene)* You are witnessing an actual meeting of a college student organization filmed live on location at an unnamed American University. This filming is presented as part of the Crisis Management series "Danger in the Streets" and will serve as a warning to the prudent to use extreme caution when travelling in our nation's cities.

KILLING INSTRUCTOR. *(gives a signal and the participants sit. He distributes pistols. His tone is commanding, sinister.)* This room won't be used until one o'clock. That gives us half an hour. *(returns to platform, clicks heels, the PLAYERS assume combat poses)* Put your pistols away immediately. *(The PLAYERS resume their seated positions. INSTRUCTOR hands out dossiers)* Here's the dossier on your victim's height, weight, eye color, hair color, class or work schedule, address, telephone number, regular hangouts, make of car.

(There is knock at the door. EVERYONE whips off their hoods and lowers their heads.)

STUDENT. *(offstage)* Isn't this where Psych. 4 meets? The door seems locked.

KILLING INSTRUCTOR. Sorry, it's jammed again. *(keeping his back to PLAYERS, he opens the door)* Can I help you?

STUDENT. Yes, I'm new here on campus. I'm looking for Dr. Morgenstern's Psych. 4 class in the Wermeier Building, room 103.

KILLING INSTRUCTOR. This is the *Student Union* room 103.

STUDENT. Oops, sorry. Everything is so confusing here in Washington. *(exits muttering)* I don't know if I'll ever figure it out.

(At the sound of the door closing, the PLAYERS replace their hoods. They look at no one else, and their motions are crisp, military, ritualistic.)

KILLING INSTRUCTOR. Did everyone observe the rules? *(the PLAYERS nod)* No one looked at anyone else?

(THEY turn their heads from side to side and then return their fixed gaze to the INSTRUCTOR)

KILLING INSTRUCTOR. Then let's continue. In the rear pocket of your dossier...*(PLAYERS snap open dossiers)*...you will find a recent photograph of your victim.

PLAYERS. *(responding to the photographs severally)* This one deserves it. Too bad, honey. Well, well, well. This is one hit I will not mind at all.

KILLING INSTRUCTOR. Now remember...*(the PLAYERS snap their

dossiers shut)...when you kill your victim, you must do it either when he is alone, which is preferable, or in the presence of no more than three witnesses, and then always in disguise.

PLAYER 1. (*stands*) I was just thinking...

(*here and throughout the scene, EVERYONE turns their head toward the PERSON speaking*)

PLAYER 1. ...maybe this is what happened to the President. Maybe one of the generals eliminated him.

(*PLAYER 1 sits as EVERYONE laughs. Their heads snap toward the INSTRUCTOR.*)

KILLING INSTRUCTOR. (*imparting information with salacious satisfaction*) Possibly. The game is no longer confined to college campuses. All sorts of people in places you would not imagine are beginning to play it.

PLAYER 2. (*standing*) What about Detroit? Anyone play in Detroit?

(*PLAYER 2 sits as EVERYONE laughs*)

KILLING INSTRUCTOR. (*with condescension*) One of the more distasteful aspects of the Detroit take-over is its puritanism. As in Cuba and China, all the truly beautiful things in life—drugs, prostitution, profit—are strictly taboo. (*PLAYERS are laughing at his wit*) The only thing genuinely new about the "new politics" in Detroit is the level of boredom it inspires. (*the PLAYERS applaud*) Any more questions?

PLAYER 3. (*standing and approaching the INSTRUCTOR*) Yes. Please review the categories for which the awards are given.

(*PLAYER 3 walks back to seat and sits*)

KILLING INSTRUCTOR. The most people killed. The most creative kill. The best threat. The best last words.

PLAYER 1. (*standing*) And if we should fail in the attempt? (*sits*)

KILLING INSTRUCTOR. If you fail in the attempt, then you must sound your signal of temporary truce.

(*The INSTRUCTOR snaps his fingers twice. The PLAYERS repeat snapping theirs twice.*)

PLAYER 2. (*standing and approaching the INSTRUCTOR*) Someone has started a rumor that the winner gets a scholarship to the Army Intelligence Training Bureau here in Washington and the loser gets Detroit.

KILLING INSTRUCTOR. (*with a faint supercilious smile, as PLAYER returns to seat*) The way I heard it, the Army Intelligence Training Bureau wants to study with us...(*ALL laugh*) ...so they can figure out what to *do* with Detroit. (*ALL applaud*)

PLAYER 3. (*snapping hand up and down*) Does the cloud affect us?

KILLING INSTRUCTOR. Obviously, it's bad for your health, but just as obviously it's a plus for the game. As you've noticed, even in broad daylight it's difficult to make out the details of people's faces. (*ominous*) As the cloud becomes more dark and dense, the time range in which you are able to make a hit and escape undetected, expands correspondingly. (*back to business*) Any more questions?

(*all PLAYERS are quiet, indicating there are no more questions*)

KILLING INSTRUCTOR. Then leave through the door by which you entered.

(*the PLAYERS rise and march out*)

KILLING INSTRUCTOR. Immediately before exiting, and without looking to the right or left, remove your masks.

ANNOUNCER. (*speaking over KILLING INSTRUCTOR'S last words*) This has been a report from the Crisis Management Bureau. Please stay tuned to this frequency for emergency bulletins.

(*KILLING INSTRUCTOR turns and exits*)

ANNOUNCER. We now return you to your regularly scheduled broadcast.

Scene 6. THE CLUB

(*Sound of people talking and cocktail music. CARMENSITA, the bartender, pushes in her bar, sets it up as MRS. BEIDOFF enters. MRS. BEIDOFF is rich, proper, of German extraction, and has had just enough to drink to bring out her true self.*)

CARMENSITA. (*over her shoulder, while entering*) Sure, just let me get set up out here.

BEIDOFF. Carmensita, that Pink Lady please, and do you suppose you could produce a blue gentlemen to go with it?

(*HERTZ and BLAKELY enter, having just come from the officers' club briefing. They signal to CARMENSITA for drinks*)

HERTZ. Excellent plan of yours, Walnut, excellent!

(*DIXON enters and hands BLAKELY a communique*)

DIXON. Colonel Blakely.

(*A YOUNG ACTRESS crosses the stage and waves. HERTZ waves back and follows her with his eyes. MISS ZIMMERMAN enters and orders a drink.*)

HERTZ. Isn't that your secretary?

BLAKELY. (*finishes reading communique and hands it back to DIXON, speaks to HERTZ with the tension of new information. DIXON exits.*) What do you know about Major Cauldwell?)

HERTZ. (*jarred out of his flirtation*) Oh, Major Cauldwell. I've seen his dossier. Hard worker. Comes from a poor family. Enlisted at eighteen. Got his commission on the battlefield.

BLAKELY. Not a West Point man.

HERTZ. (*sarcastically*) No, Sir, he came up the hard way—through the ranks.

BLAKELY. Continue.

HERTZ. He's been here about a year. Before that he spent five years at Selfridge Air Force Base in Detroit.

BLAKELY. Detroit?

CARMENSITA. (*presenting drinks*) Gentlemen. (*goes offstage to answer a phone call*)

HERTZ. Well, yes Sir. That's why we included him in our Crisis Management team.

BLAKELY. I want a complete security check run on him.

HERTZ. Yes, Sir.

CARMENSITA. (*entering*) Colonel Blakely.

(*BLAKELY puts a credit card on her tray*)

Thank you, Sir. There's a call for you.

(*BLAKELY exits*)

CARMENSITA. Captain Hertz, another Wild Turkey?

(*MRS. BEIDOFF talks to HERTZ, who eventually turns his back on her. It is difficult to tell if MRS. BEIDOFF is drunk, an eccentric, or telling the total truth.*)

BEIDOFF. A captain, huh? I would not be afraid of you even if you were a general. I'm a member of the Red Brigade. Everyone always says a rich person cannot be a Red, but at my age, I can do what I want. Do you want to know why I became a terrorist? Because when I was three years old I was frightened by a capitalist, and nothing to be observed about their behavior since that time could allay ones fears.

(*Suddenly the lights go out. PEOPLE scream. A low frantic babble underscores the rest of the scene. BEIDOFF exits muttering indignantly.*)

CARMENSITA. (*shining a penlight on her face and attempting to calm the frightened clientele*) Everyone relax, it's just another power failure. Our emergency generator will be coming on in just a few minutes. Until then, please use your penlights.

(*BLAKELY returns from his phone call and shines his penlight on HERTZ*)

BLAKELY. Hertz!

HERTZ. (*shining his penlight on BLAKELY*) Colonel?

BLAKELY. Down your drink. We're going back to the Crisis Management Center.

HERTZ. What's happened, Sir?

BLAKELY. (*with controlled alarm*) Yellow alert. The Detroit rebels now have complete control of the Army communications center outside the city, and they are attempting to disarm our nuclear missiles.

HERTZ. (*disbelieving*) Disarm our missiles!

(*CARMENSITA extends the credit slip for BLAKELY to sign*)

CARMENSITA. Your signature, Sir.

BLAKELY. (*signing it automatically in the dark*) There's one way and one way only they could get past the security systems to that center—by gaining access to highly classified codes in the files of the National Security Agency, *which they have done!*

HERTZ. Jesus God!

BLAKELY. We have a double agent on our hands. *Let's move!*

(*HERTZ and BLAKELY exit*)

HERTZ. Double agent, Jesus God!

CARMENSITA. (*with penlight ominously illuminating her face as she exits*) Everyone, the lounge is now closing but the dining room will remain open for service.

Scene 7. BUS STOP

(*A blue light slowly illuminates an area of the stage. We see a uniformed FIGURE emerging from the darkness. A SECOND uniformed FIGURE follows.*)

SOLDIER. (*whistles*) You there! License, employee identification number. (*recognizing*) Oh, Major Cauldwell. I didn't recognize you. It's so dark here with this electrical failure. Proceed, Sir. (*exits*)

(*CAULDWELL continues across the stage to the bus stop where he puts his briefcase down and waits. Soon ZIMMERMAN enters. She stands beside CAULDWELL but does not now, or ever throughout the course of the scene, look directly at him. A sense of danger prevails.*)

ZIMMERMAN. How long have you been waiting for the bus?

CAULDWELL. Not long. Be patient. It will always come. (*the code accomplished, THEY speak to the issue*) Your report.

ZIMMERMAN. Blakely is running a security check on you. Are you in immediate danger?

CAULDWELL. It will take him time to gather sufficient data, and that's all we need—a little more time. Anything else?

ZIMMERMAN. Colonel Blakely now knows the U.S. Military Communications Center is under control of the Detroit take-over.

CAULDWELL. Does he have a plan?

ZIMMERMAN. Not that I could overhear.

CAULDWELL. (*nods silently, then*) With emergency information you can reach my contact on extension 229, at the GPO. Otherwise continue to use our usual channels.

ZIMMERMAN. In dead drop 64 you will find my written reports on Blakely, and I can continue to meet you every Tuesday and Thursday evening.

CAULDWELL. Call 229 for exact time and place. Anything else.

ZIMMERMAN. We jammed the power circuit in time; so I got Blakely's signature on another supply order. The credit card is helping our side almost as much as it is theirs.

(*ZIMMERMAN covertly passes the supply order to CAULDWELL surveying the area as she does so*)

CAULDWELL. Be careful of Blakely. Never underestimate his intelligence.

ZIMMERMAN. I don't. For one moment.

CAULDWELL. (*the mood changes slightly*) The work you are doing for the take-over is dangerous. Are you frightened?

ZIMMERMAN. I'm terrified.

CAULDWELL. So am I.

(*THEY notice the bus offstage left*)

There's the bus.

(*ZIMMERMAN picks up the briefcase CAULDWELL has brought onto the stage and exits. After a moment, CAULDWELL exits.*)

Scene 8. *ELEANOR ROOSEVELT*

(*The BAG LADY bustles on. A whistle sounds.*)

SOLDIER. (*offstage*) Where do you think you're going?

ELEANOR. (*entering*) Right over here.

SOLDIER. What's your real name?

ELEANOR. My real name is Eleanor Roosevelt. I got it tattooed on my chest, right next to the Coke sign.

SOLDIER. Where is your place of employment?

ELEANOR. Right here on this corner 'til six o'clock. After that you can find me over on Twelfth Street.

SOLDIER. You're free to go. (*spots another VAGRANT and blows whistle*) You, over there, license, place of employment. (*the SOLDIER exits as ELEANOR busies herself with her collection of rags*)

ELEANOR. God! There's guns everywhere since the President pulled another one of his disappearing acts, or someone pulled it for him. That man can disappear better than Houdini. (*she is picking up rubbish*) We hear his voice on tape-like messages from Santa at the North Pole. But no live body. Just the Generals, strutting around, operating under their emergency power. Well. I say they got the emergency power all right, but it's you and me got the emergency. (*to someone in the audience*) What're you starin' at? You never seen a sexy dame before? Sure us dames can still be sexy after sixty. All we gotta do is keep on lookin' sixteen. How do we do that in times like these? Eat good garbage! Orange peels, eggshells— the brown ones are the best... (*pointing to someone else in the audience*) Hey you out there, wanna' hot tip for a quick quarter? (*catches it and snatches it down the front of her garment*) I just found out who the President says can still get social security and food stamps—you know, who the truly needy are. The dead! Yup, the stiffs. (*as though this were a logical deduction*) They're the only ones he says really can't work. Personally, I got nothing to worry about. (*confiding*) Got me a second career goin'. Fashion model! (*taking out folder*) Four bits for a look at my portfolio. Yes... (*opening it*) ...it's peppered with pictures of me in the buff. (*snapping it shut*) I only did it because it was necessary for my art. Art, fart, dart, cart, smart. (*catches another coin and looks delighted*) Four bits! (*unscrewing the wine skin*) I'll drink to that and anything else anyone cares to mention. (*drinks*) My sources tell me the best way to keep from getting a hangover in times like these is not to stop drinking. (*whistle signaling another SOLDIER appearing*) Gotta get a move on. Like my mother always said, "Head for the round house, Eleanor, they'll never corner you there." (*exits*)

Scene 9. BLAKELY'S OFFICE

(*DIXON brings on stool and then stands guard. ZIMMERMAN enters with steno pad and reports. BLAKELY enters and sits at his desk.*)

BLAKELY. Is the supply order ready for Walnut?

ZIMMERMAN. Yes, Sir. I have it for you right here: two million in dehydrated food products, three million in medical supplies, one thousand night vision scopes, one-point seven million in light arms and field munitions.

BLAKELY. Add to that five green berets, two electronic engineers, five parachute experts, four demolition engineers.

ZIMMERMAN. Yes, Sir. Is that all for Walnut, Sir?

BLAKELY. See to it that the order is sent immediately. Are there any messages?

ZIMMERMAN. The White House press office wishes to know what our official position is re: the fact that the CIA has not been able to turn up any evidence that the Soviets are using the St. Lawrence Seaway to transport armaments to Detroit.

BLAKELY. It's never in the CIA's interest to agree with Army intelligence about anything. Besides, we are getting good public support by beating the anti-Soviet drum. So our official position in all Crisis Management bulletins remains that the Soviets are the suppliers for the Detroit take-over.

ZIMMERMAN. Yes, Sir.

BLAKELY. Is Major Cauldwell waiting?

ZIMMERMAN. He's been here for half an hour.

BLAKELY. Good. Patch me through to Captain Hertz at the Crisis Management Center.

ZIMMERMAN. (*getting phone for BLAKELY*) Captain Hertz is already on the line, Sir. He called just before you sent for me. (*exits*)

BLAKELY. Good. (*into phone*) Captain Hertz, what is the word from Operation Checkpoint?

HERTZ. (*over phone*) Michigan traffic is still relatively heavy, but nothing unusual has been reported.

BLAKELY. I want a complete security check run on anyone from the Detroit area coming through your checkpoint. If that gang of rebels is smart enough to get control of the communications center outside the city, they're smart enough to get through checkpoints. And I don't want to see Detroit sympathy groups springing up all over the country. I am particularly...(*BLAKELY presses buzzer*)...concerned about anyone coming from Detroit who might have access to, or in any way be connected with, top-level security. Something does not add up.

(*ZIMMERMAN has entered. BLAKELY whispers "CAULDWELL" to her. She exits to the anteroom.*)

HERTZ. (*over the phone*) Yes, Sir. I'll see to it that those policies are put in motion immediately, Sir. By the way, Sir, the Command Post asked me to apologize for retaining your secretary, Ms. Zimmerman, at one of the checkpoints.

BLAKELY. I would expect their apology had she not been detained. They could not have known she was operating under my orders.

(*BLAKELY hangs up phone, sits a moment thinking. ZIMMERMAN ushers in CAULDWELL and removes phone.*)

ZIMMERMAN. Major Cauldwell. (*Exits. CAULDWELL stands at attention. BLAKELY rises and salutes, then hands CAULDWELL a dossier. CAULDWELL opens it and reads as BLAKELY speaks.*)

BLAKELY. I'm interested in Detroit, Major. How long were you there?

CAULDWELL. Five years, Sir. It's in my dossier.

BLAKELY. That is a list of the leadership of the take-over. Do you recognize any of those names?

CAULDWELL. No, Sir.

BLAKELY. You're certain of that?

CAULDWELL. Yes, Sir.

BLAKELY. Why do you think the rebels would be interested in dismantling our nuclear system? Are they pacifists? Or are they being paid by the Russians?

CAULDWELL. Sir, I have no concrete data, but I would imagine there are contingents from both groups who would seek to dismantle our nuclear capabilities.

BLAKELY. You can be no more specific than that?

CAULDWELL. (*returning portfolio to BLAKELY*) No, Sir. Sorry, Sir.

BLAKELY. Where is the master electrical grid for Detroit?

CAULDWELL. On the lake, Sir, north end.

BLAKELY. How many men would it take to knock it out?

CAULDWELL. At least a dozen, Sir.

BLAKELY. I need eight helicopter landing points inside the city limits. Can you get me a list?

CAULDWELL. Yes, Sir.

BLAKELY. That will be all, Major.

(*BLAKELY salutes. CAULDWELL returns the salute, then exits. Intercom on BLAKELY'S desk sounds.*)
Yes?

ZIMMERMAN. (*over intercom*) Mr. Taft to see you, Sir.

BLAKELY. (*sits in silent thought for a moment then replies*) Send him in.

ZIMMERMAN. (*offstage*) Mr. Taft.

(*ZIMMERMAN ushers TAFT in and exits taking the phone from BLAKELY'S desk*)

TAFT. (*obviously upset and out of breath*) Colonel Blakely.

BLAKELY. (*sensing the extreme emergency*) Mr. Taft, what's wrong?

TAFT. The latest Federal Reserve report has precipitated a profound weakening in the private sector support for the government. (*handing BLAKELY a report*) The bond investors are pulling out.

BLAKELY. (*reading the report in undisguised alarm*) Pulling out? What the hell are you talking about, "pulling out"?

TAFT. (*turning pages of report*) They're pulling their money out of U.S. markets, and not just a few of them. It looks massive.

BLAKELY. In other words...

TAFT. They might all go.

BLAKELY. (*in a rage*) Can we stop them?

TAFT. Sir, we lack the legislative mechanisms to forestall them.

(*BLAKELY rises*)

TAFT. In addition, there are some alarming shifts of capital occurring within the international banking community.

BLAKELY. You're the economic *wunderkind* on this committee, Mr. Taft. What do we do?

TAFT. (*taking papers out of briefcase and handing them to BLAKELY*) I've been on the phone all day. Our contacts in the business community have made a number of specific demands at this point. From the Federal Reserve Bank, they are calling for an immediate easing of tight money, and they demand that the federal government do whatever is necessary, including the imposition of total martial law, to stop inflation. From Crisis Management, they demand more upbeat programming, so instead of scaring Americans off the streets we'll get them buying again. And they want an immediate invasion of Detroit.

(*there is a pause*)

BLAKELY. (*crumbles paper and throws it, then with analytical shrewd-ness*) If the large capital investors arc pulling theii money out of the United States, why do they care about what happens in Detroit?

TAFT. You're not the only one asking that question, Sir, and no one seems to know the answer.

BLAKELY. (*snapping into action*) All right, here's what you do. Go to your NSC data bank.

(*TAFT takes out notebook and writes assignment*)

BLAKELY. Get all the information you can on insurance, stock sales, and proposed mergers of large corporations operating in Detroit prior to the take-over.

TAFT. Isn't this a job for SEC?

BLAKELY. I'll want a meeting with the SEC economists *after* I've seen the data. You just get it and have it in my office by COB tomorrow. (*exits*)

TAFT. You'll have it by five o'clock tomorrow, Sir. (*exits*)

Scene 10. *CRISIS MANAGEMENT NEWS BULLETIN*

(*Production PERSONNEL and technical CREWS pour onstage carrying out their various tasks to make everything ready for the broadcast of a special bulletin. A continual stream of directions fills the air as the moment for the live broadcast approaches. Lectern is brought on. HERTZ enters and stand at his lectern reviewing his speech. Regimenting the entire scene is DIXON, speaking through a megaphone over the hubbub.*)

DIXON. Okay, People, we're going live in two minutes. Please use your Crisis Management script number six-three-four: "Humorous Quote of the Week with Invasion of Detroit Supplement." Okay camera one, bring it in tight on the talent's face; camera two, up on the right; camera three, same thing on the left; camera four, I want you to come in close and catch the logo during the intro, then pull it way back, full face-front, through to the end of the speech.

(*a production ASSISTANT is powdering HERTZ'S nose*)

Sir, could you speak directly into the microphone please, I'd like to set a sound level?

HERTZ. Could you give me a liquid powder. This one is drying my skin.

DIXON. That's good on the level. Okay, ten-second warning people, please clear the studio.

(*Makeup ASSISTANT, exiting, accidentally leaves her makeup bag to the right of the lectern. REYNOLDS watches monitor as he walks into the house.*)

And...three...two...one...go.

ANNOUNCER. We interrupt this broadcast to bring you a special message from the Crisis Management Bureau.

HERTZ. I am pleased to inform you that the President's condition is improving every day, and he should be up and around in no time. Only yesterday he demonstrated that wonderful sense of humor of his: as his barber was preparing to shave him, the President looked up at the sharp razor and said: "I hope you're not one of those Democrats fighting for the clean air bill." However, the President is greatly disturbed by the rumor that he is contemplating military action against Detroit. *Detroit will never be invaded.* That is a promise from your commander-in-chief. Only if the citizens of Detroit were to ask the Army to come in, would we set one foot inside their city limits. This is not a communist country where dissent is ruthlessly crushed. We are not invaders! This is the United States of America, which is built upon the rock of freedom and which champions freedom all around the world. Thank you; God bless you; and good night.

(*HERTZ smiles as ANNOUNCER gives closing announcement*)

ANNOUNCER. This has been a special message from the Crisis Management Bureau. We now return you to our regularly scheduled broadcast.

HERTZ. (*Not having received the necessary information, speaks sotto voce, through a frozen smile in case he is still on camera*) Is this thing off?

DIXON. (*from back of house*) Sorry.

HERTZ. (*still through his smile*) Sorry "yes," or sorry "no"?

DIXON. Sorry "yes." It's off. Sorry.

(*An ASSISTANT enters to remove lectern. HERTZ mutters to her.*)

HERTZ. Jesus, they got a place for that kind of cement-head in Detroit. (*turns to exit, trips on makeup bag and accidentally falls on module, setting off the nuclear alarm*) My God: did I trip the alert? Where's my key? Help me turn off the nuclear alert! Who has the god damned key.

(*HERTZ runs offstage screaming. ZIMMERMAN enters with papers and is not immediately aware of what is happening, thinking it may be a trial alert.*)

ZIMMERMAN. Captain Hertz, I have your reports typed. (*She sees it is no test. She stops, stiffens. A look of unbelieving horror spreads over her face. Finally she finds her voice and screams.*) Oh my God, it's the alert! The nuclear alert! Someone help me! Get me out of here!

(*ZIMMERMAN runs into the house to escape the inevitable. GUARDS with guns appear and pursue ZIMMERMAN. Other WORKERS appear, some screaming, some dumb struck, some crying pitifully. The GUARDS retrieve ZIMMERMAN and then control the rest of the people at gunpoint.*)

DIXON. (*re-entering from back of house*) What is this? What's going on down there?

HERTZ. (*re-enters speaking through megaphone*) Has this gone out to the entire country? Were the communications systems on? Did this go out to the entire nation? Were the...

(*DIXON comes onstage as GUARDS try to push PEOPLE back out of studio*)

DIXON. (*shouting at the top of his lungs through megaphone*) Yes Sir, we'll rectify that immediately. We're going live in thirty seconds. (*hands HERTZ script*) Use your Crisis Management Emergency Broadcast script. It begins, "This has been a trial alert." Got that?

HERTZ. (*desperate, unable to comprehend anything*) No!

DIXON. (*not waiting for a reply from HERTZ, but speaking directly to CAMERAPERSON*) Okay, cameras one and three in real close. Shoot it from the waist up and narrow the frame. (*to GUARDS*) Get these people down and out, down and out! Okay, ten seconds people, please clear the studio!

(*HERTZ hands megaphone to REYNOLDS and does final preparations before cameras are operating. DIXON runs around clearing the stage of reports, the makeup bag, and other debris.*)

And...three...two...one...go!

(*DIXON exits as HERTZ speaks over an undercurrent of offstage whimpering, crying, and hysteria*)

HERTZ. This has been only a trial alert, a service of the Crisis Management Emergency Network. Had this been a real emergency, official information, news or instructions would have been given. This concludes the test of the Crisis Management Emergency Network. This had been a test. This has only been a test.

(*DIXON speaks as HERTZ breathes a heavy sigh and numbly walks out of studio*)

DIXON. (*offstage through microphone*) That's a wrap, Captain Hertz. You covered pretty well, but we're probably giving the entire nation a nuclear nightmare.

(*blackout*)

Scene 11. NUCLEAR NIGHTMARE

(CHORUS of grotesques begins chanting offstage over electronic and atonal piano music. One VOICE sings a wailing obligato. One by one THEY enter, pushing or riding modules, appearing and disapppearing through the upstage doors, standing as individuals, or forming clumps. They are masked and robed in rags and debris.)

VOICE. (chanting over microphone)

> Nuclear War.
> One hundred-forty million Americans dead.
> Twenty-five million severely burned.
> Medicine useless.
> Evacuation plans useless.

(During the song, lights change from blue to green to yellow and back again. The movements of the chorus are angular, contracted and non-human. Two of the GROTESQUES move among the others.)

GROTESQUES. (singing)

> MX, Titan Three
> Nuclear submarine.
> Crisis in the Middle East.

(throughout the song, on "kill over-kill," ALL freeze as the stage is bathed in red light)

> Kill. Over-Kill.
> Kill. Over-Kill.
>
> Air Superiority,
> All-Weather Air Superiority.
> Crisis in West Africa.
>
> Kill. Over-Kill.
>
> Strategic Air Command.
> Missiles, Ballistic Missiles.
> Intercontinental Ballistic Missiles.
>
> Kill. Over-Kill.
>
> Crisis in Latin America.
> Based or Air-Mobile.
> Least Vulnerability.
> Maximum Flexibility.

Kill. Over-Kill.

(*the GROTESQUES advance on the audience with sweeping legato movements*)

First Air Strike.
Launch Strategic Weapons.
On Warning! On Warning!
On Warning!

Kill. Over-Kill.

(*spastic, contracted, angular frenzy resumes*)

Crisis in Detroit.
Problem with F-One-Eleven.
Computer Malfunction, Computer Malfunction.
Killer Satellite, Killer Satellite.
In Crisis! In Crisis!
In Crisis!

Kill. Over-Kill.
Over-Kill.

(*Chanting and wailing resume in low barely audible tones. Two GRO-TESQUES form configurations. Electronic sound continues during remainder of act. HERTZ appears in upstage doorway, dials phone. Telephone rings. BLAKELY enters to answer it.*)

BLAKELY. C-4.

HERTZ. Sir, I want to apologize about that false alarm on our nuclear alert system today. You see, I tripped on a cord and landed—

BLAKELY. (*deadly urgent*) It was a most fortuitous accident.

HERTZ. (*not comprehending*) Sir?

BLAKELY. When we invade Detroit, we must make certain that the rebels receive no aid from other cities in the region; so we broadcast a phony nuclear alert and evacuate all the people from Toledo, Lansing, Flint. Our Army moves in, does whatever is necessary.

HERTZ. (*vindicated and intensely relieved*) Excellent.

BLAKELY. What did your security check on Cauldwell yield?

HERTZ. Everything he's told us checks out to the letter.

BLAKELY. He's smart. Disclosures of classified information have been leaked from this office to the Detroit take-over.

HERTZ. When do we arrest him?

(CAULDWELL enters. He is in a different location. He stops, surveys the area, then dials pay phone.)

BLAKELY. Not yet. We will let the noose get very tight around his neck before we slap his horse on the ass.

(THEY hang up phones and exit. Chanting and wailing cease, but GROTESQUES remain onstage. Cauldwell's CONNECTION in Detroit answers and begins to speak in code. Only the intensity of tone would indicate to an eavesdropper that the conversation might not be what it seems.)

OPERATIVE. Capitol Sporting Goods.

CAULDWELL. Coach Cauldwell, here. Have my letter jackets come in yet?

OPERATIVE. Yes, Coach Cauldwell. Your jackets are here, but the *letters* have not arrived yet.

CAULDWELL. How's the weather out there?

OPERATIVE. Clear. But Wilson thinks the Washington coaches have sent scouts to spy on you.

CAULDWELL. Wilson is correct, but my team has prepared an end around sweep to the left side to set up a screen.

OPERATIVE. Good. Is the latest order to Walnut being processed?

CAULDWELL. The full order of four point eight million in sporting goods is being sent. It will be shipped through the usual corridors, arriving next Wednesday. It will include a full playbook on the first half.

OPERATIVE. And the second half?

CAUDWELL. Instructions and diagrams are for a long bomb on the fourth down from a shotgun formation.

(Two GROTESQUES cross to modules and slowly close their lids as kneeling GROTESQUES sink into modules)

OPERATIVE. Does the Washington team have any clue about how we are getting our sophisticated sporting equipment?

CAULDWELL. They think Russia is supplying our Detroit team with equipment shipped in fishing boats travelling the St. Lawrence.

OPERATIVE. My God!

CAULDWELL. They are actually beginning to believe their own propaganda. It was only a matter of time.

OPERATIVE. Yes, it was only a matter of time.

(CAULDWELL hangs up phone and exits. Lights fade as GROTES-QUES pull modules off and disappear. Blackout.)

REYNOLDS. (*simultaneously coming onstage*) You gotta slow your circles down, Lorraine, and you're bumping too much. When you see Bobby coming in for a close-up—(*sanctimoniously*) You know what a close-up is? Slow it down.

(*Hubbub throughout. LORRAINE has returned the soda to the ASSIS-TANT, and the ASSISTANT adjusts LORRAINE'S costume, make-up and hair. REYNOLDS has been closing the upstage doors. He hands a megaphone to the ASSISTANT.*)

REYNOLDS. Take this. Now Bobby, get in close. (*BOBBY follows his directions*) Music. (*Music and mood lighting resume. LORRAINE dances.*) I want a shot of the Canary driving down her nose, over her throat, then right through the cleavage. We'll call it "Flying through the Mountain Pass."

(*Unable to control themselves, BOBBY, LORRAINE and the ASSIS-TANT break up laughing. REYNOLDS explodes throwing clipboard across the stage. Music stops. ASSISTANT exits.*)

REYNOLDS. Would the two of you like to hear something that won't sound so funny? The Canary used to be our largest account? They're broke! And the petrochemical cloud smothering half the country is hardly an inducement to buy *any* gas-powered car. Now the boys with the bucks at Canary say that soft-core pornography is no longer selling cars, so we're going hard core. Are you two "artists" ready to deliver? (*snaps his fingers for his clipboard and BOBBY retrieves it*) Music. (*Music begins. Dancing and photography resume.*) Now if the two of you wish to continue picking up your inflated paychecks— (*he gives a direction to the dancing LORRAINE*)—a Canary is supposed to be *exciting*, Lorraine—it is incumbent upon us to develop a promo for Crisis Management that would sell dust to a man dying of thirst.

(*LORRAINE drops to the floor in a sinuous choreographed routine. REYNOLDS explodes.*)

REYNOLDS. There's no excitement here. Break for dinner...(*BOBBY goes to his bag to replace camera*)...and when I get back I want a shot of the Canary...(*LORRAINE has started to rise, but at REYNOLDS' gesture drops back to the floor*)...flying through the mountain pass. Bobby, try finding a slimmer model of the Canary. (*REYNOLDS stares at LORRAINE and gestures to signify a slimmer car*)...the one she's got on her might get stuck. And, LORRAINE...(*explodes as if pushing apart mountains*)...widen the pass a little! (*He exits. BOBBY helps LORRAINE to her feet.*)

BOBBY. (*whistles*) Whew!

LORRAINE. They've gone from a Falcon in your future to a Canary in your cleavage. (*both exit*)

Act II

Scene 1. THE CANARY

(*Crisis Management recording studio bathed in red and blue light. A video taping is in progress. Far Eastern music fills the air. LORRAINE, a dancer, emerges like a mirage. She dances her lovely, almost surreal, dance, appearing and disappearing through the upstage doors. There are toy cars attached to her arms. MR. REYNOLDS, the director, sits in the front row of the house, clipboard in hand. He is talking to the MAN in the sound booth through a megaphone. LORRAINE continues dancing throughout the following dialogue.*)

REYNOLDS. (*to the MAN in booth*) Okay, Dave? Run that leader back for the intro. We'll try it over the dance before the ad copy. I want to pick it up on the segment that's coming up. (*suddenly snapping directions at LORRAINE*) Keep going, Lorraine! (*back to DAVE*) Okay, run it.

ANNOUNCER. This has been a special program from the Crisis Management Bureau. Stay tuned to this frequency for emergency bulletins.

(*BOBBY, the photographer, enters from the house to prepare his camera. He is late.*)

ANNOUNCER. And now a word from General Auto, maker of the all-new Canary sedan and station wagon with gasoline-powered engines that make Canary superior to any electric car.

REYNOLDS. That's good, Dave. Couple that with some action stills and get it off to D.C. by Friday. Bobby is shooting the stills. (*to BOBBY*) Are you ready, Bobby? Okay, shoot. (*watches LORRAINE dance for a moment*) Hey, Dave, this is being filmed in tri-tone, right?

DAVE. (*from offstage*) It's in tri-tone.

(*BOBBY continues to photograph LORRAINE. The music picks up in tempo, and LORRAINE continues, stopping periodically as BOBBY says, "hold."*)

REYNOLDS. (*as LORRAINE pauses in the middle of a back bend*) What's the matter, Lorraine?

LORRAINE. The goddamn cars are coming off!

REYNOLDS. Cut!

(*Music stops. Lights restore to normal room light. Production ASSISTANT comes onstage to check LORRAINE'S makeup, carrying a soda.*)

LORRAINE. (*to assistant*) Could I have a drink of that?

(*The ASSISTANT hands her the soda. BOBBY goes to change lenses.*)

426

Scene 2. *CAULDWELL EXCHANGES INFORMATION WITH INSIDE AGENT, ZIMMERMAN*

(*CAULDWELL enters and dials a phone. It rings. ZIMMERMAN, offstage, answers it.*)

ZIMMERMAN. C-4.

CAULDWELL. Cauldwell here.

ZIMMERMAN. The documents implicating General Duallin in the cartel pullout are in his office, File Box D, Folder X-L-1.

CAULDWELL. Excellent. Could you get me placed on the bride selection committee?

ZIMMERMAN. I already have. You're to be at the General's home at two o'clock to view the six finalists.

CAULDWELL. Excellent.

ZIMMERMAN. But Blakely will be sure to have you under constant surveillance. Scott and Muntz are already there.

CAULDWELL. How much time would you estimate I have to complete everything?

ZIMMERMAN. I would say that within seven hours Blakely will have all the information he feels he needs about you and your network. Then he will most certainly arrest you. How much time do you absolutely need?

CAULDWELL. About as long as Blakely. It's going to be a photo finish.

ZIMMERMAN. Good luck. (*hangs up phone*)

(*CAULDWELL hangs up phone and exits*)

Scene 3. *ELEANOR ROOSEVELT*

ELEANOR. (*shouting from offstage*) Hey, what's wrong! (*Entering she stops to address an imaginary heckler. She is tougher and more bitter. Her speech is acid, biting.*) What's the matter with you, Bimbo, didn't they clean your cage today? (*to another heckler*) No, I didn't get up on the wrong side of the bed. I had a good night's sleep, thank you, in an all-night movie. (*to another*) Don't worry, dough-head, I got ways of sneakin' in. The problem in this country anymore ain't how to get *in* places; it's how to get *out*. Am I right? (*puzzling, trying to remember*) Nazi... Nazi...*Nazi Brides*. That was the movie they were playing. (*ominous*) You notice how things is becoming more like them Nazis every day? (*taking out newspaper clipping*) Like this U.S. Army General Duallin. You gotta hear this to believe it. He's advertisin' for a wife in the paper. Two hundred and fifty women have already applied, it says here. Well, you can understand that—beats the breadline. Picture of the old geezer here—looks like a well-fed billy goat. Come to think of it, goats is nicer lookin'. Never saw a mean-looking billy goat in my life. Know what I think? He ain't gonna marry none of 'em—just get his jollies watching women crawl. (*as she is talking an organ is pushed onstage*) Thanks, Chip. He never asks, but I always give him a cut of the take. (*goes to organ and plays a little Mozart, stops*) Wolfgang Amadeus. (*turns in sharp scorn*) Thought I was going to do a Presley imitation, eh? Up your bebopaluba. This is what they throw money in the cup for. Everyone says, "go down to Twelfth Street and see the old hag play classical music." They throw in a quarter and laugh. Call me an anachronism. (*staring into distance*) Little do they know my past or their own future. (*directly to audience*) Listen to me, my young fawns, those three-eyed pirates running things have a place saved out here in the street and in the death-cold cellars for just about everyone. (*Leaves, pushing organ offstage, talking to audience*) No, Cyclops, I decided not to go to Detroit. You need me too much here. I'm one of the few honest people you got left in this town, and maybe the only one with guts. You lose me, you get what you deserve. Yup, *they granted you the freedom not to think in this country and, by God, you've exercised it.* I'll give you that. (*exits*)

Scene 4. CRISIS MANAGEMENT SPECIAL ON THE MORAL MAJORITY

(*Military music. CHOIR in robes enters in two lines to fill the stage. MINISTER carrying a Bible passes through them to center stage and addresses the audience.*)

REVEREND. Detroit! (*CHOIR faces front*) Detroit! (*whirls around to direct CHOIR*)

CHOIR.   The devil walks across the land
         With many forms and faces.
         He carries a hammer and sickle
         To put the righteous through their paces.

REVEREND. (*to audience*) The children of God are writing me. Detroit! Father, why has such godlessness been unleashed in our land? And I tell them the answer is as simple as damnation and the devil. And like those simple yet profound concepts, it can be stated in one word: communism.

CHOIR.   Death to the Devil!
          Death to the Devil!
          Death to the Devil!

(the REVEREND walks to the extreme right side of the CHOIR, each head turning to follow him as he passes)

REVEREND. In a land where the races are allowed to mix freely, even cohabit, a land where women can destroy their unborn children, a land where liberals have ruled our sacred institutions...*(whirls around)*...did I say ruled or ruined? I said *both*! *(points to the audience and walks to left of center)* A land where homosexuals are allowed to walk the streets and teach our children. You show me such a land and I tell you, communism is the next step. And that step has been taken in Detroit. *(directs CHOIR)*

CHOIR.   The devil is a congressman.
          The devil is an author.
          The devil is a Communist.
          The devil is a homosexual.

REVEREND. *(smiling, hand held high)* Oh, Detroit doesn't call it "communism." *(gesturing and bringing hands to rest around the bible)* They call it "people's democracy." But they lie as the snake in the garden of Eden lied. Detroit says they have free housing?

(throughout, REVEREND points for CHOIR to sing, then when he is about to speak he cuts them off by making a fist)

CHOIR.   Death to the Devil!

REVEREND. I call that "cohabitation." Detroit says they have free health care?

CHOIR.   Death to the Devil!

REVEREND. I call that "theft." Detroit says they have day-care centers?

CHOIR.   Death to the Devil!

REVEREND. I call that "destruction of the family." Detroit says they have taken over the auto plants and are manufacturing electric cars and selling them to their fellow travelers and are sharing the profits with all the workers?

CHOIR.   Death to the Devil!

REVEREND. I say, "they will drive to hell in those cars!" *(crossing to the extreme right of choir)* Yes, all that Detroit is trying has been tried before and it has failed. And it will fail again. *(weaving in and out of CHOIR, to end center stage)* It has failed in El Salvador, Nicaragua, Yugoslavia...

(CHOIR sings "Death to the Devil" throughout this list)

REVEREND. ...Albania, Russia, Poland, East Germany, Czechoslovakia, China, North Korea, Vietnam, Cuba, Grenada, Angola, Tanzania, Namibia, Ethiopia, France, Spain, Greece, Portugal, Mozambique. And it will fail in Detroit.

CHOIR. Death to the Devil! (*marches out*)

REVEREND. And now let me introduce the military arm of our mission, an arm not always publicly visible, but which has finally been honored by this administration for its courage and patriotism.

(*the GRAND DRAGON with a concealed machete held behind his back enters to center*)

REVEREND. I present the Grand Dragon, the general of God's own battalion. (*Crosses to upstage right. CHOIR offstage sings "Death to the Devil" theme. The DRAGON speaks.*)

DRAGON. We are training for a race war. We're training every able-bodied man, woman and child sympathetic to our goals. I am personally and presently training a squadron of twenty-eight little boys and girls. My own daughter, I'm proud to say, is among them. They are learning the fine art...(*revealing machete*)...of the machete: wounding, maiming, decapitation—aggressive tactics to be used against your marauding colored and Communists, like in Detroit. I have a master's degree from Harvard which qualifies...

(*BLAKELY, who has been viewing the footage, shouts from offstage*)

BLAKELY. Enough!

(*Blackout as TECHNICIAN stops film. The lights come up as BLAKELY enters.*)

BLAKELY. That's enough of this, Hertz!

HERTZ. Goddamn it, Dixon, you know my ass is on the line. What were you...

BLAKELY. (*not buying that this was an accident*) Hertz, what the hell is the matter with you? I told you that the big money boys want footage to inspire the American public into getting out and having a good time: buying clothes, food, cars, whatever. And you show me footage on the right-wing militant church and the Klan. Sixty-seven percent unemployment among blacks and uneducated whites, and you show me *this*. How would you like to be inspired into having a good time by the Klan?

HERTZ. Sir, it was a mistake. Dixon put on the wrong reel.

DIXON. I put on the reel, Sir, I was told to put on, Sir.

HERTZ. Well, actually I may have handed him the wrong reel by mistake, but he's supposed to know—

BLAKELY. *(interrupting)* Dixon, when you have a moment, would you teach Hertz the goddamned Dewey Decimal system!

HERTZ. I'm sorry, Sir. *(taking out his frustration on DIXON)* Dixon, are you ready to announce the next reel? Dixon?

DIXON. Yes, Sir. We are ready for archive number 4-8-L, "Stock Market Rag," segueing into "Get Your Job."

(Blackout. Film begins. A TRIO wearing business suits and hats appear through the upstage doors, dancing and singing.)

The Stock Market Rag

TRIO.   What's the name for the phenomena
          That controls big bucks from here to Omaha?
          That owns the oil and the coal.
          The cities and the farms?
          Convinces people not to eat
          So it can stockpile arms?
          What is that centralized power
          That knows how to bend the law
          'Til monopolies own the country,
          Own us all?
          It can sleep like a grizzly or be bullish—
          Or it can be meek as a lamb—
          But never ask it for kindness,
          'Bout people it don't give a damn!
          Its only aim is money;
          Gold puts it in a thrall.
          It's the stock market, you guessed it,
          Makes cattle of us all.
          The stock market, you guessed it,
          Makes cattle of us all—

BLAKELY. *(entering)* Enough!

HERTZ. *(rising)* Dixon, will you get the lights. And make sure "Stock Market Rag" gets put back into reel casing 4-8-L.

DIXON. Yes, Sir.

HERTZ. *(over DIXON'S words to BLAKELY)* Did you like it, Sir?

BLAKELY. *(apparently seeking information)* What was that supposed to be, a satire?

HERTZ. Oh, well, it is slightly satirical, Sir, but very upbeat. I thought we might get people singing, "dah-dah-dedah, Stock Market Rag," Sir.

It's like those late-night talk shows, slightly satirical, but definitely on the side of big money.

BLAKELY. *(letting fly)* Crisis Management programming must be blatant, no room for innuendo. Nationalistic. It must convince the public into going out to *buy.*

HERTZ. *(over BLAKELY'S last words)* Yes, Sir. You're right, Sir. I'll cut it; I'll cut it!

BLAKELY. You're damn right, you'll cut it. Where's Cauldwell?

HERTZ. He should be here momentarily, Sir. He was to attend a meeting of General Duallin's Bride Selection Committee.

BLAKELY. Scott and Muntz are with him, I presume?

HERTZ. Yes, Sir. He is accompanied. He is not alone. And I will personally escort him back to General Duallin's office after this briefing.

BLAKELY. Well, then, I suggest we get on with the—

(DIXON'S announcement interrupts BLAKELY. CAULDWELL arrives.)

DIXON. *(presenting CAULDWELL)* Major Cauldwell, Sir.

CAULDWELL. Sorry I'm late, Sir. I've just been selected to weed out the semi-finalists in preparation for General Duallin's wedding. And the General wanted me to—*(he is peremptorily cut off)*

BLAKELY. Well, we have a little "weeding out" of our own to do here, Major. So if it won't crimp your style—*(he purposely does not continue)*

CAULDWELL. Yes, Sir, Sorry, Sir. *(sits)*

BLAKELY. We are viewing new footage for the Crisis Management Network to bring our programming more in line with the demands of the business community. Our charge in Crisis Management is to get the country up and moving again.

CAULDWELL. *(asking permission to give his assessment)* Sir, if I may?

BLAKELY. Major Cauldwell.

CAULDWELL. Since our most recent intelligence indicates that Pittsburgh appears to be following the same revolutionary path as Detroit, getting the country up and moving might take more than Crisis Management.

BLAKELY. Crisis Management is but an intermediary step, Major. This country must learn to walk again before it can run. We will assist in that process.

HERTZ. Dixon, will you announce? Dixon!

DIXON. We are now ready for Archive Number 6-6-Y: "Finding a Job Can Be an Adventure," featuring Mrs. Margaret Mellon Dupont.

(Blackout. Film begins. Margaret Mellon DUPONT is on camera. She is the perfect lady. Her mannerisms are prim, her tone optimistic. Her laugh is indescribably absurd, though to her, perfectly real.)

MRS. DUPONT. Never think, "I'm out of a job and desperate." That negativism communicates immediately to an employer. Think rather, "Finding a job can be an adventure. I may end up doing what I should have been doing all my life."

(SHE laughs her laugh. A WOMAN dressed smartly as a secretary and a MAN like a young executive enter with identical movement, illustrating MRS. DUPONT'S advice.)

MRS. DUPONT. So start your adventure by making a good impression at the job interview. Dress correctly. Quality and versatility. Yes, buy the best. Always buy the best. And when you need a change, change your accessories. If everything in the closet of yours can hold its head high, you will be able to hold your head high. *(she laughs her laugh and smiles at and applauds each of them)* Now that you have the right attitude and are dressed correctly...*(as if to a child)*...where do you go to find the job that's right for you? Let us *answer* that question by *asking* some questions. Do you like motors? *(excited)* You might get a job servicing cars or laundromats.

(One at a time, FOUR ACTORS enter through the doors with properties representing the various jobs MRS. DUPONT describes)

MRS. DUPONT. Do you enjoy making places clean and ordered? You could be a chamber maid. *(expansively)* Do you like the great outdoors? You could always become a sanitation engineer. Or do you like serving people? Good for you. That field is wide open—waiters, waitresses, busboys. One last tip, to flavor the broth, so to speak—and this is the *piece de resistance*: *(laughs her laugh)* open your interview with a joke, something like, "one cannibal says to another, 'who was that lady I saw you with?' That was no lady, that was my..." *(laughs)* "...lunch." This will relax the situation and prove you have a sense of humor. *(laughs)* As our President is so fond of saying in his inspirational messages to us: *(terribly jolly)* "All the problems in this country could be solved overnight if only we could learn to laugh at them." Now we are not saying that sixty percent unemployment and the breadline are in and of themselves funny. We are saying follow these examples.

(the ACTORS with properties pirouette to DUPONT'S advice)

MRS. DUPONT. Think positively. Dress right. Know what you can do. Convince your employer you can do it. And there is a job for you.

(End of film. Blackout.)

ANNOUNCER. This has been "Get Your Job" with host Margaret Mellon Dupont.

(*DIXON restores the lights*)

HERTZ. (*obviously nervous and anticipating any possible criticism*) Dixon, ah, is that the correct sound track? I could have sworn it was supposed to be that...

(*BLAKELY enters*)

Colonel Blakely, what did you think of that one?

BLAKELY. "Better." Not "best" but "better." It will pass muster.

(*HERTZ sits*)

Before going on to the regular agenda, the reason I was late this morning was the length of my breakfast meeting with the Quintra-Lateral Commission. I would like to begin today's session with a brief review of that meeting.

(*DIXON passes out folders to the OFFICERS and TAFT. THEY stand and respond*)

OFFICERS AND TAFT. Thank you, Sir. We'd appreciate that.

(*OFFICERS and TAFT sit*)

BLAKELY. Gentlemen, the Quintra-Laterals are asking assistance of the U.S. military in getting rid of those small companies that continue to exist in this country despite the Licensing Act passed under the last administration which stipulates that only the brand names of Commerce-Department-approved conglomerates can be bought and sold in this country.

HERTZ. (*rising*) Sir?

BLAKELY. Captain Hertz.

HERTZ. If I may, Sir, I thought it was necessary for this country's image to maintain the impression that we were still operating under the free enterprise system.

BLAKELY. There's no time for that anymore. Time has run out.

HERTZ. My principal concern, Sir, is that if the U.S. military is called in to stamp out small business, Sir, surely the world press will crucify us.

CAULDWELL. (*rising and speaking*) Sir, they'll have ammunition to fuel their charges that we are a single party, indeed, a totalitarian government—

BLAKELY. (*crossing to right of lectern and shaking his head in condescending disbelief*) Gentlemen, gentlemen. (*HERTZ and CAULD-WELL sit*) Whatever the world press, or anyone may say, what the Quintra-Laterals are asking is really no more than what big business has always asked of the military: to protect big business. In years past we did this by fighting wars abroad. Now the war has come home to our own shores. That represents a change of location only, not policy.

(the OFFICERS and TAFT stand)

OFFICERS AND TAFT. *(responding individually)* Yes, Sir. We understand, Sir. *(OFFICERS and TAFT sit)*

BLAKELY. *(crossing back up to lectern and opening report)* Now, Dixon...*(DIXON steps forward)* if I were to put you in charge of assembling personnel who could go forward with this project, henceforth referred to as File Number 55-818, could you handle it?

DIXON. Yes, Sir, I'll have a list for you tomorrow, Sir.

(buzzer sounds)

BLAKELY. Captain Hertz, would you get that, please?

HERTZ. Yes, Sir.

(HERTZ exits, brings back a folder, hands it to BLAKELY and sits. BLAKELY glances at the folder, revealing nothing.)

BLAKELY. Now let us get on with the reports from the regular agenda.

OFFICERS AND TAFT. *(standing)* Yes, Sir. *(they sit)*

BLAKELY. Major Cauldwell.

CAULDWELL. *(stands)* Sir, I have the list of supplies for Walnut. They are assembled and ready for transport. Could I have the destination and Walnut's timetable, please? *(sits)*

BLAKELY. Just read the list, Major. I'll see that everything gets there in time.

CAULDWELL. *(stands)* Yes, Sir. Twenty-five thousand pounds of plastic explosives, one-point-three mil in electronic equipment, one thousand night vision scopes for rifles, three-point-five mil in assorted—

TAFT. Was that three-point-four million?

CAULDWELL. That's three-point-five mil in assorted military hardware, and a ground-to-air Stinger missile. *(sits)*

BLAKELY. Very good. And now, Major, I suggest you go to your office...

(CAULDWELL stands)

...and make preparations for the Selection Committee for General Duallin's wedding.

CAULDWELL. Sir, I don't think I need any more preparatory time for that assignment.

BLAKELY. Out of deference to General Duallin's trend-setting approach to marriage, I'm authorizing you to take the necessary preparatory time.

CAULDWELL. Yes, Sir. Thank you, Sir. *(salutes and prepares to leave)*

BLAKELY. (*stopping CAULDWELL in his tracks*) And if I need you?

CAULDWELL. (*turns to face BLAKELY*) I can be reached in my office. (*salutes and exits*)

BLAKELY. (*obviously waiting until CAULDWELL'S exit to impart high security information*) Corporal Dixon...

DIXON. Yes, Sir.

(*Corporal DIXON locks the doors to the bureau room*)

BLAKELY. (*crossing down from lectern with an air of extreme gravity*) Gentlemen, here's the situation. One American city has already fallen into rebel hands. To prevent others from following suit, these steps are being taken. The U.S. Army and Walnut will be ready to move on Detroit within three weeks.

TAFT. Excellent, Sir.

HERTZ. A master plan.

BLAKELY. As a cover to that invasion, General Duallin has approved our plan to stage a mock nuclear alert and evacuate the civilian populations from Indiana, Ohio, and Michigan.

HERTZ. (*agreeing again*) Excellent.

TAFT. A necessary contingency plan.

BLAKELY. But as you both know, there's another situation developing that could pull the rug out from under the entire operation. The higher echelon of the U.S. business community has been acting in clandestine— perhaps conspiratorial—ways in the past six months. In this closed session, we will examine the course and consequences of their behavior— wherever it may lead. Your reports are prepared?

OFFICERS AND TAFT. Yes, Sir. (*THEY sit*)

BLAKELY. Captain Hertz?

HERTZ. (*rising*) Some of this may be ancient history.

BLAKELY. A review is in order.

HERTZ. Thank you, Sir. For years, General Motors, Ford, Chrysler, etc.

TAFT. (*interrupting and knowing the answer to his question*) Sir, should I tape this for the National Security Council?

BLAKELY. There will be no taping of this report. (*he nods for HERTZ to continue, begins to pace slowly as he listens to the remainder of the report*)

HERTZ. The major auto manufacturers have been making their largest profits from overseas' production. They have, therefore, allowed their domestic plants to become outmoded, blaming their consequent inability to compete with Toyota, Volkswagen, *et cetera* on unions.

BLAKELY. Proceed.

HERTZ. Yes, Sir. The remainder of my report may be a bit of a bombshell.

BLAKELY. I have no doubt.

HERTZ. Immediately before the take-over, the Quintra-Lateral Commission took out with Lloyds of London inflated insurance policies on their auto plants in Detroit.

TAFT. Sir, I think I will not take this information back to the National Security Council.

BLAKELY. Agreed.

HERTZ. This meant, Sir...

BLAKELY. (*taking over with rising but controlled rage*) This meant that if the Army had gone in and those plants had been destroyed, the conglomerates would have collected billions of dollars; that if Detroit had been burnt to the ground in pitched battle with the U.S. military, the conglomerates had everything to gain, nothing to lose.

HERTZ. Only the U.S. stood to lose, and massive amounts. (*sits*)

TAFT. (*rising and speaking over HERTZ'S words*) I have some additional information, Sir.

BLAKELY. Yes?

TAFT. Seventy-five percent of the top executives of Fortune Five-Hundred companies operating in the United States have been neither seen nor heard from in the past six months. (*sits*)

HERTZ. There is a pattern forming here, Sir.

BLAKELY. (*over HERTZ*) Mr. Taft... I want you to go to the FAA. Find out all the information you can on flight plans, routes, and points of destination that these top executives have been taking for the past six months. I want to know where they're going, and I want to know why.

TAFT. Right away, Sir. (*exits*)

BLAKELY. To review: Dixon, you'll be in charge of assembling personnel to make a list of the small companies left operating illegally in this country, and prepare a plan to throw a scare into them.

DIXON. Yes, Sir.

BLAKELY. Captain Hertz, you will continue with your work on the conglomerates. Taft will get back to us on the FAA. That will be all.

(*OFFICERS rise and salute. BLAKELY returns it.*)

BLAKELY. Captain Hertz, may I see you for a moment?

HERTZ. Right away, Sir. (*walks up to BLAKELY*) News on Cauldwell?

BLAKELY. I would say there's something new, yes. (*hands information to HERTZ*) This is a list of phone numbers and addresses of suspected radicals in Detroit with whom Cauldwell has communicated in the past two and a half weeks.

HERTZ. Jesus God!

BLAKELY. We will have Walnut put a trace on all the people living at those addresses, and then we will know where Cauldwell "lives." (*exits*)

HERTZ. I'll get on it right away, Sir, and see to it that Cauldwell is kept under watch twenty-eight hours a day. (*HERTZ exits*)

(*the intercom sounds, ZIMMERMAN hurries into the room*)

ZIMMERMAN. Colonel Blakely.

BLAKELY. (*entering*) You want to see me?

ZIMMERMAN. Sir, we've just received a communique from the Detroit take-over.

BLAKELY. Read it.

ZIMMERMAN. "To the Nations of the World:" (*hesitating*)

BLAKELY. Read it!

ZIMMERMAN. "The people's government of Detroit, Michigan wishes to announce the take-over of the United States Military Communications Center outside our city. We have begun the process of disarming the controls for several hundred nuclear missiles operated from that center. Our intention is to stimulate an international program of total nuclear disarmament. To that end, we have initiated unilateral disarmament conferences with European and Soviet bloc nations. We invite all governments to participate in these conferences—

BLAKELY. (*interrupts, having heard enough, grabs the communique from ZIMMERMAN*) Get Captain Hertz in my office immediately.

ZIMMERMAN. Sir, at your request Captain Hertz had himself placed on the committee to view the wedding finalists so that Major Cauldwell would not be left alone in General Duallin's home. Hertz and Cauldwell should be arriving together.

BLAKELY. I need to talk with Captain Hertz and Mr. Taft before I see Major Cauldwell.

ZIMMERMAN. Yes, Sir. As soon as they arrive, I'll ask Major Cauldwell to wait in the anteroom.

(*BLAKELY and ZIMMERMAN exit*)

Scene 5. *WEDDING SELECTION COMMITTEE*

(DIXON enters and executes a precision military maneuver as he positions sequined and feathered swans on either side of the stage. CAULDWELL and HERTZ are interviewing bride finalists in DUALLIN'S suite of offices. HERTZ addresses the applicants from the house, but his real concern is CAULDWELL.)

HERTZ. Will the next applicant come in.

(MISS PEARSON, a young, very nervous woman enters)

HERTZ. Hurry, please. We're behind schedule. Just a few questions.

CAULDWELL. Are you presently employed?

PEARSON. Well, I'm a singer, but there are no jobs now...

HERTZ. *(aside)* Corporal, would you get me a glass of water. This is taking longer than I thought.

PEARSON. ...so I was working as a receptionist at the GE plant in Millpond, but they moved it to Taiwan, and I don't speak Chinese.

HERTZ. You can be described as happy, and you like being touched?

PEARSON. *(looks quickly, ashamedly to CAULDWELL, then HERTZ)* Yes.

HERTZ. *(putting out cigarette)* You understand the General would like his wife to be able to sing or dance, to have some artistic talent. Would you like to begin your performance now?

PEARSON. *(nodding to her accompanist)* Certainly.

> Time was when life was,
> Lived by you and me.
> Time was...

(As PEARSON sings there are various interruptions. She continues singing but her apprehension obviously increases.)

PUBLIC ADDRESS SYSTEM. Call for Captain Hertz. Call for Captain Hertz.

HERTZ. *(to CAULDWELL)* I'll be right back. Keep the interview going.

(HERTZ leaves, then pops back to check on CAULDWELL, then exits. CAULDWELL then slowly makes his way offstage.)

PEARSON.   ...When life was
>   A long mystery.
>   Time was when life was...

(*SUSAN WASGAT, another semi-finalist, enters. Realizing that she is premature, she embarrassedly leaves.*)

PEARSON.   Time was, then life was.
             People aren't people...

(*HERTZ reenters looking for CAULDWELL. Not finding him, he becomes frantic*)

HERTZ.   Cauldwell? Major Cauldwell? (*runs to intercom and presses, buzzer sounds*) Muntz? Muntz, are you there?

   PEARSON. (*still singing*)
             ...Not anymore.
             People aren't people
             They're a sale and a score.

(*HERTZ cuts her off, terrified by CAULDWELL'S absence*)

HERTZ.   That's fine. Thank you.

PEARSON. Wasn't that selection to your liking? I mean, the ad said General Duallin was old fashioned, and the title of the song is "Time Was" and—

HERTZ.   Next! We'll be back to you within the hour.

(*PEARSON exits dejectedly. SUSAN WASGAT enters.*)

WASGAT. (*to HERTZ*) Are you General Duallin?

HERTZ.   (*desperately searching for CAULDWELL*) Uh, yes, yes, why don't you...(*realizing what she has asked*) No, I'm not General Duallin! (*calls*) Major Cauldwell!

WASGAT. (*to HERTZ again*) Oh, how do you do, Major Cauldwell.

HERTZ.   (*looking off*) Where?

(*CAULDWELL arrives, but stands in the shadows*)

CAULDWELL.   I'm right here, Captain Hertz. (*the two OFFICERS eye each other*)

WASGAT. (*to CAULDWELL and very pleased*) Oh, are you General Duallin?

CAULDWELL. No, Miss...?

WASGAT. Wasgat, Susan Wasgat.

CAULDWELL. Where did you see General Duallin's ad for a bride?

WASGAT. In *The Examiner.* (*cautiously*) Is that paper still alright to read?

HERTZ. (*nervously watching CAULDWELL*) Where are you from?

WASGAT. (*mouthed, with no sound*) Detroit.

CAULDWELL. Where? (*rustling of papers*)

WASGAT. (*terrified of guilt by association*) Detroit. But I got out of there before the whole mess began, and I would never go back there. Never!

CAULDWELL. Thank you. Do you have something for us to see?

WASGAT. (*horrified, thinking they expect her to disrobe*) What? (*covering herself*)

CAULDWELL. Do you sing or dance?

WASGAT. Oh, yes. I tumble. Is tumbling artistic enough?

CAULDWELL. Yes.

WASGAT. Then I tumble.

(*WASGAT performs a lovely balletic tumbling routine as singing of "Time Was" continues offstage. This routine can change to fit the ability of the actor.*)

VOICES.   Time was when life was
            A good three-score and ten,
            But that was way back,
            Way back then.

            Time was when life was,
            Time was, then life was.

(*WASGAT finishes in a beautiful pose*)

HERTZ. Thank you. You can relax, Miss Wasgat.

WASGAT. (*still holding pose*) What?

HERTZ. Relax.

WASGAT. (*realizing she is still holding pose, she abruptly drops it*) Oh.

CAULDWELL. When the General interviews you, he would like to get some idea of how his wife would look on the wedding day, so would you mind trying on a gown? It's in the dressing room, behind you off the hall.

WASGAT. (*ecstatic*) Does that mean I'm one of the finalists?

CAULDWELL. Yes. It's not the exact gown you would be wearing, but it gives the General an idea, you know. (*exiting after WASGAT and speaking to HERTZ*) If you'll excuse me, I'll put this information on General Duallin's desk.

HERTZ. (*going after CAULDWELL*) I can do that, why don't you...

(*a young WOMAN in a tutu enters en point, entangling HERTZ, thereby allowing CAULDWELL to escape*)

STOCKWEATHER. My name is Pearl Stockweather, soon to be Mrs. General Duallin! (*she exits*)

WASGAT. (*from offstage*) Captain Hertz, if General Duallin chooses me to be—

HERTZ. (*cutting her off*) Don't Captain Hertz me. (*he is almost beside himself, dashes to intercom, buzzes*) Muntz!

MUNTZ. (*over intercom*) Yes.

HERTZ. Cauldwell has slipped out again. He's on his way to the General's office. (*to WASGAT*) I'm sorry, what did you say?

WASGAT. If General Duallin chooses me to be his wife, I get everything the ad promised—travel to Acapulco, Fiji...?

CAULDWELL. (*re-entering*) the General has duties in Europe, the Middle East, Latin America, wherever the U.S. has vital military interests. If you become Mrs. Duallin, you'll get all the travel the ad promised and more.

(*WASGAT has reentered attired in wedding gown*)

CAULDWELL. You look lovely as a bride.

WASGAT. Thank you.

CAULDWELL. (*to HERTZ*) If we hurry, we'll be just in time for our meeting with Colonel Blakely. (*to WASGAT*) The General will be with you in a few minutes.

(*from the other side of the stage, a SECOND WOMAN, dressed in an identical gown, enters*)

SECOND WOMAN. I'm sorry, I just got a little sick to my stomach. I'm alright now. Will General Duallin still see me?

(*another WOMAN, again in an identical gown, enters and the THREE WOMEN look forlornly at one another*)

THIRD WOMAN. (*gesturing to swans onstage*) General Duallin said we should take these as momentos.

(*during the song, WOMEN pick up the swans, turn slowly and exit upstage as voices sing*)

VOICES. (*offstage*)
      People aren't people,
      Not anymore.
      People aren't people;
      They're a sale and a score.

It's progress, they say,
A new life up ahead;
When I look that way,
Everything I see is dead.

Scene 6. *CRISIS MANAGEMENT BUREAU*

(*TAFT and BLAKELY enter agitated but determined to bring matters to a conclusion*)

BLAKELY. Hertz will be here shortly.

TAFT. Shall I begin without him, Sir?

BLAKELY. Begin immediately.

TAFT. Here, then, are the parameters of the situation. (*gives BLAKELY a paper*) Of the thirty largest multinationals in the world, only eight are currently using the U.S. as their base of operations.

BLAKELY. So the multinationals have been pulling out of this country for some time?

TAFT. Well over a decade.

BLAKELY. Where are they going?

TAFT. According to the FAA—Sir, if I may? (*removes jacket, rolls up cuffs, loosens tie*) ...the corporate jets have not been supplying flight plans; so I checked with Air Force intelligence, and they report heavy increases of air traffic over the Caribbean.

BLAKELY. But there are no large islands available to them in the Caribbean!

TAFT. According to my source they will use the Caribbean only to house their families and their think tanks. It will not be their manufacturing base.

BLAKELY. I'm not even sure it matters anymore, but for my information, did your source tell you why the multinationals have been pulling out of the United States when this government has given them virtually everything they've ever wanted?

TAFT. If you would prefer asking my source these questions directly, he is waiting in the anteroom.

BLAKELY. (*nods, goes to buzzer*) Miss Zimmerman, send in whoever is waiting to see me.

(*ZIMMERMAN ushers in CAULDWELL and HERTZ. HERTZ sits, CAULDWELL remains standing on a level with BLAKELY.*)

BLAKELY. Miss Zimmerman, pull file 4-8-L, please. (*DIXON readies his rifle. BLAKELY speaks to CAULDWELL*) I have had you under surveillance for nine days and I now have more than enough information to hang you. (*ZIMMERMAN hands him the file*) If you give me all the information I want, I will...

CAULDWELL. (*interrupting*) If you have me arrested, which of your superior commanders would you prefer to be the first appraised of your treasonous acts?

HERTZ. Treason!

BLAKELY. (*over HERTZ*) What in the hell are you talking about?

CAULDWELL. I suggest Taft not tape what I am about to say.

BLAKELY. Get on with it!

CAULDWELL. The U.S. Army under your jurisdiction has been supplying the counterrevolutionary organization in Detroit, code named Walnut, for six months. Is that correct, Colonel Blakely?

BLAKELY. Go on.

CAULDWELL. You have supplied this organization, code named Walnut, with millions of dollars worth of armaments. Is that correct, Colonel Blakely?

BLAKELY. Get to the point.

CAULDWELL. Others objected to your arming Walnut, suggested you do more preliminary investigation. But you overrode those objections as you readily agreed to Walnut's ever-increasing demands for more supplies. Is that correct, Colonel Blakely? (*bombshell*) Walnut is not a counterrevolutionary force. It is an arm of the Detroit takeover.

(*EVERYONE listening is jolted. DIXON takes aim at CAULDWELL*)

HERTZ. (*rising*) Jesus God, Sir, Walnut is what? You know I never trusted Walnut from the start. I'm going to be...

BLAKELY. Shut up!

CAULDWELL. Every time you authorized a shipment of money and armaments to Walnut, you were directly supplying the people's government in Detroit. That, Sir, however you slice it, is treason. Moreover, you supplied Walnut with more than you thought. Almost every time you signed your credit card at the press club bar, you were signing another supply order for Walnut.

HERTZ. (*exploding*) Sir, you mean the U.S. Army and not the Soviet Union has been the suppliers of the Detroit takeover?

BLAKELY. (*to HERTZ*) Will you shut the hell up! (*to CAULDWELL*) Why did you give Taft this information, and why are you confiding in me?

CAULDWELL. For a price.

TAFT. Sir, if I may, I suggest you let Major Cauldwell continue.

BLAKELY. As if I had a choice. (*gestures CAULDWELL to lectern as he takes CAULDWELL'S seat*)

HERTZ. But, Sir, you are relinquishing...

CAULDWELL. (*passes out documents to all present, then goes to lectern, addresses BLAKELY*) I think by the time you have heard everything I have to say, you might decide that the U.S. Army would be better off were they to switch their allegiance from the multinationals to the people's take-overs. (*passes out documents to all present*) And I am speaking from both patriotic and financial considerations.

(*DIXON maintains rifle aimed at CAULDWELL*)

BLAKELY. I would appreciate it if I could be spared your political analysis. (*to TAFT*) Where did he get all this information?

TAFT. From the corporate offices in Detroit at the time of the takeover.

BLAKELY. Alright, let's hear it. Why have the multinationals been pulling out of this country?

CAULDWELL. First, even though...

HERTZ. (*barely audible*) I think I'm going to be sick.

CAULDWELL. ...the union movement in this country has been virtually gutted ever since the last administration, the multinationals do not want to gamble on a business climate where unions might spring up again.

BLAKELY. (*unflinchingly demands the information*) The second reason the multinationals are pulling out?

CAULDWELL. Air and water pollution in this country are too high, making it an unsafe climate for their families. The petrochemical cloud is but the tip of the iceberg.

BLAKELY. Third.

CAULDWELL. Third. While past administrations have made the corporations virtually tax exempt, the multinationals are taking the ultimate step. Sometime within the next forty-eight hours, they will announce to the world that they have left the U.S. and formed a separate nation, tax free, totally under their own control.

BLAKELY. Fourth.

CAULDWELL. Since the event of the Detroit take-over, the multinationals are afraid the U.S. population won't stand idly by and watch their country be destroyed.

BLAKELY. That's a matter of opinion.

CAULDWELL. Yes, it's their opinion.

BLAKELY. Continue.

CAULDWELL. Of course, you already know the multinationals expected to collect massive insurance money had the Army marched in and burned Detroit.

BLAKELY. (*walking toward the lectern and spitting out his words*) Does this new self-appointed master race have any plans for the United States?

CAULDWELL. Once they have effected their pull-out, they are preparing to treat the U.S. as they would any colony.

ALL OTHERS. Colony!

(*burst of ad libs*)

BLAKELY. Explain. Could you please explain?

(*DIXON cocks gun, aims at CAULDWELL, then HERTZ, then CAULDWELL*)

TAFT. If I may assist here—once the multinationals have left this country, there will remain no large scale finance, capital goods or manufacturing. So the United States will be in the condition of many of the contiguous countries in Latin America—lots of natural resources, lots of cheap labor.

BLAKELY. (*his rage quivers in his words*) Suppose us natives get restless? Who would police this colony?

CAULDWELL. You know what out-sourcing is?

TAFT. (*to BLAKELY*) So they don't have to pay union wages. Ford, General Motors have all their auto parts, *et cetera*, manufactured by cheap labor in the Third World and then shipped back to the U.S.

CAULDWELL. The multinationals are going to out-source the police force in the United States.

HERTZ. (*dumfounded*) Why not use the U.S. military already available to them?

CAULDWELL. There are too many poor and disaffected people in the ranks of the U.S. military. The multinationals are afraid there could be a *coup*.

HERTZ. (*under his breath*) Coup?

BLAKELY. Cauldwell, who is overseeing this pullout?

CAULDWELL. (*a pause*) Your commanding officers, including General Hoffman and General Duallin.

(*this hits everyone hard*)

BLAKELY. And where is our absentee President in all of this?

CAULDWELL. Like his predecessors, he's in the Caribbean with the multinationals, protecting his investments.

BLAKELY. If I don't cooperate...?

CAULDWELL. You invade Detroit, probably burn the city to the ground, and start a civil war in this country. The multinationals fiddle while we burn.

BLAKELY. If I cooperate...

CAULDWELL. You supply other people's movements in Boston, Providence, New York...(*handing folder to BLAKELY*)...here's a complete list—with money, personnel and supplies.

BLAKELY. And assist you in setting up your people's democracy? You're talking about communism, Major Cauldwell.

CAULDWELL. I am not concerned with your political analysis or labels, Colonel, any more than you are with mine. I'm telling you the way it is. Call it what you want. Obviously you need some time to think this over.

(*CAULDWELL starts to exit. At the door he stops, slowly turns to BLAKELY, and snaps to attention. BLAKELY walks to a level with CAULDWELL. CAULDWELL salutes, BLAKELY returns it, CAULD-WELL exits. In that momentous salute there is mutual respect and understanding.*)

HERTZ. Shall we arrest him, Sir?

BLAKELY. (*with control*) When bad news comes, Captain, you don't punish the messenger.

HERTZ. But he's more than the messenger. He's a partisan of the Detroit takeover.

BLAKELY. When the face of the enemy changes, Captain, you don't arrest the soldier who saw it first.

HERTZ. Sir, I realize that the multinationals leaving the U.S. are now in some sense the enemy, but surely you don't agree with Cauldwell that our friends are now those rebels taking over cities?

BLAKELY. (*a most profound question*) What?

HERTZ. Surely you don't agree with Cauldwell that...

BLAKELY. Gentlemen, at the Academy you learn to defend your country. The question now is: *from what and for whom?* I need some time, Gentlemen, you understand?

HERTZ. Yes, Sir.

TAFT. Yes, Sir, we understand. Whenever you wish to discuss this matter, we'll be here. We will remain as long as is necessary.

BLAKELY. Captain Hertz, you had some footage for us to preview today?

HERTZ. *(standing, extremely shaken)* Uh...um...Yes, Sir. Ever since the administration gave the go ahead, the CIA has been infiltrating domestic groups. I have some footage on a dissident group, a singing group, a theater which has dared to call the government of this country "fascist."

BLAKELY. I think I would like to see that footage.

HERTZ. Dixon, will you please announce.

DIXON. *(lights darkening)* We will now view "New Rise of the Master Race," archive number 0-2-4-1.

(ZIMMERMAN runs onstage holding telegram)

ZIMMERMAN. Sir, I've just received an urgent communique!

BLAKELY. *(from offstage)* Read it!

ZIMMERMAN. "To the nations of the world: the citizenry of Pittsburgh, Pennsylvania wish to announce our solidarity with the people's coalition of Detroit. We have today, after several weeks of meetings with labor, small business and political leaders effected a peaceful takeover of our city. The majority of businesses and social institutions remain intact. We have taken control of the property owned by large corporations...

(As speech continues, all three doors open slowly to reveal the WORKERS who have taken over Detroit. ZIMMERMAN fades back to join them.)

COMPANY. It's beginning!
          It has begun!
          It's beginning!
          It has begun!

          It's not what you think.
          It's not what we thought.

          It's beginning!
          It has begun!
          It's a beginning!
          It has begun!

(blackout, then in a whisper)

COMPANY. It has begun!

END OF PLAY

NEW RISE OF THE MASTER RACE

MANANA

Left to right: David Carl Olsen, Gerard Hirsh from "New Rise of the Master Race." Photo: James Oestereich.

WINDFALL

by Maxine Klein
Music by James Oestereich

"Windfall," produced by Little Flags Theatre, written and directed by Maxine Klein with music composed by James Oestereich, premiered in Boston on February 28, 1978.

Lyle Fine .... *James Oestereich*

Biddie Gazinski .... *Ellen Field*

Scoop MacNamara .... *Sidney Atwood*

Dottie Hemingway .... *Judith Black*

Contact
District Manager .... *Gerard Hirsch*
Merle

Manager
Zach .... *David Carl Olson*

Irene .... *Kathryn Pintar*

Barrelhouse .... *Bill Johnson*

Set design by Michael Anania, costumes by David Carl Olson, lights by John Polglase.

ACT I

At the Barrelhouse Bar, Scoop's gas station, a subway station, and a job interview at an office.

ACT II

A truck, the dumpsite, Biddie's apartment, and the Barrelhouse Bar.

TIME: The present.

STORY OF THE PLAY

"Windfall is a musical play. Three embattled survivors who have been automated out of their jobs—a one-armed mechanic, a jazz trumpet player, and a sixty-three year old grandmother—come up against a comic-tragic world where machines talk, music is pre-packaged, and the backroads at night are alive with trucks delivering poison waste to our children's playgrounds and kitchen faucets.

Over their on-going poker game at the neighborhood bar these three unlikely heroes from the world of pick-up jobs pick up a possible fast buck that leads them into an unexpected nightmare in a nuclear graveyard. "Deal the cards. The stomach's emptier, the trap tighter. Times are tough. So whose business is it anyway how we survive?" "Ours" they decide as they take on the bigger battle for the survival of us all.

The play is alive.
It is relentless.
It is humorous.
It is *today*.

DESCRIPTION OF CHARACTERS

BIDDIE GAZINSKI: Biddie is a tough, tender, sixty-three year old woman, a survivor. She has worked all her life at any job she could find. Biddie lives alone with stuffed animals as companions, and often spends the evening at the Barrelhouse playing cards and bantering with her two great friends, Scoop and Lyle.

LYLE FINE: Musician at the Barrelhouse. He learned early and well that those who have get more. He also learned who and how to hustle for the little that was left. His wit is sharp and fast like his piano-playing fingers. Under this man grass does not grow.

SCOOP MACNAMARA: A close friend of both Lyle and Biddie. He is a one-armed gas station operator, an ex-steelworker, who lost his arm in an industrial accident. He is an expert card player—a student of the odds.

DOTTIE HEMINGWAY: Bartender and manager for the Barrelhouse tavern. She is efficient, a down-to-earth caring woman with a bartender's savvy: she knows when to talk and when to keep still and listen.

ZACH and IRENE: Singing waiters at the Barrelhouse.

DISTRICT MANAGER and ASSISTANT DISTRICT MANAGER: Representatives for a large oil company.

BARRELHOUSE: Plays piano at the Barrelhouse.

CONTACT: Connection with organized crime.

Left to right: James Bright, James Oestereich, Ellen Field from "Windfall.".

Prologue

(Lights come up on the Barrelhouse Tavern, a home away from home for its clientele, a place to play poker, have a beer, shoot the breeze. LYLE is at the piano. WAITERS and WAITRESSES are on platforms singing.)

> *Buyer's Market*
> It's a buyer's market; they can get what they want cheap.
> It's a buyers's market, turning people into sheep.
> It's a buyer's market; anything they want is theirs.
> Buyer's market; they take all the traffic bears.
>
> It came down to a choice between profit and people,
> In that moment the die was cast.
> In the land of the free, profit won out.
> The people came in last.
>
> It's a buyer's market; they can get what they want cheap
> It's a buyer's market; turning people into sheep.
> It's a buyer's market, the people's life is fated;
> Buyer's market, they're auto-or-assimilated.
>
> It came down to a choice between profit and people.
> In that moment the die was cast.
> In the land of the free, profit won out.
> The people came in last

(WAITERS and WAITRESSES exit)

Act 1

Scene 1. "The Barrelhouse"

(offstage piano is playing "The Barrelhouse")

LYLE. *(calling from the piano)* Dottie you got a paper?

DOTTIE. *(Entering with paper open to racing results. She hands it to LYLE, her customary dry wit prevailing.)* Why? You don't read.

LYLE. *(looking furiously to find whether his horse won)* I look at the pictures.

SCOOP. *(calling from offstage)* Anybody home?

DOTTIE. *(setting up her bar)* There they are, 5:45 on the button—you can set your watch by them. *(calling)* Red carpet's down, Biddie, Scoop.

BIDDIE. *(entering with the pizazz of a clown claiming center ring)* Your VIPs are here. Now don't embarrass us by getting nervous. Just act like you always do. Us rich folk is just like you poor ones.

SCOOP. *(following a few paces behind her majesty)* Only cleaner.

(EVERYONE laughs)

DOTTIE. *(to BIDDIE)* How's the moving and hauling?

BIDDIE. To make money driving truck anymore, you got to give up eatin', sleepin', and peein'; and I can only give up two out of three. *(moves down bar to LYLE'S piano)* Speakin' of which, Lyle, about that tip you gave me.

LYLE. *(a tone that says he can't understand how it happened)* Sweet pea in the fourth.

BIDDIE. I don't like your tone of voice and I need that money.

LYLE. She was scratched.

BIDDIE. Scratched! You're gettin' worse. Before when you gave me a tip at least the horse *ran* before it lost. You pick every loser from here to Cincinnati.

LYLE. I told you the horse was a long shot.

BIDDIE. There's a difference between *long* and *never*. *(crosses to table)* Come on Hot-Shot. Let's see if you're any better at cards than you are at pickin' horses.

LYLE. *(swaggering over from piano and doing one of his many voices)* Now lookee here, Little Missey, you can run down my woman, and you can step all over my country but don't say anything about my palomino, pal.

BIDDIE. *(to SCOOP and referring to LYLE)* Big time operator. A couple of voices, a little trumpet and two bucks to his name.

SCOOP. *(shuffling and dealing)* That's seventy-five cents more than I

458

got. Okay, down to the rough stuff. Hundred dollar limit, three raises, nothing wild but the dealer.

(*In the ensuing card game, like the ones they have played almost every night for years, THEY talk about everything that comes to mind. Tonight as always, this talk is full of one-liners and pin-jabs as well as the serious stuff of their lives.*)

BIDDIE. (*pulling out match sticks and dividing them as DOTTIE delivers drinks to the table*) Ten for you, ten for me, three for Hot Shot—

LYLE. (*protesting*) Hey!

BIDDIE. (*gives him the remaining seven*) Each stick's worth five cents; deal 'em down and dirty.

LYLE. That's the only way grease monkeys can deal.

SCOOP. Actually, grease ain't dirty. It's more sterile than your own spit. You can wash your cuts out with it.

BIDDIE. (*to SCOOP*) I get so sick of your know-it-all attitude, your damn know-it-all attitude. Ugh! This is the worst hand I've had all week. Why don't you learn how to deal instead of studying spit?

SCOOP. Is it true what I heard, Lyle? They're turning this place into a disco joint?

LYLE. I'm taking a night class to learn how to be a phonograph needle. if I can't make the adjustment, I'm out of a job Good Friday.

SCOOP. Well, you knew that was going to happen some day, right?

LYLE. I know I'm gonna die someday too; that don't make it any easier when it comes.

SCOOP. You'll find another gig.

LYLE. Yeah, sure, I see a lot of openings in the paper for architects and photo voltaic engineers.

ZACH. (*calling from offstage*) Hey Dottie, can you give me a hand out here?

DOTTIE. Be right with you. (*exits*)

LYLE. You meeting me at the track tomorrow?

SCOOP. Not tomorrow. I'm being visited by the goose that lays the golden egg.

LYLE. (*whistling admiringly*) Top brass. You win another trophy for volume sales?

BIDDIE. (*shaking her head "no"*) Uh-uh. Market for hot air dried up.

LYLE. They'll probably give you a paid vacation for all the extra time you been putting in.

SCOOP. (*direly*) You never know what they'll do.

BIDDIE. I do not come here to talk about problems; I come here to forget 'em. (*shielding mouth with cards as she confides to LYLE*) And if one-arm don't start dealin' me better than these, I'm gonna kick him in the balls.

SCOOP. I heard that.

BIDDIE. How come you always hear everything I say under my breath and nothing I say to your face?

(*Phone rings. LYLE throws down cards and goes quickly to it. Obviously he is waiting for this call.*)

SCOOP. You folding?

LYLE. What's it look like?

BIDDIE. (*looking at her cards*) Wonderful, wonderful.

SCOOP. You're lying.

BIDDIE. (*slamming down her winning hand*) You think so? Read 'em and weep. I think I'll celebrate my winnings with a good cigar.

SCOOP (*taking out his disappointment at losing*) Why do you smoke cigars? Don't look good for a lady to smoke cigars.

BIDDIE. I don't smoke them, Sonny Boy. I chew them.

SCOOP. (*taking out a pad and calculating*) I now owe you $12,420.

BIDDIE. (*from memory*) $12,423. But don't despair, Pal. (*finds brochure puts it on table*) I got something from Harry today could put us on easy street.

(*It is clear she is in dead earnest and it is equally clear that this is not the first time this TRIO has been involved in such wild schemes as the one she is about to put forth.*)

BIDDIE. Grow chickens in your living room and make $150 a day in eggs alone. *Apartment pullets!*

LYLE. (*having finished his phone call and gone back to the bar, laughs and spills drink all over himself*) Anybody got a towel?

BIDDIE. Let him drown. (*pointing to brochure*) Look at this, Scoop. This is a chicken coop, turns into a sofa at night or when the landlord comes around. *Soundproof!* And this, looks like bookcases? Chicken coops. These are false books!

(*LYLE starts whistling, not interested. BIDDIE drives him.*)

If a couple of people I know had their own personal supply of chickens, they could survive, as well as make a little scratch selling eggs to the neighbors. This is the ticket, I tell you, apartment pullets!

LYLE. What do we do with the shit?

BIDDIE. What are we doing with it now?

LYLE. (*standing*) I ain't gonna hold my breath 'til you fry your first omelette.

SCOOP. *(trying to divert BIDDIE'S frustration at LYLE'S rejection)* Whatta you know about raising animals anyway?

BIDDIE. I got a house full of 'em.

SCOOP. They're not real. They're stuffed.

BIDDIE. What's the difference?

LYLE. Barrelhouse, could you take five?

(Offstage piano stops. LYLE has set the stage for serious talk. He crosses toward BIDDIE and SCOOP.)

LYLE. All right, I got some real business to talk over with you.

BIDDIE. *(to SCOOP)* When that one talks real business...*(flips bill of her hat to the other side of her head which she does whenever she gets nervous.)* ...I get real nervous.

LYLE. That call was from Danny.

SCOOP. *(direly)* Danny Morrison?

LYLE. He's got a job for us.

BIDDIE. Whatever he's peddling ain't healthy.

LYLE. *(challenging)* What's he peddling?

BIDDIE. I don't know but...

LYLE. *(interrupting)* Then how do you know it ain't healthy?

SCOOP. Everytime we touch that louse we get burned.

LYLE. *(to SCOOP)* You ain't had a gas delivery in a month. *(to BIDDIE)* You get laid off every time you turn around. Now Daniel Morrison may not be the Junior Chamber of Commerce, but he's got paying work which is more than anybody else is offering us.

SCOOP. *(not a question but a challenge)* Doing what?

LYLE. Hauling some barrels.

SCOOP. Barrels of what?

LYLE. That's up to the guy that's hiring us.

BIDDIE. *(pauses, then with finality)* If Danny has anything to do with it, I just lost my license.

SCOOP. *(equally final)* And I threw my back out.

LYLE. Okay, start your chicken ranch and starve. *(exits, angry at their decision)*

BIDDIE. *(to SCOOP but loud enough for LYLE to hear)* Hey! Hey! What does the man mean, "starve"? There's always jobs in this country for cripples like you and rich, beautiful chicks like me.

(SCOOP begins to sing)

Windfall

SCOOP.   Got a handicap plain to see
         But it can't slow down a guy like me!
         They put a handicap on a winner.
         They put a handicap on a winner.

BIDDIE. You've heard of a diamond in the rough
         This one's old as she is tough!
         She plays it lean and close to the belt.
         She plays it lean and close to the belt.

ALL.   Place your bets on the winning team.
         The stakes are high; the game is mean.
         Soon we'll turn the winning card.
         We warn you all, be on guard.

DOTTIE. *(re-enters with ZACH and IRENE as song ends)* Sorry folks, morning comes early. Gotta close it down.

(WAITERS remove glasses, bottles, table as DOTTIE talks to BIDDIE)

Tell me, Biddie, what are you gonna do with all your winnings from the game?

BIDDIE. Do with my winnings? I'm gonna build me a tin roof.

DOTTIE. What are you going to put it on?

BIDDIE. I'll figure that out after I get the roof built. Been startin' from the bottom all my life—time I started from the top.

(ALL laugh)

DOTTIE. I got another trophy for you. *(pulls out a stuffed animal)*

BIDDIE. *(pleased as punch)* Will you look at that! Thanks Dottie. I'll take Bouncer home and tuck him in with the family.

SCOOP. What's the tab?

DOTTIE. *(pouring a drink and motioning it to SCOOP and BIDDIE)* You two don't have to leave yet. I'm just locking up to keep the tourists *out* and Lyle *in*. Stick around awhile.

BIDDIE. Well, if I had another drink to wet my whistle...*(gets a drink from DOTTIE)* Did I ever sing you that song about the bums of the road?

SCOOP. About a hundred times.

BIDDIE. One more crack out of you, Sonny Boy, and I'll turn you in for being a male impersonator.

(ALL laugh. LYLE starts to play, BIDDIE sings.)

Bums of the Road

BIDDIE. We're as shrewd as we can be.
         We can add two and two and make it come out three.

LYLE.   *(joining)*
                 Anything that's not nailed down we take
                 'Cause life for us ain't a piece of cake.

TRIO.   When stocks go down, they fall on us.
                 When profits rise, we're squeezed in a vise.

ALL.   *(joining)*
                 There's no other way that we can win,
                 Unless we peddle flesh and sell used tin.

CHORUS.   We're the bums of the road,
                 The other side of the track,
                 What it takes to win
                 Is what we lack.

SCOOP and   To stay alive takes all our time
WAITERS.   Our life savings are minus a dime.

LYLE and   If we don't look out, if we doze or slumber,
WAITERS.   The next thing you know, we'll be six feet under.

TRIO.   Morals and ethics don't buy butter.
                 My do-good mother ended up in the gutter.

ALL.   Live today, cry tomorrow
                 Let a good drink drown the sorrow.

ALL.   *(prepare to exit as chorus is sung)*
                 We're the bums of the road,
                 The other side of the track.
                 What it takes to win
                 Is what we lack.

(BARRELHOUSE continues playing the song offstage as the others leave)

SCOOP. 'Night now. *(exits)*

DOTTIE. Good night, Friend. *(puts bottles away, exits)*

BIDDIE. Come on, Bouncer, Ol' Biddie's hittin' the road too. Gotta get up early tomorrow and pound the pavement—again. Wish I had a steady job like Scoop.

IRENE. Good night, Biddie. Good luck.

BIDDIE. I'll need it.

(*lights touch black then come up revealing a small rectangle, stage center*)

Scene 2. *"Scoop's Gas Station"*

(*sound of cars on a busy thoroughfare*)

SCOOP. (*nervously holding door open for District Manager who enters*) Come on in. Haven't seen you in a long time, huh? Nice weather.

(*Assistant DISTRICT MANAGER enters. SCOOP periodically stutters as is his wont when he is nervous.*)

SCOOP. They sent two of you this time, huh? Must be pretty important. How you doing? How you doing?

DISTRICT MANAGER. Fine. Yourself?

ASSISTANT DISTRICT MANAGER. How's the Scoop scooping?

SCOOP. Great, great, never better. And you? (*nervously remembering*) Guess I already asked that. L-l-look, um, sit down, let me get you a chair. (*pulling out stools*) Got these s-s-straight from Windsor Castle.

DISTRICT MANAGER. Scoop?

SCOOP. Yeah?

DISTRICT MANAGER. We don't have a whole lot of time; so let's get right to the point.

SCOOP. Sure.

DISTRICT MANAGER. Your sales are down.

SCOOP. (*not believing what he has heard*) W-w-would you run that by me again?

ASSISTANT DISTRICT MANAGER. Your sales are down.

SCOOP. You don't give me enough gas to keep a skateboard going, and you tell me my sales are down? That's some shrewd calculating. You got a business degree from Harvard or something? I mean that is shrewd. Just go back and tell them it's hard to sell what you don't have.

ASSISTANT DISTRICT MANAGER. (*pleasant*) We're with you Scoop, we're with you all the way. But you've got to understand the company's predicament.

DISTRICT MANAGER. They can't afford to keep a station open that's not selling gas, no matter what the reason.

SCOOP. (*with fierce sarcasm*) Look, you give me some of that gas you got stored in them secret tanks, and I'll make the company a million. W-wait, wait, I read the company's annual profit report. What's another million compared to the billions they've already made off this trumped-up energy shortage?

(*DISTRICT MANAGER tries to protest*)

SCOOP. Funny the way it goes. Everytime the company's profit rate drops, like a miracle, there's this shortage. Prices go up, company's profit rate goes up a hundred percent. The only shortage is in the customer's pocket.

DISTRICT MANAGER. The current energy shortage is real, Scoop. With the Arabs fouling up the supply process, crazy things are happening to the market. You're faulting the company for making money off it? That's what they're in business to do, just like you. Money's the name of the game. Secret storage tanks I know nothing about.

SCOOP. (*outrage getting the best of him*) Don't come on like some innocent bunny rabbit with me. I helped make some of the deliveries. Remember the guy who lifted with a scoop? That was me!

ASSISTANT DISTRICT MANAGER. We're not going to argue with you. If the company says there's a shortage, there's a shortage. They've got to have a little something on reserve.

SCOOP. (*furious*) A little? They got enough gas stored up to keep every car in this country running for as many years as I got birthdays. You watch the pumps out there read eight bucks a gallon—then there'll be plenty of gas and oil!

ASSISTANT DISTRICT MANAGER. You never fail to amaze me, Scoop. You know more things than an encyclopedia. Hell, you ought to write an encylcopedia—call it "The Scoop!"

(*ASSISTANT MANAGER gets out a notebook*)

DISTRICT MANAGER. This is getting us nowhere. What the oil companies do is their business.

ASSISTANT DISTRICT MANAGER. It's your business we're talking about. (*tears off a form and hands it to SCOOP*) We understand you've been watering down your gas.

(*Silence. This hits hard.*)

SCOOP. Considering the quality of the gas you guys give me, that's like trying to water down the Atlantic Ocean.

ASSISTANT DISTRICT MANAGER. (*starting to leave*) Look Scoop, be careful, okay? We're on your side. (*like a buddy*) Hell, I had a station myself 'til I got eased out. If the company hadn't had this job for me, I'd be out flatter than a pancake, like a hundred other guys I know. We're just sent to tell you the situation looks bleak.

DISTRICT MANAGER. The company appreciates all you've done.

SCOOP. (*still numb*) All I done! I was top sales for three straight years. I got a goddamned brass plaque to prove it.

ASSISTANT DISTRICT MANAGER. You're good at sales, Scoop, but like you said, you can't create miracles. You can't sell what you don't have.

DISTRICT MANAGER. Now nothing's going to happen right away, but if I were you, within a month or so, I'd try finding myself another job.

SCOOP. (*numb*) They want to push me out and automate this place, don't they? No people, no payroll, just profits.

DISTRICT MANAGER. You got to admit, being a smart businessman yourself, self-service stations make more money.

ASSISTANT DISTRICT MANAGER. Just like you and me, Scoop, the company's always looking for ways of making more money.

DISTRICT MANAGER. (*asking for understanding*) Can't blame them for doing what they do. Can't blame a cat for killing birds. (*starting small talk*) By the way, I ran into that brother of yours the other day. He's going right to the top at Allied Chemical, eh?

SCOOP. Right to the top.

ASSISTANT DISTRICT MANAGER. (*continuing small talk*) How's Biddie, by the way?

SCOOP. (*dry as a bone*) Didn't you hear? She died. She found some gas for sixty cents a gallon and got so excited, after she filled the tank, she drank another five gallons.

ASSISTANT DISTRICT MANAGER. (*laughing*) You had me believing you for a minute. (*exits*)

DISTRICT MANAGER. (*returning to slap SCOOP jovially on the back*) You got humor. That's why you're such a good salesman: you got humor.

SCOOP. I ain't laughin' much anymore.

DISTRICT MANAGER. Cheer up. Things will get better. (*exits*)

SCOOP. For who? (*louder and angrier*) For who? (*sings*)

Two Classes of People

There are only two classes of people
Those who own, those who work for them.
There are only two classes of people
Those who own, those who labor in boredom.

Understand when I say own,
I don't mean a telephone,
Or an over-taxed house on a pot-holed road
On a twenty-year loan.

By economic deduction, it's the means of production,
Own the means of production, own the means to our end.
Our future is dire,
Our soul is for hire.

There are only two classes of people
Those who own, those who work for them.
There are only two classes of people
Those who own, those who labor in boredom.

They can own plenty of things that I lack
But not the sweat off my back.
My labor is mine and what my labor brings;
I won't play serf to their king.

By economic deduction, it's the means of production,
Own the means of production, own the means to our end.
Our future is dire,
Our soul is for hire.

There are only two classes of people
Those who own, those who work for them.
There are only two classes of people
Those who own, those who labor in boredom.

(*LYLE enters SCOOP'S gas station*)

LYLE. I saw the sign out front on the Chevy, twenty-nine, ninety-five. That price for the gas only or does the car come with it?

SCOOP. Ask the computerized cash register they're hiring to take my place.

LYLE. Does it look anything like the juke-box that's replacing me? You're not kidding are you? Jerkowitz give you the business?

SCOOP. He took the business.

LYLE. How long you got?

SCOOP. A month—maybe less.

LYLE. It's a good thing we bought all that gold, Scoop—got all that bullion stashed away.

SCOOP. (*going along with the dry humor*) My financial advisor told me to liquidate my gold and invest in toilet paper. I told him he was full of it.

LYLE. How about your brother—can't he tide you over?

SCOOP. (*covering up*) Nah, he would if he could, but he's got a family and all, you know. Biddie's got a job interview today. If she gets lucky, she'll throw a sandwich my way.

LYLE. (*sensing his chance*) I got some more details from Danny. You know that warehouse out by Monsanto? We go there, pick up some barrels, throw them in a truck, dump them a few miles out of town, we get a nice piece of change.

SCOOP. (*moving away in silence, visibly wrestling with the idea*) I know what's in them barrels—some kind of chemical waste, right? I've been hearing about this job. I don't know. I've never done anything like that before, you know? Always left the heavy criminal stuff to the government. (*silence, then...*) No, I don't think so. I'll keep my head above water somehow. I got my disability coming in.

LYLE. You can't survive on disability.

SCOOP. Whatta you mean, I can't survive? All I got to do is cut down my eating to once a week.

LYLE. (*getting up to leave*) Well, Scoop, if you don't want what Danny's offering, there is one other way out for us.

SCOOP. What's that?

LYLE. The bridge. (*exits*)

(*SCOOP is left alone*)

CUSTOMER. (*sound of bell offstage at the gas pumps*) Hey buddy, what's the highest octane you got?

SCOOP. We like to keep it right around 20. (*Exits. Lights cross-fade from one area to another.*)

Scene 3. "Barrelhouse"

(*Immediately phone rings at the Barrelhouse. Enter DOTTIE and LYLE racing each other to the phone. DOTTIE gets there first. LYLE signals, demanding the phone.*)

DOTTIE. (*into phone*) Barrelhouse.

CONTACT. Lyle Fine.

DOTTIE. (*to LYLE*) You get more calls than my bookie. (*goes back to bar, just within earshot*)

LYLE. (*into phone, not wanting DOTTIE to hear.*) Yeah.

CONTACT. Be waiting at the turnstile at the Bell Street entrance in half an hour.

LYLE. I got to work tonight.

CONTACT. You want to *keep* working, be there in half an hour.

LYLE. Listen, you going to tell me anything more about this job, like do I bring a truck, or...?

CONTACT. We provide the truck. We don't want you to rent a piece of junk. Some of those barrels leak a little. Just get yourself a couple of helpers with gloves.

LYLE. All right, I'll meet you in half an hour. (*hangs up*)

DOTTIE. That about your PTA meeting?

LYLE. As a matter of fact, it was. You may not know this, Dottie, but I happen to be a lifetime member of the Pool-Player's Theological Association. Would you pour me a drink, please?

(*DOTTIE turns to pour the drink allowing LYLE to slip out on the run*)

DOTTIE. I'll pour you a drink and then we're gonna have a little chat about Danny Morrison—(*seeing LYLE is not there*) LYLE?! LYLE!!

(*Phone rings, DOTTIE moves to answer it. Blackout. Then immediately the blinking light indicating a subway train.*)

Scene 4. "Subway Station"

(*Inside subway station. Lights flash intermittently with sound of subway train coming into station. CONTACT is seen waiting. As LYLE runs in, CONTACT slips out of sight.*)

LYLE. (*looking around*) Where the hell is this guy?

CONTACT. Relax, Lyle. I'm right here.

LYLE. Where are you? (*he looks around*)

CONTACT. Just watch the trains. You don't see me. (*reappearing*)

LYLE. (*looking at train*) I want to thank you for the tip. That is a very nice train.

CONTACT. Let's make this quick. Are you in or out?

LYLE. Well, I don't know so soon—First, I got to bring the information to my board of directors, and they'll have to review the findings—

CONTACT. (*interrupting, contemptuous*) Look, Hot Lips, there's plenty of money to be made here for smart people and nothing for wise guys, you understand?

LYLE. Okay, okay, so I need the dough. But what's all this hush-hush bullshit?

CONTACT. What, I got to draw you a picture? The Feds have the entire waste-disposal business tied up in red tape, so they don't have to deal with the problem. So by the time we get through all the legal bullshit, we got millions of barrels piled up around our ass, with thousands of independent truckers looking for hauls. The Feds look the other way, we do the dirty work for them. We're forced to dump the stuff in the morning before the sun comes up, using whatever I.T.A.'s we select on the black market. That's where you come in.

LYLE. Suppose we get caught?

CONTACT. They don't want to catch you. Like I said, no one knows what to do with the stuff; so the cops have blinders on.

LYLE. Yeah, but if we do get caught, we pay the fine!

CONTACT. Relax! We'll pay the fine for you.

LYLE. (starting to turn around) So where do I make the pick-up?

CONTACT. (disappearing) Watch the trains, Lyle!

LYLE. Oh, I almost forgot. (train passes) I want to thank you for reminding me. That is one very interesting choo-choo.

CONTACT. (reappears and starts approaching LYLE from behind) Watch it then. You get twenty dollars a barrel, as many as you can handle. Dumpsite is given out when you show up to receive the delivery. (at LYLE'S back now, he hands him money) Here's twenty bucks. Buy lunch tomorrow. I want you to make your decision on a full stomach.

LYLE. (reluctantly taking the money) So when do I have to confirm the deal?

CONTACT. (backing away) Someone will stop by your bar day after tomorrow. When he walks by the piano and offers you a number, you nod "yes" or "no." You'll hear from us.

LYLE. That's the usual nod, right? You don't want me to stand on my head and do it with my feet or nothing?

CONTACT. You're a real funny guy, Lyle. (He exits. But LYLE is unaware of it.)

LYLE. By the way, are any of these chemicals dangerous? (the train comes and LYLE tries to joke to cover his nervousness) Wait don't tell me now. I don't want to miss out. (train passes) Like I said, are any of these chemicals dangerous? (there is no response) Are you back there? Hey, where are you? Hey! Hey!

(*LYLE runs off. Blackout. Then lights come up on another area.*)

Scene 5. *"Biddie's Job Interview"*

BIDDIE. (*offstage*) Is this Freeze-Dried Funeral Florists, Inc.?

OFFSTAGE RECEPTIONIST. Yes, right through that door for the interview.

BIDDIE. Thank you. (*she enters to muzak, looks around, bewildered at finding no one*) Hello? Hello? Anybody here? Is this the interview place? I'm applying for the job as cashier, and the woman out there said to come in here and be interviewed.

COMPUTER. Hello. Please make yourself comfortable.

BIDDIE. (*dumbfounded*) What is this, some kind of practical joke? You got talking walls or something?

COMPUTER. Please do not be alarmed by the automatic hire-a-clerk.

BIDDIE. (*sotto voce*) My God! I don't believe it!

COMPUTER. The interview will now begin. Listen closely to the questions. Your ability to absorb detail quickly and accurately will tell us a great deal about you.

BIDDIE. I gotta be dreaming this. It's gotta be those chocolate doughnuts I ate last night.

COMPUTER. What is your name?

BIDDIE. Biddie Gazinski, I think.

COMPUTER. Last name first.

BIDDIE. (*stutters*) Why? Bazinsky Giddy—

COMPUTER. What is your social security number?

BIDDIE. (*fumbling in pockets to find card*) Oh, just a minute, it's four-nine-six-six-five—

COMPUTER. (*the pre-timed machine cuts her off*) Do you own your own home?

BIDDIE. Does a chicken have lips?

COMPUTER. Do you have any credit references?

BIDDIE. I never even had any credit. Look, I ain't applying to be economic advisor to the president—though God knows he could use one. I just want the job of cashier, and it's the job I done in the past so I know I can do it now. If you'll give me a cash register I'll show ya. (*dawning awareness*) I'm probably *talking* to a cash register.

COMPUTER. What was the last educational level you successfully completed?

BIDDIE. Moron, same as you.

COMPUTER. How old are you?

BIDDIE. Too old for this.

COMPUTER. What was the last job you held?

BIDDIE. (*Dead-on seriousness*) I was a gunrunner for the Apaches.

COMPUTER. Why did you leave that job?

BIDDIE. They made it a civil service appointment.

COMPUTER. Why do you want this job?

BIDDIE. Beats the shit out of me.

COMPUTER. What makes you qualified for this job?

BIDDIE. World travel, social leadership, and I'm kinky.

COMPUTER. You will now be given a series of simple multiple choice questions. Try and relax and enjoy these questions.

BIDDIE. You try and relax and enjoy the answers, Tootsie.

COMPUTER. I would rather (a) add a column of figures (b) read poetry (c) fix a clock.

BIDDIE. (*pretending to consider the options*) Lemme see. My answer is "no."

COMPUTER. I would rather (a) cook a meal (b) mow the grass (c) fix a car. I would rather (a) add (b) subtract (c) multiply.

BIDDIE. (*speaking over the machine*) All right, Machine, before I answer any more questions, I got one for you. You know what this is? (*holds up five fingers of one hand*) Five of these! (*BIDDIE clenches four of her fingers, effectively giving the computer the remaining finger. She begins singing.*)

> *Automation*
> I've bundled and bagged
> Worked the line
> Picked grapes for my Lady's wine.
>
> I've sold shoes
> Drove a truck
> Cut grass to make a buck.

(*Chorus begins chanting "Automation, Automation," then sings chorus while BIDDIE speaks the words over song*)

CHORUS.   The cutting machine with its deadly edge
           Pushes me right out to the ledge.
           Tells me to jump from here to nowhere,
           Tells me to jump from here to nowhere.

BIDDIE.   I've waited tables
           Typed letters
           Washed the floor for my betters.

           Ask me, I've done it all
           No job too large or small
           So why should I be out of work
           Until I die?

(*CHORUS chants "Automation, Automation," then sings*)

CHORUS.   Automation's the word they use
           It's good as any for the abuse
           Of turning out the old
           Of turning blood into gold!

(*BIDDIE exits in proud anger. As VOICE starts again, BIDDIE holds up five fingers.*)

COMPUTER. Will the next applicant please come in.

(*lights cross-fade to reveal the bar*)

Scene 6. "The Barrelhouse"

(*The Barrelhouse. DOTTIE brings in table, chairs and sets up bar. LYLE runs in out of breath. Barrelhouse is playing the Barrelhouse theme.*)

DOTTIE.   Where have you been? Barrelhouse had to play the last two sets by himself.

LYLE.   Just out doing something honest for a change, Dottie.

DOTTIE.   The strange phone calls I've been taking for you lately, I doubt it. By the way, the same voice that caused your disappearing act, called again. Said he'd be late.

LYLE.   Late for what? He must've had the wrong number.

DOTTIE.   The number he had was correct.

LYLE. How do you know?

DOTTIE. I'm Jewish.

LYLE. Dottie, maybe you don't have to know about everything I'm doing.

DOTTIE. Whatever you're doing I should not know about is *exactly* what I should know about.

(*BIDDIE and SCOOP enter*)

Who died? I ain't seen gloomier mugs since that police line-up when I pretended not to recognize Lyle.

SCOOP. Funny we should look that way, it's been a spectacular week.

BIDDIE. Spectacular.

LYLE. Yeah, but behind every cloud...

BIDDIE. There's a tornado.

DOTTIE. What'll you have?

BIDDIE. Whatever you've got.

LYLE. (*definitively*) The way thing's been going for us, I trust you're ready to talk sense now.

BIDDIE. For us? For the whole damn country!

SCOOP. Anyone who ain't crazy these days just ain't thinking.

LYLE. Cut the wise talk and listen.

(*DOTTIE is delivering drinks to the table*)

Dottie, what are you doing here?

DOTTIE. Whatta you mean what am I doing here? I work here.

LYLE. Well, go to the pool room and wait for your cue.

DOTTIE. Yer Mother! Come on Barrelhouse, I'll spot you five for a game. (*Cooly exits. Music stops.*)

BIDDIE. What's up you don't want Dottie to know about?

LYLE. (*ignoring her*) All right, the job is on for tomorrow night. All we need is a truck and some gloves. (*to BIDDIE*) You can handle a big one, right?

BIDDIE. The truck ain't been built I can't drive.

LYLE. We take the truck out for a little spin and we're in the chips.

BIDDIE. (*Rising from the table. This sounds too easy.*) I don't know what Danny's got up his sleeve, but I ain't robbing no bank. I'm just a small-time, honest crook. I don't want nothing to do with robbing no bank—unless it's absolutely safe.

LYLE. Just sit down. We don't rob a bank. The bank is probably a partner in this operation.

BIDDIE. *Me* do something with a bank? This has got to be crookeder than a pig's tail. Just a minute, I get to check this out with my Sunday School teacher. (*goes over to ask question in SCOOP'S ear*) It's all right what I said, "pig's tail"? Shouldn't be "snail's ear" or something?

LYLE. (*firmly*) Will you listen to me. We get some barrels, put them in a truck, dump them a few miles out of town. We get twenty dollars a barrel.

BIDDIE. (*backing up*) What's in them barrels? Dead bodies?

LYLE. Chemical waste.

BIDDIE. (*not wanting to deal with it*) Uh, Scoop, how about a game of blackjack?

(*SCOOP gets out cards and deals a hand*)

LYLE. (*walking angrily back to piano*) I'm not going to talk you two into this. This place is going to fill up pretty soon; we haven't got much time. If you want to throw away our one chance to make a buck, that's fine with me. I don't feel any better about it than you do, but what's our option, if we want to eat, that is? (*slams fist against piano*) Look. We do one job. We don't, you can bet somebody else will. (*begins to play "It's a Cold Winter"*)

SCOOP. (*silence then, to BIDDIE, trying to justify the inevitable*) You know. Lyle's right. We don't, somebody else will. I mean the stuff's just sitting there and sooner or later someone will dump it. Hell, even if it just sits there, it's as dangerous as if it was dumped. The danger's in the stuff being there in the first place, not where we dump it, right?

BIDDIE. (*staring at him as she seriously considers what she does not want to consider*) Dottie, bring me a drink!

DOTTIE. (*from offstage*) What?

BIDDIE. Come here!

LYLE. I don't want Dottie to know about this, okay?

DOTTIE. (*coming on stage, talking to customers in the poolroom*) Somebody needs me. Be with you in a minute.

LYLE. (*as she enters*) Dottie, will you get out of here?

DOTTIE. (*turning to leave*) Yer Father! (*exits*)

SCOOP. You know who I'm thinking about?

LYLE. Yeah, I know. Ernie Zimmerman.

SCOOP. He died last week. Got cancer from working with them chemicals over at Carlyle Van Han.

BIDDIE. (*trying to quell her anxiety*) Yeah, but they was working around where all the fumes was concentrated. Out in the open the air would dilute 'em—wouldn't it?

LYLE. *(feeling things may be going his way)* Stands to reason what Biddie said. Air dilutes them.

SCOOP. *(knowing the die has been cast)* Dottie, bring me a drink.

DOTTIE. *(enters)* Beer?

BIDDIE. Bourbon.

SCOOP. Double.

LYLE. Bring the bottle from out back.

(DOTTIE exits)

BIDDIE. *(whispering, angry)* The crazy thing is, we should be sitting here worrying. How come the people who manufactured it in the first place ain't bustin' their hump to get rid of it safe?!

LYLE. That's what I mean. It doesn't bother them.

(DOTTIE enters with the bottle they requested. THEY wait until she leaves to resume their discussion.)

BIDDIE. How many barrels could we get in the truck, Scoop?

SCOOP. Depends on the truck. They probably got one that carries forty to fifty, right Lyle?

(BIDDIE gets out a calculator and starts to figure)

LYLE. Yeah, there's 287 barrels, that would take six or seven trips. I figure we would start tomorrow night around 9:00 and finish before the sun comes up.

BIDDIE. *(completing her calculation)* 287 barrels at twenty dollars a barrel, that's 5,740 dollars.

SCOOP. Where'd you get that calculator?

BIDDIE. My last job, kind of like severance pay. Either I could turn my back and get a kick in the ass, or the boss could turn his and I get a calculator. I chose his back and...*(hits calculator twice)*

LYLE. You two think it over, okay? I'm not pushing. You want it, it's yours. Otherwise I suppose we could learn to live on ice-cream wrappers and beer cans.

CHORUS.   *(sings from offstage)*
           It's a cold winter
           That's coming our way.

BIDDIE. What are you thinking?

SCOOP. I ain't thinking.

BIDDIE. You're thinking we got to do it.

SCOOP. You askin' a question or giving an answer?

BIDDIE. I'm Norwegian and Polish. I do both at once.

CHORUS.   (*sings from offstage*)
           We won't make it through
           Unless we turn a trick today.

SCOOP. What should we do?

BIDDIE. Don't ask unless you really want to know.

SCOOP. You can drive any truck?

BIDDIE. Yep.

SCOOP. I hear it gets into water, causes cancer and stuff. Don't that bother you?

BIDDIE. The question is, did it bother the people who made it?

SCOOP. Yeah, that's the question.

BIDDIE. Besides, I've been reading that it ain't as dangerous as they're making it out to be. I mean it ain't all *that* dangerous.

SCOOP. Yeah, my brother works with chemicals all the time.

(*CHORUS sings offstage, underscoring rest of the dialogue in the scene*)

CHORUS.   It's a cold winter
           That's coming our way.
           We won't make it through
           Unless we turn a trick today.

           It's a cold winter
           That's coming our way.
           We won't make it through
           Unless we turn a trick today.

           Won't make it through
           Unless we turn a trick today.
           Won't make it through
           Unless we turn a trick today.

BIDDIE. I mean, if it was that dangerous they wouldn't dump it. They've got kids growing up too, right? They wouldn't do something to kill their own kids.

SCOOP. They wouldn't kill their own kids. Even the Rockefellers ain't that bad.

BIDDIE. What are the odds?

SCOOP. You've got a calculator, you figure it out. (*exits*)

(*CHORUS sings last line*)

BIDDIE. (*Goes to door, stops. Turns to LYLE.*) Tell them a ten-wheeler with a lift-back will be best for the job.

(*fast blackout*)

END OF ACT I

Act II

Scene 1. "The Connection"

(*The stage is black. Sound of a truck motor is heard. A MAN is gesturing with flashlight and calling loudly to drivers.*)

MAN. All right, it's loaded now. Here's the map. Keep your lights out 'til. you hit 294 and stay away from the Interstates. Now move it out. Come on, move it out!

(*CHORUS sings offstage*)

CHORUS.   It's a cold winter
          That's coming our way
          We won't make it through
          Unless we turn a trick today.

(*Lights come up. BIDDIE, SCOOP, and LYLE are discovered in the truck. BIDDIE is driving, cigar in mouth. SCOOP and LYLE are studying the map. They are wearing boots, gloves and outdoor work clothes. Offstage singing continues as they drive.*)

CHORUS.   Take what you can get
          When you can get it.
          Time is running out
          So bag your limit.
          Tomorrow is too fine a word.
          It's for the rich
          Or haven't you heard.

(*Dialogue begins. All are extremely agitated. Under the dialogue the offstage singing continues, low, tense, relentless.*)

LYLE. Maybe we should've brought face masks or something.

479

SCOOP. Did you put batteries in the flashlight?

BIDDIE. No, I filled it with poker chips.

SCOOP. (*gesturing to something on the road*) Watch out!

BIDDIE. (*swerves*) I saw it.

SCOOP. Biddie, we don't want to go so fast. We'll spill the barrels all over the highway.

CHORUS.   It's a cold winter
           That's comin' our way
           We won't make it through
           Unless we turn a trick today.

           It's a cold winter
           That's comin' our way
           We won't make it through
           Unless we turn a trick
           Won't make it through
           Unless we turn a trick
           Won't make it through
           Unless we turn a trick today.

           Guys at the top
           Stack the deck, make the law.
           The deal we get
           Is a deal that's raw.

           Get the cast-offs
           Crumbs from the table,
           Gobble them up
           While we're still able.

BIDDIE. There's a pheasant—did you see it?

SCOOP. Getting close to the dump, huh?

LYLE. Yeah. Our turn's coming up right here.

CHORUS.   It's a cold winter
           That's coming our way.
           We won't make it through
           Unless we turn a trick today.

(BIDDIE makes the turn. Blackout. CHORUS continues to sing.)

> It's a cold winter
> That's coming our way.
> We won't make it through
> Unless we turn a trick...

(Abruptly, before completion of the phrase, song ends, followed immediately by SCOOP'S shout.)

Scene 2. "The Dumpsite"

(Beam of flashlight punctuates the silence. The TRIO has arrived at the dumpsite. SCOOP is the first to appear, finding his way in the dark with a flashlight. There is a terrible edginess throughout this entire scene.)

SCOOP. Biddie!

BIDDIE. *(from offstage)* Yeah?

SCOOP. Turn on the headlights!

BIDDIE. What?

SCOOP. The headlights!

(She turns them on. Two rays of light cut through the darkness.)

LYLE. *(enters breathless with shovel)* Tell her to turn the engine off. The ground's too rough. We'd better carry the stuff the rest of the way.

LYLE. *You* tell Biddie. It's not your leg you're missing, it's your arm.

BIDDIE. *(entering breathless)* I figured the truck would never make it, so I turned the engine off and came down. You guys better carry the barrels the rest of the way.

SCOOP. Yeah, that's what I was...*(unable to continue, looks around, dazed)*

BIDDIE. That's what you was *what? (following his look, then snarling at him)* Finish your sentence! You never finish anything.

SCOOP. *(awed)* God, there's something spooky about this place. I mean we're out in the country and all, but there's not a sound, not a cricket, not an owl...nothing.

BIDDIE. Yeah. Sounds like death.

LYLE. How do you know how death sounds?

BIDDIE. I know.

SCOOP. Yeah? How does it sound?

BIDDIE. Like this place.

LYLE. Enough of these spooky tunes! Let's move some of this stuff and get digging. Come on, let's move!

(*LYLE and SCOOP start to move barrels*)

SCOOP. A lot of stuff's been dumped here already. The companies have dumped enough to poison the whole damned country if these barrels spring a leak, and by the looks of them if they don't, it'll be a miracle.

LYLE. (*anger to cover fear*) What's that to us? You the tour guide or something? What's a little more where a lot is already? Now give me that flashlight and get to work.

(*Exits to get barrels. SCOOP starts to dig.*)

BIDDIE. (*frantic*) You heard him! Get to work.

SCOOP. (*after a minute of digging*) Oh my God, will you look at that!

BIDDIE. What? Where?

SCOOP. Biddie, you better not.

BIDDIE. (*seeing the horrible graveyard*) Oh no. It's a bird, a dead bird.

SCOOP. Not just one of them. Right under the topsoil over these barrels. There's hundreds of them. Rabbits and mice, too. All dead.

LYLE. (*entering over the platform with a barrel, spying the two of them immobilized*) Will you two get moving? (*then sensing something*) What's wrong?

BIDDIE. This stuff killed the animals, the birds, everything.

LYLE. (*false bravura*) Well, let's get moving, or we'll look just like them.

(*SCOOP sticks shovel in dirt and goes to help LYLE*)

BIDDIE. (*barely audible*) Oh my God. (*puts her head down in misery, then stiffens*) Here's one still alive! I'm gonna take it home and get it well. You guys dump the stuff! I'm gonna look after Mexico.

SCOOP. You named it already.

BIDDIE. Yeah I named it, where I'm gonna live once we get the money from this rotten job. I'm gonna pack up my family and move to Mexico. In Mexico I'm going to get me some live animals, 'cause there they let you have all you want.

SCOOP. How do you know that?

BIDDIE. How do you know any different?

LYLE. Come on, Scoop! Leave Biddie with the bird. Get that shovel and let's bury this stuff.

SCOOP. (*shaken, pulls the shovel out of the dirt*) Jesus! The shovel. Will you look at the shovel? I had it stuck in the dirt over here, and it's changing color. I mean the edge of it. It's changed color.

BIDDIE. (*covering bird protectively*) Don't look, Mexico.

SCOOP. Jesus!

LYLE. (*carrying barrels, trying to ignore the mounting horror*) Will you get back to work? (*suddenly arrested in his own work*) Hey, look at this barrel. It's not like the other ones. It's got some kind of graffiti on it. This thing right here—look at this. Like on air-raid shelters, you know? Air-raid graffiti.

SCOOP. (*mounting terror as he stoops to examine the barrel*) No, no, not air-raid shelters. I seen that sign someplace else.

BIDDIE. (*rising fear*) You always gotta know everything.

SCOOP. I tell you, I seen it—in the papers.

BIDDIE. The racing form?

SCOOP. No, idiot, I don't remember, I don't know exactly. I seen that sign and it wasn't on no air-raid shelter.

LYLE. (*a little wild*) Will you stop this? You're making everything sound so spooky. You're driving me nuts!

BIDDIE. (*beginning to look for a way out of this*) I've been thinking, with this place being so full and all, there ain't enough room for our load, and there ain't enough top-dirt to cover it, and the shovel wouldn't last long anyway...

SCOOP. So we don't cover it.

BIDDIE. But that was the deal, right? We dump the stuff and cover it with top dirt?

LYLE. She's right, Scoop. We wouldn't get paid at all if we was to dump the stuff and not cover it.

SCOOP. Look, it's you got us this rotten deal. I ain't going to play evil honcho here. You don't want to dump the stuff, we don't dump it. Idiot! Coward!

BIDDIE. Neither of us...did either of us say that?

LYLE. No! It's just that we...

BIDDIE. We just want to find a place, you know, where we can do the job proper!

SCOOP. While we've been standing here talking, we're being poisoned with this stuff. It's like twelve x-rays an hour or something.

LYLE. Chemical waste don't radiate you to death, that's nuclear waste. Even I know that.

SCOOP. That's it!!!

BIDDIE. (*sharp*) That's what?

SCOOP. (*stuttering*)That grraff...

BIDDIE. (*urgent*) What? (*screaming as SCOOP continues to stutter*) That's what, you stuttering son-of-a-bitch! You got one arm, you can't talk?

SCOOP. ...graffiti means nuclear waste! (*all three run back in total horror and stare at the barrels. They are immobilized.*)

BIDDIE. There's chemical *and* nuclear? This place is crawling with death.

SCOOP. Let's do something. I don't want to stand around here being killed, and I don't care if I'm poisoned to death or radiated to death, right? I don't want to stand around here being killed while you two go soft.

BIDDIE. (*hysterical*) Soft! You want me to do it? Let's dump. Come on Lyle, I've got enough age left in me to out-carry a cripple!

SCOOP. I didn't say I didn't agree with you!

BIDDIE. So who's soft, you poached egg!

LYLE. (*getting desperate*) Look, no one's soft. Let's do it! It's not our fault; it's the companies made this stuff in the first place, and they're making a lot more whether we dump it or not.

SCOOP. (*the first to confirm what they all feel*) I don't want to dump it.

BIDDIE. So what do we do? Murder the sonsa bitches?

LYLE. Look, we don't dump it, it's here; we dump it, it's still here, and what's more, they're making more!

BIDDIE. (*yelling and shoving LYLE, who doesn't move*) So dump! DUMP! Big guy! (*to her bird*) Come on, Mexico, let's find Pancho Villa and get us a revolution going.

SCOOP. Pancho Villa's dead.

BIDDIE. Not the way I heard it.

LYLE. (*trying to get control*) So what are we going to do? We gonna unload this stuff or what?

BIDDIE. (*with finality*) Mexico says no.

(*THEY slowly turn and look at the barrels*)

LYLE. Well, I'll tell you what we should do. Gift wrap the stuff and send it back to the guys who made it.

SCOOP. Let their wife and kiddies open it up for breakfast; then put armed guards around the house so no one can get out.

BIDDIE. (*taking a deep breath and deciding*) Here's what we do, it's clear. (*screaming*) Scoop, will you stop that?!

SCOOP. I'm just breathing!

BIDDIE. Well don't! It makes me nervous! Here's what we do. We take the barrels back, we tell them the place was surrounded by cop cars—we don't know why or nothing, but we couldn't dump the stuff with the fuzz all around.

SCOOP. (*starting to exit with BIDDIE and LYLE eagerly following*) Brilliant! Let's get the hell out of here. For an old boot, you're pretty smart.

BIDDIE. Aw shucks, I just seem smart to a cripple.

LYLE. (*stops suddenly*) Did you hear something?

SCOOP. (*frantic*) Only the sound of you asking me if I heard something!

BIDDIE. (*equally frantic*) Well, I heard it too! His hearing went when his arm did. Let's get out of here! This place is lovely and all, but I had in mind something with an ocean view.

SCOOP. (*looking out*) Look at that. That sign there, McDonald Construction Company. Look at that. What does that say, Lyle?

BIDDIE. (*reading it all too clearly*) Oh my God.

LYLE. "Future site of the Riverside Nursing Home." They're going to put old people right next to this dump.

BIDDIE. My God...old people.

(*LYLE and BIDDIE exit*)

SCOOP. Some things just ain't worth making a buck.

(*sound of truck motor*)

LYLE. Bus is leaving.

(*SCOOP exits*)

(*from offstage*) Turn around, Biddie and let's get the hell out of here!

(*Truck lights swing around and sound of truck motor disappears as two CHILDREN enter the dumping ground dressed to play Indians. The scene is almost surreal in its simplicity.*)

GIRL. Come on! Let's play. (*starts motion of Indian dance*)

BOY. (*sensing something*) I don't want to play here. It smells bad.

GIRL. Come on! We can play Indians here.

(*BOY joins the dance for a moment*)

BOY. (*stopping*) It smells awful here! Let's go to the playground.

GIRL. (*continues to chant and dance*) No. Woo, woo, woo, woo, woo, woo...

BOY. (*upset*) Let's go down to the playground!

GIRL. Oh all right! But we'll take these barrels for teepees.

BOY. (*agrees to anything just so they will leave.*) We can roll them. It's downhill all the way to the playground.

(*THEY tip barrels over and roll them away as they continue their chant. Blackout*)

BOY AND GIRL. Woo woo woo...

Scene 3. "The Long Way Back"

CHORUS.   It's a cold winter that's coming our way.
            We won't make it through
            Unless we turn a trick today.

(*Light comes up on the truck. CHORUS sings verse and chorus of "Take What You Can Get" under the truck dialogue. BIDDIE, LYLE and SCOOP are driving the truck back to the pickup site.*)

LYLE. I'm sorry I got you guys into this. We're probably going to get sick, we're gonna have to burn our clothes; and I don't even have any clothes to burn. (*rambling, not at all aware of what he is saying*)

SCOOP. Hey, it's all right. We were broke; you were trying to help.

LYLE. It's one thing to hustle a job in the alley. It's something else to kill people.

SCOOP. We may be losers but we ain't killers.

BIDDIE. We ain't losers either. We're like any other guy that's been pushed out of his job in a country that don't care two cents about us.

SCOOP. We ain't alone. We ain't killers. But we're hungry.

LYLE. If we get out of this in one piece, we can worry about eating.

BIDDIE. What's this "we," paleface?

LYLE. Don't worry. I didn't give them your names. It's me they're gonna be looking for.

SCOOP. We ain't going to leave you alone, Lyle. Whatever hole you hide in, me and Biddie'll be right there beside you.

BIDDIE. (*a moment's silence*) Lyle, I've been thinking. When we get back, should we tell people about that place?

SCOOP. There's nothing you, me and a trumpet player can do. Those illegal chemical dumps are all over the country.

LYLE. Sorry to mention this, but who's going to talk to the guy when we bring this stuff back?

(*THEY all ponder this dilemma*)

SCOOP. Biddie should. They won't beat up a woman—I don't think.

BIDDIE. The only time a man ever admits a woman can do something better than him is when he'll get his ass kicked if he does it.

SCOOP. They'll believe Biddie, won't they?

LYLE. (*seeing the pickup site ahead*) We're about to find out.

(*BIDDIE stops the truck. LYLE exits.*)

SCOOP. Biddie, you don't have to talk to them.

BIDDIE. Get out of here, idiot.

SCOOP. Okay, okay, but...but just relax and act natural. Tell them the fuzz was all around. Whatever you do, don't panic and run. We'll be waiting in the ditch right outside the gate.

(*SCOOP exits. BIDDIE drives the truck a little further, then stops, rolls down the truck window and leans out. A flashlight shines on her.*)

HARRY. What are you doing here?

BIDDIE. (*yelling back at him*) We brought back the barrels.

HARRY. You brought back the barrels!

BIDDIE. That Lyle Fine was supposed to dump.

HARRY. Was *supposed* to? What happened?

BIDDIE. Well, we got there and the fuzz was all around, and...

(*BIDDIE turns off truck lights, scrambles out of the truck and runs for her life. All is dark except for the flashlights of the night watchmen at the pickup site.*)

HARRY. Ed, get your ass out here! (*calling to BIDDIE*) Wait a minute. (*back to ED*)

ED. I can't see.

HARRY. Get out here! (*calling to departed BIDDIE*) Wait a minute will you! God, look at that old bag run! We ought to enter her in the Olympics.

Scene 4. "Biddie's Room"

(*BIDDIE enters her room, panting and clutching her stuffed animals. She sets them down, takes off her gloves. She is in near tears. She talks and answers herself in the animals' voices.*)

BIDDIE. You've always been proud of your mother, ain't you? Well, you ain't gonna be proud of her after what she done tonight.

BOWPEEP. Aw Biddie, you're the best.

BIDDIE. No, I ain't. Take my word for it, I ain't. (*picks up Bow Peep*) You know, I had a present for you but I lost it.

BOW PEEP. Was it a bone?

BIDDIE. (*picking up Big Phant, holding and rocking both animals*) No. It was a little bird named Mexico. She was terrible sick, and I thought we could all pitch in and get her right as rain again, so she could be company for you while I was out hustling.

BOUNCER. We gotta go find her.

BIDDIE. (*very still*) I lost her where there's no finding her. And that ain't the half of it. Grandmas and grandpas are gonna die too, just like Mexico. Animals and old people don't count for much any more. (*voice becoming low and fierce*) I'm going to tell you a story, and I want you to listen careful so's you can take care of yourself if anything should happen to old Biddie here. (*sings*)

Pistol Packin' Mama

When you feel like a hungry lion
Be smart as a fox.
Watch who's walking behind you
Always look behind rocks.
Crafty like a beaver, quick like a hare,
Or you'll end up on one leg,
The other in a snare.

Sparrow fakes a broken wing,
Lures the snake away.
The ways of the wild
Keep the wild world at bay.
Keep a tough old hoof ready under your rag,
Keep it sharp as claws
Hid in an old brown bag.

When on the far side of fifty
Look dead ahead my friend.
The view will not be pretty,
Old age ain't for sissies.

Lay low like the leopard
Get your dinner fast.
Pickings may be lean
Every scrap your last.
Hunt with the sun, dig in by night

Keep on the run,
Snarl, spit and bite

The wise old bear
Guards her winter's rest.
All the other animals
Stay away from her nest!
This country is a forest, a grizzly panorama,
To make your way through it,
Come out a pistol-packin' mama.

When on the far side of fifty
Look dead ahead my friend.
The view will not be pretty,
Old age ain't for sissies.

(at song's end BIDDIE exits talking to her animals)

BOW PEEP. Are we going to bed now?

BIDDIE. Yes.

BOUNCER. We'll go right to sleep.

BIDDIE. *(back to the present)* You better 'cause I got some business to attend to. No rest for the wicked.

(lights cross-fade to illuminate a small rectangle around the bar)

Scene 5. "The Barrelhouse"

(Early morning at the Barrelhouse. DOTTIE is cleaning the bar. SCOOP runs in out of breath.)

DOTTIE. Where's Lyle?

SCOOP. He's coming through the alley.

DOTTIE. Well, I'm not here at 5:45 a.m. waiting on the two of you. I just had to clean the place up.

(LYLE enters)

DOTTIE. It's all neat now. I think I'll set the tables.

(Phone rings. LYLE brushes past DOTTIE.)

LYLE. I'll get it. *(into phone)* Yeah?

DANNY. Lyle.

LYLE. Danny! (*a fast lie*) I've been trying to reach you all morning. You heard how it went out there, right—cops all around the place and everything. (*laughs nervously*) Your friends aren't going to break my legs or nothing, right?

DANNY. They're not happy. So there better not be any mistakes next time.

LYLE. (*sinking*) Next time?

DANNY. Tomorrow night.

LYLE. Tomorrow night? Damn, wouldn't you know, there's a White House dinner in my honor tomorrow night...

(*BIDDIE enters. SCOOP motions her to silence.*)

DANNY. Friend, in this organization, once you pull out with a load, you're on hand for as long as they need you. And they need you tomorrow night.

(*WAITER enters to set up the tables and is motioned to by DOTTIE to do it quickly and leave*)

LYLE. Uh, look, Danny, I'm...

(*phone goes dead as DANNY hangs up and LYLE does likewise*)

SCOOP. (*wanting to know what DANNY has said and gesturing the words out of him*) What?

LYLE. His friends will have another load for us tomorrow night.

SCOOP. We don't come through this time, we end up at the bottom of the Bayonne sewer system or in a can of chopped liver, right?

SCOOP. No, we're penny-ante. They might push us around a little, but the rough stuff they reserve for their better class of clientele.

SCOOP. I always knew being a bum had its fringe benefits.

BIDDIE. (*still thinking hard, not really listening to the others*) So, we go along with them, dump the nuclear stuff and glow in the dark for the rest of our lives, or we blow the whistle on them.

SCOOP. Who would listen?

LYLE. Exactly. So we get some money and get out of here fast.

SCOOP. How do we do that?

LYLE. That's what I like: a man with an intelligent question.

BIDDIE. If we were to—

SCOOP. (*cutting her off so as not to interrupt his thought*) Sssh! (*thinking hard*)

LYLE. You know who'd have an angle? Fat Eddie!

(*SCOOP cuts him off; he has an idea*)

DOTTIE. Why don't...(*SCOOP puts up hand to silence her*)

SCOOP. I got it! My brother.

(*ALL smile with intense relief, except BIDDIE*)

BIDDIE. Your brother. You think he'd help?

SCOOP. He's my brother!

BIDDIE. (*all innocence and dead-pan*) That's what I mean.

SCOOP. Biddie, he's into all this. He's in the top echelon at Allied Chemical. The lake in front of his summer house got polluted? He got the state to clean it up...for free. He knows all the angles.

LYLE. So he can help us make some money so we can get out of here 'til this thing blows over?

SCOOP. Make us some money? He made a pile!

BIDDIE. Scoop, you may not be as useless as I thought. (*grabs his shirt*) When are you gonna call him?

SCOOP. Uh—right now! Why not?

BIDDIE. This had better be our windfall.

SCOOP. (*begins to make his way to phone as others encourage him*) Maybe I can get him over here tonight, huh? I haven't seen him in over a year, you know, when I helped him move. He owes me one. (*Starts to dial. Then looks at BIDDIE who is at the foot of the stairs.*) This is a private call. Go out and gaze at the stars a minute will you?

(*BIDDIE exits*)

DOTTIE. Don't ask me to leave, I'm sensitive.

LYLE. You want me to go?

SCOOP. No, stay. (*on phone*) Hey, Ace! It's me! What do you mean "who is it?" Who else would call you Ace? (*listens*) Yeah, it's me. The one who grew up in the same house with you, had the same mother and father and all? (*listens*) No, I don't want any money. I've never asked you for money—may have thought about it, but I never asked. Listen, it's been a long time since we've seen each other. Yeah, yeah, I know how busy you've been, but this here's real important.

(*SCOOP continues a conversation the audience will not hear as LYLE sings*)

Windfall

LYLE.   I've played the red, I've played the black.
            I've lost it all, I'll win it back!
            A windfall's spinning her way to me.
            A windfall's spinning her way to me.

SCOOP. Great, tonight then. Down where Lyle plays, you remember. Yeah, that's the place. I'll wear a gas cap on my lapel so you'll recognize me. (*Laughs. Hangs up phone then sings.*)

SCOOP.
It's five card stud and a shot of gin.
My pair of aces is sure to win!
Bet it all, this is the day.
Play her close, as she lays.

CHORUS,
SCOOP,
and LYLE.
Place your bets on the winning team.
The stakes are high, the game is mean.
Soon we'll turn the winning card.
We warn you all, be on guard.

BIDDIE.
(*entering*)
You've heard of a diamond in the rough.
This one's old as she is tough!
She plays it lean and close to the belt.
She plays it lean and close to the belt.

LYLE.
The champion has challenged me.
Might knock me down to my knees.
I'm not a fighter we both know it well.
But the round is beginning, there's the bell.

BIDDIE,
LYLE,
SCOOP,
and
CHORUS.
Place your bets on the winning team.
The stakes are high, the game is mean.
Soon we'll turn the winning card.
We warn you all, be on guard.

(*DOTTIE enters*)

SCOOP. He's coming. He's coming tonight! Dottie, clean this place up, will you? Lyle, you got a clean shirt?

LYLE. No. (*exits*)

SCOOP. Dottie, you got a comb?

DOTTIE. (*passes it to him*) Try and return this one, huh?

BIDDIE. (*looking around*) Where'd Scoop go?

DOTTIE. He's in the gentlemen's room. They said they'd make an exception just this once.

SCOOP. (re-entering) Dottie, you wanna turn this dollar into some drinks?

DOTTIE. You got one going. (motions to table)

BIDDIE. It ain't your eyes your missing, it's your arm.

SCOOP. You're making fun of a cripple now?

DOTTIE. Making fun...God must have bleached your brains when he bleached your hair.

SCOOP. Leave my hair out of this.

BIDDIE. Angel fuzz, would we talk this kind of foolishness if you wasn't our special friend? Talking mean to a friend is a compliment.

SCOOP. Why is it, Friend, everytime you pay me a compliment, I think you're attacking me instead? You know, you're the kind of person who would compliment the big guy who just walked in the door by saying, "for a fat guy you don't sweat much."

(MERLE enters, looking around to find SCOOP. He is obviously far more successful and sure of himself than his brother.)

SCOOP. Oh my God, there he his!

BIDDIE. The fat guy who don't sweat much?

SCOOP. No, my brother! (goes to his brother)

MERLE. (seeing SCOOP) Harold!

BIDDIE. Who's Harold?

SCOOP. Good to see you! How you doing? (sotto voce) Uh, call me Scoop, huh?

MERLE. Sure, call you anything you say. Scoop!

SCOOP. (a joviality pervades) This here is my brother Merle. That's Dottie Hemingway.

DOTTIE. Nice to meet you Scoop—I mean Merle!

(BIDDIE unconsciously gets out a cigar)

SCOOP. This is Lyle, you know Lyle.

MERLE. How's it going Lyle?

SCOOP. (snatching cigar out of BIDDIE'S mouth before MERLE can see it) This here's Biddie Gazinski.

MERLE. I've heard a lot about you! Pleased to meet you, Biddie.

(BIDDIE unconsciously wipes her hand off. Then extends hand to MERLE. They shake. BIDDIE snatches back her cigar from SCOOP.)

LYLE. Hey, Merle, how's it going? Long time no see, huh?

MERLE. Oh, you know how it is. Business. I haven't seen my wife and kids in about four years.

(*EVERYONE laughs a little too loud*)

SCOOP. You look great. Tell me how everything's been going, huh? Sit down. Wish I got some of the brains in the family; all I got was the beauty.

(*EVERYONE laughs again as though the joke were fresh and funny*)

DOTTIE. Bourbon okay for you, Merle?

MERLE. Sure.

SCOOP. (*hinting THEY should leave*) Where are you two going?

BIDDIE. (*catching on*) Oh, I was just going to the back room to play a little pool. (*exits*)

DOTTIE. Hell, I got customers back there ordered drinks four years ago. Been so busy I ain't had time to serve 'em yet.

(*again, the big laugh*)

SCOOP. Close the door, will you Dottie?

(*DOTTIE exits. Silence. Finally MERLE breaks it.*)

MERLE. Harold...

SCOOP. (*stopping him midway*) Scoop.

MERLE. So. What's this big life and death issue? Must be pretty important.

SCOOP. The way things are going anymore, it all depends on whose life or death it is as to whether it's important or not, huh?

MERLE. It's a dog-eat-dog world.

(*silence*)

SCOOP. Now that I got you here, I don't know where to begin.

MERLE. (*toasting SCOOP to cover the awkwardness*) Good to see you, Scoop. Good to see you.

SCOOP. I called a couple times. You never made it down.

MERLE. Business keeps you busy. (*awkward pause*) So...?

SCOOP. (*he takes the plunge*) Biddie, Lyle and me are all getting shafted from our work.

MERLE. You were doing so well, I thought! You're getting the ax?

SCOOP. Not yet, but the writing's on the wall. And we were getting a little desperate, right? What with being so dependent on food to live and all; so this guy comes up to Lyle and offers us a lotta money if we was to dump these chemicals...

(*Instrumental music cuts in as door opens. DOTTIE comes in the bar to get some bottles. MERLE and SCOOP continue talking underneath all the noise. Their conversation is not audible. They are discussing what we already know.*)

DOTTIE. Just gotta get a bottle from out back.

SCOOP. Close the door on your way out, will you Dottie?

(*DOTTIE exits, closing door and closing off the sound of instrumental music. Conversation is once again audible.*)

MERLE. (*perplexed*) So you didn't dump the chemicals, you want to stop them from building on the land next to the dump, and you want to make some money out of it all...

SCOOP. (*anticipating that his brother will help*) Right.

MERLE. That's a tall order. How are you going to do it?

SCOOP. What?

MERLE. How do you plan to accomplish all that?

SCOOP. No. You're the one with the smarts in c-c-chemistry and all. And you know personal some of the King Kongs in the upper echelon. I thought maybe you could help.

MERLE. (*incredulous*) Me?

SCOOP. Yeah, I thought maybe you could go up to one of them and g-g-get them to outlaw the land or something. Then give us a reward for being such good scouts.

MERLE. Back up a minute, Scoop. You're suggesting something...My company has been dumping chemicals for years in places just like that dump you went to.

(*Silence. SCOOP has been hit hard by this information. MERLE feels and responds to the silent accusation.*)

MERLE. Wait a minute. You couldn't get through a day without the things we produce. And there are chemical by-products. What are we going to do with them? There's only a handful of legal dumpsites in the entire country. What do you want us to do—eat the stuff?

SCOOP. (*still numbed; not at all responding to the last self-serving question*) You mean you're dumping out in the countryside where people live?

MERLE. My company is.

SCOOP. You are!

MERLE. (*anger rising*) Let's get something straight, right here and now. They tell me what to do, I do it. It's taken me twelve years to get where I am. Twelve long years. And now you want me to make like a radical or something, protest what my company's doing? All that would do is get me fired while some greedy bastard gets my job! Wake up, will you?

SCOOP. Well, who is going to do something about toxic wastes, Merle? If the guys who make it don't have enough guts...(*doesn't go on with the thought*) Jesus, Merle, you should see the dead birds from this stuff. And the old folks, they'll die before they knew what hit them. One year of inhaling that stuff...

MERLE. (*getting control of himself and reassuring SCOOP*) Scoop, Scoop, let me tell you a few things. Nobody's going to die in the first year from fumes. From a car accident, maybe, but fumes? (*shakes head, "no."*) And you know money's been appropriated to start cleaning up those dumpsites. Now, there's always a little lag time so there might be some minimal damage due to the radioactivity, but the long-range effects of low-level radiation have not been determined. There's probably less radiation there than you'd get from a set of chest x-rays or a suntan.

SCOOP. (*his rage finding its voice*) That gets me. I hear it all the time: "Nothing's been determined." Guys are dropping dead like flies and you haven't gotten around to determining. Well, why haven't you? Why don't you take some of that time you spend making invisible glue for false eyelashes and determine?

MERLE. I didn't know you were interested in all this.

SCOOP. (*really angry now*) Just because I haven't got a college degree rammed up my ass don't mean I can't add two and two. Yeah, I'm interested. In fact, I'm so interested, I determined, all by myself, that chemical and nuclear waste is bad so you shouldn't go around dumping it on the outside chance someone else is going to clean it up for you.

MERLE. Scoop, stick to pumping gas, huh? You don't know what you're talking about. You're in way over your head. Even the experts don't know how much radiation is safe; and as for chemical waste...

SCOOP. (*interrupting with unharnessed rage*) Let me get this straight. You experts don't know; you haven't determined; so you're finding out by watching workers drop like flies and counting the corpses...

(*THEY overlap one another*)

MERLE. That's my job.

SCOOP. ...and then subtracting that from the number of workers still alive...

MERLE. You figured it out—I count corpses for a living...

SCOOP. ...and multiplying that by the number of corporations making a profit...

MERLE. That's the computation...

SCOOP. ...and adding that to the number of chemists who need a job and are willing to kiss ass to keep it...

MERLE. You've said about enough...

SCOOP. ...and coming up with a billion-dollar profit margin that justifies murder!

MERLE. Come on, Harold!

SCOOP. The name is Scoop!

MERLE. Whatever your name is! This doesn't sound like you. You were always a good-time Charlie, out to see what's in it for yourself! A little gin, some five-card stud and you were happy.

SCOOP. I'm the same guy, but Charlie's got to stay alive to have a good time!

MERLE. You're not buying the land, Dope. You're safe!

SCOOP. For how long? We could be on top of a dump right now!

(*silence*)

MERLE. (*trying to reverse direction with a joke*) Well, I think we can withstand the radiation long enough to have another drink, what do you say?

SCOOP. I don't think so. I feel a little queasy already.

MERLE. Suit yourself. (*starts to exit*)

SCOOP. Thanks for the advice.

MERLE. (*after a pause, turns to face SCOOP*) Look, Scoop, I'm sorry, but you're barking up the wrong tree. *I'd just lose my job.* I don't know, maybe if enough of you guys got mad enough you could make Allied Chemical and Hooker and all the rest do something. You don't stand to lose as much as me.

SCOOP. Sure, Merle. I'll take care of it. You'd better go home and get some sleep. You've got a "job" to go to in the morning.

MERLE. Say goodbye to the women for me.

LYLE. (*steps in with trumpet*) So long, Merle. You leaving so soon?

MERLE. I'm afraid so.

(*LYLE steps back sensing the mood*)

MERLE. (*trying one last time, MERLE walks back to SCOOP and holds out his hand*) Scoop.

(*SCOOP extends his half-arm. MERLE looks silently at it. Exits. DOTTIE enters, senses the mood.*)

DOTTIE. You look like you could use a stiff one.

SCOOP. Thanks. I already had my allotment.

DOTTIE. (*shaking her head "no"*) Uh-uh! This one's on the house.

SCOOP. You got enough of this house stuff to drink me under the table?

DOTTIE. Yep.

(*BIDDIE enters with cue stick, stands looking at SCOOP, sensing what has happened*)

SCOOP. What are you staring at?

BIDDIE. Nothing.

SCOOP. You're not going to ask me about my brother?

BIDDIE. No, Friend. (*innocently to bring SCOOP out of his despair*) Where'd you get the money to buy a drink? You lying bastard! You got enough money for a drink, you buy me one.

SCOOP. (*having been lured unwittingly into conversation*) Why should I buy you one?

BIDDIE. 'Cause you happen to owe me six billion dollars.

SCOOP. That's a lie. I won almost as many games as you did.

BIDDIE. (*touching his good arm*) You count on this side, you do fine. You get over here...(*moving to stump*)...you get in trouble. No fingers.

SCOOP. What are you doin' with that cue stick?

BIDDIE. (*mimes shooting pool on platform*) Getting the feel of it in my bones. I'm studying to be world "champeen." I read you got to eat, drink and sleep the stick 'til it's almost a part of you. ¡

SCOOP. You're not going to ask me about my brother.

BIDDIE. (*from deep caring*) Uh-uh.

SCOOP. Well, actually he ain't my brother anymore. He's a clone for Allied Chemical. He's kind of like them little fish that live off the sharks. They swim right beside them, and when the shark makes a killing, they eat the leftovers. If the shark killed their mother, they'd be right there, eating the leftovers.

BIDDIE. Dottie, bring me a beer.

LYLE. (*enters and, like BIDDIE before him, ignoring the brother issue*) Where'd you get your money? You're supposed to be broke.

BIDDIE. I won it at pool.

(*Phone rings. ALL look at phone, then at each other. DOTTIE goes to phone, hesitantly.*)

DOTTIE. Barrelhouse.

DANNY. Lyle Fine.

DOTTIE. He is not here.

DANNY. You tell that trumpet player that walks on two legs to get out front by the phone booth if he wants to keep walking on them.

DOTTIE. (*hangs up phone*) He's outside waiting for you.

(*After a tension-filled pause, LYLE goes to the door. SCOOP and BIDDIE run to stop him.*)

SCOOP. I'm coming with you.

LYLE. (*shaking his head "no"*) This is a solo act. (*starts to leave*)

BIDDIE. (*as always, she has the best scam*) Lyle, Lyle, wait. wait, a-a-a-act like you was drunk. They'd never let you drive if you was drunk. You could get picked up.

(*That stops LYLE. It's a good idea. SCOOP gets up, grabs a bottle, gives it to LYLE. They open the door and assume a drunken stupor. BIDDIE and DOTTIE yell at them, helping the act.*)

LYLE. (*as though his speech is affected by alcohol*) Where are the keys, Pal?

DOTTIE. (*speaking simultaneously with BIDDIE*) This is a decent bar. Get out of here you drunken bums. We don't need this here.

BIDDIE. Hey, you two, get out. Don't come around here again 'til you sober up.

DOTTIE. We don't need your kind in here. You start breaking stuff, you're out.

(*Ad lib until LYLE and SCOOP have exited. DOTTIE and BIDDIE freeze looking at each other in silence and terror. After a moment, SCOOP enters, goes to table. BIDDIE and DOTTIE move closer to him, wondering what has happened and where LYLE is. Then LYLE enters. There's a moment of relief. LYLE goes to the piano and sinks onto the stool.*)

LYLE. They bought it. They think we're a couple of drunken bums. What they don't know is we'd never drive again for them, drunk or sober. (*LYLE plays and sings, at first almost to himself; then the song gradually rises in intensity*)

> *Even a Bum Like Me*
> I'm not a hero, holding evil at bay.
> I've only done for myself
> 'til today.
> But there's something even I will not do,
> Something evil, an evil brand new.
>
> Even a guy like me can say no.
> There's a distance even I will not go.
> There's a rule guiding all under the sun.
> There's even a rule guiding this one.
>
> It says the life of the race
> Of animals and earth, all in space,

Has been honored since life was begun
Can't be destroyed for the profit of some.

Even a guy like me now speaks out,
Now that I know what your evil's about.
And I'll fight you with all that is mine.
To save the children and the earth,
Even what's thine.

(the offstage piano continues to play the song and the TRIO reflects)

SCOOP. We probably know some of the guys that work that construction site next to the dump, bringing home toxic chemicals on their boots.

LYLE. And there's a water table running underneath that land, poisoning people through their kitchen faucets, drop by drop.

BIDDIE. A doomsday clock, ticking off the minutes.

SCOOP. Maybe my brother was right about one thing, maybe people like us got to move in on the big shots, push them around a little, *make* them think about something besides their profit margin.

LYLE. It's not only the big shots, Scoop. There's a lot of little guys like us who know what's happening and been keeping our mouths shut.

SCOOP. Yeah, but we got more than enough to do scrounging after jobs and keeping food in our bellies. Why should it be up to us?

BIDDIE. Because we know about it, I guess.

SCOOP. *(exploding)* So do a whole lot of other people. And what are they doing about it?

BIDDIE. I don't know, One-Arm, but I do know we'll never find out if we don't ask.

SCOOP. *(turns to LYLE)* What are the odds out there?

LYLE. Friend, when its the only game in town, you don't ask the odds. You go for broke.

(BIDDIE begins singing as COMPANY variously enters the stage and joins singing)

To the People

BIDDIE. When you've gone every place that you can go,
Lies around you continue to grow,
Evil so thick you can cut it with a knife
Nothing left to lose but your life.

ALL. Take it to the people.

DOTTIE. A flower needs the same conditions to grow
         As a lot of children that I know.
         Clean air and water, plenty of food,
         'Til we get that, stay in a fighting mood.

ALL.   To the people, to the people.

LYLE.   This country won't move, this country won't eat
         'Til the rich man feels this poor man's heat.
         Burning up privilege and greed,
         Our fuel isn't oil, it's human need.

ALL.   To the people, to the people.
         Friends and neighbors, the woman next door.
         Guy without a job, the working poor.
         To the people, to the people.

         When a people revolt, don't happen overnight
         Takes a lot to get people to fight.
         When we act in our majority,
         We change history!

         To the people, to the people.

BIDDIE. (*spoken*) Take it to the people.
(*lights gradually fade to black*)

END OF PLAY

WINDFALL

M. ANANIA